AF785636

ARCHITECTS OF THE EURO

Architects of the Euro

Intellectuals in the Making of European Monetary Union

Edited by
KENNETH DYSON
and
IVO MAES

OXFORD
UNIVERSITY PRESS

OXFORD
UNIVERSITY PRESS

Great Clarendon Street, Oxford, OX2 6DP,
United Kingdom

Oxford University Press is a department of the University of Oxford.
It furthers the University's objective of excellence in research, scholarship,
and education by publishing worldwide. Oxford is a registered trade mark of
Oxford University Press in the UK and in certain other countries

© Oxford University Press 2016

The moral rights of the authors have been asserted

First Edition published in 2016

All rights reserved. No part of this publication may be reproduced, stored in a retrieval system, or transmitted, in any form or by any means, without the prior permission in writing of Oxford University Press, or as expressly permitted by law, by licence or under terms agreed with the appropriate reprographics rights organization. Enquiries concerning reproduction outside the scope of the above should be sent to the Rights Department, Oxford University Press, at the address above

You must not circulate this work in any other form
and you must impose this same condition on any acquirer

Published in the United States of America by Oxford University Press
198 Madison Avenue, New York, NY 10016, United States of America

British Library Cataloguing in Publication Data
Data available

Library of Congress Control Number: 2016931582

ISBN 978–0–19–873591–5

Links to third party websites are provided by Oxford in good faith and for information only. Oxford disclaims any responsibility for the materials contained in any third party website referenced in this work.

Preface

> 'I am not an economist. I am an architect. But I know political economy better than the economists do.'
>
> (Jaffé 1935)

These words of the eminent Lausanne economist Léon Walras offer an insight into the character of the intellectuals who contributed to the epic process of designing European monetary union with which this book is concerned. They were neither the political leaders who drove the process nor narrow expert economists. At the same time their qualities as active networkers and as interrogators of ideas led them to cross these boundaries during their often long careers. The architects of the euro were intellectuals who grappled with the acutely difficult, large-scale, and practical challenges of designing Economic and Monetary Union (EMU) in Europe, often under acute political pressures. Their habitat was political economy. The architects occupied the difficult terrain between often very constraining and unwelcome political constraints and the frequently conflicting prescriptions of professional economists.

The intellectual challenge was to flesh out the nature of EMU. What should be its economic and monetary constitution? How to design EMU on a sustainable basis, not least on terms that would satisfy the political leaders who commissioned the work? The architects were intellectuals in the highly complex EMU policy process rather than experts in a narrow specialist sense.

In assessing their individual contributions and legacies, one needs to bear in mind the distinction between architects and architecture. The EMU architecture that was agreed by the European Council in Maastricht in December 1991 bore the imprint of the European political leaders, especially those of France and Germany, who commissioned this ambitious project (Dyson and Featherstone 1999). The design defects were very much inherent in the commissioning, above all in considerations of limiting the loss of economic and fiscal sovereignty and of protecting domestic institutional interests, for instance in banking supervision and regulation.

The result was an asymmetric design of EMU (Dyson 2000; Maes 2002). On the one hand, monetary policy became supranational. There was to be a new single currency—the euro—and an independent European Central Bank (ECB) with a mandate to secure price stability. On the other hand, Member States were to retain sovereignty over fiscal policy, banking supervision and regulation, and policies that affected competitiveness, like labour markets, social provision, and wage bargaining.

The architecture was unbalanced. The euro was a 'market-making' project that eliminated transaction costs in doing business. In this way it reinforced the European single market, including the single market in financial services. However, the euro was deficient as a 'market-correcting' project, one that could address market failure and consequent systemic risk. This unbalanced design reflected an exceptional feature of its architecture. It was a monetary union without a state. Overall, the Maastricht architecture of the EMU was deemed unsatisfactory—if in different ways and to different degrees—by the individual architects. No architect would wish to claim that this architecture was their own; and all perceived it as larger and as more economically and politically heterogeneous than they had envisaged.

Throughout the period in which we have led and managed this cross-national research project, we have been able to draw on the support and encouragement of numerous people and institutions. In a short acknowledgement it is far from easy to express just how grateful we are to all those involved. They range from our own institutions—Cardiff University and the National Bank of Belgium—to the wide range of sponsoring bodies, our expert advisory group, and not least the colleagues working on the project. All have contributed insights and comments, as well as energy and time, to the project. Without their commitment the book would have been immeasurably poorer.

We are delighted that the governor of the National Bank of Belgium was kind enough to contribute a foreword to the book and grateful to the National Bank of Belgium for its support of this project from its inception to its completion. It illustrates once again the way in which over decades the National Bank of Belgium has been a pace-setter in contributing not just ideas to the process of European monetary union but also to our understanding of the history of this remarkable historical project.

Particular thanks are due to the institutions that provided financial and moral support for this project. In addition to the National Bank of Belgium, they included the British Academy, the Centre virtuel de la connaissance sur l'Europe (CVCE) in Luxembourg, the European Central Bank (ECB), the Gutt Foundation, Robert Triffin International, the University of Luxembourg, and the Pierre Werner Foundation. Their support enabled us to organize three research workshops which brought together the contributors. They were held in London in October 2013, in Luxembourg in April 2014, and in Brussels in March 2015. The discussions at these workshops extended beyond contributors to include a wide range of discussants with practical experience of the making of EMU as well as external academic reviewers.

The three research workshops were invaluable in offering deeper insights into the role of intellectuals in the making of EMU. They helped to establish a common framework of questions and a process of convergence in how we addressed these questions. At the same time the workshops also revealed the remaining diversity of views amongst the contributors about how best to understand the nature of EMU and the role of individual architects. The reasons for this diversity, like the structure/agency problem and the problem of levels of analysis, are examined in Chapter 1.

We also benefited from panel discussions at various conferences, including the University Association for Contemporary European Studies (UACES), the European Society for the History of Economic Thought (ESHET), the Italian Association for the Study of Economic Thought (AISPE), and the Italian Association for the Study of Political Economy (STOREP).

A distinctive and important feature of the project was the work of its expert advisory group, which comprised veterans of the EMU process. We owe special thanks to them for the interest that they showed in the project and for devoting so much time in offering both general advice to the editors and comments on individual chapters. The members also participated actively in the workshops.

The advisory group comprised Charles Goodhart, FBA, Emeritus Professor at the London School of Economics and former chief economist and former member of the Monetary Policy Committee of the Bank of England; Francesco Papadia, formerly at the Banca d'Italia and economic adviser at the European Commission, as well as director-general for market operations at the ECB from 1998 to 2012; Robert Raymond, formerly at the Banque de France, later director-general at the European Monetary Institute (EMI) from 1994 to 1998, and then ECB representative at the International Monetary Fund (IMF); Fabrizio Saccomanni, formerly deputy governor of the Banca d'Italia and Italy's minister of economics and finance; André Sapir, Emeritus Professor of the Université Libre de Bruxelles, Senior Fellow at the Breugel think-tank in Brussels and long-time adviser to the European Commission; Hanspeter Scheller, formerly at the German Bundesbank, later general secretary of the EMI from 1994 to 1998, general director of the ECB, and later special adviser to the ECB executive board; and Niels Thygesen, Emeritus Professor at the University of Copenhagen and former member of the Delors Committee and of various earlier committees on European monetary integration.

We also benefited from the advice of numerous scholars, notably Frédéric Allemand (CVCE), Michele Chang (College of Europe), Thierry Grosbois (CVCE), Jack Hayward (Hull University), Jean-Claude Koeune (Université catholique de Louvain), René Leboutte (University of Luxembourg), Jean-Victor Louis (Université libre de Bruxelles), Susana Munoz (CVCE), Paolo Tedeschi (CVCE), and Ad Van Riet (ECB).

As editors we owe a great debt to the continuous and enthusiastic support of Oxford University Press. Dominic Byatt and his colleagues showed once again how it is possible to be congenial as well as efficient in helping to guide a project of this type to a successful conclusion.

In the final analysis, as ever, the usual disclaimer applies. The contents of this book remain the exclusive responsibility of the editors and the authors. Neither the various institutions nor the members of the advisory group are responsible for any of the views expressed in this volume.

Kenneth Dyson
Cardiff University, Wales

Ivo Maes
National Bank of Belgium
Université catholique de Louvain

24 November 2015

Contents

List of Archives

Archives nationales de Luxembourg (ANLux)

Bank of England Historical Archive, London (BoEA)

Bank for International Settlements, Basel (BISA)

Commission of the European Communities, Brussels (CECA)

Diplomatic Archive Center of the Ministry of Foreign and European Affairs, La Courneuve (FDAC)

European Central Bank, Frankfurt (ECBA)

European University Institute, Fiesole (EUIA)

German Federal Archives, Koblenz (BArch)

Historical Archives of the European Union (HAEU)

Historisches Archiv der Deutschen Bundesbank, Frankfurt (HADB)

Italian Historical Diplomatic Archives, Rome (IHDA)

Jean Monnet, Fondation Jean Monnet, Lausanne (JMA)

National Bank of Belgium, Brussels (NBBA)

Pierre Werner family archives, Luxembourg (PWLux)

Robert Marjolin, Fondation Jean Monnet, Lausanne (ARM)

Robert Triffin, Université catholique de Louvain, Louvain-la-Neuve (RTA)

Tickell Papers, All Souls College, Oxford (TP)

Notes on Contributors

Eric Bussière is a Professor at the Université Paris IV—Sorbonne and holder of the Jean Monnet Chair in the History of European Integration. His research focuses on the history of European integration, especially the monetary and financial dimension. His publications include *La France, la Belgique et l'organisation économique de l'Europe, 1918–1935* (CHEFF, 1992); *Paribas, l'Europe et le monde, 1872–1992* (Fonds Mercator, 1992); and *London and Paris as International Financial Centres* (Oxford University Press, 2005, with Y. Cassis).

Elena Danescu is a Research Fellow at the University of Luxembourg. She was previously a Researcher in European Integration Studies at the Centre Virtuel de la Connaissance sur l'Europe, Luxembourg. Her research areas include the transition in Central and Eastern Europe, EU enlargement and EMU. Her current research is based on the Werner family archives and deals with Pierre Werner and Europe. Recent publications have focused on reinterpreting the Werner Plan, for instance 'The Werner Report and the Financial Crisis during the 1970s' in *Eurochange: European responses to economic and social changes. From the 1970s to the New Millennium* (P.I.E. Peter Lang, forthcoming, with P. Tedeschi); 'Pierre Werner: l'homme et son oeuvre' *in Pierre Werner and Europe: His Approach, Action and Legacy* (P.I.E. Peter Lang, 2015); and *La revue d'histoire économique et sociale du XVIe au XXe siècle* (2011).

Kenneth Dyson is a Fellow of the British Academy, a Fellow of the Royal Historical Society, a Founding Fellow of the Learned Society of Wales, and Research Professor in European Political Studies at Cardiff University. His research interests encompass the European state, German policies and politics, comparative and international political economy, and the EU. His best-known books include *States, Debt and Power: 'Saints' and 'Sinners' in European History and Integration* (Oxford University Press, 2014)—winner of the UACES Best Book Prize); *The State Tradition in Western Europe* (republished in the ECPR Classics Series, 2011); *Elusive Union* (Longman, 1994); *The Road to Maastricht* (Oxford University Press, 1999, with K. Featherstone)—*Choice* academic book of the year; *The Politics of the Euro-Zone* (Oxford University Press, 2001); and the two-volume *European Economic Governance and Policies* (Oxford University Press, 2010, with L. Quaglia).

Dermot Hodson is Senior Lecturer in Political Economy at Birkbeck College, University of London. Earlier he was an economist at DG Economic and Financial Affairs of the European Commission. His research focuses on EU policy-making, global economic governance, and UK public policy. He is author of *Governing the Euro Area in Good Times and Bad* (Oxford University Press, 2011) and of articles in the *Journal of Common Market Studies*, the *Journal of European Public Policy*, and the *Review of International Political Economy*.

David Howarth is Professor of Political Economy at the University of Luxembourg and has written extensively on banking and financial regulation, economic and monetary union, and the Euro Area crisis. His books include *The French Road to European Monetary Union* (Palgrave Macmillan, 2001); *The ECB: The New European Leviathan* (Palgrave Macmillan, 2005, with P. Loedel); and *Market-Based Banking and International Financial Crisis* (Oxford University Press, 2013, edited with I. Hardie).

Harold James is Professor of European Studies at Princeton University and has written extensively on economic and financial history and on modern German history. His books include *The German Slump, 1924–36* (Clarendon Press, 1986); *International Monetary Cooperation since Bretton Woods* (Oxford University Press, 1996); *The End of Globalization: Lessons from the Great Depression* (Harvard University Press, 2001); and *Making the European Monetary Union* (Harvard University Press, 2012).

N. Piers Ludlow is Associate Professor in the Department of International History at the London School of Economics and has written extensively on the history of Western Europe since 1945 and in particular on the historical roots of European integration. His books include *Dealing with Britain: The Six and the First British Membership Application* (Cambridge University Press, 1997); *The European Community and the Crises of the 1960s: Negotiating the Gaullist Challenge* (Routledge, 2006); and (ed.) *Visions of the End of the Cold War, 1945–1990* (Berghahn, 2012). He is currently writing a monograph on Roy Jenkins' period as president of the European Commission.

Ivo Maes is Senior Adviser at the Research Department of the National Bank of Belgium and Professor, Robert Triffin Chair, at the Université Catholique de Louvain and at ICHEC Brussels Business School. He is President of the Council of the European Society for the History of Economic Thought. In 2003, he was a member of the Committee for Institutional Reform of the West African Monetary Union. His research focuses on the history of central banking and European monetary and financial integration. His books include *Economic Thought and the Making of European Monetary Union* (Edward Elgar, 2002); *Half a Century of European Financial Integration: From the Rome Treaty to the 21st Century* (Mercatorfonds, 2007); and *Alexandre Lamfalussy: The Wise Man of the Euro—A Conversation with Christophe Lamfalussy, Ivo Maes and Sabine Péters* (LannooCampus, 2014).

Fabio Masini is Associate Professor at the University of Rome III and has worked as a consultant on EU affairs. His research interests include the history of economic thought, the international political economy, and EMU. His most recent journal articles have appeared in the *European Journal of the History of Economic Thought*, *Constitutional Political Economy*, *Storia del Pensiero Economico*, and *History of Economic Thought and Policy*.

Katja Seidel is a Visiting Lecturer at the University of Westminster. Her research interests include the history of the European Commission, the origins and development of European policies (such as competition policy and the common agricultural policy), and biographical studies of European elites. Recent publications include *The Process of Politics in Europe: The Rise of European Elites and Supranational Institutions* (I.B. Tauris, 2010); *Europeanization in the 20th Century: The Historical Lens / Pour une lecture historique de l'européanisation au XXe siècle* (Peter Lang 2012, ed. with Matthieu Osmond et al.).

Foreword

The Euro Area crisis has led to profound debates, not only in the academic community, but also among economic policy-makers and society at large. It has rekindled the issue of the relationship between monetary union and political union. So, this book is very timely, as it places these discussions in a broader historical context. It focuses on the challenges and dilemmas of intellectuals as policy-makers in the construction of EMU, torn between the academic and political worlds.

The sovereign debt crisis highlighted the structural defects of European Economic and Monetary Union. It demonstrated that membership of a single currency, in a common economic and financial market, creates extremely deep and complex interdependencies. Much more advanced integration of economic policy is thus absolutely vital.

Over the last few years, there have been significant reforms in economic governance in the Euro Area. They include the so-called 'Six-Pack' legislation to strengthen macro-economic coordination, with the new Macro-Economic Imbalance Procedure; the Euro Area's Fiscal Compact Treaty; and the Single Supervisory Mechanism as a key first pillar of European banking union. Moreover, a new blueprint for EMU was drawn up, in a report by European Council President Herman van Rompuy, in close collaboration with the presidents of the European Commission, Eurogroup, and the European Central Bank, entitled *Towards a Genuine Economic and Monetary Union* (Van Rompuy 2012). The report put forward a vision for EMU with a banking union and moves towards a political union to complement its economic and monetary arm. This vision has been elaborated and refined in the so-called 'Five Presidents Report' published in June 2015.

It was not the first time that these types of ideas have been formulated. In fact, they are close to the traditional Belgian vision of a symmetric economic and monetary union (Smets et al. 2003). They were clearly present in the January 1970 Snoy Plan, named after the then Belgian Finance Minister: 'Un Plan de Solidarité Monétaire Européenne en Trois Étapes 1971–1977' (Ministère des Finances 1970). The Belgian plan argued that for a 'European monetary community' two conditions had to be fulfilled: a unification of economic policies and a certain homogeneity of the economies of the Member States. It further emphasized that major institutional reforms were necessary for the final phase of EMU. Establishment of two new supranational Community institutions was essential: first, a 'Community Monetary System', like the Federal Reserve System in the United States, and, second, a kind of supranational European economic government, 'made up of Community organs endowed with the necessary powers to conduct a single economic policy'. Economic policy was defined as encompassing budgetary and income policies. For budgetary policy, the new Community institutions would establish the general framework wherein the Member States had to administer their budget. The Community budget should, gradually, gain in importance and certain Community transfer mechanisms should be developed. The Belgian plan further proposed that the European Community should become an 'autonomous entity' vis-à-vis the rest of the world.

As Jean Monnet observed, crises often act as a catalyst for change. The Euro Area crisis has followed this pattern. It highlighted the fragility of its institutional architecture. The crisis made clear that the Euro Area needs a quantum leap towards a stronger and more efficient institutional architecture, making EMU more resilient and remedying its fragilities.

The Euro Area's present institutional framework is still too fragile with respect to economic, fiscal, and financial affairs. A major weakness is that the ECB does not have a strong political counterpart. This weakness became very obvious during the financial crisis. It points to a major difference from the United States. The US Federal Reserve could focus on fighting the financial crisis, without having to worry about the integrity of the dollar area. This contrasted with the ECB, which played a key role in maintaining the integrity of the Euro Area.

As a consequence of the crisis, significant efforts were made to strengthen the institutional framework of the Euro Area. However, some of the new instruments, particularly the financial assistance programmes to help Member States in difficulty, are characterized by intergovernmental decision-making mechanisms, which are not conducive to the development of shared responsibilities. They run the risk of a conflict between the legitimate democratic interests of individual Member States, without offering sufficient legitimacy at European level. To remedy this deficit, we should share decisions that affect the future of the Euro Area within common institutions with a European mandate and democratic oversight at European level. The history of the ECB illustrates the merits of such an institutional approach.

Naturally, one has to accept that a deepening of EMU, and shared responsibilities, go together with shared risks. More solidarity should then go hand in hand with domestic ownership and national responsibility. It is evident that a monetary union brings not only new rights but also new obligations and reinforces the importance of establishing a level playing field for all economic actors.

Moreover, for a monetary union, resilience is crucial in the face of shocks that lead to consistently higher unemployment and economic divergence between Member States. Structural reforms are essential, not only to increase potential output, but also to strengthen the resilience of the economy to shocks, which have direct implications for the integrity and coherence of the

Euro Area. A stronger common governance of structural reforms is certainly necessary for this.

For these reasons, the Euro Area needs to build institutions that reinforce the cohesion of economic, monetary, and political union. To this end, it must recreate a sense of shared responsibility. This book on the architects of the Euro is an important contribution to this process. It shows that, whatever their background, the architects cooperated to make a success of this historical project. They accepted the trust which Europe's leaders had bestowed on them, to advance the European integration project, which has brought peace and prosperity to a continent that was formerly divided with tragic consequences.

Jan Smets

Governor of the National Bank of Belgium
Member of the Governing Council of the European Central Bank

1

Intellectuals as Policy-Makers

The Value of Biography in the History of European Monetary Union

Kenneth Dyson and Ivo Maes

The creation of the Euro Area was one of the most extraordinary and momentous events in modern European history. It centred on the launch of a single currency, the euro, managed by a European Central Bank (ECB) whose independence was guaranteed by the Maastricht Treaty, as agreed in December 1991. The Euro Area represented an ambitious and bold political commitment to the promotion of European unification, an affirmation of the importance of political leadership, above all by France and Germany (Dyson and Featherstone 1999). In addition, European monetary union remained an extraordinary technical feat of construction—both in complexity and in scale—encompassing eleven European Union (EU) Member States in 1999.

However, from the outset many economists, especially Anglo-American, raised serious doubts about the viability and sustainability of the project. Thus Martin Feldstein (1992) concluded that monetary union was not necessary to achieve the advantages of a free-trade area. Moreover, it posed risks to future peace and stability in Europe. Closer to the launch of the euro, he warned in even starker terms of the possibility of future war in Europe (Feldstein 1997). Bernard Connolly, a senior official in the Commission's monetary department, was scathing: 'The true lesson of the ERM [Exchange-Rate Mechanism] story is that a Europe, even a Rhenish Europe, built on its money would be a Europe sitting atop the fault lines of an earthquake zone. Those fault lines correspond with the borders of nation-states, for the Commission slogan "One Market, One Money" is no more than a prediction of discredited "neo-functionalist" theory' (Connolly 1995: 378). Milton Friedman (1997) argued that politics had triumphed over economics. Monetary union would 'exacerbate political tensions by converting divergent shocks that could have been readily accommodated by exchange-rate changes into divisive political issues . . . Monetary unity imposed under unfavourable conditions will prove a barrier to the achievement of political unity.' Early assessments of its construction concluded that it was a fair-weather project, vulnerable to the political economy of bad times, its design lacking instruments of crisis management (e.g. Dyson 2000).

The critics were also to be found within continental Europe. In June 1992 over sixty German economists signed an open letter attacking the weaknesses in the Maastricht Treaty. They claimed that the convergence criteria for euro entry were too lax, argued that convergence must come before a specific date, doubted that there was a shared stability culture, and concluded that the outcome could endanger rather than promote European integration (for details see Dyson and Quaglia 2010a: 493–4). In May 1992 the Bank for International Settlements, the central bankers' bank, pointed to the risk that political considerations could triumph in applying the convergence criteria. It noted that too little thought had been given to the implications of the wide variation in wage and price levels in the European Community (Dyson and Quaglia 2010a: 491–3).

The unfolding financial, economic, and sovereign debt crisis of the Euro Area—just ten years after its birth—exposed in vivid terms the design faults of the Euro Area, notably in banking and financial market union as well as in economic and fiscal union. The imperfections of European economic governance, the naïvety of assumptions about Member State compliance, and the failure to consider issues of state capacity were clearly revealed (Dyson 2014). The highly respected economic journalist Martin Wolf (2014) wrote of the euro as a disaster, an exercise in blind arrogance and wishful thinking. Thomas Mayer (2012), former chief economist of Deutsche Bank, went so far as to suggest a Plan B of 'monetary unions in EMU': a 'softer' Latin monetary union; a hard parallel currency for Germany and the Nordic Member States; and peripheral Member States with softer parallel currencies of their own. Fears of a transfer union and of serial circumvention of fiscal rules heightened risks that German elites might begin to disengage from the EU.

Against this background, it is timely to assess the contribution and legacy of the architects of the euro. The crisis poses questions about the quality of the original design of the Euro Area; and about whether the architects were part of the design problems or were disregarded on key issues and can be seen as still providing a source of inspiration for solving the design problems. Just how prescient were the architects in identifying the problems to which monetary union would give rise and in suggesting solutions that were overlooked at the time?

This book also fills a niche by examining the history of European monetary union through the lens of biography. It employs the metaphor of architect to examine the role of individuals who were directly involved in the process of constructing Economic and Monetary Union (EMU) and contributed ideas to its design in the period before the launch of monetary union on 1 January 1999. Some of these architects—like Robert Marjolin, Robert Triffin, and Pierre Werner—were most heavily involved in the period before the process of negotiating the Maastricht Treaty, which committed the EU to monetary union. Others made their main contribution during the relaunching of the EMU process and the negotiations of the Maastricht Treaty, for instance Jacques Delors. Certain architects—notably Hans Tietmeyer—spanned both periods.

QUESTIONS AND THEME

The book addresses a set of questions that arise as the Euro Area confronts the implication of its own extraordinary character. Who were its architects? From what sort of backgrounds did they come? Notably, with one exception, they came from the six founding Member States. What kind of attitudes and beliefs inspired their engagement with EMU? Was there a shared factor of generational experience? In their various ways, they had in common shared personal exposure to the horrors of European war and the aftermath of the Versailles Treaty and the Great Depression. It led them to hold a profound core belief in building a new and different Europe. EMU was inexorably bound up in a much larger sense of historic purpose: to create a Europe in which war was no longer a possibility. German unification in 1990 was to reawaken this sense of historic purpose. EMU was to be a means of anchoring more firmly a more powerful united Germany into Europe. The character of many of the architects had also been influenced by the early post-war revival of Christian social ethics. It helped endow them with a shared, strong moral earnestness and sense of public duty. The demise of the Bretton Woods system and its aftermath, including the oil crises, was another shared formative influence. It highlighted the intimate connection between external and internal economic stability and its importance to European integration. Many shared a sense that Bretton Woods had to be recreated on a regional scale.

What kind of project did the architects seek to construct, how, and with whom? There was no consensus of purpose. For Raymond Barre, it was a matter of exchange-rate stabilization, a tool for disciplining and modernizing Member States, not least France. For Triffin, and for Tommaso Padoa-Schioppa in the early 1980s, monetary union was very much about a European currency, also as a contribution to the design of a multipolar international monetary system. Like Marjolin, Triffin's conception of EMU was embedded in a strongly Atlanticist approach. For Karl-Otto Pöhl and for Tietmeyer, monetary union was about a single currency and a single monetary policy. The question of 'how' to create a monetary union involved a division of views about whether economic convergence or a gradualist monetary integration should take primacy. There was more consensus about 'with whom' a monetary union should be formed. Despite what happened later (a Euro Area of eleven Member States in 1999), the architects had envisaged a small monetary union built around the original founding Member States. On this issue the thinking in the German 'core Europe' paper of Wolfgang Schäuble and Karl Lamers in 1994 was close to the views of the architects (for details see Dyson and Quaglia 2010a: 541–3). Five or six Member States would initially form this core.

How successful were the architects in embedding their ideas in the final design? Here there were significant differences. The Maastricht design went well beyond the expectations of Barre and Triffin. Though they would emphasize the limitations of the design of the euro, Pöhl and Tietmeyer were more successful than other architects in this respect. However, seen from the perspective of the crisis, had the architects been prescient in recognizing design requirements and faults? All of the architects thought something was missing in the Maastricht Treaty. Nevertheless, they differed about what they thought was missing and what should be done. Seen in the light of later developments, Alexandre Lamfalussy proved perhaps the most prescient of all the architects.

Were the design failures attributable to the architects' lack of warnings about the risks involved? Or were the design faults attributable to the failure of politicians to listen and to wishing the end of monetary union without paying sufficient attention to the means? Pöhl, Tietmeyer, and the German Bundesbank had issued numerous warnings about setting deadlines and about the risks in establishing monetary union without the preconditions of firm fiscal discipline, economic convergence, and political union. In his paper for the Delors Committee in 1988 Lamfalussy had pointed to the risks in not having a strong macro-economic policy framework. On the whole, it is remarkable that all the architects were in favour of a much more 'symmetric' EMU than the one negotiated in Maastricht.

In addressing these questions the lens of biography draws out the complex and dynamic interplay of conviction and expediency in the thinking of architects. Their thoughts involved a compound of ideas with interests. This theme arose with respect to the relationship of the pursuit of EMU with national interest, for instance in Werner's promotion of Luxembourg as a laboratory for the development of new ECU (European currency unit) business. It also surfaced in the conflict of institutional interests between the European Commission and European central banks. Which was to be empowered by EMU? A further instance of the complex interplay of conviction and expediency was evident in the different incentives and constraints facing architects when in and out of office. In office, they were disposed to think in more cautious and diplomatic terms; out of office, they were likely to be more forceful, whether in expressing their disappointment, like Marjolin in the 1970s, or in advocating bolder reforms, like Padoa-Schioppa after leaving the ECB.

DESIGN FAULTS

In the first pre-crisis decade of the euro the record of policy outcomes associated with the euro was mixed (for details see Dyson 2008). On the positive side, there was evidence of the quality of the work of these architects in the trouble-free launch of European monetary union on 1 January 1999. The new ECB took charge of the single monetary policy for the Euro Area, as well as a euro payment and settlement system. This step was followed by the smooth introduction of euro banknotes and coins on 1 January 2002. Also, for longer than the first decade of the euro, the ECB proved capable of locking-in long-term expectations of Euro Area inflation in a manner consistent with its price stability target of 'below but close to' 2 per cent.

On the negative side, there were problems. The convergence criteria for euro entry were not applied strictly, notably in the case of Greece. Economic growth was lacklustre, not least for France, Germany, and Italy. Member State fiscal discipline was weak. Aggregate public debt remained above the Maastricht reference value of 60 per cent of gross domestic product (GDP). Sharp divergence in unit labour cost development was linked to serious and growing trade and financial imbalances within the Euro Area. Interest-rate convergence led to cheap credit and serious asset-price bubbles in the housing and property markets of certain Member States, notably Ireland and Spain.

This ambivalent pre-crisis record suggested a discord between relative—though still partial—success in the monetary dimension and relative failure in the economic and financial dimensions of EMU. It attested to design faults linked to asymmetry in the design of its two central pillars, economic union and monetary union.

The Euro Area's construction was exceptional in a number of senses. It was an impressive feat in overcoming problems of sheer technical scale and complexity. However, it rested on Member States jealously guarding their sovereignty in economic, fiscal, and banking policies, whilst delegating sovereignty in monetary policy to the supranational level—and thus giving up exchange-rate and interest-rate instruments of domestic adjustment. Its institutional construction took on the distinctive and problematic form of 'a monetary union without a state'. A durable construction on such terms seemed to be without historical precedent. Huge responsibility was vested in the institutionally lonely and exposed ECB, which lacked the supportive framework of a European banking union and a European fiscal union.

Above all, EMU was a rule-based construction. In effect, the Euro Area was 'a monetary union with many states', a construction that proved the source of many of its problems. The Euro Area lacked the formal attributes of independent sovereign powers over fiscal and economic policies and over banking and financial markets, not least to ensure financial stability in conditions of deepening market integration. Possession of these attributes presupposed an institutional framework of European political union. Such a framework was not in evidence (in 2005 France and the Netherlands had rejected the European Constitutional Treaty). Political union was essential to provide the democratic legitimacy that such far-reaching transfers of sovereignty, above all in fiscal policy, require.

This institutional vacuum created serious doubts about the robustness and sustainability of the construction of European monetary union and posed questions about the quality of the work by its architects. It was by no means clear whether—in existential crisis—the bonds of political solidarity would prove strong enough to hold the construction together. The architecture had to be resilient enough to cope with contagious cross-national financial panic, to contain the dynamics of market disintegration, and—not least—to be able to manage cross-national political contagion. As we shall see, few architects anticipated just how serious this problem of institutional vacuum was in their thinking about the design of monetary union.

Moreover, the construction of European monetary union did not rest on a consensus amongst its architects about who bears liability for adjustment to internal trade and financial imbalances within the Euro Area. This issue had haunted the European integration process from the outset. It was central to the Bretton Woods negotiations in 1944; to the design and operation of the European Payments Union (EPU) in the 1950s; and to the European Monetary System (EMS), which was launched in 1979 and formed an important part of the context of the Maastricht negotiations (Dyson 2014). The problem of imbalances was not centrally addressed in the early architecture of the Euro Area. The emphasis in the Maastricht Treaty was on nominal criteria of convergence rather than on real convergence as conditions for euro entry. Most telling was the absence of a collective financial assistance mechanism to help manage adjustment and the discursive victory of the 'no bail-out' idea. The implications were clear: debtor states must bear responsibility for problems of adjustment that were seen as 'home-made'. The crisis was to reopen this central issue as a contest not just of economic belief but also of political solidarity and its limits.

The design faults of the Maastricht framework, notably in crisis management, were to be graphically highlighted as the financial, economic, and sovereign debt crisis unfolded from 2007. The period from the inception of the Greek crisis in 2009–10 led to a major reconfiguration of institutional arrangements and policy instruments. European economic governance evolved to include stronger and more intrusive economic surveillance, with greater attention to trade and financial imbalances; tougher monitoring of fiscal rules; new financial assistance mechanisms; the strict conditionality associated with rescue programmes for Member States in debt crises; and the new pillars of European banking union. The ECB used its longer-term refinancing operations to provide liquidity to the Euro Area financial system and the economy. It also bought bonds of Member States facing market difficulties, like Italy and Spain. This cumulative process of radical change led to executive empowerment. The element of 'integration by stealth' also stimulated new, highly politically sensitive debates about sovereignty, national identity, technocracy, and democracy in Europe.

The construction of the Euro Area could be seen as having evolved from a 'monetary union of Member States' into a new form of 'monetary union beyond the state'. It was one in which the EU and the Member States could be seen as joint sovereigns behind the euro (Hoeksma and Schoenmaker 2011). This shift to a conception of joint sovereignty was evident in major political breakthroughs: the creation of the European Financial Stability Facility (EFSF) in May 2010—later the permanent, treaty-anchored European Stability Mechanism (ESM); the fiscal compact treaty in December 2011; and European banking union, with a Euro Area Single Supervisory Mechanism (SSM) and a Single Resolution Mechanism (SRM) and fund for restructuring and winding-down banks.

THE LENS OF BIOGRAPHY

The distinctiveness of this book lies in its attempt to answer questions about the role of architects of the euro by using original archival sources and, where possible, elite interviews and by drawing on established experts in the history of European monetary integration. Methodologically, the book rests on a range of historical sources. They include archival records; autobiographies, diaries, journals, unpublished papers, testimonials, and personal correspondence; and oral history, which involves the individual architect and/or collaborators, as well as senior people still active in EMU, not least to assess the reputation of the architect (cf. Weintraub 1991).

Characteristically, when confronted by acute threats to its identity, coherence, and survival, a polity looks back for inspiration to its architects. The Euro Area crisis provides an opportunity to re-examine their contribution and legacy, in particular the adequacy of the ideas on which monetary union was constructed. Despite certain shared aspects of generational background, experience, and belief, the architects of the euro had often very different visions of Europe and very different understandings of EMU. Padoa-Schioppa was a European federalist. In contrast, Barre opposed a supranational Europe. Others, for instance Delors, were more reticent or ambiguous about the kind of Europe in which EMU was to be embedded. For some, EMU was a self-contained project; it did not require political union. Solidarity was a matter of fulfilling commitments by respecting fiscal rules and by implementing supply-side reforms, for instance to labour markets and to welfare state provisions. Despite these differences of understanding, each in their own way contributed ideas that shaped the way in which European monetary union was debated and created. Their importance stems from the way in which they were institutionally embedded within the EMU policy process. They occupied nodal positions in the key policy networks, notably in and around the European Commission and in European central banking. Four of the nine architects in this book were European Commissioners; five worked at some stage in central banking; whilst the career paths of two architects, Lamfalussy and Padoa-Schioppa, involved a commercial banking background.

Using the lens of biography helps to provide a corrective in writing about the history of European monetary union. Its history has been viewed from various perspectives, each shedding light on particular aspects of what is a highly complex phenomenon. Structure has proved a particularly influential perspective, pointing to the logic at work in European monetary integration, however fuzzy. It focuses on the way in which individuals are caught up within particular settings which for them take on an impersonal and objective character, to which—consciously or unconsciously—they adjust: economic, financial, political, or ideational, and typically international (e.g. Dyson 1994). These external realities include financial globalization, the evolving institutional arrangements of European integration, the Franco-German relationship, beliefs about markets, and the ideational power of Germany over macroeconomic discourse. They are seen as locking the choices of individuals into a particular trajectory of development. Emphasis is placed on historical path dependency and on the institutional constraints on what individuals can do and think they can do.

A variant of this type of account is functionalist narratives of EMU. In this account individuals are enmeshed in the logic of 'spill-over' from processes of international capital market liberalization, of making EU common policies like customs union, the Common Agricultural Policy (CAP), and the single European market work effectively, and of power balancing in the Franco-German relationship. Marjolin was strongly motivated by this kind of view of monetary union.

A particular variant of structural accounts is that in which individuals are seen as entrapped within mainstream or 'hegemonic' economic ideas. Here EMU is situated in the process of paradigm change from an ascendant Keynesianism in the 1950s–60s to monetarist and supply-side economics from the 1970s onwards (e.g. Maes 1998a; Marcussen 2000; McNamara

1998). This type of ideational change is typically seen as contingent on the accumulating policy problems and failures associated with established economic institutional arrangements and policies, international and domestic. The association of mainstream economic ideas with persisting and mounting policy failures undermines their credibility and opens space for new thinking. Seen in this way, European monetary union was designed in the 1980s–90s within the 'sound money, sound finances' paradigm (Dyson 2000). EMU as designed in the Delors Report of 1989 was very different from that envisaged in the Werner Report of 1970. The paradigm of 'sound money, sound finances' gained mainstream ascendancy after the collapse of the Bretton Woods system, the oil crises, and the 'stagflation' of the 1970s. These events and developments had diminished the credibility of Keynesian ideas of counter-cyclical demand management through activist fiscal policies and macro-economic policy coordination. Increasing emphasis was placed on the role of monetary policy in delivering price stability as the basis for sustainable economic growth and on supply-side reforms as the engine of economic growth and employment. This ideational change was linked to the crucial role of the central banks in creating European monetary union and in the way in which it was designed.

European monetary union has also been depicted as an essentially political process, in which political leaders played a decisive role in driving forward the project (e.g. Dyson and Featherstone 1999). German Federal Chancellor Willy Brandt and French President Georges Pompidou played this role in the first attempt to put EMU on the agenda in 1969–70. Chancellor Helmut Schmidt and President Valéry Giscard d'Estaing were central to the launch of the EMS in 1978–9. Above all, Chancellor Helmut Kohl and President François Mitterrand had a sense of 'making history' and binding their successors by ensuring the irreversibility of European monetary union with the Maastricht Treaty. From this perspective, European monetary union is an exercise in 'high' politics. Political leaders provide historical legitimacy and help shape history by timely strategic interventions. In the case of EMU they managed the process by establishing institutional venues to circumvent potential veto players or to bind them into the process, by setting tight time deadlines, and by asserting the primacy of the European Council (Dyson and Featherstone 1999).

This book seeks to contribute to our understanding of the history of European monetary union through a lens of biography that focuses not on the political drivers of the process of EMU but on the architects of its substance. Two premises lie at its heart. The first is that individuals matter. The question is in what ways they matter. The role of architects is important if we are to understand 'what happened when', how a particular type of monetary union was constructed, and why the Euro Area faced certain kinds of challenge later. Their importance rested in giving substance to the project of monetary union through their exceptional engagement with, and knowledge of, the often esoteric technical issues and through their networking skills within complex European governance structures. The architects contributed ideas and proposals that shaped institutional development and policies. Alternatively, if not adopted, their ideas and proposals retained a relevance to later challenges that faced European monetary union. The architects contributed more than just a unique intellectual milieu to EMU. They also built up personal networks and institutional structures of support for their ideas, as both intellectuals and policy advocates.

The second premise is that debates at a technical level about how to construct a viable and sustainable European monetary union, about its substantive content, and about the management of the policy process matter. These debates were the provenance of the architects of the euro, individuals who sought to design a European monetary union with firm foundations, whilst divided on what those foundations should be. The questions that form the heart of this book are: what form these technical debates took; and who contributed to them, in what ways, and leaving what kind of legacies.

Biography poses a number of challenges. First and foremost, it is possible to become seduced by the individual experts about whom one is writing. In the process one loses both critical perspective and the possibility of arriving at a balanced judgement about their role and impact within the context of the times they lived in and the circumstances they encountered. In stressing what they contributed to European monetary union, one risks overlooking the ways in which they failed to contribute. Biography should be as much a study of failures as of successes if it is to avoid creating mythology and degenerating into hagiography.

Secondly, we must not forget that, in the final analysis, the history of European monetary union was a collective enterprise, not simply the story of one person or a small group of individuals. It is important not to lose sight of the fact that the making of European monetary union involved the ideas and efforts of a wide range of experts. It could not have succeeded without their collaboration. Moreover, the individuals changed over time. Some were active over long periods. Triffin was an active contributor from the period of the EPU, through the protracted demise of the Bretton Woods system, to the design and operation of the EMS. Tietmeyer remained actively engaged from the Werner Committee in 1970 to the establishment of the ECB in 1999. Others, like Roy Jenkins, had a much briefer involvement. It is impossible to include all who played a role and had an impact, and we have had to be selective. In being selective, we should not forget that the story of European monetary union is about the complex dynamics not just amongst the architects chosen here but also with significant others. The significant others included the political leaders who had entrusted them with a negotiating mandate and timescale and on whom they relied for their negotiating space.

Despite these qualifications, some architects merit close attention in writing the history of European monetary union. One reason is that they were representative of larger debates. They played a leading role either in agenda setting or in clarifying and giving content to debates. They stood out as unusually and productively reflective, inquisitive, questioning, and comfortable in exploring across boundaries. The longevity and/or intensity of their engagement with issues of monetary union gave them a personal intellectual authority that could be readily translated into influence. Another reason for focusing on certain architects is that they understood how to negotiate the complex interface between economic and monetary ideas and the structures of power in Europe. They were not just fascinated by, and comfortable with, the world of ideas. They were also engaged in trying to realize them through governance structures, above all in European and central banking structures. They were, in short, not simply 'experts with influence'. They were 'intellectuals as policy-makers'.

SHARED UNDERSTANDINGS: THE SHADOW OF HISTORY, EUROPEANIZATION, AND THE LIMITS OF EXPERTISE

This book does not attempt to present the individual architects of the euro in a tightly preconceived format. Space is left for the individuality of architects to emerge. At the same time, the book brings out a number of themes that cut across the various chapters. These themes invite authors to critically assess the larger role and impact of individual architects of the euro and the ideas and the schemes with which they were associated. In addition, this assessment needs to be qualified by a recognition that, however great their diversity of views on how best to construct a monetary union, and what form to give it, these architects were bound together by a set of shared, often implicit, understandings that facilitated consensus building.

At the heart of these shared understandings were two historical factors. The first was that they were part of a common generational experience, coming to maturity in the aftermath of terrible and ruinous wars and convinced that what Europe needed was a new basis of peace, order, and stability. The second factor was shared experience of adaptive learning about how best to make economic and monetary policies within the new institutional framework of European integration, with its attendant unanticipated consequences. This experience included the demise and the aftermath of the Bretton Woods system and a world of capital liberalization. It also involved factoring out restructuring of Member State sovereign and bank debts as a design issue. The shared assumption was that debt restructuring was relevant to developing states, not to 'developed' EU Member States, which could be relied on to respect rules of sound public finances. Moreover, there was a third factor: a shared recognition of the limits of their expertise in designing European monetary union.

The Shadow of History

Despite their many and varied differences over how to construct a European monetary union, and what form to give it, the architects of the euro shared a certain broad world-view. They looked to the past, above all inter-war Europe, not for models of economic and monetary policies but in order to learn from the mistakes that had led to hyper-inflation, currency instability, the Great Depression, and the slide into war. The past was deeply unattractive. They had in common a distrust of models of the 'national economy', engaging in bilateral arrangements in pursuit of individual state advantage. Albeit to varying degrees, they were committed to multilateralism and sceptical of appeals to economic sovereignty. They were part of a whole generation of educated elites for whom promoting European unification offered unrivalled opportunities to use their technical knowledge and skills to forge a new and better Europe that would ensure that past horrors of economic dislocation, misery, fascism, and total war were not repeated.

These shared attitudes bound them together as a particular post-war, post-fascist generation. The economic and political turmoil of inter-war Europe and ruinous conflict cut through their personal biographies or at least those of their immediate families. They shared the notion of a different post-national Europe living together in more civilized terms within a framework of common institutions. In this context the revitalization of Christian social ethics, and in particular Catholic social thought, was a major influence on how many of them thought about Europe. It reinforced their moral earnestness and their profound sense of public duty.

The shadow of history was deepest and most profound in European states that had directly lived under fascism—Germany and Italy—and under Nazi occupation, notably France and the small European states like Belgium, Luxembourg, and the Netherlands. As Europe's largest economy, and its major creditor state from 1952–3, German participation was indispensable for a sustainable European monetary union. Crucially, the deep reservations of German Ordo-liberals about European monetary union were counterbalanced by the way in which the shadow of history led Germany's own founding fathers to write a responsibility for promoting European unification into the preamble of the Basic Law of 1949. Promoting European unification was recognized by the German Federal Constitutional Court as a 'constitutional duty'. In Italy there was a shared understanding that the post-war republic had to regain respectability by ensuring that it had, and retained, a seat at Europe's high table. Elites in the small European states were determined that Europe's big powers find a new way to live together on more civilized terms. In these ways the shadow of history helps us to understand why Belgians, French, Germans, Italians, and Luxembourgers were active as architects of European monetary union. It also shows why they could reconcile their differences.

Europeanization

From the 1950s a second historical factor was at work. Initially, European economic and monetary cooperation was pushed onto the agenda by the terms of US Marshall Aid, the Organization for European Economic Cooperation (OEEC), and the EPU. For Triffin, who was also an architect of the EPU's monetary dimension, the EPU was a fundamental experience which would serve as a source of inspiration for his plans for EMU (see Chapter 2). In particular, the EPU Managing Board occupied itself with the issues of what constituted good and bad behaviour not just by debtor states, like France, but also creditor states, like Germany (Kaplan and Schleiminger 1989). Many of the later issues within European monetary union were rehearsed within the EPU of the 1950s, notably who should bear the burden of adjustment to trade and financial imbalances (Dyson 2014).

The Treaty of Rome in 1957 made no explicit commitment to monetary union. Nevertheless, it served to stimulate debate—and divisions—about what the customs union, the CAP, common trade policy, and the longer-term commitment to 'ever closer union' implied for European economic and monetary policy coordination and integration. This debate was evident within the German Federal Economics Ministry. As early as 1958–9, the State Secretary with responsibility for European integration, Alfred Müller-Armack, was advocating a European Counter-Cyclical Board with associated funds to stimulate infrastructural investment (see Chapter 7). He sought to use European integration to spur a domestic debate about a second phase of the social market economy. Whilst blocked by his minister, Ludwig Erhard, these ideas were later to flow into the so-called Schiller Plans for EMU in 1969–70. They retain relevance today as the EU considers how it might use public investment to strengthen Europe's growth potential.

Importantly, the debate about Europeanizing economic and monetary policies evolved, and gained momentum, with the widening policy scope and deepening institutional integration of Europe. The collapse of the Bretton Woods system in 1973 triggered debate about the relative gains and costs of seeking to restore exchange-rate stability within Europe. A crucial issue was whether a 'Bretton Woods for Europe' should be designed in more symmetrical terms than Bretton Woods, as demanded by France. However, the EMS became, to a large extent, a new D-Mark zone, like its predecessor, the European monetary 'snake'. The commitment to a European single market in 1985–6, including freedom of capital movement, acted as a catalyst in the debate about monetary union. What did the ERM and the single market, in combination, mean for European economic and monetary policies?

By the late 1980s technical elites in European central banks, finance ministries, and the European Commission could not avoid engagement in debate about Europeanization. There was a basic consensus that economic and monetary policies had to be rethought in the context of European integration, the complex dynamics that it unleashed, and the unanticipated consequences and the unstable states to which it gave rise.

Architects of the euro were caught up together in a process of adaptive learning both about the practical requirements of a sustainable monetary union and about the scope for finding mutually acceptable outcomes. Addressing these problems was not possible on the basis of a simple dichotomy between 'objective' economic laws and 'subjective' politics. Objectively, constructing EMU had to deal with the problem of how to create incentives for the domestic ownership of the project and of its implications by Member State governing elites and their citizens. This consideration forced the architects of the euro to pay greater attention than academic economists to the political acceptability of the project, including norms of reciprocity in burden sharing. They learnt to recognize the importance of moral sentiments like dignity and respect, and of avoiding humiliation and shaming, and the anger that they would provoke, in arriving at sustainable negotiated outcomes. EMU rested ultimately on its cultivation of a sense of shared belonging (cf. Nussbaum 2013). This recognition was widely shared, though not necessarily the answer to the question 'belonging to what?'

The Limits of Expertise

A third factor was shared recognition of the limits of their expertise as architects of EMU. In the first place, they had to work within the limits of the political mandate, including time deadlines that they were given by the heads of state and government in the European Council. Heads of state and government—or, acting on their behalf, the Council of Economic and Finance Ministers (ECOFIN)—could engineer the process by choosing the institutional venues and the kind of expertise that they wished to involve (see Dyson and Featherstone 1999). Thus the membership of the Werner Group on the Study of EMU in 1970 was based on the chairs of the key European Economic Community (EEC) committees and thus included finance ministry representation. In contrast, the Delors Committee in 1988–9 was primarily composed of EU central bank presidents acting in a personal capacity. A centre for decision-making on economic policy figured more prominently in the Werner Report than in the Delors Report. In contrast, the Delors Report placed greater emphasis on fiscal rules to bind Member State governments. It laid the foundations for the 'rules-based' economic policy framework of the Maastricht Treaty. Choice and composition of institutional venues for the study of EMU had implications for the kind of expertise that was included and excluded.

Secondly, European political union—and the associated and fundamental questions of political legitimacy—was essentially out of bounds for the architects of the euro. They could recognize and stress its indispensability and address the issue indirectly as part of the functional prerequisites of a sustainable monetary union. Thus the German Bundesbank made repeated references to the importance of European political union. However, its expertise and responsibility did not extend to giving substance to this area, which was the domain of heads of state and government.

The central problem was that the economic, fiscal, and banking policy pillars of EMU touched on highly sensitive political issues of sovereignty. Indeed, a central consequence of EMU was its role as a catalyst for revival of debate about sovereignty and constitutional identity. This debate provoked a new and greater role for legal as opposed to economic and monetary experts, exemplified in the growing body of German Federal Constitutional Court rulings on EMU, as well as rulings by other Member State constitutional courts (Chalmers 2013). At the same time, monetary union touched on sovereignty in a more restricted manner than economic policy union. Once central bank independence became accepted as a principle within EU Member States, linked to a narrow mandate of price stability, it became less 'sovereignty sensitive'. Also, monetary policy had the feature of being less overtly redistributive and direct in its effects on individuals than fiscal and economic policies, which had an impact through taxes, spending, benefit levels, wages, and working conditions.

Nevertheless, this limitation of their expertise left architects of the euro exposed to critique. EMU was judged to be flawed by its entrapment in a narrow economic and technocratic rationality. Even in these narrow terms it could be criticized for a naïve faith in compliance with fiscal rules and for neglecting debt restructuring of sovereign and bank debt as a policy instrument (Dyson 2014; Sandbu 2015). In more general terms the edifice in whose construction they had participated could be condemned for its 'authoritarian managerialism', its subversion of democracy (e.g. Beck 2013; Habermas 2013; Heisbourg 2013; Joerges 2010). It was accused of being driven by technocratic elites and of facilitating a process of executive self-empowerment at the expense of parliamentary participation and effective accountability at both national and European levels. The European economic governance structures associated with monetary union, and above all with post-2010 crisis management and reforms, were seen as hollowing out the substance of Member State democracy (Streeck 2013). They were accused of contributing to citizen disempowerment, political alienation, and heightened mistrust of political processes: in short, of deepening the 'democratic deficit' at the heart of the construction of the EU.

In the final analysis, public disaffection with the democratic deficit of EMU could not be ignored by European policy-makers, including its architects. The December 2012 report 'Towards a Genuine Economic and Monetary Union', drawn up by European Council President Herman van Rompuy, in close collaboration with the presidents of the European Commission, the Eurogroup, and the ECB, contained a section on democratic legitimacy and accountability. Their conception of a genuine EMU was one that included a fiscal union, an economic union, a banking union, and political union. In the ensuing years, new proposals to remedy the democratic deficit were put forward (cf. Maystadt 2014).

Nevertheless, the critique of the absence of a political union was in many respects unfair if addressed to the expert architects. They were after all trained in economics and finance and active in central banking and in European Commission circles. Crucially, they were limited by the mandate which they were given by Europe's political decision-makers. This mandate was fundamental to their own political legitimacy and the basis of their accountability. They were not asked whether the mandate was sensible. At the same time, the political foundations of sustainable European monetary union constitute vital aspects of the architecture of the euro. Any assessment of the architects' role has to take this aspect into account.

More directly telling for the expert architects were critiques of the economic rationality of their shared understanding of EMU construction. Some of the strongest critiques came from Anglo-American economists, often based on the so-called 'Optimum Currency Area' (OCA) theory. OCA theory had various strands, identifying a range of factors—traditionally exogenous—that were deemed indispensable to a sustainable monetary union. They remain controversial both independently and as an interdependent package. OCA theory spread in the 1960s, following Mundell's (1961) seminal article (cf. Maes 2002: 13–28). It focused on the adjustment mechanisms in a monetary union when hit by an asymmetric shock, creating unemployment in part of the union. The main adjustment mechanisms were identified as labour mobility, wage and price flexibility, and federal budget and solidarity mechanisms, which lead to transfers between the regions in case of asymmetric shocks. Compared to the United States, and its internal migration, the Euro Area appeared inadequately prepared to manage asymmetric shocks. It lacked not only a fiscal transfer mechanism but also cross-border labour mobility and wage flexibility (Dyson 2000: 193–5; Goodhart and Smith 1993; Krugman

1993). However, sustainable currency union is at least as much a political as a technical phenomenon. It needs the political glue provided by a sense that the union as a whole is acting in ways that support collective interests, including those who are disadvantaged by asymmetric shocks. In this respect the absence of a well-designed Euro Area fiscal shock-absorber mechanism was a failure in political design of the euro.

In the final analysis, the architects of the euro did not design European monetary union on the basis of a shared OCA theory. Many of them questioned the effectiveness of some of the mechanisms of adjustment in federal systems like the United States. They noted that monetary unions seemed sustainable despite being only weakly correlated with OCA attributes. Far more important was the understanding amongst architects of the euro that the chief risk facing Member States and any structure of European monetary integration were exchange-rate crises. They were part of a generation that had lived through the collapse of the post-war Bretton Woods system of stable and managed exchange rates and through the subsequent crises that followed attempts at European exchange-rate coordination first in the 'snake' and then in the ERM. This shared understanding was confirmed by the ERM crises of 1983, 1987, 1992, and 1993 and the strains that they put on the Franco-German relationship. They pointed to the increasing vulnerability of the EU to exchange-rate crises from the combination of the ERM with capital market liberalization. EMU was, in their view, the least bad alternative; it offered escape from exchange-rate crises. Many of the architects had the deep conviction that, over time, a single market was only sustainable with a single currency.

The architects of the euro could be criticized for failing to fully anticipate the complacency that would follow once the exchange-rate constraint was removed in a currency union. Market pressure to correct imbalances was reduced, at least until the bond markets woke up to the scale of risks within the monetary union. The problem of persisting imbalances suggested that neglect of OCA theory had been unfortunate. The sheer diversity and heterogeneity of economic structures, and of traditions of macro-economic discourse and practice within the Euro Area, begged the question of whether the criteria for euro entry had been sufficiently robust, for instance in focusing too narrowly on criteria of price stability and public finances. Economic adjustment was politically and socially more costly in the absence of attributes of an OCA.

A further critique of the inadequate shared understandings of European monetary union focused on the architects' neglect of the importance of financial stability for a robust and sustainable construction of the Euro Area. Here Lamfalussy was more prescient than others. Missing elements in the initial construction of European monetary union were pan-European banking and financial market supervision and regulation; common provision for the resolution of failed banks; a shared deposit guarantee mechanism; and the creation of a capital markets union.

Financial integration deepened significantly after the euro was introduced (Maes 2007). However, the global financial crisis caused that process to go into reverse, in substantial part because of the incomplete nature of financial integration in the Euro Area (Draghi 2014). Price convergence in many asset classes created an appearance of financial integration. In practice, financial integration was relatively shallow, particularly in the banking sector. While the inter-bank market was fully integrated, retail banking remained fragmented. In this situation banks used short-term and debt-based funding to increase lending to favoured domestic sectors such as property and construction. As banks' assets were not well allocated, nor well diversified geographically, they were more vulnerable to domestic shocks. And, as their foreign liabilities were mainly inter-bank, they could not share the subsequent losses with other jurisdictions (ibid). Hence, when the crisis hit, the cost of repairing balance sheets fell largely on the domestic fiscal authorities of banks. The result was the infamous bank–sovereign nexus, again an issue neglected by the architects of the euro.

The economic critique of the limits of the expertise of the architects of the euro went beyond OCA and banking union. It also pointed to another design problem, very much related to the asymmetry of EMU and the absence of a political union. The Euro Area suffered a credibility problem because of the weakness of its capacity to act in supreme emergency. The Maastricht Treaty had, for political reasons, committed to the principle of irreversibility in creating a monetary union. However, the question remained whether the EU and the Member States were committed to defend the monetary union in its current configuration by reference to this principle. The original architecture of the euro did not include an institutional capacity to manage extreme conditions, above all a combination of financial market panic, deepening economic recession, and political turmoil (Dyson 2012). In such circumstances the ECB stood as the one lonely supranational actor with serious instruments at its disposal, unlike the European Commission. It was in a dangerously exposed position, at risk of acting without adequate political support and of being accused of encouraging moral hazard.

Nevertheless, the Euro Area crisis altered the institutional and decision-making structures of the EU. The Commission gained wider responsibilities for the surveillance of national economic policies. However, it is more difficult to assess how the overall influence of the Commission has evolved. A UK House of Lords report (2014: 20) commented: 'Some authorities have grown stronger, notably the ECB and the Eurogroup ... By contrast, the Commission's power and influence in determining the crisis response has diminished ... it is noticeable (and perhaps inevitable) that it is euro area authorities, as opposed to those representing the EU 28, that have grown in power and influence.'

During the crisis the responsibilities of the ECB have been significantly extended. These changes were very much in line with the preoccupations of Lamfalussy, one of the architects of the euro and the founding president of the European Monetary Institute (EMI), the precursor of the ECB. Following the de Larosière Report on the strengthening of European supervisory arrangements in 2009, the European Systemic Risk Board (ESRB) was established (Dyson and Quaglia 2010b: 109–14, 131–9). The main task of the ESRB was to focus on the stability of the financial system as a whole, compared with the supervision of individual firms. The ECB has an important role in the ESRB, for which it also provides the secretariat. In addition, the Single Supervisory Mechanism (SSM), a crucial pillar of banking union, marked a watershed not just in the history of the ECB but also in the history of European integration. With the start of the SSM in November 2014, the ECB assumed responsibility for directly supervising significant Euro Area credit institutions and can also decide at any time to take responsibility for a less-significant credit institution.

TRADITIONS, INDIVIDUALITY, AND ADAPTIVE PRESSURES

In examining the various architects of the euro it is important to have a sense of the different traditions that helped to structure their thinking. Indeed, the history of European monetary union is typically conceived of as a contest between different 'schools' of thought.

The sense that architects were caught up in different schools is evident in the debate about how best to construct a monetary union. The creation of monetary union was pictured as a debate between two coalitions, the so-called 'economists' and 'monetarists'. The 'economists', led by Germany, believed that the foundations for a sustainable monetary union lay in 'home-grown' stability. Member States must first put their own houses in order. They needed sustainable, disciplined domestic fiscal policies and domestic economic policies that ensured speedy, flexible, and smooth adjustment through market mechanisms, not least promoting labour mobility. In these ways a foundation of economic convergence was to be put in place before monetary union. The legacies of this school of thinking are the convergence criteria for euro entry and the design of the excessive deficit procedure, both with a strong focus on fiscal convergence. The 'economist' school could, in part, draw on traditional OCA theory for support.

In contrast, the 'monetarists', with France as a major player, believed that a process of monetary integration would help promote economic convergence. Exchange-rate stabilization could be used as an instrument to externally discipline Member State monetary, fiscal, and economic policies; whilst monetary union would promote convergence through closer trade and financial integration. Monetary union was viewed as a process of common institution building. It would involve learning by doing, by gaining experience of exchange-rate, monetary, fiscal, and economic policy coordination. The 'monetarist' school gained intellectual support from the endogenous OCA theory of Andrew Rose (2000), which stresses the trade gains from monetary union. However, when put to the test, this monetarist faith was to be shaken as convergence proved not to be a simple one-way street but a dynamic process in which regression—and the conditions for crisis—was possible.

These differing views on monetary integration can be situated within deeper and longer-standing French and German conceptions of economic policy-making (Maes 2004). In France, there was a long tradition of a 'voluntarist' approach to economic policy-making with an active role for the state in the economy, traditionally characterized as 'Colbertism'. The 'monetarist' approach, with monetary integration having a leading role in the integration process, fitted into this voluntarist tradition. In Germany, Ordo-liberal thought was very influential in the post-war period, with its belief that market competition required as a precondition a strong robust domestic institutional framework. Consistent with the 'economist' approach, it emphasized the responsibility of Member States for creating the conditions for convergence by building stability at home. These contrasting traditions of economic thought reflected in turn more fundamental differences in 'meta-beliefs'. The 'republican tradition' in France stressed the sovereign nation as the source of legitimacy and, consequently, the political direction of economic policy. Post-war German beliefs rested on the vital ordering role of law, the division of power in a federal system, and the important role accorded to non-majoritarian institutions like the Bundesbank. The convergence of French and German economic policy conceptions was an indispensable condition for the realization of EMU. However, the deeper meta-beliefs that informed different approaches to monetary union remained resilient. France typically tends to favour a more discretionary approach; Germany emphasizes the importance of rules.

Individual architects can be seen as manifestations of different traditions of economic thinking and the construction of monetary union as an ongoing contest between these traditions. The ideas that Triffin, Marjolin, Delors, and Padoa-Schioppa brought to the construction of monetary union bear important Keynesian traces. In contrast, Barre, Pöhl, and Tietmeyer are more representative of the Ordo-liberal camp. With respect to the approach to monetary union, Triffin can be identified as a 'monetarist'; Pöhl and Tietmeyer as 'economists'. Though French, Marjolin was no strict 'monetarist'. He stressed the importance of promoting the convergence of economic structures.

However, biography is a tool that has the potential to deconstruct these categories. Individual architects may have theoretical commitments that are consistent with a particular school. At the same time, they are deeply engaged with complex, multidimensional, and multilevel issues of monetary union at the European level. The architects were acutely aware of the practical political problems of forging agreement, notably in a context of asymmetric power that favoured Germany. This experience led them to adopt positions that suggested a more differentiated picture at the level of practical engagement. The complex dynamics that are associated with this engagement generate adaptive behaviour, distancing them at times from the more abstract attachments of academic economists. Architects of the euro and academic economists operated to a certain extent in different peer-group contexts, establishing different measures of esteem and success.

In particular, individual architects had to position themselves with respect to the underlying power structures of European monetary integration, specifically Germany's systemic power. In the negotiation of EMU Germany appeared to be a semi-hegemonic power, one whose participation was essential for any credible form of collective action. As such, Germany possessed agenda-setting capability and bargaining resources denied to other Member States (Dyson 2014). This power stemmed from the combination of the relative size of the German economy with its status, since 1952–3, as Europe's major creditor state. Quite simply, agreeing a credible and sustainable monetary union depended on German willingness to participate.

Hence, in the period before 1999, the non-German architects of the euro faced the practical challenge of how to engage Germany and to retain German support during the long transition to a monetary union. In this sense the 'road to Maastricht' ran through Bonn, Germany's then political capital, and through Frankfurt, its monetary capital. In 1969–70 Jean Monnet and Werner sought actively to engage the new German Chancellor, Brandt, behind Triffin's proposal for a European Reserve Fund. In 1988–9 Delors focused on mobilizing Chancellor Kohl behind a new initiative for monetary union. And in November–December 1991, just before the Maastricht European Council, the emphasis in European diplomacy was on ensuring that Chancellor Kohl would commit to 'irreversibility' of monetary union in the Maastricht Treaty, specifically a fixed, final date (on which see Dyson and Featherstone 1999).

The practical exigencies of negotiating around German positions were evident in the establishment of the EMS in 1978. The outcome was a system of exchange-rate coordination that involved asymmetric adjustment based on linkage to the D-Mark. The Bundesbank emerged as 'the bank that rules Europe' (Marsh 1992). The planned stage two of the EMS, with a European monetary fund, never materialized in the face of German opposition. Later in

1989–9 the Delors Committee negotiated primarily around the plan that was presented by the Bundesbank. It was recognized that the signature of its president was indispensable if monetary union was to make progress; that the ECB would have to look like the Bundesbank 'writ large' (Dyson and Featherstone 1999).

Responding to German power was in many ways the key practical issue for architects of the euro. For Barre it was an opportunity. The ERM was a valuable instrument for disciplining and stabilizing the French economy. However, for many architects asymmetric adjustment to trade and financial imbalances was a major problem that had to be addressed. This problem characterized the EPU in the 1950s, the 'snake' exchange-rate system in the 1970s, the ERM after 1979, and EMU as negotiated in the Maastricht Treaty (Dyson 2014).

Individual architects also had to live with the power of the international financial markets. In the period before monetary union this power was exhibited in exchange-rate crises under the Bretton Woods system and later the EMS. Exchange-rate volatility had disruptive effects on trade and financial flows and reduced the benefits from the customs union and from the single European market programme. Many, though by no means all, architects of the euro had witnessed at close hand market panic and the way in which waves of optimism and pessimism could lull policy-makers into complacency or overwhelm them. Triffin, Padoa-Schioppa, Delors, and Lamfalussy did not share a neo-classical faith in financial market efficiency. However, the implications of financial-market integration through a single market in financial services and currency union constituted a major challenge for banking and financial-market supervision. Before the post-2007 crisis banking supervision remained within the realm of Member State sovereignty and subject to the inducement to protect national banking champions. European banking union was the missing element in the thinking of most architects on the foundations of monetary union. This gap was an aspect of a wider underestimation of the scale of consequences from European monetary union.

ARCHITECTS: WHO ARE THEY?

The study of architects of the euro faces problems of definition and of selection. This book focuses on the architects of the euro as opposed to its political founders and its ideational founders. The political founders made a decisive contribution, resolving the question of *whether European monetary union should take place*. Their contribution took the form of their mastery of driving the process of European monetary integration at EU and domestic levels. It involved providing historical legitimacy for the project; selecting institutional venues to progress the project; binding-in potential opponents; and setting deadlines for decision and action (cf. Dyson and Featherstone 1999).

There was considerable variety amongst the political founders. Helmut Schmidt had greater substantive policy expertise on issues of European monetary integration and union than Brandt or Kohl; the same applied to Giscard d'Estaing in comparison with Mitterrand. Nevertheless, they all shared a dependency on the expertise of the architects of EMU for design of the project. The political founders were not equipped to answer the question of *how monetary union was to take place*, as well as its detailed institutional architecture, questions that made exceptionally high cognitive demands.

The architects of the euro are also different from the ideational founders. The ideational founders were essentially academic economists whose peer-respect within their discipline translated into influence on debate. Thus Francesco Giavazzi and Marco Pagano (1988) contributed ideas on the value of 'tying hands' in economic and monetary policies as a device for securing credibility with financial markets. It provided a theoretical rationale for Member States to bind themselves within a 'hard' ERM, anchored on the German D-Mark. In this way European monetary integration could serve as a device for importing stability.

Earlier, in a seminal article, the economist James Meade (1957) discussed the balance of payments problem in a European free-trade area. Meade distinguished several factors which made the adjustment between regions in a country easier than adjustment between countries. Foreshadowing OCA theory, he singled out as important elements: mobility of goods, labour, and capital; a single banking system; a single budgetary policy; and national solidarity with regions affected by adverse shocks. Meade concluded that, in the absence of these mechanisms in Western Europe, a flexible exchange rate was the preferable mechanism of adjustment.

Robert Mundell (1961) pioneered the literature on OCA theory and the conditions for a sustainable monetary union. Much of this literature was to provide the basis for a critique of the Euro Area. EMU was not established on the *ex ante* basis of fulfilling the often highly restrictive conditions of OCA theory. Rather, it was a political project, based on the optimistic belief that European monetary union could move towards an OCA through the combination of market pressures, above all the European single market, and peer pressures. One of many variants of OCA was McKinnon's (1997) 'market-preserving fiscal federalism', which argued for the transfer of sovereignty as necessary to remove the ability of Member States to encroach on markets by suppressing competition. This variant offered a useful rationale for the kind of monetary union that was emerging in Europe and that was advocated by the ECB.

Another influential contribution from ideational founders was the Mundell–Fleming model of the 'impossible trinity'. It posited a trilemma: a fixed exchange rate, free capital movement, and an independent monetary policy could not be realized together. The 'impossible trinity' had clear relevance to the way in which European integration was evolving. Padoa-Schioppa adapted and applied to it the European integration project as the 'inconsistent quartet', adding the single market in goods. In this form it provided the basis for the argument that monetary integration and union were a logical progression from the single market and capital liberalization (Dyson and Quaglia 2010a: 354–7). In sharp contrast, Friedrich Hayek (1976a) inspired British interest in an evolutionary and market-based 'competing currency' approach to EMU (Dyson and Quaglia 2010a: 407–12). In these various ways, the ideational founders contributed ideas that were relevant to the substantive design of EMU and that fed into debates amongst architects of the euro.

At the same time, both the political founders and the ideational founders were key parts of the context within which the architects of the euro worked. Moreover, these analytical distinctions were not so clear in practice. Many of the architects crossed fuzzy boundaries. Delors, Jenkins, and Werner had political careers; Barre had both an academic and a political career; Triffin had an academic career, as well as working closely with the European Commission. In short, individuals do not fit neatly and simply into the categories of political founders, ideational founders, and architects. Nevertheless, at the heart of the creation of the euro it is possible to identify a set of 'intellectuals in policy-making'. Their expert technical contribution on how to design a sustainable monetary union was decisive to the realization of a politically-driven process.

The architects of the euro were individuals of exceptional intellectual power and energy, combined with qualities of moral earnestness and public duty. They helped to build EMU in various ways. One role was as agenda setters, advocating innovative schemes for developing monetary integration and union, like Triffin with the European Reserve Fund (ERF) proposal. Another role, evident in the cases of Pöhl and Tietmeyer, was in bringing substantive policy knowledge to bear on institutional and policy design issues. As with Delors and Werner, they also contributed by their superior information about the range of negotiating positions to be reconciled and by facilitating agreed negotiation outcomes on the basis of their expertise in managing negotiation processes. The architects of the euro combined high levels of expertise on the substantive issues in EMU, on the policy and negotiation processes and how to use European institutions, and on the negotiating positions of other participants so as to be able to craft outcomes that were convincingly workable and that could command political consent (cf. Beach 2005; Tallberg 2008).

SELECTING ARCHITECTS

The challenge of defining architects leaves open the vexed question of who to select from a large number of individuals active in designing European monetary union. At a basic level we exclude those whose main contribution came after 1 January 1999, like the presidents and chief economists of the ECB. Besides this exclusion we have worked with a set of criteria of selection. In applying these criteria, we have sought to achieve a measure of balance in Member State representation. We have also been guided by the availability of adequate historical archive material to produce satisfactory biographies.

The criteria of selection focus on the key resources of influence that enabled certain individuals to make an exceptional contribution to the debate about the construction of European monetary union. The first criterion was their substantive economic and monetary expertise. This quality was particularly striking in the cases of Barre, Lamfalussy, Marjolin, Padoa-Schioppa, and Triffin. Alternatively, as with Werner, an architect possessed a particular facility in engaging in technical arguments about monetary union. Command of relevant expert knowledge increased the capacity of an individual to shape the technical boundaries of agreement.

The second criterion was the longevity and intensity of involvement with EMU. Here Padoa-Schioppa, Tietmeyer, Triffin, and Werner excelled. Their experience and familiarity with the issues of international and European policy coordination meant that they enjoyed an exceptional credibility in helping to frame debates about EMU.

A third criterion of selection was the occupation of nodal positions in the world of policy-making on EMU, above all in the European Commission or in central banking, at critical junctures. In consequence, certain individuals were able to acquire high levels of information about the negotiating positions of others. In certain circumstances they gained a capacity to impart valuable information to others. This capacity was important in the cases of Pöhl and Tietmeyer. Their Member State, Germany, was indispensable to a credible negotiated outcome. In this way certain individuals were able to locate common ground in EMU negotiations or—as with Pöhl—shape where the common ground was to be found. Barre, Delors, Lamfalussy, and Werner excelled in these skills.

A related criterion was skill in administrative network building. This skill included creativity in finding, creating, and using institutional routes to build alliances and to influence negotiating processes. As European Commission presidents, both Jenkins and Delors sought to advance EMU by using the European Council to bypass traditional structures like the Committee of EEC Central Bank Governors. They recognized the particular importance of creating institutional routes to EMU that would bind-in German actors to the process. Marjolin was a supreme networker in the United States, France, and Germany. Triffin was fully immersed in the network of Jean Monnet and his Action Committee for Europe, which called on him to disseminate his thinking about a European Reserve Fund.

A fifth criterion was the good fortune of structural privileging from which certain individuals benefited. The underlying policy performance of Member States mattered in lending credibility to technical arguments. Individuals had greater capacity for deploying convincing arguments when their Member State was seen as indispensable to the final agreement. Indispensability was a function of size and systemic significance, of economic and monetary policy record, and of a creditor position. In these circumstances, the arguments of certain individuals gained traction from the implicit threat of exit from negotiation by the Member State on whose behalf they spoke. This criterion favoured the selection of German architects, notably Pöhl and Tietmeyer. It endowed them with a pivotal importance.

Finally, certain individuals possessed a particular persuasive power based on their framing of technical issues in monetary union within a long-term vision of European unification, even if this vision remained unclear. Examples included Delors, Jenkins, Lamfalussy, Padoa-Schioppa, and Werner. This criterion draws attention to the missionary zeal that characterized certain individuals who contributed to the design of EMU. Their dry technical arguments and promotion of institutional and Member State interests often concealed a deep emotional engagement with the idea of Europe.

The problem of selection is aggravated by the complexity of interactions amongst architects of the euro. Sometimes analysis of these interactions confirms our selection: for instance, the close relationship of Triffin to Marjolin and to Werner and of all three to Jean Monnet and his Action Committee for Europe. In other instances, these interactions introduce difficulties into selection. Thus Pöhl depended heavily on his Bundesbank economists, led by Helmut Schlesinger, who succeeded him as president in 1990. Nevertheless, Pöhl occupied the nodal position in negotiations not just because of his presence in the Delors Committee but also because he was chair of the Committee of EC Central Bank Governors during the drafting of the Statutes of the ECB and of the EMI.

Tietmeyer is clearly the obvious choice amongst German architects. However, Horst Köhler represented Germany in the Inter-Governmental Conference (IGC) on EMU in 1990–1. Jürgen Stark was the key German figure in the negotiation of the Stability and Growth Pact (SGP) in 1996–7. Their engagement was, however, much briefer. Alfred Müller-Armack was in many ways a more original contributor of ideas during the period 1957–63 than Tietmeyer was to be later. In particular, he tried to steer the EEC towards the idea of European counter-cyclical policy, based on developing its capacity to invest in cross-national infrastructure. Also, Otmar Emminger in the Bundesbank was more important than Tietmeyer in the negotiations of the EMS in 1978–9. These difficulties are in part managed in the book by integrating these relationships into the individual biographies.

An important issue that we faced in relation to Member State balance was the absence of a Dutch architect. This absence seems all the more surprising because we have two Belgian and one Luxembourger architects. The explanation is to be found in a strong Dutch orientation to German views on monetary union. This Germanic focus went back at least to the Rome Treaty negotiations and to the close cooperation of Jelle Zijlstra at the Dutch central bank with Emminger at the Bundesbank. Also, as in the case of André Szasz at the Dutch central bank, there was scepticism that monetary union could be workable in the absence of fiscal and political union. Dutch thinking was more clearly aligned than Belgian thinking with this type of German scepticism. Belgium might even claim a third architect in Hubert Ansiaux at the National Bank of Belgium.

Ultimately, the book offers a selection that has been tested by seeking the advice of a panel of euro veterans. The outcome was a remarkable consensus. Nevertheless, certain individuals retain a claim to particular significance. Ansiaux was chair of the Committee of EEC Central Bank Governors at the time of the Werner Group. Bernard Clappier was important in both the Werner and the EMS negotiations. Jacques de Larosière, governor of the Banque de France, was pivotal within the Delors Committee in gaining acceptance by President Mitterrand for the principle of central bank independence in the final report (Dyson and Featherstone 1999: 124–5). Jean-Claude Trichet led the slow reluctant conversion of the French Treasury to this principle. He also played an important part in the adoption of the 'hard franc' (*franc fort*) policy in the 1980s as central to retaining French negotiating power vis-à-vis Germany (Dyson and Featherstone 1999: 210; Aeschimann and Riché 1996). In addition, Trichet represented France in the IGC on EMU. However, neither Clappier, nor de Larosière, nor Trichet advocated ideas around which others negotiated. The concept of the ECU as the reference currency for the EMS and for symmetric adjustment to imbalances was associated with Triffin. Moreover, the concept of a European 'economic government', which found favour in Paris, had no impact on the Delors Report. It remained weakly developed in the subsequent EMU negotiations. It was seen as likely to deter rather than encourage German agreement to monetary union. Other individuals came to prominence after 1998–9, notably Wim Duisenberg and Otmar Issing, respectively first president and first chief economist of the ECB. They were less significant players in the time period before 1998–9.

STRUCTURAL DYNAMICS AND PERSONALIZATION: THE PROBLEM OF BALANCE IN BIOGRAPHY

Two biases infect the writing of history and find expression in sharply contrasting attitudes to biography. The first bias is associated with structural accounts and explanations. In this type of approach individuals tend to fade into the background in favour of hegemonic discourses, institutions, policy communities, and networks. They are subsumed within categories like 'economist' and 'monetarist' theories of monetary union, 'Keynesian' and 'monetarist' thought. They are seen as embedded within a 'sound money' policy paradigm or within an institution like the Bundesbank or the European Commission.

In rescuing individuals from the insignificance to which this type of approach subjects them, it is important to remember—paraphrasing Karl Marx—that they were making EMU but not in circumstances of their own choosing. As circumstances changed, architects of monetary union were under pressure to rethink EMU. Marjolin and Triffin found themselves in this situation in the 1970s as progress on the Werner plan was disrupted by the demise of the Bretton Woods system, the oil crises, and currency volatility in Europe. They had to confront the disappointment of their earlier hopes.

The second source of bias stems from isolating 'great individuals' and their 'big ideas' from their contexts and from subjecting them to specialized treatment. In this form of narrative, history writing pivots around 'celebrity memoirs', painting portraits of larger-than-life characters in propelling certain ideas to the centre of policy-making and creating 'schools' of thought. It involves constructing the history of European monetary union as a dramatic narrative of heroes and villains. Individuals take on a mythological character.

Steering clear of bias towards an over-personalizing of the history of European monetary union involves situating the role of architects of the euro in a deeply layered contextualized account (cf. Popkin 2005). The process of European monetary union entwined individuals in complex structural dynamics, which they understood in different ways. These structural dynamics offered them changing constellations of opportunities and constraints. They provided them with competing ideas that they could recombine in different ways. Ultimately, the economic and monetary knowledge of architects was embedded in larger social structures, including their university training, their institutional location, and their career progression. It was socially embedded in communities of scholars and practitioners, its evolution having the character of a shared product. Moreover, the capacity of architects to gain influence over policy development and negotiated outcomes rested on structures of power. It was enhanced when individuals negotiated on behalf of a creditor state, above all one with systemic significance and a track-record of successful policy performance (Dyson 2014).

At the same time, the history of European monetary union cannot be fully understood without the personal, intimate, and often passionate engagement of the architects with the process (cf. Nora 1987; Szenberg 1992, 1998). This lived experience is bound up with the specific spatial and temporal contexts that shaped them. It is grounded in their education and career paths; in the disciplinary paradigms that they used, and adapted; in the institutions with which they interacted and sought to change; in their presence and use of often transnational policy networks that transcended these institutions; in the collaborations and disputes in which they engaged; and, not least, in the particular blend of creativity and energy that they brought to bear on the design of EMU.

Inevitably, a book of this type illustrates both the possibilities and the limits of individual creativity and inventiveness. It examines how certain exceptional individuals attained pre-eminence and reputation by seeking to reframe how economic and monetary policies were made in Europe; by building networks to develop and disseminate their ideas; and by contributing to the dynamics that made European monetary union possible through a combination of expertise, networking skills, and administrative skills. This book seeks to retrieve the personal voices of these architects in history-writing about European monetary union and the threads of personal, emotional, and subjective engagement that run through this history (cf. Popkin 2005; Weintraub and Forget 2007).

The picture that emerges is one in which the history of ideas about European monetary union is far from linear. It is not a simple story of one architect building directly on the ideas of others, let alone of one architect prevailing in how European monetary union was constructed. As developments after 2010 continue to show, it is a story of interruptions, dead ends, defeats, odd turning points, and surprising advances. The role of the architects is not to be understood as part of a teleological process. The interest lies in how they interpreted these interruptions, dead ends, defeats, odd turning points, and sudden advances. It is to be found in their lesson-drawing from these experiences and in how they become personally engaged in disseminating these lessons. Not least, it is a story of how ideas once thought lost—like Triffin's ERF and Lamfalussy's macro-prudential supervision—found later echoes in Euro Area institutional reforms.

2

Robert Triffin

The Arch Monetarist in the European Monetary Integration Debates?

Ivo Maes and Eric Bussière

> If my main concern were to make safe forecasts, I would agree with you and be proven right nine times out of ten. But I prefer to be wrong nine times out of ten, if I can contribute once in ten times to divert us from catastrophe, and help build a better future. (Triffin 1981: 247)

Robert Triffin (1911–93) played an important role in the international monetary debates in the early post-war period. He became famous with his book *Gold and the Dollar Crisis*, published in 1960, in which he predicted the end of the Bretton Woods system. Triffin's personality and approach to economics were nicely summarized by Alexandre Lamfalussy:

> He had an insatiable appetite for detecting the weaknesses of our international monetary and financial system and trying to understand the underlying causes. He had the courage and intellectual honesty of defending his views—even when they looked iconoclastic in the eyes of powerful politicians and a number of economists. But, more important, he wanted to 'solve' problems—and in his endeavours to find solutions he was definitely forward-looking, while not neglecting the lessons of the past. (Lamfalussy 2001: 9)

This chapter focuses on Triffin's role as an architect of the euro. It argues that there was a remarkable continuity in his work. From his earliest writings, he developed a view that the international adjustment process was not functioning according to the classical mechanisms. This view was based on thorough empirical analyses of the Belgian economy during the Great Depression and shaped by a business cycle perspective with the emphasis on disequilibria and the transition period (Maes 2013a). His doctoral dissertation on imperfect competition theory at Harvard and his Latin American missions for the US Federal Reserve further reinforced this view. Like so many economists of his generation, the Great Depression of the 1930s, and especially the pound sterling's demise, left a deep mark on Triffin. For Triffin, the policy conclusion was to put international liquidity and economic policy coordination at the core of the international monetary system.

Triffin's analysis has been the topic of major debate in the academic and policy-making world. Indeed, his thinking is still very much present in current debates on the international monetary system. The late Tommaso Padoa-Schioppa (2010b) argued that Triffin's analysis transcended the Bretton Woods system (see Chapter 9 by Fabio Masini). He built his own views about European monetary union on the foundation of Triffin's 'general dilemma': that 'the stability requirements of the system as a whole are inconsistent with the pursuit of economic and monetary policy forged solely on the basis of domestic rationales in all monetary regimes devoid of some form of supranationality'.

For Triffin, and later for Padoa-Schioppa, the so-called domestic 'house-in-order' approach—that international stability rested on every country pursuing domestic stability, a view advocated by Germany—was not sufficient for a sustainable and stable international monetary system. Triffin took a 'systemic' view of the international monetary system, always looking for the 'counterpart' in the international adjustment process. This view had later relevance in debate about the proper principles of design of the Euro Area and differed in its implications markedly from the structure agreed in the Maastricht Treaty in 1991.

In his policy proposals, Triffin followed a double-track approach, looking both at the international and at the European dimensions. Here, he was strongly influenced by the early post-war experience, in which the failure of a global restoration of convertibility was followed by the big success of the European Payments Union (EPU), for which he claimed some credit. He came up with proposals for reforming the international monetary system. However, as he doubted that they would come to fruition, he also developed proposals for regional monetary integration, particularly in Europe. In his eyes, these two approaches were strongly complementary, aiming at a new multipolar international monetary system, with the European Community as an essential pillar. So, he became a great partisan of European monetary integration. As he observed in *Europe and the Money Muddle* (1957: 30): 'Countries whose peace, progress and welfare are intimately interdependent must, in their own interest, learn to use or limit their national sovereignty in the light of their interdependence.' This gave his work an important political dimension too.

There are two main reasons to consider Triffin as an architect of the euro. First, he was highly influential in shaping the intellectual debates about the international and European monetary system. He was one of the main advocates of international cooperation and a stern critic of the so-called domestic 'house-in-order' approach. Second, as a policy-maker, Triffin held very important advisory positions, for instance for Monnet's Action Committee, providing German Chancellor Willy Brandt's paper for the Hague Summit of December 1969, as well as for the European Commission. In these positions, he came forward with innovative ideas, especially for a European Reserve Fund (ERF) and a European parallel currency. It is also important to stress the longevity of Triffin's involvement in the process of European monetary integration, spanning four decades, from the EPU to the European Monetary System (EMS).

TRIFFIN'S FORMATIVE YEARS

Triffin pursued his undergraduate studies at the University of Louvain, obtaining a degree in economics in 1935. As a young economist, he was active at the Belgian Institut des Sciences Économiques. In the inter-war period, this institute became the first modern economic research centre in the Low Countries (Maes and Buyst 2005). The dominant figure was Léon-H. Dupriez, who had studied at Harvard and who was also at the National Bank of Belgium. Dupriez was a leading scholar in business cycle analysis.

At that time, Belgium, as a small open economy, was badly affected by the Great Depression. It was hit hard by sharply contracting world trade and falling international prices. This critical situation prompted major debates. In the spring of 1934, Dupriez argued that devaluation was the only solution. In March 1935, Paul van Zeeland, a colleague of Dupriez, was appointed prime minister. He immediately devalued the franc by 28 per cent. The young Triffin was responsible for the calculation of the devaluation percentage.

Triffin was one of Dupriez's pupils. In 1935, he wrote a statistical article explaining the calculation and interpretation of differential group indices of prices. Triffin argued that the differential movement of prices, especially the rigidity of domestic costs, was leading to serious losses in Belgian manufacturing, leading to closure of firms: 'The seemingly favourable sales prices constituted starvation prices for our industrialists, leaving half the country's enterprises trading at a loss in 1934' (Triffin 1935: 290).

Notably, Triffin also concluded that agricultural prices were much more sensitive to the business cycle (Maes 2013a). This observation formed the basis for an important theme in his later work, which emphasized that deflationary policies at the centre of the world economic system would have even greater deflationary effects in the periphery.

In 1937, when he was a graduate student at Harvard University, Triffin published an article entitled 'La théorie de la surévaluation monétaire et la dévaluation belge' ('The theory of currency overvaluation and the Belgian devaluation'). Here he went further into the theoretical and empirical background of the Belgian franc devaluation. Triffin started with a trenchant critique of Cassel's purchasing power parity theory, especially for not being suited to situations of disequilibrium (Maes 2012). In line with his earlier article, Triffin's fundamental criticism was that Cassel did not look at the structure of prices in a country. Like Dupriez, Triffin made a distinction between 'sheltered' and 'non-sheltered' sectors of the economy. In the non-sheltered sector of the economy, sales prices had to be aligned with world-market prices. However, costs in the non-sheltered sectors were largely determined by domestic factors, leading to a profit squeeze, a decline in production, and rising unemployment.

Triffin went to Harvard in 1935 for his doctoral work in economics. There, he fell under the spell of Joseph Schumpeter and pure economic theory. As he wrote in an autobiographical article, 'A few weeks at Harvard, however, sufficed to convince me that what I missed most was an adequate training in pure theory, then taught at Harvard by Professor Schumpeter whose broad culture in that field, and others, was as unique as his class showmanship' (Triffin 1981: 241). At the centre of economic theory, for Schumpeter, was general equilibrium theory. As observed by fellow Harvard student Paul Samuelson (1951: 103), Schumpeter was 'surprisingly un-Austrian' in his approach towards economic theory, and much more Walrasian.

Triffin wrote his dissertation on *Monopolistic Competition and General Equilibrium Theory* (Triffin 1941), under the direction of Schumpeter, along with Leontief and Chamberlin. In this work, he tried to reconcile imperfect competition theory, which had its origins mainly in Marshallian partial equilibrium theory, with general equilibrium theory. In this way Triffin became an authority on imperfect competition theory, a theory that would further shape his perception of international monetary phenomena.

After obtaining his doctorate, Triffin moved back to Belgium. However, as he could not find a suitable job, he returned to Harvard in 1939. From 1942 to 1946, Triffin worked for the Board of Governors of the Federal Reserve System in Washington, focusing on Latin America. He was more and more absorbed by what one might characterize as a 'progressive Keynesian' spirit. The Triffin missions to Latin America represented a remarkable episode in US financial diplomacy and constituted a break with the earlier approaches to 'international money doctoring'. US central bank officials not only rejected the classical liberal policies; they also 'went out of their way to consult with, and learn from, their Latin American counterparts as well as to tailor and differentiate their advice to the specific needs of each country' (Helleiner 2009: 24). Triffin himself emphasized that his aim was to put monetary and banking policy at the service of the 'overwhelming development objectives previously ignored in central bank legislation copied one from the other and trying merely to imitate a distant and largely inappropriate Bank of England or U.S. Federal Reserve model' (Triffin 1981: 243).

For Triffin, the economic cycle in Latin American economies was not so much determined by domestic savings and investment, as in the older industrial countries, as by the inflow or outflow of foreign exchange. Triffin was further critical of exchange-rate adjustments as an economic policy instrument in these countries. He questioned the efficacy of devaluation to bring about a readjustment of the balance of payments in such highly specialized countries, with few export products, facing inelastic demand. Triffin's analysis was clearly shaped by his background in imperfect competition theory: 'The situation recalls the case of oligopolistic competition in which none of the sellers are usually able to profit for very long from price-undercutting policies' (Triffin 1944: 112).

TRIFFIN'S ANALYSIS OF THE INTERNATIONAL MONETARY SYSTEM

During his period at the US Federal Reserve, Triffin became more interested in the international adjustment process. He wrote a first, important essay on the international monetary system, entitled 'National Central Banking and the International Economy' (Triffin 1947). Its focus was on the problem of reconciling domestic monetary policies with the prerequisites of international balance. This problem did not arise under the gold standard as the domestic money supply escaped the control of national authorities. However, in the new post-war world, it became a big issue as countries were now much more attached to national economic policy objectives.

Triffin raised the question whether the international monetary system in the inter-war period was a gold standard or a sterling-exchange standard. In his view, as the United Kingdom was the major centre of world trade and finance, changes in the British discount rate had significant effects on capital movements. Consequently, the British discount policy immediately affected not only the domestic economy and prices but also other countries, thus transmitting British cyclical fluctuations. According to Triffin's statistical evidence, a restrictive British monetary policy would lead to an improvement in Britain's terms of trade and balance of payments, as prices in other countries were more affected than those in the United Kingdom. Thus the main result of orthodox gold standard policies was to spread internationally cyclical disturbances arising in major industrialized countries. Eichengreen (1992) calls this the 'Triffin effect'.

In Triffin's view, this analysis had an important policy conclusion: compensatory policies should be followed to the fullest possible extent. This conclusion put global liquidity at the core of the international monetary system. Triffin had a clear ranking of policy instruments, preferring exchange controls to devaluation. 'When reserves are insufficient, foreign or international assistance—such as is contemplated under the International Monetary Fund—will be necessary. Failing this, exchange control should be used as a third line of defense, in order to continue compensatory policies and avoid the greater evils inseparable from deflation or currency devaluation' (Triffin 1947: 80).

In 1946, Triffin went on to the International Monetary Fund (IMF), where he became head of its exchange control division in Washington, before moving to Paris to lead the IMF's Representative Office in Europe. From 1949 to 1951, he was a Special Adviser to the (US) European Recovery Administration (ERA) in Paris. During these years, his focal point of interest was the EPU. Then, in 1951, he became a professor at Yale.

In 1960, Triffin published *Gold and the Dollar Crisis*, the book that made him famous. In line with his earlier work, its focus was on international liquidity and the vulnerability of the international monetary system. Triffin emphasized the fragility of the gold exchange standard system, stressing the contradiction of an exchange standard 'whose operation becomes increasingly dependent on one or a few *national* currencies as major components of *international* monetary reserves' (Triffin 1960a: 19, original italics).

Triffin distinguished two types of balance of payments deficits which had to be financed by international reserves: temporary deficits and more fundamental disequilibria, for which the adjustment would take some time (Triffin 1960a: 34). For someone so deeply affected by the experience of the 1930s, the alternative was gloomy: 'In both cases, an insufficient level of reserves will force the deficit country to resort to otherwise unnecessary measures of deflation, devaluation or restrictions' (Triffin 1960a: 34).

Triffin argued that the world's liquidity requirements were being increasingly met by the growth of foreign-exchange reserves, especially US dollar balances. He was most concerned about this development and turned to the inter-war period and the experience with the sterling exchange standard for lessons. For Triffin, the international monetary system in this period had been a very fragile construction, as funds could move in and out of London as a consequence of changes in relative interest rates and/or changes of exchange-rate expectations. Moreover, the return to gold at the pre-1914 rate made pound sterling highly vulnerable. The financial crisis of the 1930s put the pound further under pressure: 'The final blow came in the summer of 1931, when the development of the world crisis put into difficulties the Credit-Anstalt of Vienna, triggering a financial panic which spread rapidly throughout Central Europe and led to further and massive withdrawals of funds from London' (Triffin 1960a: 57). The devaluation of sterling in September 1931 had devastating implications for the global monetary system and international liquidity. It marked the end of the sterling exchange standard and an implosion of global liquidity. 'The conversion of pounds into gold and dollars was accompanied and followed by similar conversions of dollars into gold. The foreign exchange component of the world's monetary reserves was nearly wiped out in the process, except for the countries of the sterling area' (Triffin 1960a: 57). The fall in international monetary liquidity contributed to the Great Depression.

By the end of the 1950s, Triffin became more and more worried about the international reserve position of the United States due to the country's gold losses and the increase in dollar liabilities. In his view, the continued deterioration in the US net reserve position would undermine foreigners' confidence in the dollar as a safe medium for reserve accumulation. For Triffin, the conclusion with regard to international liquidity was clear: 'further increases in dollar balances cannot be relied upon to contribute substantially and indefinitely to the solution of the world illiquidity problem' (Triffin 1960a: 63).

So, in Triffin's eyes, the gold exchange standard was not sustainable, leading to his famous dilemma:

> The gold exchange standard may . . . help in relieving a shortage of world monetary reserves. It does so only to the extent that the key currency countries are willing to let their net reserve position decline through increases in their own gross reserves. If they allow this to happen, however, and to continue indefinitely, they tend to bring about a collapse of the system itself through the gradual weakening of foreigners' confidence in the key currencies. (Triffin 1960a: 67)

Triffin did not fear a US dollar collapse, but the return of a liquidity shortage and a repeat of the gloom and doom of the 1930s, predicting that: 'the growing inadequacy of world reserves would be most likely to lead, within a relatively short span of years, to a new cycle of international deflation, devaluation and restrictions, as it did after 1929' (Triffin 1960a: 70).

Like Keynes, Triffin sought a more 'international' solution for the world liquidity problem: namely, 'the true "internationalization" of the foreign exchange component of the world's international reserves, protecting the world monetary system from the instability resulting from arbitrary shifts from one reserve currency into another or into gold' (Triffin 1960a: 71).

TRIFFIN AND EUROPEAN MONETARY INTEGRATION

The debates on European monetary integration are widely known as the controversy between the 'monetarists' and the 'economists'. The 'monetarists', with France as a dominant player, were in favour of plans for greater exchange-rate stability and exchange-rate support mechanisms (Maes 2002). The 'economists', under the leadership of Germany, emphasized the coordination of economic policies and the convergence of economic performances, especially inflation, as a precondition for Economic and Monetary Union (EMU). In this discussion, Triffin belonged firmly in the monetarist camp. In his book *Europe and the Money Muddle*, Triffin already urged the (future) European Economic Community (EEC) members to forge ahead and set up a plan for the realization of a monetary union. Furthermore, he argued that: 'Monetary unification would not require, in any manner, a full unification of national levels of prices, costs, wages, productivity, or living standards. Neither does monetary unification require a uniformization of the budgetary, economic, or social policies of the member countries . . . The problem of monetary unification is therefore a political rather than an economic problem' (Triffin 1957: 288). Later, after the monetary turmoil of the 1970s, he became more cautious about EMU.

A further reason to consider Triffin as a 'monetarist' is that he was a strong advocate of the introduction of a European currency unit (ECU) as a parallel currency. This was an important continuity in his thinking and policy proposals. He had already, back in the 1950s, argued for the use of the EPU unit of account as a parallel currency. For Triffin, wider use of a parallel currency would pave the way for monetary integration. With these views, Triffin went squarely against the German paradigm of the indivisibility of the currency and monetary policy.

In an article in honour of Triffin, entitled 'European Monies and European Monetary Union', Padoa-Schioppa (1991d: 201) is quite positive about the ECU as a parallel currency on the path to EMU. However, he observes that his article is 'limited' as it does not address the 'hardest issues' raised by EMU: economic union and the operational arrangements of monetary union. The article stemmed from a conference in December 1988, when the work of the Delors Committee, which rejected a parallel currency approach, was underway.

Furthermore, Triffin made no significant distinction between a monetary union and a system of stable exchange rates:

> From an economic point of view, the prerequisites for the successful preservation of monetary unification are practically identical with those for the successful preservation of free and stable exchange rates. The participating regions or countries must, in either case, subordinate their internal monetary and credit expansion to the maintenance of equilibrium in their balance of payments . . . From an economic viewpoint, monetary unification would even impose a somewhat less stringent monetary discipline on the participating countries, since the elimination of exchange risks would be even more complete than under a system of free and stable exchange rates, and would therefore stimulate the cushioning of temporary deficits through readjusting capital movements rather than aggravate them through speculative capital flight. (Triffin 1957: 289)

However, Europe's monetary union showed that, with accommodating capital movements, disequilibria were not corrected, leading to significant imbalances and bubbles, which, eventually, burst and contributed to the crisis of the early 2010s.

In a footnote, Triffin dismissed the argument for fiscal federalism: 'It is sometimes asserted that fiscal redistribution between richer and poorer regions of a single country plays a major role in regional balance of payments adjustments. This is extremely doubtful' (Triffin 1957: 288). He advanced two arguments:

> (a) such redistribution was extremely limited in scope in all countries until 20 or 25 years ago and is still very limited in many countries with poorly developed fiscal and social security systems; (b) this redistribution is not designed primarily to smooth out balance of payments disequilibria and may often aggravate them rather than reduce them... The regional pattern of federal expenditures on military production is also very likely to disturb rather than equilibrate regional balances of payments.

With hindsight, this was certainly a major weakness of Triffin's analysis. The Euro Area's sovereign debt crisis clearly demonstrated that EMU created very close and complex interdependencies between the participating countries, requiring a strong economic policy framework and close coordination of policies, posing also the question of political union.

With the Marshall Plan, the US government acknowledged the need for an approach to economic reconstruction that was specific to Europe, based on a return to trade on a multilateral basis. As a member of the (US) European Recovery Administration, Triffin was influential in setting up the monetary dimension of the Marshall Plan, embodied in the EPU. Eichengreen (1993: ix) even describes Triffin as the 'EPU's architect'.

It was against this backdrop that Triffin's thinking on monetary regionalism developed. Triffin (1950) set out the broad lines of his plan in a note *La multilatéralisation progressive des devises en Europe*. In Triffin's view, the process of reintegrating Europe into the international economy could only be gradual and involve 'multilateralization of trade and payments' in stark contrast to the 'bilateral and discriminatory techniques' still being used at the end of the 1940s. While he admitted the inevitable nature of restrictions on goods trade and monetary transfers at that time, he also pointed out that bilateral restrictions were by far the most harmful and should be tackled as a matter of priority.

In the monetary area, progress was hampered by the ideas of universal convertibility that had prevailed at Bretton Woods. As conceived at the time, the IMF found itself being given objectives and instruments that were only suitable for the long term. Moreover, the way it operated was ill-adapted to managing transitions and to tackling problems that were specific to regional areas. The Fund's statutes actually 'said nothing about the possibility of mutual and simultaneous commitments by a group of nations as regards liberalization or multilateralization of exchange controls' (Triffin 1950: 19–21).

For the functioning of both the compensation mechanism and the multilateralization of net debts or claims, the EPU needed a monetary unit in which all accounts could be denominated. This was a sensitive issue, as the choice of this unit would also determine the exchange-rate guarantee attached to the EPU's credit operations (Triffin 1957: 172).

The EPU agreement created a special EPU unit of account, initially defined by a gold content equal to that of the 1950 US dollar. This gold content could be changed at any time by a decision of the Organization for European Economic Cooperation (OEEC) Council. However, the unanimity rule for OEEC decisions made any such change highly improbable: the creditors would always have an interest in vetoing devaluation, and the debtors an interest in vetoing an appreciation of the EPU unit (Triffin 1957: 173). So, it was stipulated that no country could veto a change equivalent to, or smaller than, the appreciation or depreciation of its own currency. This effectively implied a definition of the EPU unit of account in terms of the member currency which remained most stable in terms of gold.

In a footnote in *Europe and the Money Muddle*, Triffin claims paternity for this formula and points to its significance for the future of European monetary integration: 'My own objective in proposing and defending this formula . . . was also to define a form of exchange guarantee that might be used later to encourage a resumption of capital movements in Europe, and a monetary unit that might be adopted in future agreements on European economic integration' (Triffin 1957: 173). Triffin was to be actively involved in this process himself.

Thus, as early as 1950, Triffin laid the foundations for monetary regionalism, with Europe serving as a kind of test laboratory. Bilateral agreements would have to be gradually extended to the regional level, then coordinated with other regional systems, or with third countries, as part of the transition back to an international system. In this way, he defended monetary regionalism not just as an essential solution to the internal imbalances of a particular region in the world, but also because of 'profound imbalances between the different regions'. The regional solution of returning to currency convertibility was less risky and brutal than the global approach. In Triffin's eyes, it was, in the first instance, a question of coping with a transition to which 'the regional approach is perfectly adapted', without however 'acting as a substitute for the fully international methods of cooperation that are the basic objective and the very *raison d'être* of the International Monetary Fund' (Triffin 1950: 23).

In the mid-1950s, the six so-called Schuman countries that founded the European Coal and Steel Community (ECSC) followed two rather different paths to economic integration. The Six opted for regional integration of the goods markets, with the establishment of the EEC. However, monetary cooperation was approached from a worldwide perspective, with the restoration of full external convertibility under the Bretton Woods system (Abraham and Lemineur-Toumson 1981).

The EEC Treaty was, *de facto*, of a constitutional order and would transform economic and legal rules in the countries of the European Community. However, the Treaty left macro-economic and monetary policy-making mainly in the hands of the individual Member States. The Commission's responsibilities were chiefly concerned with the orientation and coordination of the national policies. Triffin (1958: 1) described the limited monetary dimension of the EEC Treaty as 'a Hamlet in which the role of the Prince of Denmark is almost totally ignored'.

The most extensive discussion of macro-economic and monetary issues can be found in the 'Balance of Payments' chapter of the Rome Treaty. It illustrates that these issues were tackled from a 'common market' perspective, as balance of payments disequilibria would threaten the creation and functioning of the Common Market (Maes 2006). Article 104 stated that each Member State should pursue an economic policy 'to ensure the equilibrium of its overall balance of payments and to maintain confidence in its currency, while taking care to ensure a high level of employment and a stable level of prices'. It reflected very much the domestic 'own-house-in-order approach', advocated by Germany.

Article 108 discussed the situation where a Member State has serious balance of payments difficulties which could threaten the functioning of the Common Market. It stipulated that the Commission should investigate the situation and gave it the right to recommend measures for the Member State to take. Moreover, the article provided for the possibility of granting 'mutual assistance'.

After the establishment of the EEC, on 1 January 1958, Triffin became an official adviser at the European Commission. He had very close links with its vice-president Robert Marjolin, who was responsible for economic and financial affairs (see Chapter 3 by Katja Seidel). They knew one another from the Second World War, when they were both in Washington. They had also been in Paris together in the early 1950s, when Marjolin was the first secretary-general of the OEEC and Triffin was the head of the European office of the IMF. When Triffin came to Brussels, they usually stayed up late, discussing Europe's and the world's monetary problems.

Triffin's relations with Raymond Barre, who succeeded Marjolin in 1967, were much less close (see Chapter 4 by David Howarth). Barre had a much more 'pragmatic' and 'realist' approach, which clashed with Triffin's more 'utopian' vision of European monetary integration. Later, with Roy Jenkins as Commission president in 1977, who also took a more 'monetarist' and voluntarist approach, Triffin became again more important (see Chapter 6 by Piers Ludlow). In his *European Diary*, Jenkins (1989: 296) observes that Triffin 'was of great assistance to us in the run-up to the EMS'.

Inside DG II, the Directorate-General for Economic and Financial Affairs, Triffin was very close to Frédéric Boyer de la Giroday, the director for monetary matters. They had been colleagues together at the IMF in the late 1940s and were both actively pressing for European monetary integration. In a letter to Triffin, Boyer acknowledges his debts to 'the Triffin Treasury of smart ideas'.[1]

In the second half of the 1950s, Monnet became very interested in European monetary integration. This interest was a consequence of the French financial crisis at that time, which threatened France's participation in the Common Market project. Typically, he put the French problem in a European framework and turned to his network for technical advice. This advice came from Pierre Uri, Paul Delouvrier, Marjolin, and, 'above all', from 'Marjolin's Belgian friend' (Duchêne 1994).

The French macro-economic and monetary situation was also a matter of serious concern for the European Commission, leading it to reflect on how it could fulfil its role in the macro-economic and monetary area (Maes and Buyst 2004). In close collaboration with Triffin, Marjolin drew up a proposal to set up a European Reserve Fund (ERF). The ERF project became one of Triffin's most important topics of analysis during his time as an adviser at the European Commission.

The cornerstone of Triffin's European project, the creation of an ERF as an instrument for European monetary regionalism, was elaborated in the context of the EEC in 1957. But the proposals followed on from a lengthy debate. The issue of the continuity of the regional system set up in the EPU framework had already been raised by Triffin in a note, *Convertibility and EPU* (Triffin 1953). He contested the provisional nature of the EPU and instead recommended its consolidation. In his arguments, Triffin made a link between justifications specific to the concept of regionalism and its contribution to the functioning of the international monetary system as a whole. He especially stressed the risks of instability associated with the dominant role of the American economy and the central role of the US dollar in the international monetary system. Triffin emphasized the 'fear of a resurgence of the dollar shortage, in the event of an economic recession or a new protectionist offensive in the United States' (Triffin 1954: 360).

In the mid-1950s, this concept of regionalism became a protective and stabilizing regionalism for Europe, in the face of asymmetric effects and domestic tensions in Europe associated with a potential crisis in the United States that might cause a dollar shortage. Triffin admitted that the ideal context

[1] Letter from Boyer to Triffin, 2 August 1967, RTA, 8557.

for convertibility was 'the world itself or, at very least, the free world'. But Triffin refuted the 'myth of systematic and uniform universalism', preferring instead a regional shock-absorbing context within which interdependencies and similar shared interests would facilitate economic policy compromises, as the OEEC experience had shown. Thus there emerged the vision of an economic and monetary federalism involving 'delimitation of the respective boundaries of action for regional integration and global integration' (Triffin 1954: 372). Triffin recommended making the EPU a permanent fixture via a regional union in charge of managing internal EPU transfers and those to the dollar zone. After this option failed to materialize, implementation of the Rome Treaty offered the prospect of putting Triffin's plan into practice in the framework of the EEC Six.

Triffin severely criticized the limited scope of the European Monetary Agreement (EMA), signed in 1955. In the framework of the EMA, a European Fund was created that provided EMA members access to non-automatic credit facilities in case of temporary balance of payments difficulties. In addition, a Mutual System of Settlements was set up that encouraged the settlement of international payments through the foreign-exchange markets, rather than through central banks as had often been the case until then (Kaplan and Schleiminger 1989). In Triffin's view, these EMA arrangements, which would become operational after the dissolution of the EPU, were not ambitious enough. He argued in favour of taking advantage 'of the next EPU revision to transform EPU into a clearing house for all European central banks, and to require them to hold all their European currency reserves—and possibly a specified portion of their overall gold and foreign-exchange reserves—in the form of EPU deposits' (Triffin 1957: 285). He advocated the transformation of the EPU into a European clearing house, which could pool about 20 per cent of the total gold and foreign-exchange reserves held by European central banks. The European clearing house would use these reserves to intervene in international exchange markets, approximating the open market operations performed by national central banks in their domestic markets. Triffin considered the European clearing house as a powerful collective European instrument to combat speculative currency movements (Triffin 1957: 292).

Hence, in developing his ideas for an ERF, Triffin drew inspiration from his experience at the EPU. In his view, the first function of the ERF would be as a clearing house between central banks (note the resemblance with John Maynard Keynes' Bretton Woods proposal for an International Clearing Union). This would pave the way for the ERF to turn naturally into the 'European Monetary Authority':

> All payments between central banks, within the Community, would be made by a simple and mandatory transfer onto the deposit account that each central bank would be required to hold with the European Reserve Fund. The constitution of

> these deposits would give the Fund a vast '*masse de manœuvre*' that could be used to ensure the financing of the mutual assistance foreseen in the Treaty of Rome, to steer developments in the Community's overall monetary policy and to gradually pave the way, both practically and functionally, for the creation of a European Monetary Authority capable of 'steering the ship' and ultimately ensuring full monetary integration between the six countries of the Community. (Triffin 1958: 9)

The ERF could be constituted by pooling 10 to 20 per cent of the international reserves of the Member States' central banks, a proposal that was sure to incur the wrath of the central bankers. The Fund could provide different types of loans, both to assist countries with balance of payments difficulties and to support economic growth. Triffin (1989: 9) even argued that it could play a useful role in banking crises.

This idea—that the Community should dispose of resources to facilitate financial solidarity—would become a recurring theme in Commission proposals. There is a resemblance here with the later European Stability Mechanism (ESM), established in 2012. The underlying principle is the same: such mechanisms, by demonstrating a collective stance, are a more efficient way of averting speculation than isolated national measures. Also, it makes it possible to offer 'carrots' to Member States which had to adjust policies, increasing the influence of the Commission's policy recommendations.

There was, moreover, an important rivalry with the IMF. In a confidential note for Jean Monnet, Triffin argued that financial assistance should be arranged preferably within the EEC itself, as long as the balance of payments and reserve position of the Community as a whole was strong enough. He further observed that the EEC procedures were far less satisfactory than those of the IMF, as the IMF provided in advance stable sources of financing for the assistance required: 'Prospective borrowers, therefore, would be unwilling to relinquish in any way their full freedom of access to the I.M.F. without being firmly assured of at least equivalent and expeditious borrowing facilities from the Community.'[2]

Triffin also advocated the introduction of a European unit of account: 'the European Reserve Fund deposit accounts would be... denominated in a European unit of account, defined so as to give it the same stability as that of the most stable among the participating currencies' (Triffin 1958: 9). In a footnote, he again referred to the example of the EPU: 'The legal definition of such a unit of account would be similar to the formula used for setting the current E.P.U. unit of account.'

Triffin proposed several measures to promote this European unit of account, including as a parallel currency: 'A first step in this direction could

[2] Confidential note on the need for a European Community Reserve Fund, 11 November 1959, JMA, AMK 25/4/15.

be to legalize the use of the aforementioned European unit of account in all contracts, both public and private, domestic and international.' He saw this as a clear strategy to advance towards monetary union:

> A second measure, of a more spectacular nature, and already effectively implying acceptance of full monetary unification as the ultimate goal, would involve the conversion of existing national monetary units into new monetary units, still national and independent of one another, but having the same value . . . the new national banknotes could, by joint agreement, be given the privilege of being about to circulate freely throughout the territory of the European Community. Combined with the *de-facto* equivalence of national monetary units, this 'privilege of intercirculation' would enhance resistance to any future exchange rate fluctuations. (Triffin 1958: 16)

As indicated earlier, Triffin saw a strong connection between his proposals for the international monetary system and for European monetary integration. He was convinced that regional monetary integration would contribute to a more stable international monetary system. In his view, the ERF would help strengthen the international monetary system: 'the dual mechanism of clearing and lending of a European Reserve Fund would help solve a problem that, paradoxically, has been neglected or even ignored today . . . that of the liquidity needed for the satisfactory functioning of the international monetary system itself' (Triffin 1958: 12).

The European Commission discussed the ERF plan at its meeting on 20 November 1958. It agreed in principle with the project, but it postponed the debate on the implementation to a future meeting.[3] Triffin also promoted the idea actively in Paris (Triffin 1958). However, in December 1958, President Charles de Gaulle devalued the French franc and introduced orthodox economic policies. The countries participating in the EPU restored the external convertibility of their currencies in the framework of the Bretton Woods system. In this changing context the proposal for an ERF lost its *raison d'être*, even though Monnet tried to revive it in the early 1960s.

The ERF idea returned to the agenda in 1969, when Willy Brandt became German Chancellor. Brandt was a member of Jean Monnet's Action Committee for the United States of Europe, which he consulted in order to prepare for the Hague Summit. Monnet appealed to Triffin, who drew up a new proposal for an ERF (Monnet 1976: 610). The December 1969 summit of heads of state and government at The Hague ended with an agreement that 'a plan by stages should be drawn up by the Council during 1970 with a view to the creation of an economic and monetary union'. The communiqué noted that 'The Heads of State have agreed that the possibility should be examined of setting up a

[3] Minutes of the meeting of the Commission of 20 November 1958, COM(58) PV 38, secret part, CECA.

European reserve fund to which a common economic and monetary policy would lead.'

The Hague Summit marked a fundamental break in the process of European integration, with EMU now officially on the agenda. As argued by Monnet in a letter to Triffin:

> Last year, you drafted your reports and the proposal for a European Reserve Fund, in light of Great Britain's accession and the problems to be solved in order to achieve this . . . We must now take the perspective of Economic and Monetary Union. The Hague Summit decided that a plan would be drawn up for an Economic and Monetary Union in stages. Implementation of this decision is starting now.[4]

In March 1970, a committee was established under the chairmanship of Luxembourg Prime Minister Pierre Werner to map out a concrete plan for EMU. In the Werner Committee, the concept of an ERF was watered down. In the end, the Werner Report stated that a European Fund for Monetary Cooperation (EFMC) with more limited functions should be set up. Triffin, who was still an official adviser at the Commission, was active in the elaboration of ideas for the EFMC. However, his influence was limited. In reality, the Fund became a bookkeeping agency, virtually run as a subsection of the Bank for International Settlements (BIS) in Basel (Szász 1999: 49). Even though he was not involved in preparing it, Triffin regarded the plan that emerged from the work of the Werner Group as a both an institutional and a political opportunity. As he said in a note addressed to Jean Monnet in November 1970:

> The second merit of the Werner Report is to drive home the message that the objective pursued cannot be attained by *ex-post* intergovernmental consultations—even if they are given more clout through accepting majority voting procedures—nor by laying down in a treaty, *ex ante*, specific solutions that unforeseeable future problems will require. The roots of Economic and Monetary Union basically lie in the transfer to joint decision-making Community bodies of responsibilities and competences hitherto in the hands of national organisations, at both the administrative scale and the level of governments and their national parliaments. In all domains . . . when compatibility of decisions and policies is the very condition needed for them to be effective, the interpenetration of national administrations themselves and their deliberations is essential for forging common views and avoiding frequent disputes that need repeated and difficult arbitration by the Council of the European Community.[5]

Triffin's 'monetarist' approach towards European monetary integration came clearly to the fore in his advocacy of the creation of a European currency and

[4] Letter from Monnet to Triffin, 2 March 1970, JMA, AMK C 25/4/163.

[5] Note de Robert Triffin, *La réalisation par étapes de l'union économique et monétaire dans la communauté*, 24 novembre 1970, JMA, RT1/136.

in his proposals to promote this European currency as a parallel currency, alongside the existing national currencies, both in the official monetary circuits (e.g. among central banks) and in commercial circuits (e.g. the bond markets). Remarkably, Triffin was acting not only in the official sector, notably as an adviser at the European Commission, but also in the private sector, for instance as an administrator of Kredietbank Luxembourgeoise, the leading bank for bonds denominated in the European unit of account, thanks again to Triffin's advice.

After retiring from Yale University, Triffin came back to Belgium in 1977. He was involved, with the help of funding from the Ford Foundation, in the establishment of the Centre for European Policy Studies (CEPS) in Brussels. As a prelude, he organized four international conferences on the, just launched, EMS, 'with the help of an advisory committee on which Rudiger Dornbusch, Alexandre Lamfalussy, Alexander Swoboda, Niels Thygesen and Jacques van Ypersele de Strihou have kindly agreed to serve' (Triffin 1979: 10).

As argued earlier, a European unit of account was a key element of Triffin's proposals, both for the EPU and for an ERF. The breakdown of the Bretton Woods system in the early 1970s would give further impetus to his ideas. Triffin called for a fundamental overhaul of the international monetary system, fearing 'a reversion to the economic and monetary chaos that followed the collapse of the pound sterling in 1931' (Triffin 1973: 426).

Triffin advocated two-pronged action, at both world and European levels. On a global scale, he recommended the creation of an international standard along the lines of the special drawing rights (SDR), more symmetrical rules for adjustment, and a system for recycling surpluses. But putting such a programme into practice would be a long haul, requiring close transatlantic cooperation. Hence it was imperative for Europe to speed up implementation of EMU, which would 'enable (the Europeans) to play the role that falls to them in global negotiations and to keep as much stability as possible in their relations between one another and with other countries' (Triffin 1973: 425). The new situation implied giving priority to relations between the European currencies themselves. Triffin based his plan on the expansion of the functions of the European Monetary Cooperation Fund (EMCF), established in March 1973. It could develop market interventions in European currencies and no longer in dollars; pool part of the reserves; and transform the unit of account into a reserve instrument that could be transferred between the European countries' central banks and then circulated among the general public through EMCF's investment on the bond markets in unit-of-account-denominated securities. A key element of his proposals was a new denomination for the unit of account, the 'Europa', with the aim of popularizing it. The Europa was to be a basket of currencies so that the system would not be anchored on the strongest currency.

Between 1974 and 1977, Triffin proposed a series of intermediate versions of his project, adapted to the economic and political facts of the day and the outcome of intense cooperation with the Commission. He defined the Europa as a 'parallel exchange unit' intended to give the Community's economic stakeholders an instrument that 'would make them less vulnerable to [movements in] the dollar and which would gradually substitute the national currencies in domestic use'.[6] He remained absolutely set on this innovation as part of a long-term plan, the first step towards EMU pure and simple (Triffin 1977).

At the end of the 1970s, Triffin was very much affected by the failure of the reform of the international monetary system that he had really believed was possible, and despite all the efforts made throughout the 1970s. As he observed in July 1978:

> As far as the global situation is concerned, the situation is hopeless. The second amendment to the IMF charter... postpones indefinitely all reforms to the international monetary system previously declared to be indispensable... This amendment gives a belated legal setting to the chaos inherited from the illegal and widespread renouncement of the main international commitments in force up to the—'temporary'—suspension of dollar convertibility in August 1971.[7]

For Triffin, the EMS, created in March 1979, was a key part of a reformed international monetary system, rather than an isolated strategy or even one of opposition to the US dollar (Bussière and Feiertag 2012). The newly created ECU was to be the instrument used for cooperation between European currencies and would play a wider regional role. On a global scale, a decentralized system in which the ECU would play its part alongside the US dollar would emerge, becoming a system adapted to a 'heterogeneous and diversified world'.[8] Triffin helped promote his model by organizing conferences, bringing together academics, practitioners, and officials. In June 1981, a conference held at Louvain-la-Neuve was attended by representatives of the European Commission, the National Bank of Belgium, and the banking and insurance sectors, which set out the broad lines of a programme for widening the use of the ECU by economic stakeholders.[9]

The postponement of the creation of a European Monetary Fund, the so-called second institutional phase of the EMS, at the end of 1980 was a defining moment. Far from just regretting the vetoing and resistance, Triffin defined the objectives and the paths to follow: the ECU as a parallel currency

[6] RTA, Letter from Triffin to Boyer, 11 December 1975.

[7] RTA, 'L'Europe face au chaos monétaire international', 5 July 1978.

[8] RTA, 20.3, 'Quelques réflexions sur quatre controverses monétaires internationales de l'après-guerre', 13 October 1981.

[9] RTA, 17.2, Séminaire international sur les utilisations privées de l'Ecu, Louvain, 13–14 juin, CR.

for the countries of the EEC; use of the ECU by the private sector as an alternative to the euro currency market; simplification of monetary and financial support arrangements; multilateralization of the swap agreements with the United States, which would from then on be denominated in ECU; and setting up the European Monetary Fund's involvement in intra-marginal interventions on the foreign-exchange markets. Many of these ideas were also developed by the European Commission, especially under Padoa-Schioppa, who was then director-general for economic and financial affairs.

Back in the 1950s, Triffin had already promoted the idea of using the EPU unit of account for bond issues in the financial markets. This idea was taken up by the Kredietbank in 1961, under the impetus of Triffin, who was a director of Kredietbank Luxembourg from 1961 to 1988. As observed by De Beckker (1984: 129):

> The first issue in European Units of Account (EUA) has a strong claim to be considered the first bond issue ever, pre-dating what is conventionally considered to be the first issue by Autostrade in 1963. If one looks at one generally accepted definition of a Eurobond issue, i.e. an issue underwritten and placed by an international syndicate of banks and denominated in a currency which is not the currency of the borrower, then the first Eurobond issue ever was launched in 1961, by Kredietbank SA Luxembourgeoise for the Portuguese borrower SACOR.

It would contribute to the development of Luxembourg as a financial centre, an important project of Pierre Werner (see Chapter 5 by Elena Danescu).

After the creation of the EMS, Triffin was very active in promoting the commercial ECU. In June 1980, he organized a conference on 'The private use of the ECU' for commercial market participants (Triffin and Swings 1980). Alfonso Iozzo (2012: 137), who attended the conference, characterized it as a 'solemn oath'. After the meeting, many initiatives were taken, from the opening of ECU-denominated current accounts to the issue of traveller cheques. In two sectors in particular the operations in ECU made a quantum leap: the issue of bonds, first from banks and companies and then from states, Italy in particular; and the setting up of a daily clearing system. Triffin further played an active role in the development of the ECU clearing system. Padoa-Schioppa (1987: 63) tells how, when he was director-general of DG II at the Commission: 'In February 1982, prompted by Robert Triffin and Paul Caron, I convened the banks that were then active in the ECU market and invited them to set up a study group for the creation of a multilateral clearing system.'

The success of the private ECU created a momentum for further policy initiatives. As argued by Iozzo (2012: 138):

> Alongside the stream of ECU-bonds issued in increasing volumes that had reached significant shares of the world market and were 'officially' registered in the international statistics, the promoters of the European Monetary System, the former French President Valéry Giscard d'Estaing and the former German

> Chancellor Helmut Schmidt, resumed in 1986 the initiative by setting up the 'Committee for the European Monetary Union', which included important politicians, industrialists and representatives of the financial sector of the main European countries.

However, under the influence of Renaud de la Genière, a former governor of the Banque de France, they rejected a parallel currency approach, just as the Delors Committee would do.

CONTRIBUTION AND LEGACY

Triffin was one of the dominating intellectuals in the international monetary debates of the early post-war period. His analyses were not only based on a broad theoretical and historical understanding of the international monetary system, but also on sharp empirical observations of the economic and financial situation.

Above all, he was a major critic of the international monetary system's domestically focused 'house-in-order' approach. As Baffi (1988: 16) noted: 'Triffin's proposals are based on the well-grounded conviction that "keeping one's own house tidy" without the fulfilling additional obligations at the international level is not a sufficient condition to ensure monetary stability.' In Triffin's view, a sustainable international monetary system also depended on an appropriate provision of international liquidity, to finance temporary disequilibria, and economic policy coordination.

One of the most important questions raised by Triffin was that of policy coordination in an international monetary system that comprised states with significant dissimilarities, which have their origin in their economic and social structures or in their economic and political cultures. Monetary regionalism was Triffin's solution to the basic contradictions that he had singled out. His solution did not try to deny these contradictions but to get round them. It was based on empirical analyses, anchored in history, and could be adapted to changes that Triffin perceived.

Triffin never doubted the intrinsically political nature of his ideas and the need for economists to take action. More fundamentally, his proposals linked economic and monetary considerations with political issues in a synthesis of federalist inspiration, put forward as early as 1950. This did not mean that he saw this project as simple and straightforward. But, as Triffin said himself: 'countries that are closely linked by geography and tradition . . . will agree more easily amongst themselves on certain procedures for coordinating their monetary and economic policies'.[10]

[10] RTA, 20.3, Quelques réflexions sur quatre controverses monétaires internationales de l'après-guerre, 13 October 1981.

Monetary regionalism was thus at the heart of Triffin's approach, but only gradually so. In 1950, he saw it as a transitional solution, intended to enable Europe to integrate into the universal scheme of Bretton Woods. Increasingly, during the 1950s, and even more so after the establishment of the EEC, this regionalism developed within a bipolar global context that, from an economic point of view, resembled Atlanticism. Triffin sought to symbolically join together the two sides of an ocean that shared very close economic and political conceptions. The break in the early 1970s consolidated Triffin's monetary regionalism, but put it also into a new perspective. After the failure of reforms of the international monetary system, regionalism became a goal enabling the best possible management of a multipolar international system in a heterogeneous world.

Triffin can be considered as the 'arch monetarist' in the EMU debates. As such, he was certainly a utopian, developing policy proposals that were often too ambitious, given the economic and political realities. This weakness lost him influence on more pragmatic policy-makers like Raymond Barre. Nevertheless, many of the other architects were influenced by Triffin, like Marjolin, Werner, Jenkins, Padoa-Schioppa, Delors, and Lamfalussy. His more utopian proposals, like the ECU as a parallel currency, helped to shape the debates on European monetary integration, preparing minds for the introduction of the euro. Interestingly, the post-2012 ESM has some similarities with Triffin's proposals for an ERF. A second weakness of Triffin was his tendency to equate EMU with a system of stable exchange rates. He did not pay enough attention to the economic and political requisites of a sustainable EMU and significantly underestimated the complex interdependencies that EMU would bring.[11]

[11] The authors would like to thank all those who contributed to this project, especially E. Danescu, Ph. Duvieusart, M. Emerson, A. Iozzo, J.-C. Koeune, A. Lamfalussy, A. Sapir, N. Thygesen, P. Paesani, M. Vanden Abeele, J. van Ypersele, and participants of the ESHET (Lausanne), UACES (Cork), and Storep (Bergamo) conferences, as well as the participants of the 'Architects of the Euro' project, especially K. Dyson. The usual caveats apply.

3

Robert Marjolin

Securing the Common Market through Economic and Monetary Union

Katja Seidel

> To do everything that is humanly possible to coordinate, approximate and harmonize the economic, financial and monetary policies of the Member States in the expectation that within a future political union they will be completely unified.[1]

The French economist Robert Marjolin made a significant contribution to French and European post-war economic reconstruction. Although he was one of the pioneers of the Common Market, Marjolin remains one of the lesser-known members of the Commission of the European Economic Community (EEC) under Walter Hallstein (1958–67). During Marjolin's term in office as vice-president in charge of economic and financial affairs the flagship projects were arguably the Common Agricultural Policy (CAP), the customs union, and the common commercial policy, while Economic and Monetary Union (EMU) was not realized. Hence, his contribution to EMU has all but been overlooked, with the Werner Plan of 1970 being usually seen as the first serious attempt to bring about EMU.

With his attachment to Keynesian economics and his conviction of the merits of economic planning, Marjolin was far from being an uncontested figure. Others with a more liberal outlook, such as German Commissioner Hans von der Groeben or, crucially, German federal economics minister Ludwig Erhard, disagreed with many of Marjolin's proposals. In spite of this opposition, Marjolin was a major driving force behind attempts to achieve

[1] Archives Robert Marjolin (ARM), Fondation Jean Monnet, Lausanne, 26/9/67, Comité Économique et Social, Exposé de M. Marjolin, Brussels, 18 November 1963.

greater European unity in the economic and monetary spheres to steer the EEC through the monetary turbulences of the 1960s and to provide the conditions for a smoothly functioning common market. This chapter is the first archive-based account of Marjolin's attempts to launch EMU.

BACKGROUND AND EARLY CAREER

Born in Paris in 1911 into a working-class family, Marjolin's start in life was far from privileged. He left school at the age of fourteen to support his family. Apprenticed to an orthopaedic workshop but lacking any talent for manual work, he then started working for a firm of stock market brokers where his interest in economic, financial, and monetary questions originated (Marjolin 1986: 17). Not unusual for someone with his background, he joined the socialist party in the late 1920s. For him, the party activism and the incessant debating marked a kind of 'intellectual awakening' (Marjolin 1986: 16).

Aware of the gaps in his education, and in spite of his nascent interest for economics, he decided to broaden his general knowledge and started taking evening classes at the Sorbonne. From 1931 he was able to study full-time, first philosophy and then, from 1934, political economy. Marjolin benefited from distinguished mentors ranging from economists to philosophers such as Charles Rist, Élie Halévie, Raymond Aron, and Éric Weil who recognized his talent. In the early 1930s a grant enabled him to spend a year at Yale University where he formed ties with US scholars and came to admire President Roosevelt's New Deal.

Like many architects of the euro, most notably Robert Triffin, also born in 1911, Marjolin was deeply marked by the Great Depression, an event that had facilitated the breakthrough of Keynesian ideas (see Chapter 1 by Maes and Bussière). For him, and many others, the Great Depression had irreparably undermined the credibility of classical economics. In France, the 1930s gave rise to a rather widespread view of the (economic) weakness and decline of the country, which persisted after the Second World War. Marjolin shared this view. It motivated him to contribute to the modernization of France as an economist. His doctoral thesis on long-range economic movements ('Prices, Money and Output: Essay on Long-Run Economic Movements') led him to the theories of John Maynard Keynes.

However, one of Marjolin's character traits seems to have been the absence of ideological dogmatism. It is thus not surprising that following his return from the United States he started to work for Charles Rist, a prominent French economist and proponent of economic liberalism, at the Institut de Recherches Économiques et Sociales (ISRES). By the mid-1930s Marjolin had made a name for himself in French economists' circles; he regularly appeared on the radio and published articles. In the mid-1930s he began working with Léon Blum and the left-wing Popular Front government, first as economics editor of the socialist newspaper *Le Populaire*, then as an economic adviser to Blum. However, he resigned in 1936 as he disagreed with some of the government's decisions on social and economic policy, such as the introduction of the forty-hour working week, which he thought would undermine economic recovery.

Marjolin first encountered theories of economic planning in socialist circles in the early 1930s but only became convinced of the concept during the Second World War (Marjolin 1986: 62). The beginning of the war also opened a new chapter in Marjolin's life: his transformation from scholar to public servant. In May 1940, Marjolin was called to London by Jean Monnet to serve on the French Coordinating Committee. Following France's defeat, he remained in London to serve the Free French under Charles de Gaulle, eventually becoming head of the French Supply Mission to the United States in 1944 to forecast and negotiate France's needs in terms of aid following the liberation. In late 1944 he returned to France as head of DREE (Directorate of External Economic Relations), still in charge of procurement of supplies, a post that involved frequent trips to Britain and the United States.

When Monnet became Commissioner General of the French Plan for Modernization and Equipment in late 1945, he made Marjolin his deputy. Working on the reconstruction of the French economy, Marjolin became entirely convinced of the effectiveness of large-scale economic planning. The Plan was the first of what he saw as his three great roles; the other two were as secretary-general of the Organization for European Economic Cooperation (OEEC) and as vice-president in charge of economic and financial affairs at the EEC Commission.

SECRETARY-GENERAL OF THE OEEC: PAYMENTS AND RECONSTRUCTION

When the Marshall Plan was launched in 1947, Marjolin participated in the Paris conference of the sixteen European nations that had opted to take part in the programme, becoming its 'unofficial secretary' (Marjolin 1986: 184). He used his experience at the French planning commission to help draw up a four-year programme of European economic recovery for the period 1948–52. Not least, these negotiations provided Marjolin with some training as a European where he 'lost his national identity to some extent' (Marjolin 1986: 184). Marjolin's work was facilitated by the Keynesian outlook that he shared with US and British economists; hence the programme focused on economic growth and maximum production, as well as on the fight against inflation and the establishment and maintenance of internal financial stability.

In 1948, at the age of only thirty-seven, Marjolin became the first secretary-general of the OEEC. Once in post, the elimination of obstacles to intra-European trade, in particular quantitative restrictions, was his main concern. The other two interrelated problems preventing the rapid recovery of European economies were related to payments: the US dollar shortage, on the one hand, and the fact that European currencies were not mutually convertible, on the other.

It is clear from Marjolin's writings and speeches during this time that his focus was on achieving the goal of convertibility between European currencies, and thereby to contribute to restoring trade and competition in Europe.[2] The European Payments Union (EPU), established in 1950, was a major step towards convertibility and trade liberalization, providing a multilateral credit and payments system, but not, to the disappointment of the Americans, European integration due to British resistance to closer supranational integration (Milward 1984). Among the experts who drafted the EPU scheme was the Belgian-American economist Robert Triffin, who became a close associate of Marjolin. Both shared hopes that the EPU would evolve into a European monetary union, with a shared currency and a European central bank, something that did not materialize. Still, the EPU put an end to the inefficient system of bilateral agreements in European payments. While it did not restore convertibility within the broader Bretton Woods system, its clearing and credit facilities contributed to the liberalization of trade among European countries. Marjolin was convinced of the EPU's merits in strengthening European countries economically and thus—in a period of intensifying Cold War—politically.[3]

Given the limited time-span of the European Recovery Programme (ERP), Marjolin felt that an important part of his work was to prepare European economies to survive without American aid. For him, close cooperation was the key to thriving European economies, enabling them to compete with the American economy. He had in mind the extension of the French-originated Schuman Plan for integration of the coal and steel sectors to other economic sectors, resulting in the establishment of a 'single European market'.[4] Here he differed from Monnet who in the mid-1950s promoted further integration in the atomic energy sector. His experience at the OEEC, the shortcomings of the

[2] ARM 4/3/8, A proposal for the liberalization of intra-European trade (Note by the Secretary-General), 30 May 1949.

[3] ARM 7/2/10, Déclaration de Monsieur Robert Marjolin Secrétaire Général de l'O.E.C.E. à l'occasion de la signature de l'Accord sur l'UNION EUROPEENNE DE PAIEMENTS, Paris, 19 September 1950.

[4] ARM 4/10/2, OEEC [R. Marjolin], Programme for a lasting settlement of the Dollar problem, Secret, Paris, 4 June 1952.

organization, and the imminent end of ERP funds had perhaps encouraged him to adopt bolder ideas for the integration of European economies than many national civil servants and statesmen dared to harbour at the time.

Closer integration through the OEEC did not materialize. Marjolin left the organization in 1954, feeling frustrated by the limited progress that it was making due to its intergovernmental set-up and the number and diversity of the countries involved. Moreover, his own position as secretary-general had been designed from the outset to be politically weak, lacking any independent powers. A major set-back for him was the inability to turn the OEEC into a customs union—for him the next 'natural' step in European integration:

> For two or three years or more before leaving OEEC I tried to do my best to expand the OEEC into a customs union . . . I felt that this was a natural development. I pushed the thing as fast as I could and there I met a strong British opposition . . . so I felt in '54 when I made my decision that everything that OEEC could do had been achieved, and that therefore, I could feel free to try something else.[5]

AT THE EEC COMMISSION: ECONOMIC AND MONETARY COOPERATION

After a short spell as a professor of economics at Nancy University, Marjolin returned to the centre of French decision-making on European integration in early 1956 when a new centre-left government under Prime Minister Guy Mollet came to power. He became the adviser to foreign minister Christian Pineau and was put in charge of formulating French positions during the negotiations leading to the Treaty of Rome. Marjolin and a small group of politicians and civil servants in the French administration shared concerns about France's protectionism and lack of competitiveness to which the Common Market could be a solution. However, the majority of his colleagues, in particular at the foreign ministry, were inherently sceptical about the Common Market and about opening up the French economy to foreign competition (Lynch 1997). Deeply convinced of the benefits of closer European economic integration for the modernization of France, Marjolin worked hard to influence the French negotiation positions in the summer of 1956, rendering them more compromising and thus acceptable to France's negotiation partners (Warlouzet 2011: 79). The negotiations were successfully concluded,

[5] Interview Philip C. Brooks with Robert Marjolin, Paris, 30 May 1964, <http://www.trumanlibrary.org/oralhist/marjoln.htm> (accessed 14 January 2015).

and the French government signed the treaties establishing the EEC and Euratom in Rome in March 1957 and ratified them in July of that year.

As someone whose post-war career was concerned with European economic integration and who had an intimate knowledge of the EEC Treaty, Marjolin was an obvious candidate for the new EEC Commission. He became one of its vice-presidents and took the portfolio of economic and financial affairs. However, for his area of responsibility—economic and monetary issues—the Treaty articles were vague. The general objectives of the EEC Treaty mentioned the aim of strengthening the unity of Member States' economies and ensure their harmonious development. Article 6 envisaged the coordination of macro-economic policies between Member States more specifically; Articles 103–9 were the only ones dealing exclusively with economic, monetary, and exchange-rate policy. Article 103 decreed that Member States were to regard their short-term economic policies as a matter of common concern.

However, while it included a rather weak obligation for consultation, the Treaty provided the Commission with no procedure or instruments and did not define short-term economic policy any further, for instance whether it also included monetary policy. Article 104 set out basic objectives for the Member States' economic policies corresponding to the 'magic triangle' of price stability, high levels of employment, and balance of payments equilibrium. Article 105 dealt with economic policy coordination in view of realizing the objectives of Article 104, in particular achieving equilibrium in the balance of payments; it also addressed monetary matters, in particular it provided for the establishment of the EEC Monetary Committee in charge of monitoring the situation in the Member States. Article 107 stipulated that Member States were to treat their exchange rates as a matter of common concern. Furthermore, Articles 108 and 109 dealt with the management of balance of payments difficulties of a Member State and the procedure to be followed by the Commission and the Council. At the request of France, Article 109 also contained safeguard clauses in case of a sudden balance of payments crisis, while Articles 67–73 focused on the liberalization of capital movements.

There are at least two reasons why the Treaty did not deal with monetary policy in any great detail. First, by the time the Treaty was signed, European currencies had not yet regained their full convertibility and the Bretton Woods system was widely seen as an adequate way to organize international monetary affairs. Second, issues pertaining to currency were seen as a prerogative of the nation-state, and money was a symbol of national sovereignty. However, while monetary union was not an aim of the EEC Treaty in itself, the cooperation in and coordination of economic and monetary matters were seen as vital for ensuring the smooth functioning of the Common Market.

While the Treaty articles provided the framework for Marjolin's work at the Commission, his policy proposals were guided by the political context at the time, his experiences in France and at the OEEC, and his ideas on European integration. For example, Marjolin took his core conviction of the benefits of indicative planning to the Commission as he considered it a necessity to ensure the harmonious development of the Common Market. At his directorate-general DG II, Marjolin surrounded himself with collaborators sympathetic to the idea of economic planning.[6] He put Pierre Uri, economist at the High Authority of the European Coal and Steel Community (ECSC) and close collaborator of Monnet, in charge of two studies: one on the economies of the Member States (Commission of the EEC 1958); and one on economic perspectives 1960 to 1970 (Commission of the EEC 1962b). Monetary union came repeatedly onto the agenda whenever the instability of the international monetary system, and Member States' reactions to it, threatened the unity and the functioning of the Common Market and, in particular, its CAP.

Marjolin's 'philosophy' of European integration can also go some way to explain the shape and form of his proposals. It is often said that he did not share the federalist outlook of some of his colleagues, in particular Commission president Walter Hallstein and Jean Rey (Warlouzet 2008). However, it can be argued that Marjolin shared their goals of a European federal state as the final stage for European integration, but the means and steps of achieving this that he had in mind were distinctive and certainly much more gradual. While Hallstein almost aggressively lobbied for an extension of the powers of the Commission and the European Parliament, Marjolin thought that close cooperation would lead to policy coordination, the convergence of ideas, and eventually unity: 'Coordination goes further than cooperation. It leads to shared rules, which constitute the antechamber of unification.'[7]

Rather than strengthening supranational institutions, Marjolin aimed at closely involving experts, national civil servants, and politicians in Community-level policy-making. This, he thought, would lead them first to better understand each other's situations and eventually to share interests leading to closer integration. His proposals for the establishment of various Community committees reflect this essentially neo-functionalist outlook on European integration.

The following sections deal with Marjolin's three initiatives for EMU: first, his proposals of 1958; second, the Action Programme for the Second Stage of 1962 and the measures and policies that were implemented as a result; and, third, a last attempt to bring EMU onto the Community's agenda in 1965.

[6] Interview with Jean Flory, Paris, 8 January 2014.

[7] ARM 26/11/125, R. Marjolin, Speech to Parlementaires Mouvement Européen, Paris, 5 November 1964.

Ambitious Beginnings: The Proposals of 1958

Marjolin's aim of furthering the modernization of the French economy through European integration shaped his first proposals at the Commission. Until late 1958, when the new French president Charles de Gaulle implemented far-reaching financial reforms with the Pinay–Rueff Plan, France suffered from severe economic problems and a balance of payments crisis (Maes 2006). The proposals that Marjolin drew up in 1958 reflect this situation in that they envisaged a solidarity mechanism in which economically weaker Member States obtained access to credit, while stronger Member States would make sure that debtors followed reasonable financial and economic policies. For Marjolin, France was among the weaker countries and needed to be integrated and even disciplined by Community rules. However, the proposals were also a means of 'testing the water' and opening up the debate with the Member States about what were possible and desirable avenues to pursue.[8]

Marjolin's first proposal dated from 31 May 1958 and contained his initial thoughts on monetary cooperation.[9] As he took up many of these ideas in later proposals, this is an important document to consider. Shortly before Marjolin made his proposal, Monnet's Action Committee for the United States of Europe had launched the idea of a European Reserve Fund (ERF), financed by central bank reserves, and giving credits in European units of account which resembled an EPU among the Six. It was Triffin who was at the origin of this idea (Maes and Buyst 2004). The ERF proposal was clearly at the back of Marjolin's mind, given his close relationship with both Monnet and Triffin. However, rather than an ERF, Marjolin proposed a more general coordination of economic, financial, and monetary policies in the developing Common Market. Due to the deficiencies of the current EEC Treaty in terms of economic integration, Marjolin went so far as to propose a new treaty to realize the aim of a fully-fledged economic union where Member States would relinquish key prerogatives, such as decisions on budgetary spending, budget deficits and surpluses, credit policy, public investment, and exchange rates.

More particularly, the Commission memorandum proposed a three-stage plan. In the first phase, countries would benefit from financial solidarity if they followed a code of good conduct. The Commission would monitor the economies of the Six and make suggestions to the Council, which would then decide on recommendations to each Member State. In this first phase, these recommendations by the Council would not be binding, but there was a clear incentive to follow them as otherwise the Member State would be deprived of financial aid. In the second phase, envisaged as starting about four years after

[8] Interview Jean Flory with the author, Paris, 8 January 2014.

[9] ARM 32/1/1, Coopération monétaire dans la Communauté Économique Européenne, Brussels, 31 May 1958.

the beginning of the first phase, governments were obliged to follow the recommendations by the Council, taken by qualified majority voting. To provide financial solidarity to each other, Member States would make available a limited percentage of their currency and gold reserves to provide a Member State experiencing balance of payments difficulties with credits. This could eventually be extended to a 'total' solidarity, for example in the second phase. An ERF with limited funds would not be sufficient for this purpose, and Marjolin did not think that it would be a good idea if Member States had to give up a portion of their reserves. He believed that his method was more flexible, even though Member States potentially had to use larger parts of their reserves to support another Member State. At the end of stage two (of an unspecified duration), Marjolin considered that the Member States were in a (not further defined) 'state of monetary union', in which their balances of payments could be considered as individual chapters of a unified balance of payments. Stage three was not fleshed out.

Regarding institutional changes, Marjolin considered that in the first phase the existing institutions would be able to cope with the task. However, the EEC Monetary Committee would see its competences extended. Crucially, Marjolin proposed the creation of a Council of the Governors of the EEC Central Banks, having consultative powers in monetary affairs. This Council, together with the Commission, would also be in charge of studies and works leading to the creation of a System of European Central Banks, similar to the American Federal Reserve System. This Council would decide by qualified majority from the beginning of the second phase and would see its powers extended considerably to encompass credit policy (central banks to governments), interest rates, and medium-term credit. The Commission did not pursue these proposals any further as the European Free Trade Area (EFTA) negotiations, the launch of the CAP, and the first steps in the customs union were seen as more pressing issues.

Marjolin's second memorandum dated from 7 November 1958.[10] At this point the EFTA negotiations were floundering and the memorandum embodied Marjolin's commitment to the Common Market as the more ambitious project requiring closer integration and a far stricter discipline on the part of the Member States. The imminent dissolution of the EPU and the return of the pound sterling and European currencies to convertibility was another important factor. Exchange-rate stability thus became an important topic for Marjolin—in this and future memoranda—as he saw it as a key condition for common policies such as the CAP, launched in the summer of 1958, and the free circulation of capital. Triffin's collaboration on the text was obvious as it envisaged an ERF as the basis for creating an EPU for the Six.

[10] ARM 32/1/2, Robert Marjolin, Cooperation économique, financière et monétaire dans la Communauté Économique Européenne, COM(58)249 secret.

Marjolin proposed the following procedures for achieving closer cooperation in the economic, financial, and monetary spheres: regular studies (or monitoring) of the economic and financial situation in areas including public spending, budgetary deficit, credit policy, investments, and exchange-rate fixing, to obtain a solid understanding of Member States' situations in order to develop recommendations and improve coordination. However, Marjolin was more cautious than in the earlier May 1958 memorandum: the recommendations were not binding on Member State governments. Financial solidarity was still on the agenda. However, the situation in France had improved and was less threatening, so less emphasis was put on this issue.

The most important difference between the May and the November memorandum was that in the latter Marjolin proposed the setting up of an ERF which he had rejected in May. Each Member State would pay in a minimum of 10 per cent of its foreign reserves, in total *circa* 1 billion US dollars. The fund would have numerous functions, and its reserves could be used for all settlements between central banks of the Member States as well as with EPU members and the rest of the world. As in the EPU, the memorandum proposed to use a unit of account for managing the fund. This proposal arguably continued what the EPU had begun but went much further as it linked increased financial solidarity with deeper integration leading to monetary union. It is likely that Triffin and Marjolin used their experience with the EPU—both its achievements and its shortcomings—as a reference point for this proposal.

Featuring the ERF, the November memorandum appeared to be bolder, but in other respects it was less ambitious than the May memorandum. For instance the near unconditional solidarity of the Member States in vouching for each other with their currency reserves as proposed in May seemed far more difficult to achieve than to agree on a monetary fund for foreign reserves that was accountable and well-managed.

Crucially, in the November memorandum, economic and financial coordination took a back seat. The monetarist views of Triffin, who had become an adviser to Marjolin at the Commission, were much more prominent (Maes 2006). The expected effect of the ERF was that monetary cooperation would automatically lead to economic coordination; Triffin did not think that coordination of economic policies was a necessary precondition for a rapprochement of monetary policies (Warlouzet 2011: 199; Maes and Buyst 2004). Neither proposal was taken forward, largely due to resistance in the EEC Monetary Committee, whose members from the central banks were sceptical about the unit of account and the ERF (Bussière 2007: 394). Also, shortly after, the political context had changed again with de Gaulle pushing through reforms, a devaluation of the franc, and a liberalization of the French economy with the Pinay–Rueff Plan. The issue suddenly seemed less pressing.

Nevertheless the May memorandum expressed some of Marjolin's core ideas: integration through the coordination of economic, financial, and monetary policies and the creation of a committee of governors of the central banks of the Member States to strengthen monetary integration. The ERF idea would take a back seat in future proposals by Marjolin as it did not correspond entirely to Marjolin's conviction of the need for close economic coordination and cooperation in the Common Market. It was also likely to be rejected by the German government, above all by Erhard. Marjolin adopted more of an economist perspective on EMU, thus moving away from Triffin's monetarist approach and advocating a more balanced approach.

The Action Programme of the Community for the Second Stage and its Consequences

The 1960s were characterized by two phenomena that would threaten the unity of the Common Market: the US balance of payments problems and inflationary tendencies in some economies of the Six. The speed with which the Common Market was taking shape was another incentive for Marjolin to advance new proposals. Given the acceleration decision of 12 May 1960, the immediate abolition of the quota system and 10 per cent of additional reduction in customs duties, and advances in the CAP, Marjolin increasingly saw the harmonization of economic and monetary policies as a precondition for the smooth development of the Common Market.

In August 1960 Marjolin drafted a secret memorandum in which he proposed the idea of monetary policy harmonization.[11] Some of the content of this memorandum would eventually be taken up again in 1962 in the Commission's Action Programme: notably, the coordination of exchange rates and long-term capital movements, and tackling internal and external (in particular as a result of US balance of payments problems) monetary problems in a coordinated fashion. However, the memorandum was more 'monetarist' than 'economist' in its approach to EMU and bore Triffin's signature. It conferred three tasks on the EEC Monetary Committee: namely, a study of the reform of the International Monetary Fund (IMF), the creation of an ERF, and the entry of the United States into the European Monetary Agreement. The memorandum shows that, at that time, the Community framework was not necessarily seen as the ideal one for a solution to monetary and balance of payments instabilities. There needed to be a reform of the international monetary system—something most EEC central bankers favoured over a regional European solution. All in all, this document

[11] ARM 32/1/4, [DG II], Harmonisation des politiques monétaires nationales des pays de la Communauté, 30 August 1960.

demonstrates Marjolin's belief that, as the second largest economy in the world, the Community needed to assume its responsibilities and contribute to shaping the international monetary system.

In October 1962 the Commission launched its Action Programme for the second stage of the transition period of the Community (Commission of the EEC 1962a). Marjolin was in charge of chapters VII and VIII on economic and monetary policy, respectively. It was here that Marjolin formulated his most ambitious plans for economic and monetary cooperation in the Community. Chapter VII on economic policy focused on measures to achieve increased cooperation and coordination of Member States' economies, regarding both short-term and medium-term economic policies.

Importantly, Chapter VII introduced a project dear to Marjolin: Community-level indicative planning, carefully termed 'a programme' in the text, in deference to German sensibilities. Such a programme would be 'indispensable for a rational distribution of the limited financial resources of public authorities'; it should be a guide for the plans drawn up in many Member States. Marjolin argued that a Community-wide economic programme was necessary for implementing common policies such as the CAP. The duration of such a programme would be five years. Suggestions for Keynesian macro-economic management made their appearance. For instance, the document suggested a reinforcement of the instruments of anti-cyclical policy at the disposal of national authorities and the development of a system of economic indicators to permit rapid diagnosis of change in economic activity. A Community-wide short-term economic policy was to be created. In annual meetings national policies would be scrutinized and adjustments would be discussed. National budgets should also be analysed and, if necessary, influenced through recommendations.

In short, 'the Community must move towards the establishment of one single centre for economic policy' (Commission of the EEC 1962a: chapter VII). The EEC Monetary Committee and the Counter-Cyclical Economic Policy Committee, which had been created in 1960, were to be strengthened and to be more involved in this cooperation between the Commission and the Member States. The Counter-Cyclical Economic Committee was testament to Marjolin's Keynesianism and his experience at the OEEC with national accounts (Albert 2004).

A Plan for Europe: Introducing a Medium-Term Economic Policy in the EEC

From 1962 onwards Marjolin focused on introducing planning (*planification*) at the European level. However, the reactions in some Member States, and among some of his colleagues in the Commission, were very negative. In particular, German federal economics minister Erhard reacted strongly to anything that smacked of economic planning. His speech in the European Parliament in November 1962 was scathing about the Commission's attempts to introduce a medium-term economic programme. Competition policy should regulate economic activity in the Common Market, not macroeconomic planning, which he deemed 'primitive' and 'centralizing'.[12] In 1963, against the background of this level of resistance, Marjolin embarked on a promotional campaign in favour of planning or 'programming' in the EEC.[13]

Marjolin also presented specific proposals to the Council on the establishment of a medium-term economic policy and a Medium-Term Economic Policy Committee (Commission of the EEC 1963b). To appease those Member States and Commissioners critical of indicative planning, he underlined that this proposal did not seek to limit the freedom of the markets. It offered a framework in which Community institutions, government, and private sector could work together and could achieve more transparency of their activities. The task of the new committee would be to put together a draft programme for a medium-term economic policy for the period 1966–70, setting targets for growth. It would also monitor medium-term economic policies in the Member States and watch over their compatibility with the programme. In addition, it would publish opinions independently or at the request of the Commission. The Commission suggested that this committee should collaborate with the other Community committees, thus establishing a quasi-technocratic economic government for the EEC. According to Warlouzet (2011: 352), while this proposal was 'fairly moderate in its form, it was in reality very ambitious as Marjolin presented a far-reaching societal project under the cover of economic policies'. It was a vision that was contrary to Erhard's idea of *Ordnungspolitik*, of just setting an orderly framework of rules for the competitive market economy and refraining from any intervention in the economic process.

On 15 April 1964 the Council decided on the creation of the Medium-Term Economic Policy Committee (64/247/EEC). However, it substituted a language of intentions and suggestions for that of automatism and coercion. It was clear that the Commission had little power if a Member State deviated from the programme which would be adopted by the Council. A German, Wolfram Langer, State Secretary at the German Ministry of Economics (1963–68), became the first president of the committee. Appointing a senior official who was close to Erhard was a smart move, given the German

[12] Ludwig Erhard, Planification—kein Modell für Europa. Rede vor dem Europäischen Parlament in Straßburg, 20 November 1962, in Erhard (1988: 773).

[13] ARM 26/3/1, Robert Marjolin, 'Faut-il un Plan européen?' in *TransMondia Revue Mensuelle au service de l'homme du XXe siècle*, No. 100, January 1963; 26/9/38, Robert Marjolin, 'Was bedeutet Programmierung?' in *Junge Wirtschaft. Zeitschrift für fortschrittliches Unternehmertum*, No. 5, May 1963.

economics minister's and then, since 1963, Chancellor's scepticism towards indicative planning. The committee worked well together and agreed on a set of economic policy guidelines to achieve steady economic growth (4.3 per cent per annum) while maintaining stability. The Council approved the provisional programme for 1966–70 on 9 February 1967, shortly before Marjolin left the Commission.

Monetary Policy Cooperation

The Action Programme's chapter VIII was dedicated to monetary policy. Here Marjolin reverted to a more balanced position between the monetarist and the economist approaches to EMU, arguing that the far-reaching plans for economic policy outlined earlier necessitated a parallel action in monetary policy. Fixed exchange rates were seen as paramount in a Common Market with policies with common price regimes such as the CAP. Thus, the chapter suggested fixed exchange rates with a narrow fluctuation margin from at least the end of the transition period. This was deemed 'the very essence of a monetary union' (Commission of the EEC 1962a: chapter VIII). Triffin's idea of a European reserve currency was revived as it was thought that it would contribute to the reform of the international monetary system and would facilitate international monetary cooperation. Marjolin repeated his proposal of 1958 to establish a Council of the Governors of the Central Banks. Important monetary decisions, such as changes in interest rates, reserves policy, and exchange rates should be discussed in advance in either this setting or a joint meeting of central bank governors and finance or economics ministers. Corresponding to Marjolin's view of a gradual advancement of integration, this system of prior consultations should 'naturally develop' into a system of recommendations.

With regard to the external monetary situation, the chapter envisaged consultations leading to common positions on important decisions and actions in the international monetary system, for instance recourse to the facilities of the IMF, the reform of the international monetary system, and harmonization of the central banks' reserves policy. While initially EEC governments and central banks would be free, after consultations, to take any decision they deemed fit, eventually 'the institutions will have been set up and the procedures tested which will make it possible to go further and advance from the co-ordination to the centralization of decisions' (Commission of the EEC 1962a: chapter VIII). Monetary union 'could' become the objective of the third stage. However, how this should come about was not specified any further other than the suggestion (as in the May 1958 memorandum) that the committee of central bank governors 'would become the central organ of a federal type banking system' and EEC finance and economics ministers would decide on the volume of national budgets and of the EEC budget and on their financing.

While Marjolin revived some of his earlier ideas, the context of this memorandum was crucial. In the monetary field the 1960s were characterized by turbulences, both internally and externally. Unilateral actions by individual Member States threatened Common Market unity and, crucially, the emerging CAP which relied on a system of common prices for key agricultural products such as cereals. The alarm bells rang in Brussels when in 1961 Germany revalued the D-Mark without consulting its EEC partners. Moreover, reserve currencies such as the US dollar and pound sterling were in difficulties. In a system of fixed exchange rates European countries were forced to maintain their exchange rates with what was perceived as an overvalued dollar. This put further pressure on the EEC countries to coordinate their position and formulate their interests as the second largest economy in the Western world. It 'gave an indication to the countries of the European Community that the demise of the Bretton Woods system could cause problems for the common market project' (Maes 2006: 230).

In institutional terms the 1962 proposals were characteristic of Marjolin's integration concept. A transfer of sovereignty to the European level was not meant to benefit the Commission but would proceed via a 'Europeanization' of experts, the creation of Community-level committees, a procedure of coordination *ex ante* and *ex post*, and increased use of majority voting. Only in the third stage would there be a centralization of decisions. This approach suggests Marjolin's political awareness, as he was in regular contact with French policy-makers such as Olivier Wormser and Maurice Couve de Murville and conscious of the limits of French willingness to abandon more powers to Brussels.

Between the publication of the Action Programme in October 1962 and the Commission's proposals to the Council in June 1963 (Commission of the EEC 1963a) the Community had experienced its first crisis when President de Gaulle declared an end to accession negotiations with Great Britain in January 1963. This action was followed by the signing of the contested Elysée Treaty between France and Germany shortly afterwards. The atmosphere in which the June proposals were presented was thus subdued. Nevertheless, the proposals were the result of Marjolin's broad consultations with Member States and the EEC Monetary Committee. It became clear that the Commission was taking a broader view of policy coordination. It argued that to be effective monetary policy cooperation could not be limited to central banks but needed to encompass budgetary decisions. Monetary policy of the central banks and fiscal policy needed to be coordinated in the Member States and at Community level. The document thus recommended the creation of a Budgetary Policy Committee. The rationale here was that monetary policy coordination alone would not suffice. The entire domain of public finances needed to be taken into account in order to ensure that monetary policy orientations would not be undermined. There was to be preliminary coordination before budgetary policy decisions were taken in each Member State. Having a single Community budget was the ultimate aim.

In a second proposal, the Commission proposed the establishment of a Committee of the Governors of the EEC Central Banks to allow for a more targeted exchange of view than was possible in the EEC Monetary Committee which was dominated by economics and finance ministers. The initial tasks of this new Committee of Central Bank Governors would be to conduct an exchange of information on national banking policies, follow the monetary development in each Member State, consult on the general principles of the policies of the central banks (e.g. in credit, money market, and foreign reserves), and discuss measures that a central bank was about to put in place in a Member State, ideally *ex ante* rather than *ex post*.

This proposal was followed by a third recommendation of the Commission to the Council for collaboration between Member States in international monetary relations. It proposed a closer coordination of the six Member States' policies in this domain, using the EEC Monetary Committee. The statute of the EEC Monetary Committee was to be altered to allow it to organize prior consultations before a decision and to systematize the consultation procedure preceding an exchange-rate adjustment.

The Council of Ministers adopted some of these proposals in the spring of 1964 (64/300/EEC), albeit often in a watered-down form. For instance, the Council decision on consultations on the international monetary system contained a reservation that prior consultations would take place 'unless circumstances and in particular the time limits for taking them require otherwise' (64/301/EEC). In terms of consultations prior to an exchange-rate adjustment, the Council adopted a declaration, not a decision as suggested by the Commission, to hold such consultations (64/306/EEC). The text of the decision on the Budgetary Policy Committee was also slightly altered so that the committee would not be involved in or scrutinize national budgets during their preparatory phase for their compatibility with Community economic aims. It simply said: 'The Committee shall study and compare the broad lines of the budgetary policies of the Member States' (64/299/EEC).

The Committee of the Governors of the EEC Central Banks

With regard to the creation of EMU, no decision was perhaps more important and far-sighted than the creation of the Committee of EEC Central Bank Governors. However, the reaction of the central bankers to Marjolin's proposals was less than enthusiastic. While they agreed that a coordination of monetary policies was useful, they thought that such coordination would ideally take place in a larger international framework. To mark their independence vis-à-vis the Community, they selected Basel as their meeting place and set their meetings to coincide with the bi-monthly meetings at the Bank for International Settlements (BIS). One representative of the Commission, Marjolin himself or the director-general of DG II, would participate in the meetings. The first meeting of the Committee of Governors took place on 6 July 1964.

Marjolin had high hopes for this new and important group as a driving force for EMU. He was keen to encourage the central bank governors to coordinate their actions, to agree norms and policies, and to coordinate behaviour vis-à-vis third countries. This is demonstrated by the ambitious agenda Marjolin presented to the governors in the first session where he suggested 'action to stop fluctuation in agricultural prices arising from the value of the unit of account; anti-inflationary action, since too often this was left to central banks, which tightened interest rates, restricted credit, and thus confined the possibilities of investment; and determining the usefulness of capital controls, used in particular by Germany to block inflows' (James 2012: 54). The governors' response can be described as lukewarm at best.[14]

While they were far from being united on most topics, Marjolin was acutely aware of the danger of the governors closing ranks to back a governor's decision and thus defend their independence. This was the case for instance with item number three on Marjolin's agenda, Germany's restriction of the import of foreign capital, a measure that went against the freedom of capital movement. The Commission was opposed to this measure. However, as it feared that the other five governors would support Bundesbank president Karl Blessing, Marjolin suggested a compromise to approve a moderate restrictive credit policy.[15]

One of the most controversial topics that the Committee dealt with in the first years of its existence was the question of the liberalization of short-term capital movements. Short-term capital movements were attributed an important role in the balance of payments' adjustment process and were studied for their effect on domestic monetary and fiscal policies (Hodjera 1973). The liberalization of capital movements was prescribed in Article 67 of the EEC treaty. The Council had adopted a first directive to this effect on 11 May 1960. It was amended in 1962 to unconditionally liberalize direct investment, short- or medium-term lending for commercial transactions, and purchases of securities traded on the stock exchange.

[14] Procès-verbal de la première séance du Comité des gouverneurs des banques centrales des pays membres de le CEE, 6 July 1964. ECB archives, <http://www.ecb.europa.eu/ecb/history/archive/agendas/html/index.en.html#y1964> (accessed 25 July 2015).

[15] ARM 24/1/6, DG II, Note, 3 July 1964.

Most central banks were sceptical as to whether the complete liberalization of short-term capital movements was feasible or whether having some sort of control over the entry and exit of capital would not be preferable. The Committee of EEC Central Bank Governors studied the possibilities of a liberalization of short-term capital movements at length during 1965–7 but could not agree on a common position. The documentation that each central bank submitted in 1966 showed the great diversity of opinions. However, the Commission held a strong belief in the benefits of the liberalization of short-term capital movements for economic union.[16] Marjolin put it this way: 'Liberalizing short-term capital movements will inevitably lead to a coordination of budgetary policies and to a unified business cycle.'[17] The bottom line of the central bank governors remained unchanged. An autonomous monetary policy of the Member States required the possibility of restrictions on short-term capital movements. Finally, in January 1967 the Committee put an expert group of the Commission and the central banks in charge of studying short-term capital movements.[18] Again, the experts had difficulties finding solutions given the different attitudes to the problem in the national central banks. In short, there was no common ground on this issue, and the matter was quietly dropped.

The Commission's Segré Report on the development of a European capital market has to be seen in this context (Commission of the EEC 1966). Maes (2007: 31) argued that the 'Commission's effort became increasingly focused on the opening-up of domestic capital markets'. The next major development with regard to the liberalization of capital movements only came with the single European market programme in the mid-1980s.

Implementation and Application: A Mixed Balance Sheet

The economies of the six Member States were experiencing impressive economic growth during the early 1960s: industrial production grew by 5 per cent in 1963; in 1964 the growth rates were between 8.5 and 6.4 per cent. Gross National Product (GNP) in the Member States grew by approximately 4.5 per cent. Inflation was becoming a problem in some Member States, in particular Italy and France. In 1963–4 Italy underwent a balance of payments crisis and price rises.

This economic context provided a real testing ground for Marjolin's new coordination and cooperation mechanisms. The Monetary Committee

[16] ARM 24/2/10, Note à l'attention de Monsieur Marjolin, 8 March 1966; 24/2/13, Letter Holtrop to Jacques Brunet, 21 March 1966.

[17] ARM 24/2/21, Marjolin, Gouverneurs, 11 July 1966.

[18] ARM 24/2/29, General Secretary of the Committee of Central Bank Governors to Marjolin, 19 January 1967.

discussed the situation intensively and issued recommendations for a restrictive spending and wage policy.[19] Marjolin also worked relentlessly, travelling to Rome and persuading the Italian government to adopt an action plan by the Commission which had the endorsement of the Monetary Committee. The economic situation in Italy improved. However, the Community was unable to provide Italy with the necessary capital. In March 1964 the Italian government thus decided to obtain loans from the United States, the IMF, the Bank of England, and the Bundesbank to stabilize the lira, without informing the Commission or the Monetary Committee. Marjolin was disappointed and remarked that this put into question the coordination and cooperation between Member States if a government unilaterally took such important decisions.[20] Crucially, the Italian crisis became the trigger for a range of new proposals.

Steps towards EMU 1965–7

Both 1964 and 1965 were turbulent years for the Community and the international monetary system. US balance of payments problems had placed the reform of the international monetary system at the top of the agenda of European leaders. At a press conference in February 1965 President de Gaulle even suggested a return to the gold standard.[21] At the Commission Marjolin was clearly challenged by both the US balance of payments problems and by de Gaulle.

Moreover, the Italian events in 1964 and the decision on common cereal prices in the framework of the CAP, on 15 December 1964, provided an additional motivation to relaunch the EMU project in early 1965. The CAP system of common prices was extremely vulnerable to exchange-rate fluctuations, which threatened to thwart the common market for agricultural products. Hence, from mid-1964 onwards, Marjolin sought new ideas for ways to realize monetary integration. His paperwork of this period encompassed various studies and opinions, for instance by a former colleague in the French administration as well as a speech by Otto Pfleiderer, member of the central bank council of the Bundesbank at Kiel in May 1964 ('Monetary Order and European Integration'). Pfleiderer argued for a common monetary policy and a common reserve fund.

[19] ARM 20/1/1, Comité monétaire, Rapport au Conseil et à la Commission sur la situation monétaire et financières de l'Italie, Confidentiel, Brussels, 23 October 1963.

[20] ARM 20/1/12, Aide Monétaire à l'Italie (Communication de Monsieur Marjolin), secret, Brussels, 18 March 1964.

[21] Charles de Gaulle, Press Conference on 4 February 1965. <http://fresques.ina.fr/de-gaulle/fiche-media/Gaulle00105/conference-de-presse-du-4-fevrier-1965.html> (accessed 10 February 2016).

A DG II memorandum drew on these thoughts to suggest four possible areas for action, each requiring more integration and Member State commitment. The first was to organize intra-Community swap agreements and credits; the second was to develop the European unit of account into a means of payment and reserves for banks—but not as a single currency; the third was the creation of an ERF with a fixed amount of resources; and the final step on the integration ladder was the complete pooling of Member States' reserves.[22]

In early 1965 DG II submitted detailed studies to Marjolin about the limits and possibilities of monetary union. The memorandum contained studies of historical examples of monetary union such as the United States, the Belgian–Luxembourg union, the pound sterling zone, and the gold standard. Marjolin's handwritten conclusions are characteristic of his cautious approach: monetary union was a long and complex process which could not be realized by decree.[23]

Following this preparatory work, in a meeting of the Commission on 19 January 1965, Marjolin outlined the process and form monetary union could take in the Community. He again emphasized that it would be a long process, the final phase of which was characterized by fixed exchange rates. Other conditions for monetary union were shared reserves and a common reserves policy, no limits on central banks' acquisitions of each other's foreign-exchange holdings, free short-term capital circulation, free circulation of long-term capital, and the possibility to transfer public funds, for instance in the framework of regional policy. Another precondition to stabilize the system was a close coordination of credit, budgetary and economic policies.

However, Marjolin saw a problem in the lack of a common political authority and did not believe in the possibility of a European central bank independent of the Member States. For him the post-1998 European Central Bank (ECB) would have been unthinkable: 'without doubt the governments would oppose the creation of an independent Community central bank'. Marjolin was opposed to a rigid process by stages towards monetary union and preferred a 'continuous evolution' whereby the Commission would 'exploit the favourable opportunities'.[24] He presented a version of these ideas to the European Parliament in March 1965.[25]

[22] ARM 32/1/17, Raisons d'être et modalités techniques d'une organisation éventuelle des relations monétaires entre pays de la C.E.E., 2 September 1964.

[23] ARM 32/1/20, DG II, Monnaie, Integration et C.E.E., 9 January 1965, annexed handwritten notes by R. Marjolin.

[24] ARM 32/1/21, H. Sigrist, Note à l'attention de MM. les membres de la Commission, Brussels, 25 January 1965, Très secret, and speaking notes R. Marjolin, undated.

[25] ARM 26/12/14, Extrait de la déclaration de Monsieur Robert Marjolin, Vice-Président de la Commission de la Communauté Economique Europénne, devant le Parlement Européen, le 23 mars 1965, sur certaines questions monétaires.

Shortly afterwards, DG II put these proposals into a 'Community action programme in the monetary domain', a draft memorandum for the Commission. According to this document, economic union implied the abandonment of all restrictions to currency exchange or of change of exchange-rate parities as a means to reach balance of payments equilibrium: 'This is the definition of monetary union.'[26] The document propagated a gradual approach. Anything else—including attributing powers to a Community organ able to prevent national authorities from adopting certain decisions considered as threatening market unity—would be politically impossible as it would mean abandonment of sovereignty of Member States. Once common prices became the norm, in the agricultural sector in particular, and the interests of Member States were more closely linked, they would voluntarily opt for further integration.[27]

A revised Commission paper then specified that coordination should take place in six monthly meetings of the Council. At these meetings Member States would discuss their respective problems in terms of macro-economic equilibrium. The Council would make recommendations on the basis of suggestions by the Commission, after having consulted the relevant committees. It would issue guidelines for economic policy conduct, in particular about government spending and debt. In addition, the Council would also develop an emergency procedure in the case of a crisis.[28] The French 'empty-chair' crisis broke out two weeks later and put an end to all efforts at achieving EMU through Marjolin's gradual method. The 1965 proposals came to nothing.

MARJOLIN'S LEGACY

Marjolin left the Commission in 1967 and was succeeded by the French economist Raymond Barre, who was able to build on Marjolin's work. As Howarth shows in his chapter in this volume, Barre had some success with his plan of 1969 which suggested the coordination of short-term economic policies and mechanisms of solidarity (also Bussière 2007).

Barre's and Marjolin's approaches to European integration differed. While Marjolin worked towards a logic of neo-functionalist spill-over, Barre was more of an intergovernmentalist. Barre's attitude was perhaps more suitable for the period following the empty-chair crisis. However, the two men shared similarities in that they were both 'atypical' French economists. They were

[26] ARM 32/1/26, DG II, Programme d'action de la Communauté dans le domaine monétaire (Projet de Mémorandum à la Commission), 9 April 1965.

[27] ARM 32/1/26, DG II, Programme d'action de la Communauté dans le domaine monétaire (Projet de Mémorandum à la Commission), 9 April 1965.

[28] ARM 31/1/31, DG II, Renforcement de l'Organisation Monétaire au sein de la Communauté Économique Européenne (Projet de memorandum), 16 June 1965.

open-minded, opposed the protectionism that was advocated by so many French politicians and civil servants, and advocated capital liberalization. Marjolin, like Barre, rejected a mere focus on monetary integration and advocated parallel action in economic policy coordination. Both also saw exchange-rate stability as a crucial precondition for European economic integration, in particular with regard to running the CAP. However, Barre rejected fixed exchange rates. They also differed in that Barre was less Keynesian and more 'German' with his monetarist focus on low inflation.

Of all the architects, Marjolin had the closest personal and working relationship with Robert Triffin. Triffin and Marjolin had a shared generational experience of the Great Depression, the Second World War, and post-war reconstruction in the framework of the IMF and the OEEC. Triffin became an important figure as adviser of DG II, and was able to shape some of Marjolin's proposals, in particular the early ones. However, the two also differed. Triffin was an arch-monetarist in his approach to EMU, whereas Marjolin had a more balanced view of EMU and was a proponent of economic convergence. EEC-wide planning (*planification*) became his pet project rather than Triffin's ERF.

Member State governments officially committed to the aim of EMU at the summit of The Hague in December 1969, leading to negotiations in the Werner Committee. Marjolin frequently commented on the Werner Plan and its aftermath. It appears that he had become disenchanted with his own gradual approach to EMU, which he also saw as a problem of the Werner Plan. Marjolin criticized the lack of 'common centres of political decisions, which do not exist and the creation of which is hardly contemplated'. He was sceptical about the ten-year schedule for EMU.[29]

Finally, in 1974 Marjolin was asked to chair a group of experts to draw up a study on EMU. They passed a gloomy verdict: 'without denying certain progress of a technical nature . . . the Group is of the opinion that the efforts undertaken since 1969 add up to a failure . . . Europe is no nearer to E.M.U. than in 1969. In fact if there has been any movement it has been backward' (Commission of the European Communities 1975: 1). Likewise, in the memoirs he published shortly before he died in 1987 he reserved a rather cursory treatment for his contribution to EMU (Marjolin 1986). This brevity suggests that at the end of his life he doubted some of his own achievements and their long-term impact. It also reflects the fact that he wrote his account of the 1960s under the impression of the economic crisis and eurosclerosis of the late 1970s and early 1980s.

To conclude, a few factors help explain why Marjolin was not more successful in pushing for EMU in the 1960s. First, the *legal basis* was weak, as the EEC Treaty did not have EMU as an explicit goal.

[29] ARM26/17/2, 'Status of European monetary integration and stability of existing European exchange rates'. Allocution de R. Marjolin à la Conférence Chose, 19 September 1970.

Second, with regard to *timing*, Marjolin was arguably the right man at the wrong time. With many of his proposals Marjolin reacted to major challenges such as crises in the international monetary system, the introduction of common prices in the CAP framework, or the French and Italian balance of payments crises. However, the economic situation of Member States during the 1960s was generally good. The Bretton Woods system was beginning to show its weaknesses, but finding a common European solution was not yet at the top of the agenda of Member State governments. Thus, the pressure on Member States to realize Marjolin's ideas was arguably not strong enough, nor was Marjolin himself able to exert any such pressure. The Community crises of 1963 and 1965–6 also thwarted Marjolin's attempts to realize closer economic and monetary integration. Moreover, his ideas for an EEC-wide economic programme came arguably too early. By the time Marjolin left the Commission even Germany had introduced macro-economic planning in the form of *Globalsteuerung* under the social-democratic federal economics minister Karl Schiller.

Third, Marjolin's *methods* of achieving his goals are often described as prudent, contemplative, and compromising and thus perhaps less effective in obtaining the results that he sought at the negotiation table (von der Groeben 1982).[30] It is telling that he favoured the slow process of socializing experts, who would, he expected, eventually move beyond an exchange of views and opinions to a convergence of interests, over asking for an outright transfer of powers to the Commission. While he did not doubt the necessity of EMU, during his term in office he adopted a tentative approach to its realization. His approach was keenly alert to Member States' concerns, in particular those of France. His three sets of proposals of 1958, 1962, and 1965 largely reflect this quest for carefully measured steps and methods to achieve EMU geared towards solving the economic and monetary problems of the day. Even in the heyday of the Hallstein Commission, Marjolin's chapters in the 1962 Action Programme were far less integrationist than other chapters.

Finally, Marjolin lacked politically influential *allies*. He had a distant and, for him, disappointing relationship with French president Charles de Gaulle, unlike his successor Barre. At the same time he faced a strong adversary in German federal economics minister Ludwig Erhard. Moreover, Marjolin's clientele in the committees consisted of an independent-minded and internationally orientated central bankers' community who resented the 'meddling' of the Commission.

Nevertheless, Robert Marjolin had a vital role in preparing the ground for the debates on EMU of the 1970s. He came up with a number of original ideas, some of which took time to take hold and become effective. The creation of the

[30] Interview Jean Flory with the author, Paris, 8 January 2014.

Committee of EEC Central Bank Governors was crucial as this group would be at the centre of most debates on EMU and would contribute vitally to the Delors Committee in 1988–9. Importantly, this move secured the Commission a seat at the table of the central bankers and a voice in their debates. The other committees that were created during the 1960s would also become important forums for discussing EMU. For instance, their chairmen made up the Werner Committee.

Marjolin's most original contribution to the EMU debate was arguably his advocacy of the advancement in parallel of close economic coordination and monetary union, albeit with the latter remaining rather ill-defined. The post-2007 financial and economic crisis in the Euro Area brought the lack of economic coordination in the EMU framework to the fore. Subsequent attempts to advance towards more coordinated macro-economic governance including a banking union, a fiscal union, closer budgetary coordination and surveillance, and economic policy coordination mean that Marjolin's view of the necessity of a closer economic and fiscal coordination between the Member States, in addition to monetary integration, has been justified.[31]

[31] The author is indebted to the organizers and participants of the project as well as to Dr Frances Lynch (University of Westminster) for their helpful comments on this chapter.

4

Raymond Barre

Modernizing France through European Monetary Cooperation

David Howarth

Raymond Barre's claim to be an architect of Economic and Monetary Union (EMU) rests ostensibly on his activities as the European Commissioner responsible for economic and financial affairs (Directorate-General II) and Commission vice-president from 1967 to early 1973. Commissioner Barre and his staff prepared the February 1969 memorandum and the March 1970 communication—widely known as the Barre Plans 1 and 2—which formed the basis of the discussions of the Werner Committee.

Much later, following the Maastricht European Council of December 1991, Barre became one of the leading political defenders of EMU in France, supporting painful fiscal consolidation and tax increases to move to the single currency by 1997, the earliest date allowed by the Maastricht Treaty (Mauduit 1995). Even former French president Valéry Giscard d'Estaing, one of the leading proponents of the single currency, came to argue that it would be unrealistic—given the difficulties facing the French economy and the high public sector deficit—to start EMU's final stage three by 1997 (Mauduit 1995). With Pierre Werner, Barre also became co-chair of the ECU Institute in Lyon. This private body was created in March 1992 to study the economic effects of EMU and to promote the single currency.

However, the true significance of Barre as an architect should be seen in terms of his economic convictions. They led him—far earlier than most of his compatriots, and against many detractors within French political, policy-making, and academic circles—to support the three main macro-economic stepping stones to EMU: macro-economic convergence based on low inflation; exchange-rate targeting (through an external exchange-rate regime) to reinforce domestic efforts to bring down inflation; and capital liberalization. As European Commissioner, and then as French prime minister from 1976 to 1981 with a concurrent stint as finance minister from 1976–8, Barre maintained his consistent support for these three policy goals, although without the telos of a single currency by way of official justification. Prior to the Delors Report, he never publicly stated his support for the creation of a single European currency emitted by a European central bank.[1] Barre repeatedly claimed that he was a European by conviction, but his Europeanism remained one in which Member States retained control. He was no fan of supranationalism (Lequesne 2010; Saint-Ouen 1990: 111ff.; Soutou 2010). Domestic economic concerns and the competitiveness of the French economy were always his priorities.

Unlike previous prime ministerial appointments, Barre had been a marginal political figure in France and never an official member of a political party. He was selected, at least officially, for his economic expertise by President Valéry Giscard d'Estaing. The president justified his choice on the grounds that Barre, the former academic, was 'the best economist in France' ('le meilleur économiste de France'). While this claim is debatable at best, Barre had considerable intellectual influence. He was a professor at the elite Parisian policy studies institute, Institut d'Études Politiques, periodically from the late 1950s to 1966 and the author of a political economy textbook that appeared in at least sixteen editions over a fifty-year period and was well-thumbed in universities throughout France. Barre shaped the economic thinking of a generation of students, some of whom went on to dominate the economic and financial administration of France and many of its largest banks and companies. As France's leading economist-politician, Barre played a—if not the—central role in the construction of a dominant economic vision, labelled *la pensée unique* by its detractors, which formed the ideological underpinning of French support for EMU.

[1] This claim is made on the basis of a full survey of Barre's speeches and interviews prior to 1992 (see also Balleix-Banerjee 1999: 36–40). In 1987, Barre called for a 'true monetary union within which a true European currency would circulate' ('veritable union monétaire au sein de laquelle circulerait une veritable monnaie européenne'), a position compatible with both a common (parallel) and a single currency (Barre 1987: 233). In his 1988 presidential election campaign programme (*Projet pour la France*), Barre used a very similar wording and called for a 'European Reserve System' which would coordinate national central banks, manage pooled currency reserves, promote the use of the European Currency Unit (ECU), and elaborate a common monetary policy in relation to the dollar (see also Barre 1988a, 1988b). Prior to the Maastricht Summit of December 1991, in the French political context, support for 'monetary integration' and EMU very rarely indicated support for the elimination of national currencies and the creation of a single currency emitted by a European central bank (Balleix-Banerjee 1999; Howarth 2001).

BARRE AS ECONOMIST: FROM THE IVORY TOWER TO THE COAL-FACE OF POWER

Barre's economic vision came from a synthesis of very different and often conflicting traditions (de Boissieu 2010). As a young academic economist, he declared himself a follower of John Maynard Keynes but eschewed Keynesianism as it had developed in the post-war period. Barre argued that Keynes' ideas were limited and had to be developed in a number of areas (Barre and Fontanel 1991). De Boissieu (2010) points to two main anchors of Barre's early economic thinking: late nineteenth- and early twentieth-century Swedish economists and the Austrian School. It is revealing of his search for alternative economic ideas that one of his earliest academic endeavours was to translate Friedrich von Hayek's *The Counter-Revolution of Science: Studies on the Abuse of Reason* into French and write the preface (Hayek 1953).

As prime minister and minister of finance, Barre intervened directly in the Eight Plan (1976), known as the Barre Plan, which was dominated by an explicit rejection of Keynesian reflation. From monetarism, Barre emphasized the need to use monetary policy to control the growth of the monetary supply with the aim of maintaining low inflation (Barre 1984). This determined focus also reflects the period in which he was appointed as prime minister. In the year 1975, French M2 increased by a record 18.2 per cent. Barre credits his policies with having reduced M2 growth to 10 per cent by 1980. Repeatedly, both in and out of office, he made clear that the battle against inflation was at the heart of any coherent economic *and* social policy (see, for example, Barre 1981; Fuerxer 2002b: 11). He emphasized the need for structural reform throughout the French economy to tackle inflation, insisting upon both labour-market reform and the liberalization of prices, controlled by the state since the 1940s, with the aim of increasing competition in a range of sectors to eliminate 'artificial and abusive', and thus inflationary, profits (Barre 1976; Fuerxer 2002a: 37ff.). At the same time, Barre (1981) recognized the social, political, and economic dangers of 'brutal deflation', opting instead for progressive and continual disinflation and gradual adaptation.

On budgetary policy, as prime minister, Barre did not seek necessarily to balance the government's books. However, he was concerned about the tendency of French governments to run excessive deficits and called for their reduction and for the need to run budgetary policy in tight coordination with monetary policy (Barre 1981). Control of fiscal deficits was a crucial part of Barre's monetarism (Barre 1981; Fuerxer 2002b: 61ff.). It placed his thinking squarely in the French credit-counterpart approach to monetarism of Jacques Rueff (Fuerxer 2002b: chapter 4; Daniel 2008), in contrast to the dominant American approach of Milton Friedman which focused singularly on the monetary base. Barre argued that a deficit above 1.5 per cent of gross domestic product (GDP) would 'be seriously damaging for the French economy' (Barre 1981: 52; author's translation). He regularly challenged the 3 per cent fiscal deficit limit, set by Socialist President François Mitterrand at a 9 June 1982 press conference and defended by subsequent Socialist governments (Seux 2014), as lax and inflationary (Barre 1984; Fuerxer 2002a, 2002b). However, both Barre's and Mitterrand's acceptable maximum fiscal deficit figures were arbitrarily set, although Barre's ensured a more sustainable debt load. That Mitterrand's 3 per cent was accepted by the German federal government as the Maastricht threshold for an EMU project, regularly denounced as deflationary, suggests that Barre was even more cautious on fiscal deficits than the German Christian Democrats.

Barre was a consistent supporter of free trade. Unlike much of the French political class, he saw the European Common Market and then the single market as stepping stones to gradual international trade liberalization (Fuerxer 2002b: 17ff.). As the head of the support staff of Jean-Marcel Jeanneney, minister of industry in the Gaullist government of Michel Debré, one of Barre's principal responsibilities was to supervise the abolition of tariffs and quotas, as required under the Treaty of Rome. He later claimed to have taken to this task with considerable 'energetic vigour' (Barre 1984: 178) and repeatedly denounced any return to protectionism as 'extremely dangerous' (Barre 1976). In this way Barre located himself in what was, in the French administration and political class of the 1960s and 1970s, a fringe position.

At the same time, Barre did not advocate the kind of unilateral and total trade liberalization upheld by the mainstream trade theory dominant in the English-speaking world. He was not a doctrinal trade liberal in the Frédéric Bastiat tradition in France (Fuerxer 2002a: 18ff.). In government, he called for 'ordered growth' of trade (Barre, *Le Figaro*, 15 September 1977) and accepted state intervention to 'manage' trade in sensitive sectors such as automobiles. Unlike most French academic economists and the financial administrative elite in the Treasury division of the Ministry of Finance, Barre also leaned towards capital liberalization. Again, however, he accepted the need for controls in the context of economic adjustment (Barre 1984: 208).

Barre's views on exchange rates aligned closely with mainstream French academic and political-class thinking from the 1950s onwards and differed markedly from neo-classical economists (Howarth 2001). The currency was not to be seen as a good like any other whose value was determined solely by the push and pull of supply and demand. Rather, its value should be defended in a fixed but adjustable exchange-rate regime. Barre saw exchange-rate stability as crucial to European market integration and the operation of the Common Agricultural Policy (CAP) so dear to President Charles de Gaulle. Given Barre's commitment to capital liberalization and exchange-rate stability, it is reasonable to assume that his thinking might have taken him down the

Mundellian route of the triangle of incompatibility, whereby governments can maintain only two of the three following goals at the same time: fixed exchange rates, capital liberalization, and monetary autonomy. However, Barre accepted that devaluations were inevitable and even desirable as long as their perverse effects were limited (Barre 1984; Fuerxer 2002a, 2002b).

Barre saw exchange-rate policy as the servant of his monetarism and his drive to root out inflationary elements in the French economy (Maes 2004). However, he did not see a European exchange-rate regime as a straitjacket at the complete expense of national margin of manoeuvre. In political life, both in government and as a leading opposition politician in the 1990s, Barre's economic preferences were tempered by political realism. Internal devaluations (deflationary policies) were desirable but too rapidly imposed they would result in social and political upheaval. The Exchange Rate Mechanism (ERM) of the European Monetary System (EMS), as initially conceived in the Bremen Accords, provided an appropriate balance between constraint and margin of manoeuvre.

In government and in opposition Barre frequently noted his concern for the French trade and current account deficit, a widespread preoccupation in the French political class (Howarth 2001). Combined with a determined anti-inflationary stance, the trade and current account deficit was an important motivation for the policy of 'competitive disinflation' that took root in government economic policy under Barre from 1976. It became strongly entrenched following the about-face in Socialist government economic policy in 1983, when President Mitterrand took the decision to keep the franc in the ERM and pursue deflation in France.

Barre might be best described in terms of German Ordo-liberalism, given that he wanted France to follow the German model of low inflation and export-led economic growth. In the 1970s and 1980s France was a world leader in the export of manufactured goods and services, falling behind Germany in the former but far ahead in the latter. However, France faced a constant trade and current account deficit while Germany was consistently in surplus.

There were three core economic policy ideas which encouraged support for EMU in elite French political, academic, and financial administrative circles, although none provided compelling reasons: competitive disinflation; a largely fixed, but potentially adjustable, exchange-rate mechanism to provide an external constraint; and capital liberalization. Collectively, these policy goals have been labelled by detractors as part of *la pensée unique* which in English finds its rough equivalent in Margaret Thatcher's 'there is no alternative' (Kahn 1996).

Barre is widely known in France for providing both academic and political leadership in promoting these three policies. After having struggled in the wilderness of France's economic policy landscape for over two decades, Barre's plan of 1976 represented the first impetus to *la pensée unique*. During the 1980s, this form of argument spread thanks to the conversion of important (but always minority) elements in the Socialist Party and to the brief liberal spurt of the neo-Gaullists under prime minister Jacques Chirac and finance minister Édouard Balladur from 1986 to 1988 (Balladur 1987). By the late 1980s, French academic economic thinking had also shifted. It provided few obstacles to, and considerable support for, these elements, indispensable to the move to EMU. However, it needs to be stressed that few proponents of the core elements of *la pensée unique*, in academic or political circles in the 1980s, were proactive on monetary union and very few campaigned on the matter prior to 1988. Barre certainly did not.

On 'competitive disinflation', Barre argued from the 1950s that monetary laxity risked weakening the competitiveness of French industry. The spiral of inflation, devaluation, and then even greater inflation, threatened to develop beyond the control of policy-makers. In the context of an increasingly open economy, devaluation became increasingly ineffective and even harmful. Barre (1984) argued that France should follow Germany in the pursuit of low inflation, along with domestic structural reform and micro-economic reforms, to increase the competitiveness of French industry in relation to its main trade partners. Although a fringe position in the 1970s, by the late 1980s 'competitive disinflation' became fully entrenched as unquestionable French government economic doctrine on both the centre right and the centre left, which was then in power (Fitoussi 1993). The pursuit of 'competitive disinflation' made it easier for French officials to accept the inclusion of the convergence criteria in the Maastricht Treaty, which constitutionalized the goal of price stability. However, there was considerable disagreement about the extent to which EMU was necessary to achieve this goal. It was advocated as a necessary step only by Banque de France officials and a few academics who saw the project as the ultimate guarantee of entrenching anti-inflationary monetary policies in a country, the politicians and public of which were still prone to excess (Howarth 2001).

Yet, on the issue of exchange-rate stability, Barre saw problems with the growing consensus around the EMS from the mid-1980s as a system of fixed rates (Barre 1984; Fuerxer 2002a, 2002b). He stood in opposition to the Socialist minister of finance in the late 1980s and early 1990s, Pierre Bérégovoy, who refused to accept German demands after reunification for the realignment of parities within the ERM in order to permit the revaluation of the D-Mark vis-à-vis the franc and certain other currencies (Howarth 2001). Barre had never been of the opinion that permanently fixed exchange rates were desirable (Fuerxer 2002a, 2002b). Further, the move from a system of fixed but adjustable rates to EMU was not, for Barre, an intellectually necessary one.

BARRE IN BRUSSELS

In early 1967, Barre succeeded Robert Marjolin as Commissioner responsible for economic and financial affairs (DG II) and as vice-president. His five-and-a-half years in Brussels corresponded to considerable international monetary upheaval, menacing the recently completed European Customs Union. Barre arrived in Brussels during a pound sterling crisis, followed swiftly by a French franc crisis. He left two months prior to the German government's decision to float the D-Mark, forcing the European 'snake' exchange-rate system from its US dollar tunnel.

Barre was the Commissioner responsible for monetary policy during the demise of the Bretton Woods system, the first round of intensive discussions on European monetary integration in the Werner Committee meetings, and the creation of the European exchange-rate mechanism, the 'snake'. The sea change in Member State preferences on European monetary cooperation during this five-and-a-half years impressed him. When Barre arrived at the Commission, he later claimed that Member State governments had no real understanding of monetary cooperation and 'refused' to see monetary problems as problems of common interest (Barre 2004: 19). He pointed out that many French policy makers saw his first two-page memorandum on monetary cooperation of February 1968 as unacceptable, covering matters beyond the jurisdiction of the EEC Treaty.

Barre left his mark on monetary integration most ostensibly through his memorandum of 1969 which informed discussions both among government leaders at the Hague Summit of December and in the Werner Committee, and led directly to concrete initiatives on monetary policy cooperation. He met bilaterally with French President Georges Pompidou, German Chancellor Willy Brandt, and Jean Monnet prior to the Hague Summit. Barre (2004: 16) claimed that each of them confirmed that he would intervene personally to launch discussions on monetary cooperation. The Commission was represented on the Werner Committee by Ugo Mosca. However, Barre (2004: 17) followed Committee meetings closely.

De Gaulle's appointment of Barre to the Commission was of importance—politically, symbolically, as well as in terms of economic direction. During the 1950s and 1960s, there was a real threat that French governments might resort to safeguard clauses to block EEC trade liberalization. The French 'empty-chair' crisis of 1965 and the subsequent 'Luxembourg compromise' were fresh in all minds. Maes (2006) notes that influential French officials occupied many of the crucial Community-level positions involved in an assessment of national economic situations. Thus Alain Prate was secretary of the EEC Monetary Committee; Robert Marjolin was Commissioner; and François-Xavier Ortoli was the director-general responsible for the internal market. This careful placement of French officials was intentional and designed to avoid EC economic policy recommendations that would annoy President de Gaulle (Lequesne 2010). Barre's views on the economy differed from those of most of these French colleagues and, in particular, from Marjolin, his predecessor at the head of DG II, notably in terms of his more critical appraisal of Keynesian economic theory and his monetarist focus on low inflation. Early in his half-decade term at the Commission, Barre manifested a cautious and critical approach to monetary integration. His focus was on low inflation and exchange-rate stability.

Lequesne (2010) and others insist that Barre's influence in Brussels, and over both French and other Member State politicians and officials, was considerable because he demonstrated impressive economic expertise, intelligence, and efficient administrative skills. His economic pragmatism and 'un-French' views would have been very welcome to officials from other Member States. Thus Barre had little enthusiasm for the CAP, which was sacred to de Gaulle, and saw it as something of a time-wasting burden (Soutou 2010: 78).

Soutou (2010: 73) argues that Barre played a central role, during his time in Brussels, in shifting the opinions of French political leaders away from a return to the gold standard—the solution proposed by de Gaulle in 1965—towards a more moderate reform of the international monetary system—one that limited the exorbitant privilege of the United States (see also Guindey 1973). Similarly, Barre encouraged French political leaders to accept the need for European monetary cooperation when an acceptable reform of Bretton Woods appeared unlikely. Supported by Giscard d'Estaing, the former French finance minister, and the Germans, notably federal finance minister Helmut Schmidt, Barre argued that a return to the (largely) fixed exchange rates of Bretton Woods was no longer possible and that a joint float of European currencies in relation to the US dollar was necessary (Soutou 2010). This shift to greater exchange-rate flexibility in the thinking of the French political leadership amounted to what some have described as a 'cultural revolution' (Soutou 2010). It opened the way, under Barre's leadership, for closer Franco-German monetary cooperation. Some see in the ideational approximation of Barre, Giscard, and Schmidt on monetary and macro-economic questions an important reason behind Barre's appointment as prime minister in 1976 (de Saint Périer 2013).

Barre claims that his time in Brussels resulted in changes to his thinking on the economy and the desirability of European monetary cooperation. He claims that in being exposed to the economic views of German officials, both in the Commission and in the German federal finance ministry, he began to examine even more critically the 'interventionist' approach of the French administration, its 'certain lack of understanding of the market' and its tendency toward protectionism (Barre 2000: 19). Barre (1984: 208) came to appreciate and concur with the views of his German interlocutors on capital market liberalization—and notably on the ineffectiveness of capital controls.

Well before European Commission agreements on capital market liberalization, Barre made clear his views on the subject and noted the importance of German thinking in the development of his own views. In his final report as Commissioner to the Council of Finance Ministers (ECOFIN) in 1972, Barre underlined the serious inflationary tensions appearing on the horizon and proposed a series of necessary measures to shield Member State economies. He noted that, of the members of ECOFIN, only the German federal finance minister, Schmidt, showed his agreement (Barre 2004: 25).

Barre brought about administrative changes in DG II which also reflected his economic views (Maes 2006). On his arrival, the existing DG II directorates of 'national economies and business cycle', 'monetary matters', and 'structure and development' reflected the macro-economic policy preoccupations of Commission officials, many of them French. 'Structure and development', in its focus on medium-term forecasts, sectoral analyses, and structural programmes, took inspiration from the French Planning Commission. To these, Barre added a fourth directorate to focus on 'budgetary matters', reflecting his preoccupation with fiscal deficits and their contribution to inflation. Barre also reanimated the Committee of EEC Central Bank Governors with the active support and collaboration of the then governor of the Banque de France, Bernard Clappier (James 2012). As the chapter by Seidel in this volume points out, this committee had been created by Marjolin. However, Barre claimed that it had barely functioned when he arrived in 1967. Clappier was intimately familiar with the European Communities. He had been the head of Robert Schuman's support staff from 1951 to 1953. As the head of the external relations office of the ministry of finance from 1951 to 1963, Clappier was one of France's leading negotiators on the Treaty of Rome (Badel 2005). During Barre's half-decade tenure at the Commission and subsequently when he worked at the Banque de France, he attended regularly the monthly meetings of the Committee of EEC Central Bank Governors which took place after the governors' Bank for International Settlements meeting in Basel.

Barre's criticism of French administrative economic thinking did not apply to senior Banque de France officials. After Barre's departure from Brussels, he became a member of the council of the Banque de France. In meetings at the bank, and in the Committee of EEC Central Bank Governors, he noted that central bankers were in full agreement on most matters but that governments tended to ignore them (Barre 2004). For Barre, the best mechanism for European cooperation—especially with the demise of Bretton Woods—was the Committee of Governors. In France, Barre (2004: 25), the independent economist, regularly sided with the central bank against the all-powerful French Treasury. However, the Treasury kept the central bank on a short leash, with limited opportunity to express opinions on monetary policy (Mamou 1988).

In the aftermath of the May 1968 riots and strike action in France, inflationary wage increases, and speculation against the franc, the French government made use of the EEC Treaty safeguard clauses and adopted protectionist measures. Some have argued that Barre played a crucial role in convincing President de Gaulle to avoid devaluation in November 1968 and to make use of the exchange rate as an external constraint to help rein in inflation (Aglietta and Baulant 1993; Lequesne 2010: 61). Barre (2004: 25) was opposed to the 11.1 per cent devaluation of the franc in August 1969 under President Pompidou—whom Barre describes as 'inflationist'. He argued that it further undermined the Bretton Woods fixed exchange-rate system. Barre (2004: 15) claimed that he was very much opposed to the unilateralism of the French devaluation, which was announced without any prior communication with the German government. The revaluation of the D-Mark in October 1969 further confirmed the beginning of the end of a system which had provided two decades of relative monetary stability in Western Europe. Barre (1984) saw this 20 per cent realignment as worsening an inflationary disequilibrium between France and Germany that persisted for most of the following two decades. The European Commission saw exchange-rate instability and macroeconomic imbalances as a direct threat to European market integration. French governments also perceived a direct menace to the operation of the CAP (Howarth 2001). The principal Commission response was to improve policy coordination and monetary cooperation.

The Barre Plans, 1 and 2

While Barre saw exchange-rate stability as a desirable goal, his views on European monetary and economic policy cooperation were also tinged with a heavy dose of pragmatism. Given the economic conditions of the late 1960s, he recognized the need to drop the former insistence upon fixed exchange rates, opting instead for parity changes by agreement. Maes (2006: 235) writes of a brief, two-page memorandum presented to ECOFIN in February 1968 (EC Commission 1968). In this the Commission called for prior mutual consent to precede exchange-rate adjustments, the elimination of fluctuation margins, the introduction of a system of mutual assistance, the establishment of a single European unit of account, and concerted action in international monetary institutions. These Commission proposals reflected French thinking on monetary integration and the voluntarist ideas of Robert Triffin which had dominated DG II economic thinking under Marjolin. However, they had little chance of making headway in the face of German and Dutch opposition. Such a 'one-sided monetary approach made no sense' (Szász 1999: 11).

With a two-sided approach, focused on both improved economic and monetary policy cooperation, Barre adopted a position on monetary integration that reflected a pragmatic and deliberately strategic approach, one which could help reconcile the monetarist (French) and economist (German) approaches to monetary integration and EMU. However, it is important to emphasize that this two-sided approach also conformed better to Barre's economic vision. Barre was arguably one of the few Frenchmen who could achieve some level of reconciliation between the French and German visions on acceptable monetary cooperation. He moved DG II away from Triffin's European Reserve Fund idea, which was unacceptable to the Germans, towards a mutual assistance system consistent with Article 108 of the Treaty of Rome. Barre promoted 'financial solidarity', mechanisms offering financial support to weak currency Member States under pressure to devalue in the face of speculative financial attacks. This solidarity was also to come in the form of financial carrots designed to facilitate the introduction of structural reforms, thus potentially extending Commission influence. Community mechanisms were presented as more effective to see off speculation than isolated national measures. Barre defended the economist approach of the German and Dutch governments: economic convergence was essential to ensure stable exchange-rate parities; and monetary union was the 'crowning' of economic union. Also, he was willing to make statements that would have ruffled feathers in Paris, arguing vaguely, for example, that for EMU to be successful, a stronger European political authority was needed (Barre 1968: 17). But, in doing this, he was expressing his scepticism about the probability of EMU rather than advocating further European integration.

At the same time Barre's vision of European monetary cooperation fitted well with some elements of the French Treasury and French government position. This was notably the case with regard to the need for monetary policy cooperation, specifically cooperation on interest-rate policy, and for support mechanisms. As Commissioner, Barre also promoted, albeit briefly, a single European unit of account, a French demand since the mid-1960s. However, he dropped this demand in the face of German opposition (Fuerxer 2002a). In the 1980s, he was a keen supporter of measures to promote the European currency unit (ECU) (Balleix-Banerjee 1999). Barre (2004) himself insists that he maintained close relations with French governments during his time in Brussels, with regular monthly (even weekly) visits to Paris and regular meetings with the foreign minister, presidents de Gaulle and Pompidou, and the secretary-general of the Elysée. These meetings helped to reduce the likelihood of friction between his policies at the Commission and French government preferences. By his own account, he bypassed the French permanent representation in Brussels (Barre 2004).

Barre sought to build a consensus around a two-sided approach to monetary integration that pragmatically combined German and French positions.

This approach was outlined in the so-called Barre Plan or Memorandum presented to ECOFIN in February 1969 (EC Commission 1969). The plan was far more modest and pragmatic than the Commission's Action Programme of 1962. It was also more balanced than the memorandum of February 1968. The Barre Plan called for a progressive narrowing of the margin of fluctuations among EEC currencies; convergence of medium-term economic policies; the coordination of short-term economic policies; and support mechanisms. Barre blended the medium-term approach of French planning with the German insistence upon economic convergence. Thus convergence was to be focused on inflation rates and also on national economic growth rates and balance of payments situations. Maes (2006: 236) notes an important shift in Commission thinking on inflation, reflecting heightened concern over disparities in prices and costs in Member States. This shift almost certainly reflected Barre's presence at the Commission, given his long-standing preoccupation with inflation. On the coordination of short-term economic policies, Barre proposed the reinforcement and more effective application of existing consultation procedures and a system of 'early warning' indicators.

The 1969 Barre Plan had a direct impact on policy. Following a French government initiative, in July 1969 ECOFIN agreed to the extension of a May 1964 obligation to consult on exchange-rate changes to cover all economic policy measures having an impact on other Member States. On support mechanisms, the plan called for both unconditional short-term monetary support and conditional medium-term financial assistance. While the position of EEC central bank governors on the Barre Plan was mixed, with the Germans, Dutch, and Italians openly hostile, the plan's proposal led to an arrangement among national central banks to create in February 1970 a Community Mechanism for Short-Term Monetary Assistance. ECOFIN also agreed to create (in March 1971) a medium-term financial assistance facility to assist countries suffering from balance of payments difficulties. However, Germany, the Netherlands, and Italy refused to move beyond limited central bank swaps (Dyson 1994: 65–71).

Following the Hague Summit, Barre set to work on a communication that was presented to ECOFIN on 4 March 1970 (EC Commission 1970). This communication—often referred to the Second Barre Plan—reiterated the elements of the February Barre Plan. Specifically, it placed emphasis on the convergence of national guidelines that should go hand in hand with 'concerted action in the field of economic policy'. However, it also proposed three main steps and a ten-year working calendar for the move to EMU. The Second Barre Plan focused on 'attempts to offset the imbalances created by separate action by Governments and to make for some degree of coordination'. However, it failed to spell out the permanent instruments for common policies (Dell'Amore 1970; Danescu 2012). Furthermore, it called for the harmonization of national fiscal policies—again without precision. Barre also proposed—as in the February 1968 memorandum—the creation of a common, not a single, currency. Effectively then, the Second Barre Plan contained the key elements of both the EMS of 1979 and the Single European Act of 1985.

The role of the Barre Plan in the history of European monetary integration, and thus Barre's role as an architect, must also be seen in terms of sequencing. The first plan was Barre's arguably more realistic response to Pierre Werner's far more ambitious proposals for monetary union. Indeed, in important respects, the Werner Committee followed Barre more closely than Werner's preceding plan. Barre (2004: 21) claimed that the Werner Committee followed his memorandum closely: 'the work of the Werner Committee stems directly from what we put in the Commission memorandum' (author's translation). Werner made clear his support for the memorandum (Lequesne 2010; Danescu 2012).

Specifically, the Werner Plan insisted upon the parallel development of both economic convergence and monetary integration. On the former, coordination was reinforced and Member States with higher inflation were required to bring this down. On the latter, the Werner Plan called for the creation of a fixed but adjustable exchange-rate mechanism—later, the 'snake'—and the reinforcement of centralized funds to be drawn upon to support weak currencies hit by speculation. The Werner Committee similarly followed the ten-year working calendar for the creation of EMU outlined in the Second Barre Plan (Danescu 2012).

If the Werner Plan of October 1970 is to be considered the founding act of EMU, then the Barre Plans should be seen as the conceptual genesis of monetary integration, adopted with pragmatism and with full awareness of the difficulties of realizing EMU (Lequesne 2010). Barre knew what was necessary to keep the French government interested in negotiations on EMU: cooperation and support mechanisms. At the same time he understood German sensitivities and knew that a committee inspired explicitly by the work of a Frenchman, even one as credible as Barre, would be suspect (Lequesne 2010). Danescu's chapter in this volume credits Barre with the decision to appoint Pierre Werner to chair the committee.

In the context of his liberal intergovernmentalist analysis of European integration, Moravscik (1998) describes the Barre Plan as narrow, conservative, and redundant. However, he dedicates very little attention to the content and logic of the Barre Plan. The facts that it led directly to policy changes that were substantiated later by the provisions of the Werner Plan and that it set out for the first time the route to Franco-German compromises on monetary cooperation make the application of the term 'redundant' inappropriate, to say the least. Lequesne (2010), de Boissieu (2010: 24), and Danescu (2012) all stress the Werner Plan's *direct* inspiration from the Barre plans.

BARRE IN POWER

Barre is the only French member of the European Commission to date for whom the posting was a stepping-stone to a successful political career in France. His competence as Commissioner was essential for his appointment as prime minister, given his non-participation in party politics and his negligible experience in government. He had been minister for trade for little more than six months.

For Barre (1981, 1984), the clear lesson to be drawn from the economic developments of the first half of the 1970s was that Keynesian stimulation and devaluation were not effective tools to achieve sustainable economic growth. During this period, French governments experimented unsuccessfully with various schemes to shield domestic interest rates from international markets through credit rationing (Loriaux 1991). While contributing to short-term stability, capital controls were eventually circumvented and in any event reduced the confidence of international investors. A risk premium began to be charged on francs, and French domestic interest rates began moving towards and then above world market rates. French business complained and called for financial liberalization (Loriaux 1991).

In order to deal with France's inflationary problem, Barre advocated two disciplines for the French economy: exchange-rate stability and a lower rate of short-term economic growth than that of France's principal trading partners (de Ménil 2010). His policy of stabilization was only in part a success. The franc strengthened, rising 10 per cent between 1979 and 1981, while at the same time a surplus in the balance of payments was achieved for the first time in many years in 1978 and 1979, and for the last time until the 2000s. But inflation remained stubbornly high and austerity was eased in the year leading to the 1981 presidential elections.

Barre's reform efforts targeted the inherently inflationary and debt-ridden domestic 'overdraft' economy (de Ménil 2010; Loriaux 1991). The French economy was characterized by a high degree of dependence on institutionally allocated credit, the so-called 'treasury circuits'. In 1976, 85 per cent of all finance provided to firms and households was provided by banks or some other financial institutions, which received most of their funding from the Banque de France. The generous provision of credits resulted in excessively casual cash-flow management in both firms and banks which led to a high level of indebtedness of firms to banks, and of banks to the Banque de France. Alternative sources of finance were severely underdeveloped, meaning the virtual non-existence of a financial market in the mid-1970s.

The 'overdraft' economy was the product of successive governments' unwillingness to tackle the political legacy of post-war growth-oriented industrial policies (Loriaux 1991). It created structures and patterns of financial behaviour that increased the difficulty of achieving monetary stabilization in France and were politically difficult to change. It relied upon the *encadrement du crédit* or 'tightening of credit'—a clumsy tool of economic policy—to combat domestic inflation. Moreover, monetary policy-makers of the 1950s and the 1960s attributed endemic inflationary pressure in the economy to fiscal deficits—as did Barre—and sought to use fiscal policy to fight it. While the 'overdraft' economy could be tolerated during periods of low-inflationary economic growth, the inflationary impact of the Grenelle wage accords of 1968 and the rise in oil prices during the 1970s underlined its structural weakness.

Barre brought about both financial innovation and liberalization, beginning the reform of the *encadrement de credit* system that Socialist finance ministers Jacques Delors and Pierre Bérégovoy subsequently broadened. The Monory Act of July 1978 offered tax incentives for the development of the stock market: mutual funds were created in July 1979 and new types of short-term assets in September 1981. By early 1983, Delors pursued further liberalization so that, by the time the right returned to power in 1986, the financing of the largest French companies from capital markets, stocks, and bonds had risen to around 75 per cent, up from less than 25 per cent at the start of the decade.

Barre's reform efforts were supported by the big business community in France, with keen support from the CNPF (Conseil National du Patronat Français), but from few others. His discourse focused on adapting France to the changing conditions of the world economy (Barre 1981, 1984). However, Barre was isolated politically, opposed by Keynesians not only on the Socialist left but also on the Gaullist right. The combination of the failure of the previous Gaullist government of Jacques Chirac to keep the franc in the 'snake' mechanism, the devaluation of 1975, the surge in inflation and stagflation emboldened Barre as prime minister. It created a brief window of opportunity for alternative policies. As a result of his reform efforts, Barre was, by the early 1980s, an unpopular prime minister, so much so that Giscard d'Estaing pushed him aside entirely in the 1981 presidential elections (de Saint Périer 2013: 118).

Barre's support for the EMS was not about the inherent merits of European monetary integration. President Giscard d'Estaing was preoccupied with Franco-German relations and France's position in Europe and the world. However, in the case of Barre there are no indications in any of his writings from the period or since that he saw the EMS in terms of broader European or international geostrategic goals *or even* in terms of further European economic integration. Barre appears not to have shared the view, which was widespread in French policy-making circles, that European monetary integration through the construction of a more symmetric EMS, or later a single currency, could be a mechanism to contain German monetary and economic power (Howarth 2001).

Barre's appointment as prime minister was significant in that, while Gaullist in his reflexes on national sovereignty with a preference for intergovernmentalism at the European level, he was less under the yoke of a sovereignty-minded neo-Gaullism. Indeed, he was the first non-Gaullist or non-neo-Gaullist prime minister of the post-1958 French Fifth Republic. This factor gave him a certain intellectual margin of manoeuvre at both the national and European levels. Amouroux (1986: 98) quotes Barre on his time in Brussels:

> and I let it be known that if I was European, I was not a supranationalist, and that if I was Gaullist, my views were not determined solely by Gaullism. (Author's translation; see also Soutou 2010)

More importantly, Barre saw in the EMS a crucial external constraint to achieve domestic economic objectives: micro-economic austerity and renewed competitiveness for French firms; and macro-economic discipline to keep inflation down and public spending under control (Aglietta and Baulant 1993). If France was to become 'the best student' of Germany—an expression frequently and often critically applied to Giscard and the Barre government—Barre was the teacher's top assistant (Howarth 2001). Barre sought to increase French competitiveness through a strong currency, as the Germans had done, and by encouraging less price-sensitive, higher technology export industries such as electronics, automobiles, aerospace, and transport. A stronger currency would assist with domestic efforts to rationalize traditional industries, such as telecommunications and steel, and force contraction in price-sensitive, labour-intensive sectors. The aim was to emulate the German austerity of the early 1970s that had successfully prevented inflation in that country (Ludlow 1982).

While the focus of historians working on the origins of the EMS has been on the central position of Giscard and Schmidt, Barre also played a significant role in the discussions and negotiations leading to the Bremen Accords. He met Chancellor Schmidt on several occasions in 1977 and 1978 to discuss reinforced monetary cooperation (Soutou 2010). Henri Froment-Meurice (1998), the director of economic affairs at the Ministry of Foreign Affairs at the time, outlined Barre's role in detail. Barre was committed to the creation of the EMS, but he was also cautious about the need for gradual adjustment for the French economy. He would have preferred four or five years more to reform the domestic economy and liberalize industrial prices prior to the launch of the EMS. The need for readjustment to ease the burden for France reinforced his long-standing preference for 'fixed but adjustable' exchange rates.

While previously a trenchant opponent of British entry into the EEC, Barre was nonetheless very energetic in his efforts to encourage British participation in the EMS. His aim was to dilute what he saw as the inevitable asymmetry of the system with the D-Mark as the anchor currency, although he never specifically used the term asymmetry (Soutou 2010: 77). When these efforts to encourage British participation failed, he nonetheless accepted the EMS 'such as it was' (Soutou 2010: 77).

Barre was very much aware that EMS membership meant for France the pursuit of considerable reform over the long term and macro-economic convergence with Germany (Soutou 2010). Nevertheless, the Bremen Accords corresponded in large part to the aims of the first and the second Barre plans and subsequently to the broad thrust of French policy on monetary cooperation. This correspondence was apparent in the insistence upon greater symmetry in European monetary arrangements than under the 'snake' both through more generous support mechanisms and through mutual realignments and the commitment of strong-currency national central banks to preserve exchange-rate parities. However, for Barre, the creation of a more symmetric ERM was definitely not about relaxing the French push on austerity and about burden-sharing with the Germans, as it was for many other French policy-makers in the 1980s (Howarth 2001). It was about facilitating reform by decreasing the pain of the external constraint.

BARRE'S CONTRIBUTION AND LEGACY

Of all the architects examined in this volume, Barre was almost certainly the least supranationalist and his interest in European monetary integration was the most driven by purely domestic economic considerations. Nonetheless, Barre merits entry into the pantheon of EMU architects, despite his cautious views regarding EMU and his failure to demonstrate any public support for the adoption of a single currency prior to the Maastricht European Council in December 1991. Barre came out strongly in favour of the single currency only after the Maastricht Summit of December 1991 (Barre 1992).

Crucially, as a rare Frenchman of influence, favourable to the German 'economist' approach to EMU, Barre was able to forward a consensual vision of European monetary cooperation. The Barre Plan of 1969 set the agenda for discussions in the Werner Committee. It also led directly to the creation of short-term and medium-term EEC support mechanisms which facilitated French support for European exchange-rate mechanisms. Barre was one of the earliest French policy-makers to see a European exchange-rate mechanism—the 'snake' and then the ERM—as a useful disciplinary device that would help to enforce necessary anti-inflation reforms in the face of the resistance of influential domestic interests. In this way, Barre sought to increase government control over the domestic economy by surrendering some margin of manoeuvre over monetary policy. While the extent of reform was limited during the Barre government itself, this motive was nonetheless important in determining his support for the EMS. More significant reform had to wait until a Socialist government began its serious restructuring of domestic financial markets in 1984. Barre was, from the late 1960s, an ardent supporter of capital liberalization, another ideational import from his experience at the European Commission. Although he did not achieve full capital liberalization during his five years as prime minister, the French government adopted a range of liberalization measures which facilitated its subsequent agreement to the Organisation for Economoic Co-operation and Development (OECD) and EC engagements on full liberalization in the 1980s.

Barre's focus on low inflation and a strong currency, combined with micro-economic reform to improve the competitiveness of the French economy, put him at odds with most of the French political class in the 1970s. However, these ideas formed the bedrock of the ideational consensus of the late 1980s and 1990s that allowed France's participation in an EMU project, the design of which was largely dictated by German macro-economic preferences.

Despite Barre's crucial role in monetary integration history, the claim of several observers, including de Boissieu (2010: 24), that EMU was 'at the heart of the Raymond Barre project' is highly contestable. This claim is at worst ahistorical or at best relies on a very loose—indeed pre-Maastricht French—understanding of EMU, certainly one very different from the project that was finally agreed. Rather, European monetary cooperation served clear domestic economic objectives that dominated Barre's policy-making even during his five-and-a-half years at the Commission.

5

Pierre Werner

A Visionary European and Consensus Builder

Elena Danescu

> Inherently attached to the European idea—and what Luxembourger wouldn't be?—I believe that during my career I remained equidistant from Eurosceptics and pro-Europeans. It might be said that a measured, constructive optimism was my most valuable contribution to European progress. (Werner 1992, II: 171)

Pierre Werner (1913–2002) was an economist and a lawyer, a politician and a diplomat, and a leading player in the building of a united Europe, in particular in monetary integration. As prime minister and finance minister of Luxembourg for several decades, this prominent Christian Democratic intellectual and committed federalist was one of the rare statesmen who was associated with all the major issues in European integration from the Schuman Plan of 1950 to the Fontainebleau European Council of 1984. He placed the European integration process at the centre of Luxembourg policy, convinced of the need to preserve national sovereignty by adopting an international outlook.

Werner played a major role in regional integration, notably in the Belgium–Luxembourg Economic Union (BLEU) and in Benelux, and in European Economic Community (EEC) policy-making. He gained a strong reputation for his skills in forging a political consensus between larger powers, above all Germany and France, and between diametrically opposed positions on monetary integration, principally between the 'economists' and the 'monetarists'. In this way he succeeded in defending Luxembourg's vital interests, from the steel industry to the seats of the European institutions and the promotion of its financial centre.

Werner was involved in the major intellectual debates of his time and in the efforts to establish transnational guidelines and consensus on monetary matters. He was an early activist for a common European currency, both for official usage, to help bring national policies closer together, and for private usage as a banking instrument. Although he was initially in favour of a 'monetarist' approach to European integration, he was one of the first to develop arguments for a symmetrical Economic and Monetary Union (EMU). The careful balance that he sought reappeared in the Werner Report of 1970, which was offered as the official blueprint for EMU in the European Union (EU). Werner's claims to be an architect of EMU are threefold: his intellectual contribution to goal-setting, his effective political negotiation methods, and his consensus-building skills.

Based on the previously unpublished Werner family archives and on an extensive selection of original interviews, this chapter examines Pierre Werner's work in favour of EMU and reveals his role as an architect of this process. The first part focuses on Werner's intellectual background and European commitment. The second looks at his monetary thinking and political action in the 1960s. The third section considers the Werner Report and Werner's personal contribution as chair to its work in terms of both substance—a parallel approach, a balanced final outcome, and the external dimension of EMU—and the forging of a political consensus. The final part assesses his legacy.

WERNER'S INTELLECTUAL AND CAREER BACKGROUND

Werner was born of Luxembourgish parents in Saint-André near Lille, France, on 29 December 1913. In 1934 he enrolled in the higher preparatory course in law in Luxembourg. As his country did not have a university, he continued his studies at the Faculty of Law in Paris, where he also attended courses at the École libre des sciences politiques. In January 1938 he completed his PhD in Law and prepared to embark on a career as a lawyer.

From early on, Werner was an active member of the Association of Catholic University Students, which he chaired from 1935 to 1937. In 1937 he became vice-president of the International Movement of Catholic Intellectuals (*Pax Romana*). During his time in Paris he lived at the Biermans-Lapôtre Foundation, whose alumni included many members of the Luxembourg elite. In this period Werner joined the European ranks of Catholic thinkers. Inspired by the theologian Robert Picard de la Vacquerie, he began to take an interest in the 'authentic Christian politics' advocated by Jacques Maritain, whose influential political theory was one of the main bases for the Christian Democratic movement. Werner also became deeply involved in the work carried out by Robert Garric's 'social teams' (*Équipes sociales*). From that time on, the principles of social Catholicism strongly characterized his political and social approach.

During his studies, Werner was particularly interested in public and private finance, forging useful links with his teachers Jacques Rueff and Wilfrid Baumgartner, both influential French finance officials, as well as with Charles Rist, deputy governor of the Banque de France. They influenced his intellectual development and stimulated his curiosity for the study of economic and monetary questions. In Paris, he met another Luxembourg native, Robert Schuman, a member of the French National Assembly, who tried to whet his appetite for politics and who was to become an iconic figure in the launch of post-war European integration.

As a young lawyer at the Luxembourg bar, in 1938 Werner was awarded an internship at the Banque Générale de Luxembourg (BGL), in which the Deutsche Bank (DB) had taken a major holding. He escaped Nazi persecution thanks to Hermann Abs, chairman of the board and appointed by the Deutsche Bank. Abs' benevolent attitudes helped protect those who, like Werner, refused to join Nazi organizations. Werner's family was not, however, spared by the war. Pierre's younger brother was forcibly conscripted for 'labour service' (*Arbeitsdienst*) and died at a labour camp in eastern Prussia on 15 January 1945. Werner's work in the secretariat of the BGL prompted him to write a report on the monetary, financial, and banking situation in Luxembourg in 1942. He managed to send the report to the Luxembourg government in exile in London through the Martin network of the French Resistance.

At the Liberation, Werner became an attaché in the finance ministry. In 1945, he was tasked with carrying out a study of the reorganization of the banking system in Luxembourg. Subsequently he was appointed banking commissioner. In this capacity he was involved in the creation of an authority to organize and regulate the credit market and contributed to the establishment of international financial relations. He was associated with the operations for the reintroduction of the franc, the refloating of banking activities, and the re-establishment of the main Luxembourg state bank, the Banque et Caisse d'Épargne de l'État. He represented Luxembourg in international negotiations, particularly in Switzerland and within the BLEU and the Benelux. As adviser to Prime Minister Pierre Dupong on financial affairs, Werner also took part in multilateral dealings relating to defence, including NATO, the abortive European Defence Community (EDC), and the Western European Union (WEU). At a very early stage he became familiar with the International Monetary Fund (IMF). In 1947, with the support of Ambassador Hugues Le Gallais, he successfully negotiated a loan of $12.7 million from the International Bank for Reconstruction and Development (World Bank) for the reconstruction of Luxembourg.[1]

[1] Telegram from Pierre Werner to Pierre Dupong (New York, 22 July 1947). Archives Nationales de Luxembourg (Luxembourg National Archives) (ANLux)/AE-09283.

Werner worked closely with the Luxembourg prime minister, who was increasingly of the view that this competent, meticulous expert was the best man to assume the functions of finance minister. This promotion duly came about in December 1953, when Werner was asked to join the new cabinet set up by Joseph Bech, following Dupong's untimely death.

After the 1959 elections, Werner became prime minister. For twenty years—from 1959 to 1974 and from 1979 to 1984—he directed the coalition cabinets that the Christian Social Party (CSV) formed with either the liberal party or the socialist party. His role as president of the government was combined with other ministerial portfolios in what were seen as priority areas for a country that was constantly innovating and developing. He served as minister for finance (1959–64 and 1969–74), for the Treasury (1964–9 and 1979–84), for foreign affairs and justice (1964–7), as well as for the civil service (1967–9) and for cultural affairs (1969–74 and 1979–84).

As finance minister, Werner turned his attention to major projects with a view to making Luxembourg a forward-looking country and a true international platform. The development programme for the 'European quarter' on the Kirchberg (1961) was a major trump card in the country's hand during the 'battle for the seats' in 1965. He worked hard to diversify the economy, especially focusing on consolidating Luxembourg's transformation from a banking centre to an international financial centre from the 1960s onwards, nurturing the idea for a Luxembourg shipping flag, developing the audiovisual sector, and, in particular, setting up the satellite project.

For the 1974–9 parliamentary term, the CSV went into opposition and Werner was chair of his party's parliamentary group. He encouraged the CSV to pursue an approach inspired by the British tradition of 'Her Majesty's loyal opposition', which enabled it to play a constructive role in the consensus-based management of the steel crisis. One of the results was the establishment of the 'steel tripartite' (an institutionalized platform for dialogue between the government, employers, and employees), which subsequently became the Luxembourg model for social consultation.

The new Werner government took office in 1979 and worked to ensure a smooth post-industrial transition for Luxembourg. It successfully overcame the unrest in the BLEU and for the first time laid down Luxembourg's monetary status in a comprehensive, coherent way. Werner took measures to transform his party and brought Jean-Claude Juncker, aged just twenty-eight, into the government as state secretary for labour affairs. In July 1984, when his party again won the general election, Werner passed the baton to his long-time fellow-worker Jacques Santer and withdrew from political life. He remained active in public affairs, particularly focusing his energies on the promotion of EMU and the euro, notably as joint chair, alongside Raymond Barre, of the Lyon-based ECU Institute, a think-tank composed of international economic and financial experts that was set up in 1992 to promote the European currency. He also retained an active interest in the development of the media and the audiovisual sector, especially through the project for the Société Européenne des Satellites (SES). Werner passed away on 24 June 2002 in Luxembourg City.

A COMMITTED EUROPEAN

Werner had been aware of the importance of European issues since his university days. However, his commitment to European unification took firm shape in 1949, when he became convinced of the urgent need for the countries of Western Europe to undertake the economic and political construction of a united Europe. His experience of working in the international arena, 'particularly his awareness of the weakness and the divided state of Europe, made it almost an intellectual obligation' (Werner 1992, I: 34–5).

As a Luxembourger, Werner was naturally attached to the European idea. It offered a response to Luxembourg's main aspirations, which were linked to its specific geopolitical status as a small, multicultural, multilingual nation, sandwiched between two larger powers, France and Germany, as well as to its economic situation, which included a lack of natural resources, no central bank, and no national currency. The European principle of equality among states also guaranteed Luxembourg a role in decision-making and in the leadership of European organizations. By giving up part of its sovereignty—which it had already shown it was prepared to do in the monetary field as a member of the BLEU—Luxembourg has, paradoxically, actually strengthened its sovereignty. Thanks to its 'mastery of small-state diplomacy' within the context of European integration, Luxembourg took on the role of mediator between larger powers and simultaneously succeeded in defending its vital interests, from the steel industry to the seats of the European institutions and its financial centre (Dyson 2015).

Werner was associated from the very outset with the major issues relating to European integration. He made a significant contribution to shaping the outcome of the battle over the political seats of the European institutions and to the choice of Luxembourg firstly as the workplace of the institutions in 1965, then as one of their permanent capitals; he also played a major role in the 'Luxembourg Compromise' of 1966 which ended the French 'empty-chair' policy and, not least, in the Werner Report of 1970.

The 'Luxembourg Compromise', which had been based on a Benelux strategy of mediation, encouraged the idea that Werner might one day stand for the role of president of the European Commission. However, it remained no more than a rumour, as he never really considered giving up his national electoral mandate. In the mid-1960s, in his efforts to affirm Luxembourg's position of leadership on the international stage, Werner was involved, alongside Pierre Pescatore, general secretary of the foreign ministry, in organizing an independent diplomatic service, based on national intellectual elites and continuing the work begun by Joseph Bech at the dawn of the Second World War.

From 1960 to 1974 and in 1980 the Luxembourg presidencies of the EEC Council were held exclusively by various Werner governments in succession. He adopted an approach which he saw in theoretical terms as a method for any fruitful presidency:

> I regarded my presidency as an opportunity, primarily, for creating an atmosphere and a climate of negotiation which took account of the delicate sensitivities of partners aspiring to reach agreement. The agreement must not leave any losers in a squabble over minutiae of language which may disguise a persistent underlying disagreement. (Werner 1992, II: 79)

Werner's longevity in power and his European commitment enabled him to forge lasting relationships with many eminent figures and to be involved in various transnational governance networks, communities of experts, and influential groups. He also took an active role, alongside Jean Monnet and Robert Triffin, in the Action Committee for the United States of Europe (ACUSE) and the European League for Economic Cooperation (ELEC). Together with Jacques Santer, Werner also played a part in the establishment of the European People's Party (EPP), which was founded on 8 July 1976 in Luxembourg. He wrote the economic and social chapters of the EPP's electoral manifesto for the first European Parliament elections by direct universal suffrage in 1979.

WERNER'S MONETARY THINKING AND POLITICAL ACTION IN THE 1960s

As finance minister and later prime minister, Werner was well aware of the potential of the banking sector for the diversification of an economy that was entirely dominated by the steel industry. Luxembourg had several distinguishing features which gave it a competitive advantage. They resulted in part from action taken by the government and in part from various external factors, including the interest equalization tax introduced in the United States in 1963 and the German securities transfer tax (*Kuponsteuer*) introduced in 1965. In particular, the absence of a central bank meant that Luxembourg-based banking establishments were not obliged to set aside compulsory minimum reserves. Furthermore, the dual Belgium–Luxembourg exchange market, which was managed by the Institut belgo-luxembourgeois du change (the Belgium and Luxembourg Exchange Institute), created a separation between commercial and financial transactions and facilitated international activities. The supervisory authority, the Commissariat au contrôle des banques (Banking Control Commission or CCB), was a small structure, with a dynamic decision-making process and a Commissioner with extensive powers, making it particularly responsive to opportunities as they arose.

Finally, the establishment of the European Coal and Steel Community (ECSC) in Luxembourg was followed by the relocation to the country of the Community's financial institutions, including the European Investment Bank (EIB), which established its headquarters there in 1968. Their presence gave the Luxembourg financial centre a European dimension, placing it in a strong position to become an 'incubator' for monetary integration. The monetary association with Belgium meant that Luxembourg had only a 'virtual monetary authority', exercised by the CCB. However, this did not stop the country from playing an active role in international monetary debates, with its representatives regularly invited to participate, alongside the experts of National Bank of Belgium, in the Basel Committee of Banking Supervision and the Group of Ten.

The proactive policy of the successive Werner governments in the decade from 1960 to 1970 led to the development and specialization of Luxembourg's international financial centre. It became a pillar of the economy and served as a 'laboratory' for a common European currency. In 1959 the first US bank opened in Luxembourg as Crédit Européen, followed by the first Luxembourg investment fund, Eurunion. In 1961, the Luxembourg stock exchange became a founding member of the International Federation of Stock Exchanges. In 1965, the legal status of 'financial holding company' was created to attract long-term capital by eliminating double taxation. In 1967, the first branches of German, Swiss, and Portuguese banks arrived in Luxembourg. Subsequently, in 1969 Werner set up an informal think-tank on the financial centre, including Triffin, Jean Blondeel, Fernand Collin, Constant Franssens, Edmond Israel, and Raymond Kirsch, to analyse future trends with a view to identifying the prospects for Luxembourg within EMU.

Werner had a way of thinking about economic and monetary affairs which was quite his own and was built up from personal ideas and the contributions of others. He was inspired by the unique situation of Luxembourg, a country which did not have its own central bank or national currency and had therefore always favoured currency unions.

In the lecture 'What Monetary Integration Means' ('Significations d'une intégration monétaire'), Werner (1960) set out his first thoughts on European monetary integration. Evoking the lessons learned from the Benelux Union, which was based on a monetary agreement, he stressed that economic cooperation and integration come about more directly through the instrument of monetary policy, 'but that unilateral and therefore brutal decisions were not desirable':

> Between sovereign countries, monetary rapprochement can only be gradual and concomitant with the rapprochement of economic policies . . . and monetary unification comes at the end rather than the beginning of the integration process. (Werner 1960: 4)

A common market required not just a financial order within the EEC but a financial order on a broader continental or world scale. At the same time, with respect to the financial order of the EEC, it was not enough for it to join a broader monetary system: 'a stronger Community slant should be given to their financial policies'. Werner proposed the progressive introduction of a European currency of account capable of lessening the risks caused by speculative movements of capital. In the EEC's international relations, this European currency 'would supply a benchmark for value shielded from ups and downs in the national currencies, facilitate the expansion of international trade and encourage the development of savings'. Private use could be introduced gradually to 'accustom people, little by little, to this collective currency' (Werner 1960: 10).

Werner was in tune with the ideas of Robert Triffin, who looked ahead to a gradual disintegration of the international monetary system and argued for the setting up of a European monetary union. On this topic, Werner was in contact with his Belgian opposite number, Pierre Wigny, and with Belgian banker Fernand Collin. The latter, with whom Werner had had discussions since 1956 on the subject of a European unit of account for private use, was actively involved in setting up some of the special features of Luxembourg as a financial centre. At the instigation of finance minister Werner, the Luxembourg financial centre was the first to issue international bonds denominated in European units of account (EUAs). In January 1961, Kredietbank SA Luxembourgeoise (KBL), of which Collin was president and Triffin a member of the board, issued the first loan of 5 million EUAs to the Portuguese oil company Sacor. A second followed in 1962. Paradoxically, these proto-Eurobonds were never recognized. In July 1963, the first Eurobonds were listed on the Luxembourg stock exchange, in US dollars, for the Italian motorway network Autostrade.

Although he was not yet a member of the Action Committee for the United States of Europe, as early as the summer of 1961 Werner was in contact with Monnet and was familiar with the Committee's proposal for the establishment of a European union of the monetary reserves of the Six EEC Member States.

Werner kept up to date with developments in economic and monetary thinking, testing some of his ideas and initiatives in a wide range of settings. Pride of place went to regular meetings with European heads of state and government, especially when affiliation to Christian Democracy gave him an added kinship with them; to the discussions which took place within the BLEU and the Benelux; and to the meetings of the EEC finance ministers, in which he was involved for many years. He established relations of trust with his EEC counterparts, particularly with Raymond Barre and Valéry Giscard d'Estaing in France, Baron Jean-Charles Snoy et d'Oppuers in Belgium, Karl Schiller and Franz Etzel in Germany, and Emilio Colombo in Italy; with central bank governors including Baron Hubert Ansiaux in Belgium, Guido Carli in Italy, Jelle Zijlstra in the Netherlands, Bernard Clappier in France, and Karl Blessing in Germany; and with other bankers, especially Collin and Abs of the Deutsche Bank. They held regular exchanges over a long period. Werner enjoyed very close relations with his Belgian and German partners. He also had cordial relations with the British, especially with Edward Heath, taking a close interest in Britain's moves towards membership of the EEC and the problems raised by the pound sterling in the context of a European monetary identity. The good connections he had long maintained with US political and business circles added the requisite global dimension to his views, especially as regards the conclusions to be drawn from American economic liberalism and the role of the dollar as both a national and an international currency.

In November 1962, Werner was the first EEC head of government to react favourably to the Action Programme for the Second Stage of the EEC, which European Commissioner Robert Marjolin had presented one month earlier (see Chapter 3 by Katja Seidel). In the lecture 'Issues Relating to Financial Integration in Europe' ('Problèmes de l'intégration financière de l'Europe'), Werner (1962) once again asserted the relevance of a European unit of account, which he saw as a means of giving a kick-start to a European monetary system. He emphasized the need for fixed exchange rates and a common monetary discipline and solidarity in a specific institutional framework, that is to say a 'monetary institute which could concomitantly develop its role as a clearing house between the central banks'. Werner went on to say that:

> The method recommended here would enable monetary integration to proceed along the lines of development of the Community's tasks without impinging on national responsibilities and without premature dispossession . . . The unification of economic policies will never be absolute: at specific times, short-term economic measures may be imposed in this or that country. (Werner 1962: 9)

It was only in 1964 that some of the European Commission's recommendations in terms of monetary policy started to take practical shape, in particular with the creation of the Committee of Governors of the Central Banks (CGCB), which was set up in June 1963, and the establishment of collaboration between the Member States on international monetary relations in 1964. They reflected a growing concern to make further progress in European monetary integration.

In 1965, Werner was the first head of government, whilst president-in-office of the EEC Council, to emphasize the importance of monetary integration as part of the Community's internal and external policy. In an address given to the European Parliament, he stressed 'the need to set up . . . common monetary procedures and . . . the need to enshrine fixed exchange rates in a set of monetary rules' (Werner 1966b: 8). At the annual meeting of governors of the IMF in 1966, he spoke as an 'advocate for European monetary policy' (Werner 1966a: 3).

In 1967–8, the turbulence in the international monetary system became increasingly apparent. The idea of setting up an area of monetary stability in Europe and thereby protecting the European economies from the upheavals which the dismantling of the Bretton Woods system would cause began to gain strength (Van Yperseele and Koeune 1988: 41). In these circumstances, Werner used the Europaforum congress on 26 January 1968, alongside Jean Monnet and Walter Hallstein, the president of the European Commission, to outline his views of the 'Prospects for Europe's Financial and Monetary Policy' ('Perspectives de la Politique Financière et Monétaire Européenne') (Werner 1968a). He set out a theoretical structure for the means and instruments of practical action in an increasingly unpredictable international context. Six months before the entry into force of the Customs Union between the EEC Member States, Werner put forward a roadmap to European monetary integration.

His action plan was based on five pillars: the creation of a European unit of account, prior consultation between national authorities, fixed exchange rates between the Member States, internal and external solidarity (particularly within the IMF), and the creation of a Community reserve fund. He emphasized the consequences of liberalizing capital flows and of the development of the Euromarkets, subjects that he had been able to analyse within the Luxembourg financial centre. His address foreshadowed the main theme of the first Barre memorandum, which the EC Commission published the following month (see Chapter 4 by David Howarth). However, the memorandum did not refer to the monetary union and the reserve fund that had been recommended by Triffin, the Monnet Action Committee, and Werner.

Throughout 1968, Werner played an increasingly active role in Monnet's Action Committee for the United States of Europe and enjoyed fruitful exchanges with Monnet, Triffin, and Carli. The governor of the Banca d'Italia praised the pioneering nature of this 'first Werner Plan' and circulated it in international financial circles and within the CGCB. The German economics minister, Karl Schiller, wanted to see the Community progress in the direction sketched out by Werner.[2] The Benelux finance ministers were also particularly

[2] Letter from Karl Schiller to Pierre Werner (Bonn, 23 February 1968), BArch B 102, Bundesministerium für Wirtschaft (Federal Ministry of Economic Affairs)/93454, Pierre Werner family archives (PWLux).

interested in the plan, as was the Council of Finance Ministers (ECOFIN 1968b). When Werner presented his ideas at the meeting held on 9 and 10 September 1968 in Rotterdam, he emphasized the two fundamental principles that underpinned his approach: the political commitment of the Six as a basis for monetary unification, and the parallel and balanced movement between the coordination of economic policies and monetary integration.

> Monetary solidarity will only be established laboriously in line with the strengthening of economic policy, and is dependent on it. On the other hand, the establishment of legal procedures and instruments directed towards a common monetary policy will be a powerful lever for bringing national economies closer together. (Werner 1968c: 5)

However, in order to defend the Luxembourg financial centre, and in his role as prime minister, Werner moved away from this middle line in his political action, choosing instead to adopt a resolutely 'monetarist' approach. French foreign minister Michel Debré made a point of emphasizing that: 'Werner [is] the Luxembourger who, behind sweeping declarations of principle and lofty views, strictly defends the specific interests of Luxembourg' (Debré 1988: 398). Werner saw his approach as justified by the difficulties experienced first by the pound sterling and then by the French franc. These difficulties led ECOFIN to put monetary questions at the forefront of the European integration process.

THE CONSTITUTION AND WORK OF THE WERNER COMMITTEE

The Hague Summit of 1 and 2 December 1969 took place under the auspices of the 'completion, enlargement, deepening' triptych of the EEC. Regarding the 'deepening' of the Community, two aspects stood out: economic and monetary cooperation and political cooperation. As Raymond Barre put it:

> This decision by the Heads of State and Government . . . was the outcome of an agreement between Mr Pompidou and the German Chancellor Mr Willy Brandt, and Mr Monnet, whom I had seen before the summit. He had told me that he was intervening personally to ensure that the monetary question would be raised at the summit. (Bitsch et al. 2004: 16)

The six EEC heads of state and government agreed that a plan by stages should be drawn up by the Council in 1970 for the establishment of an economic and monetary union. An ad hoc committee would be set up for this purpose. They also decided 'to arrange for the investigation of the possibility of setting up a European reserve fund in which a joint economic and monetary policy would have to result' (EC 1969: 13). The proposal on the ERF, which Monnet asked

Triffin to draw up, was sent to Brandt, an active member of the Action Committee for the United States of Europe, who presented it at the Hague Summit.

The final agreement reflected the differences of approaches between the various representatives and foreshadowed the later clashes between the French and the Germans. While Brandt considered the effective harmonization of economic policies to be a prerequisite for the establishment of the ERF, Pompidou insisted on the introduction of a system for balance of payments assistance and a monetary union between the Six which would consolidate their position on the international stage.

On 6 March 1970, the EC Council decided on the composition of the ad hoc group. There were three main reasons for the choice of members. First, responsibility for examining the issues raised by the Hague Summit had to be in the hands of officials in charge of economic and financial policy in the Member States. Second, the figures concerned had to have a special commitment and considerable experience in European integration. Lastly, any solution put forward had to have the widest possible support at government level. The group was formed of the leaders of the various specialized committees of the EEC, who also held high national offices. They were the chairs of the EEC Monetary Committee (Bernard Clappier, deputy governor of the Banque de France); of the Committee of Governors of the Central Banks (Hubert Ansiaux, governor of the National Bank of Belgium); of the Medium-Term Economic Policy Committee (Johann Schöllhorn, state secretary in the German federal economics ministry); of the Anti-Cyclical Policy Committee (Gerard Brouwers, state secretary in the Dutch economics ministry); and of the Budgetary Committee (Gaetano Stammati, treasurer-general in the Italian ministry of the treasury). The Commission was represented by the director-general for economic affairs (DG II), Ugo Mosca. When the committee members chose their deputies, Schöllhorn turned to Hans Tietmeyer, an official in the federal economics ministry with responsibility for the Common Market, and Ansiaux to Jacques Mertens de Wilmars, economic adviser to the National Bank of Belgium (see Chapter 7 by Kenneth Dyson).

The experts were supposed to exercise their role on the committee in an individual capacity and in full independence. However, their behaviour increasingly reflected the positions of their governments. The composition of the group was such that Luxembourg was the only one of the Six not to be represented. The initial idea was for the committee to be jointly chaired by Luxembourg and the European Commission, and a Franco-German proposal put forward the name of Clappier as representative of the Commission. Clappier suggested that he should withdraw in favour of Ansiaux. It was at this point that Werner's name was put forward by Barre, who proposed that Luxembourg should chair the committee on its own. Baron Snoy on behalf of Belgium launched the official proposal, drafted and published the diplomatic document, and worked to secure the agreement of the three partners. But it was thanks to Karl Schiller, who managed to bypass the double-dealing by France and bring the Netherlands on board, that the initiative came to fruition (Danescu 2012b).

Werner's appointment as chair of the group was not just a highly political choice but a considered act in favour of a man with a strong reputation for forging a consensus. At the same time his 'monetarist' approach and his close involvement in the group's work gave rise to reservations. Ultimately, even those who had previously harboured reservations now came out in support of Werner. At the Council meeting, the Dutch prime minister, Joseph Luns, stated: 'I regard [this] proposal that the prime minister of Luxembourg be invited to assume the chairmanship of the ad hoc group as very timely, since, aside from his many other qualities, Mr Werner has had a great deal of quite specific experience in this field; what is more, the importance of the office which he holds will make a definite contribution to the work of the group.'[3]

The ad hoc group held a preliminary meeting in Luxembourg on 11 March 1970 and started its work on 20 March, again in Luxembourg. The main purpose of these first meetings was to approve the working method. It was agreed that there would be a quorum if at least five of the seven members were present. Decisions would be taken by simple majority. The group would do its best to present unanimous conclusions. Discussions were considered to be confidential and would only be minuted briefly. The experts decided to deliver a preliminary report by the end of May and to conclude their work by the end of July 1970. These early debates brought out the fundamental thinking of the committee. Priority issues were the pooling of the Six's reserves and the establishment of a Community central bank. The experts adopted a three-point analysis: a description of the starting point, the final goal, and the alternative routes that could be followed in carrying out the plan. They decided to focus on defining the first stage of EMU.

The task of drafting the report was delegated to the assistants, who met on 6 and 8 May under the chairmanship of the Belgian central banker Mertens de Wilmars. On 11 May their draft was ready and on 20 May the committee finally managed to reach agreement on a joint position. Werner presented the interim report to the ECOFIN meeting on 29 May in Venice, stressing that further work needed to be done on certain priority areas and emphasizing the need to achieve parallel progress in the monetary and economic fields. On 9 June in Luxembourg, the Council of Ministers approved the interim report and agreed that the committee should continue its work.

The deepening of the Werner Committee's work was carried out between June and October 1970. The preliminary draft of the final report was reworked in a select group including Tietmeyer, Looijen, Bloch-Lainé, and Mosca. The

[3] Proceedings of the 105th session of the Council of 6 March 1970, reel No 2385, direction 1—OJ 8 and 12, p. 2/Pierre Werner family archives (PWLux).

Werner Committee concluded that the establishment of EMU must be embarked on in an evolving, gradual manner, building on the measures already adopted to enhance the coordination of economic policies and monetary cooperation. While aware of the need for economic and monetary policies to be developed centrally, the committee stated straight away that it was not in a position to make proposals regarding political structures. The subsequent criticism of the final Werner Report for its failure to offer a detailed analysis of the architecture of the Community institutions has to be seen against the background of the initial decision of the group to remove this matter from the scope of its reflections.

On 7 October, the 'plan by stages for the establishment of EMU' was approved following a last-minute compromise. The next day, Werner presented it publicly in Luxembourg. Of the fourteen official meetings of the committee held from March to October 1970, nine took place in Luxembourg (consolidating its reputation as a permanent capital of the Communities), three in Brussels, one in Paris, one in Rome, and one in Copenhagen on the sidelines of the annual meeting of the IMF and the World Bank (Danescu 2012c). The Werner Committee met for the final time in this configuration at the Council of Ministers on 8 February 1971.

On 29 October, the EC Commission published its own proposals which were inspired by the report. Although they had similar aims, the proposals reflected different views. The German government voiced its dissatisfaction with the Commission's proposals, which were considered to be too limited and not to go far enough. More ominously still, the Werner Report elicited harsh criticism from orthodox Gaullists because of its supranational elements. Under pressure, the French government changed its policy, which led to the proposals being 'watered down'.

In line with the European Commission's proposals, the Six adopted a political resolution—albeit one with no legal force—on 22 March 1971, committing them to establishing EMU. However, developments in the international monetary system and the decision by US President Richard Nixon on 15 August 1971 to suspend the convertibility of the US dollar into gold were to thwart the shared ambition set out in the Werner Report, which had already been weakened by the absence of any real political will.

SEEKING A BALANCED APPROACH BETWEEN THE ECONOMISTS AND THE MONETARISTS

The placing of EMU on the EEC agenda catalysed different national visions of European monetary integration (Gros and Thygesen 1998). In January and February 1970 several governments provided the Werner Committee with their views on EMU: Belgium (the Snoy Plan), Germany (the Schiller Plan), and Luxembourg, whose position, which was penned by Werner, was based on his five-point plan from 1968 (Werner 1970a). In March, the European Commission published the second Barre memorandum, which emphasized the critical link between economic coordination and monetary solidarity. When the European Commission compared the four documents, it defined two landmark positions: first, the Luxembourg Plan, which took the most purely monetarist approach, and second, the Schiller Plan, which put most stress on the role of the measures to be undertaken in the various spheres of economic policy.

Although all the partners agreed that the ultimate aim was to achieve EMU in ten years, the ways of achieving this goal were a source of debate. From the very start, the work of the Werner Committee was marked by the conflicting approaches between 'economists' and 'monetarists'. From the outset, the Germans (Schöllhorn, assisted by Tietmeyer) and the Dutch (Brouwer) supported the position of the Schiller Plan, namely that prior convergence of economic policies was imperative. The Belgians (Ansiaux) and the French (Clappier) advocated the monetarist stance. The Italian position on EMU was influenced by both economist and monetarist views and evolved over time (Maes and Quaglia 2004). Luxembourg sided with the monetarists in its view that the economy was driven by deliberate monetary decisions. The priority was therefore for quick decisions on the margins for fluctuation between European currencies, concerted monetary action, and the establishment of a European reserve fund.

Werner attempted to arrive at a common Benelux position. However, the three finance ministers and governors of the central banks could not reach agreement: the Dutch sided clearly with the German economists. The Belgians came out in support of a currency equalization fund, to offset the floating exchange rates which were increasingly in use. At the group's second meeting on 7 April, Ansiaux raised the question of a fund in reaction to Schöllhorn, who firmly believed in the primacy of economic union. Werner appreciated the Germans' views in principle but saw them as 'too severe and not measured enough'. Although he agreed with Ansiaux, he was aware that the Member States were not ready to abandon the floating exchange rate system in favour of fixed but adjustable exchange rates.

The interim report seemed to tip the scales in favour of the 'economists', as was noted by Walter Hallstein who claimed that 'in substance, the report presents a compromise that tends towards the economists' position'. In response, Werner decided to work for a balanced solution (Werner 1989). He started by asking the EEC governments to commit to 'guaranteed parallel development' between economic cooperation and monetary coordination. Although at its meeting on 8 and 9 June in Luxembourg, ECOFIN approved this fundamental principle, the dispute between the two sides remained.

Werner also made sure that the views of the 'monetarists' were taken into account. On 12 June, he asked for an opinion from the CGCB on the exchange-rate regime in the Community. The committee was of the view that a European monetary cooperation fund should be established from the first stage of EMU. Werner shared this view. He firmly believed that a plan which made no provision for any innovation on the monetary front in the first three years, and involved nothing but pushing forward procedures for harmonizing economic and budgetary policies, without any monetary incentives to support it, would very probably become bogged down in interminable discussions at the Community level.

In the end, after heated debates into which everyone pitched, Werner sought to avoid a failure by securing a subtle compromise which was accepted unanimously. Speaking to the EEC foreign ministers on 26 October 1970 in Luxembourg, Werner stressed:

> I am happy to note that on all these aspects we forged a unanimous collective view. Of course these joint replies do not reflect all the individual preferences of the members of the group. But we do think that having looked at the question from all sides, at long sessions where we compared a range of ideas, we have succeeded in giving shape to the wish for proceeding in parallel on the measures to be taken in the economic and financial fields. What we aspired to do was, once and for all, to break the vicious circle consisting of setting prior economic and political conditions. We have tried to draw a line midway between the view that monetary union is the crowning glory of European integration and the view that would turn it into the virtually all-powerful engine driving integration. I think the proposals are in line with the existing treaties, and that they do, precisely, ensure that the objectives of the treaties will be achieved in full. Thus for stage one we can go a great deal of the way without amending the treaties. However, there must be a strong political will backing up this process all the time that it is being put into effect. (Werner 1970b: 5)

THE WERNER REPORT: AN ADEQUATE BLUEPRINT FOR EMU?

The Werner Report of 8 October 1970 offered a full definition of EMU, which was to be established in three stages over a period of ten years (1971–80). The ultimate aim was to achieve irreversible convertibility between the currencies of the Member States, the complete liberalization of capital movements, the irrevocable fixing of exchange rates, and even potentially the replacement of national currencies by a single currency as a natural and desirable further development of monetary union. Monetary policy vis-à-vis the outside world would be a matter for the Community. Only the first three-year stage, due to begin on 1 January 1971 and loosely based on the first Barre memorandum, was clearly defined. It should be noted that the characteristic feature of this memorandum is a particular association of traditional German and French concepts: 'a French-inspired medium-term analysis was applied to the German idea of economic convergence' (Maes 1998b: 42).

The report emphasized the pursuit of common policies by the Member States, the introduction of greater coordination of national budget policies (centralization of the size and balance of national budgets and how they should be funded), as well as the harmonization of fiscal policies (VAT and excise duty rates) including taxation of capital, on which matter it called on the CGCB to define the appropriate guidelines. The report stressed the need to consult economic and social sectors before defining the guidelines of Community economic policy.

From an institutional viewpoint, the report called for the creation of two new steering bodies: a 'centre of decision for economic policy', independent of governments and placed under the democratic control of the European Parliament, to be elected by universal suffrage; and a 'Community system for the central banks'. This system would be preceded by the establishment of a European Monetary Cooperation Fund (EMCF), based on Triffin's proposals but more limited in scope. EMU would serve as a 'leaven' for the development of a political union without which, ultimately, it would not be able to manage. This argument was prescient with respect to later criticisms of the architecture of the Maastricht Treaty, especially in the wake of the post-2008 Euro Area crisis.

The Werner Committee believed that these elements were indispensable for a complete EMU. The union—as described in the report—represented the minimum that had to be done and was a stage in a dynamic evolution that would be shaped by the pressure of events and political will.

Two main principles underpinned the drafting of the Werner Report: gradual realization of EMU by means of a step-by-step approach; and 'parallel movement in practice' (Tietmeyer 1971, 2015; see also Chapter 7 by Kenneth Dyson). This principle of parallelism applied in three areas: parallel movement in progress towards economic policy convergence and the imposition of additional monetary constraints; parallel movement in the imposition of monetary constraints and the transfer of powers over economic policy to the Community; and parallel movement in the development of Community powers and the corresponding development of effective European institutions.

The Werner Report could have been the basis for a common response by the then Member States of the EEC to the dramatic change that occurred in the economic and monetary environment of the Western world in the first half of the 1970s. But the implementation of the plan was *de facto* suspended, as noted by the Marjolin Report of 8 March 1975 (see Chapter 3 by Katja Seidel). The report did have some 'intrinsic weaknesses', including 'insufficient constraints on national policies, institutional ambiguities [from a monetary, economic and fiscal viewpoint], inappropriate policy conception, [and] lack of internal momentum', which might explain its lack of success in the immediate term (Baer and Padoa-Schioppa 1989: 57). It was based on a regime of fixed (but adjustable) parities, despite the obvious weakness of the Bretton Woods system. Moreover, in its definition of the second and third stages of EMU, the report provided only general indications and did not lay down a timeframe. It was imprecise as to the definition of economic union and also relatively sketchy when it came to institutional matters.

But could the Werner Group have acted any differently to reach unanimous conclusions? The compromise was finely balanced. It provided for a 'system of central banks' that would be responsible for monetary policy. However, it was not specified that this system would be 'independent', as the Germans wanted. At the same time, the 'European monetary identity' did include supranational aspects, contrary to what the French preferred. The plan also adopted a centralist approach, aiming to resolve the majority of doctrinal and constitutional problems associated with EMU despite the seeming lack of compatibility between national sovereignty and the Community interest. The Werner Report was at the vanguard, making it 'operationally, institutionally and politically incompatible with the constitutional realities of states and of the treaty' (Ghymers 2015: 198).

Nevertheless, the Werner Report became a blueprint for EMU in the European Community, as the Delors Report and the Maastricht Treaty would confirm twenty years later. The Delors Committee started its deliberations in September 1988 symbolically in Luxembourg with a thorough analysis of the Werner Report. It thus became the yardstick by which the feasibility and eventual success of the Delors Report would be measured (see Chapter 7 by Kenneth Dyson). Werner and Delors both emphasized the principles of progressive realization of EMU by stages and parallelism between economic convergence and transfer of powers to the supranational level. Moreover, their reports define monetary union in almost identical terms (Werner 1990; Delors 1992), but in some respects the Werner Report goes further and is more clear cut than the Delors Report. In its conclusions, the Werner Report firmly states that:

> B: Economic and monetary union means that the principal decisions of economic policy will be taken at Community level and therefore that the necessary powers will be transferred from the national plane to the Community plane . . .
>
> D: On the institutional plane, in the final stage, two Community organs are indispensable: a centre of decision for economic policy and a Community system for the central banks . . . (EC 1970b: 28)

Contrast this with the language of the new Article 3a inserted in the EEC Treaty by the Maastricht Treaty in February 1992, which vaguely refers to 'the adoption of an economic policy which is based on the close coordination of Member States' economic policies' (Koeune 2015: 301). The main differences reside in the manner in which the two committees addressed two fundamental issues of EMU: namely, the design of the economic pillar of EMU and the development of this pillar into a political union (Scheller 2015).

PIERRE WERNER AND THE WERNER REPORT

Werner's private archives reveal that he made a major personal contribution to the method and substance of the Werner Report. In the first place, he contributed the three-point method. On 11 March 1970, at the group's preliminary meeting, Werner proposed a three-point working method based on a starting point, a final goal, and alternative routes between them—a very basic feature of the plan by stages. He drew his inspiration from the method used for the establishment of the Common Market, as evident in his five-point plan of 1968, which had been received with such enthusiasm. The Werner Committee sided with this approach, and the Werner Report was developed on this basis.

Werner also played a vital role in deepening the Werner Group's work for the final report. At a meeting of EEC finance ministers on 29 May in Venice, he emphasized the need for further work in six priority areas. They included institutional aspects of EMU, instruments for the coordination of short-term policy and economic policy in the medium term, and budgetary coordination instruments.[4] He based his suggestions on the view that economic union and monetary union had to proceed gradually and in perfect tandem. Political union was a longer-term objective, underlying the other two.

On the subject of exchange-rate rules, Werner specifically stipulated that there should be 'consultation with the governors of the central banks'. Although the finance ministers were in agreement on many conclusions, there were still differences of opinion, notably regarding the creation of an EEC exchange equalization fund prior to a common reserve fund. Nevertheless, it seemed essential to improve the coordination of the policies of intervention by the central banks in the foreign-exchange market.

All these proposals of Werner were to appear in the Council decision on furthering the work of the group and eventually in the final report. Werner also proposed 'consulting social partners on any important monetary decision', recommending that they should be associated with the development of Community economic policy.

[4] Handwritten note by Pierre Werner for his speech to the EEC Council of Ministers, Luxembourg, 8–9 June 1970, PW047/Pierre Werner family archives (PWLux)

In addition, Werner particularly favoured giving the CGCB a leading role in EEC monetary integration and advocated the essential role of the EMCF in promoting gradual convergence between different domestic monetary policies. In this respect, he may have been reassured by Ansiaux, the chair of the CGCB, whom he knew well from their many years working together within the Belgian–Luxembourg monetary union, and also by Clappier.[5] Werner had raised the idea of a European reserve fund as early as 1962, and in a more sustained manner from May 1967. In his five-point plan from 1968, he described the role and powers of such a fund, which would encourage financial solidarity and serve as an instrument to strengthen the coordination of economic policies in the Community. His approach was decidedly 'Triffinian'.

However, the CGCB remained very cautious about the EMCF, which it saw as a Trojan horse for political control over monetary policy that would put central bank independence at risk. Its own technical study, the so-called Ansiaux Report, therefore did not recommend its establishment. It concluded that, once a Community system for the narrowing of the fluctuation margins between the Community currencies had been set up and was functioning satisfactorily, the establishment of such a fund could be envisaged, subject to prior progress towards convergence of economic policies and coordination of monetary policies (James 2012). The EMCF was set up on 1 April 1973 but was reduced to a mere accounting tool for cooperation between the central banks.

Werner also worked to further the external dimension of EMU which the plan by stages entailed. From 1969 he was in regular contact with the US Federal Reserve and political authorities and with American financial circles, particularly through the Luxembourg financial centre. One idea that kept coming up was the consolidation of the future monetary identity and solidarity of Europe by ensuring that the Six spoke with one voice in international financial organizations, particularly in the IMF. Werner had several informal meetings with Pierre-Paul Schweitzer, managing director of the IMF, following the discussions that Monnet had had with him, as well as with Arthur Burns, chair of the US Federal Reserve Board. Washington had reservations about the idea of a European monetary bloc, which would stand in the way of increased flexibility in the international monetary system and seemed to be prompted by anti-American motives.

Last but not least, Werner was directly involved in the writing of the English version of the report and its dissemination in the English-speaking world, particularly in Britain. He held regular discussions with Edward Heath, the British prime minister.

[5] Letter of 24 April 1970 from the governor of the National Bank of Belgium, Baron Hubert Ansiaux, to Pierre Werner, president of the Luxembourg government, with a confidential annex on a European exchange equalization fund, PW 047/Pierre Werner family archive (PWLux).

MEDIATION AND NETWORK DIPLOMACY: DEVELOPING A TWO-PILLAR APPROACH TO EMU

One of Werner's key contributions was in mediating to bring the differing points of view in the committee closer together and secure an agreement on the interim report on 20 May 1970 and the final report on 7 October 1970. Thorny issues included the transfer of responsibility from the national to the Community level without engendering lasting tension; short- and medium-term economic policy; the necessity for the main decisions on monetary and credit policy to be taken in common; and the need for real decision-making power to be given to the Community bodies. The controversy between the 'economists' and the 'monetarists' was so marked that it was impossible to reach any unanimous conclusions on these issues—a fundamental principle for the group's work.

The Action Committee for the United States of Europe was a strong pillar of Werner's network, and he kept in permanent contact with Triffin and Monnet.[6] He consulted them a great deal on the sources of influence into which he must tap, especially in Germany and the Netherlands, the two Member States most reluctant to agree to a common position on the final report. Werner and Monnet were close to Brandt, using this relationship to good effect;[7] whilst the approaches of Gaston Eyskens, the Belgian prime minister, and of Baron Snoy to Johan Witteveen, the Dutch finance minister and deputy prime minister, also helped to achieve the desired result.

Werner drew upon a wide range of political contacts to gain influence. He negotiated a common position within the ECOFIN Council directly with finance ministers Giscard d'Estaing and Schiller.[8] He also called Clappier and other members of the EEC Monetary Committee to mediate among the Member States. Furthermore, Ansiaux asked Triffin to exercise his good offices by persuading German and Dutch officials to agree to the parallelism principle.[9] Werner consulted central bankers, notably Ansiaux, Carli, Otmar Emminger of the Bundesbank, and Zylstra, as well as Rinaldo Ossola from the Banca d'Italia, chair of the Group of Ten.

[6] 'Groupe Werner: Antécédents, préparatifs et réunions 1968–1970' ['Werner Group: Antecedents, preparations and meetings 1968–1970'], PW 047/Pierre Werner family archives (PWLux).

[7] Letter from Jean Monnet to Pierre Werner (Paris, 26 May 1970), PW048/Pierre Werner family archives (PWLux).

[8] Letter from Karl Schiller to the Chancellor of the Federal Republic of Germany, Mr Willy Brandt, the Federal Minister for Economic Affairs (Bonn, 14 October 1970), BArch B 102, Bundesministerium für Wirtschaft/93463.

[9] Letter from Baron Ansiaux, Governor of the National Bank of Belgium, to Professor Robert Triffin, Berkeley College, Yale University, New Haven, Connecticut (Brussels, 23 June 1970), PW048/Pierre Werner family archives (PWLux).

The result of an astute compromise, the Werner Report can be considered as another 'Luxembourg Compromise', secured by Werner. From 1968 onwards, Werner was one of the first to develop arguments in favour of the 'parallelism principle':

> We can identify two schools of thought: one is of the view that the monetary community will fall like a ripe fruit from the common policy tree . . . and one maintains that the development of a real economic and stabilization policy will be hindered by the absence of monetary unification. I believe that the truth lies at the midpoint between these two extremes. (Werner 1968c: 5–6)

In discharging his duties as chair of the group of experts, Werner chose to remain neutral, advocating a parallel approach to economic cooperation and monetary coordination as the underlying principle for the group's reflections. He adopted a median position in the dispute between the various trends in monetary and economic thinking, between which it fell to him to arbitrate in order to bring the work of the Werner Committee to a successful conclusion.

WERNER'S CONTRIBUTION AND LEGACY

As prime minister and finance minister of Luxembourg over several decades, Werner emerged to play a rare statesman-like role in the process of European unification in the second half of the twentieth century. He was all too aware of the particular geopolitical and historical situation of his country. For Luxembourg, adopting an outward orientation had always been a sine qua non. Werner was convinced of the need to preserve national sovereignty and vital interests by maintaining an international outlook. Accordingly, he placed the process of European integration at the centre of Luxembourg policy. Werner's foresight and his pragmatic approach enabled him to develop long-term strategies and focus on what was achievable. His political method was based on three main principles: anticipation, innovation, and consensus (Danescu 2015).

Werner can be considered as an architect of EMU for three main reasons. First, he possessed considerable expertise as a policy-maker and was able to translate this expertise into influence on agenda-setting and decision-making in the development of EMU. Monetary policy was a major and sensitive bastion of national sovereignty, and the Member States were unwilling to make concessions. Werner was unanimously recognized as an 'honest broker' who helped to generate momentum and forward movement. He forged this consensus-builder reputation on three levels: the domestic level by promoting dialogue with both sides of industry, the 'social partners', which led to the Luxembourg model of social consultation; the regional level within the BLEU and the

Benelux as a leading proponent of small-state diplomacy; and the EEC level, above all in EMU. His name is closely linked with two key milestones in European integration: the 1966 'Luxembourg Compromise' which put an end to the 'empty-chair' crisis and reconciled France with Europe; and the 1970 Werner Report which laid the foundations for the single European currency. Alongside his key mediator role, Werner provided a vital contribution to the substance of the plan in relation to both the parallelism principle and the concept of stages.

Second, Werner contributed his own vision of EMU. From the early 1950s onwards, Werner called for the establishment of a European monetary system based on a unit of account, for both official and private usage, and on a clearing house for central banks. He made monetary policy a pivotal part of his government's action. In addition, the burgeoning Luxembourg international financial centre, which experienced major growth in the early 1960s, served as a vanguard for a European currency unit. As early as 1962, Werner raised the idea of an EEC monetary cooperation fund, as the prelude to a common monetary policy. In 1968, his 'balanced monetarist' approach was evident when he delivered a clear roadmap to get to EMU and advocated the idea of gradualism and 'effective parallelism' in European integration. For Werner, economic union and monetary union had to work in perfect tandem, with political union as the ultimate aim. In his view, social Europe and the coordination of budgetary and monetary policies were intrinsic characteristics of EMU.

Third, Werner developed a tradition of Luxembourg 'network diplomacy' and European integration leadership (Dyson 2015). He forged his ideas by cultivating long-term productive exchanges of views with other instigators of monetary innovation like Collin, Rueff, and Triffin, as well as with financial technocrats like Ansiaux, Carli, Emminger, and Zijlstra. There was also a notably strong Belgian dimension to these exchanges. In addition, Werner remained in close contact with the Action Committee for the United States of Europe, above all with Monnet, Brandt, Hallstein, and Marjolin. Although he never claimed to be an academic expert, Werner exerted his influence at various levels of Community decision-making and became a key figure in intellectual debates between monetary elites and in the efforts to establish consensual transnational guidelines on monetary matters.

Werner also served as mentor and leadership trend-setter for other leading political figures in Luxembourg who later became active on EMU matters. This process can be traced back to the time of Joseph Bech (prime minister from 1953 to 1958 and one of the key figures of the Messina Conference) and, besides Werner, included Gaston Thorn (prime minister from 1974 to 1979 and president of the European Commission from 1981 to 1985), Jacques Santer (prime minister from 1984 to 1995 and president of the European Commission from 1995 to 1999), and Jean-Claude Juncker, long-serving president of the Eurogroup (2004–13) and European Commission president from 2014. Luxembourg political leaders proved masters of the art of political consensus and the country was a rich source of 'men of providence' who were able to help find a way out of Europe's successive impasses. The influential nature of this leadership has given Luxembourg a role in the European integration process that far outweighs the country's socio-economic size.[10]

[10] The author would like to express her gratitude to all those involved in this project, especially Ph. Duvieusart, L. Frieden, J.-C. Juncker, J.-C. Koeune, J. Santer, A. Sapir, H. Scheller, H. Tietmeyer, H. Werner and M.-A. Werner, the participants in the ESHET (Lausanne), UACES (Leeds) and STOREP (Torino) conferences, as well as all those involved in the 'Architects of the Euro' project, especially K. Dyson and I. Maes. Many thanks to S. Cooper for her proofreading. The usual caveats apply.

6

Roy Jenkins

The Importance of Top-Level Politics

N. Piers Ludlow

Roy Jenkins' direct involvement with the process of Economic and Monetary Union (EMU) in Europe was remarkably short, lasting little more than eighteen months. Indeed, the period when he was, arguably, *the* key figure in kick-starting the revival of interest in the issue that would culminate in the launch of the European Monetary System (EMS) in 1979 was shorter still. It lasted only the seven months from his own decision in July 1977 that EMU should be the Commission's number one goal, to German Chancellor Helmut Schmidt's surprise revelation in February 1978 that he intended to make the issue his own priority. Unlike several of the other architects examined in this book, therefore, Jenkins was not someone for whom EMU was a linking-thread running through much of his professional career. It was merely something on which he focused, intensely and to some effect, for a short period of a lengthy and distinguished career.

Furthermore, and again in contradistinction to several of the architects discussed in this volume, Jenkins had comparatively little training in academic economics. As such he was ill-placed to contribute much to the highly technical debate about what exactly EMU might look like and precisely what getting there would entail. Instead, his contribution was essentially political, focused on the relative priority accorded to EMU as against other European policy goals, the manner in which this goal should be pursued, and the level of government and of European policy-making at which the subject could most fruitfully be debated. His presence amongst the architects is almost certainly justified; but it is justified as a reminder that the quest for EMU has never just been a highly complex discussion amongst experts on international finance and macro-economics about the feasibility or desirability of moving towards a single currency. Rather it has also involved a highly political set of choices, often made by national and European leaders with little time for, or expertise in, the finer details of macro-economic argument, but motivated by the shared conviction that EMU could be a highly effective instrument for attaining a long-cherished political goal, namely the greater integration and unity of Europe.

This chapter begins with a short sketch of Roy Jenkins' life and career prior to his arrival in Brussels. From this it should become apparent that, while Jenkins had acquired quite a lot of experience of how disruptive and damaging exchange-rate volatility could be, and a degree of hands-on experience of dealing with international macro-economic issues, he had next to no track record on EMU itself before becoming European Commission president. It is not therefore particularly surprising that he would identify EMU as something he wanted to work towards only once he was installed in the Berlaymont building in Brussels.

A second section will then examine why he decided to espouse the goal of EMU before plunging into an analysis of that brief, but important, period when Jenkins became the most important and active advocate of European monetary integration. This will involve tracing the origins of his ideas, exploring their content, looking at the manner in which they were put forward, and assessing their effectiveness. The section will then conclude with an account of how Jenkins gradually lost control of the dossier that he had helped revitalize and became little more than a cheer leader for efforts primarily carried out by others.

A third and final section will then gauge the overall impact of Jenkins' contribution on the broader EMU story. It will suggest that his brief involvement *did* matter, but more for his views on the politics of the EMU quest than as a source of economic ideas. Jenkins did little to increase the sum of European knowledge about how EMU might work or the precise economic or political steps needed in order to bring it about. Few of his ideas are directly traceable forward into the EMS as it eventually emerged, still less into more recent steps towards monetary union. But his key insights were, first, that EMU was something that could not be obtained through too gradual and cautious a process but instead required a high degree of political commitment and will; and, second, that if it was to happen it would be the product of mobilization at the highest level of European governance rather than just discussion amongst monetary experts or ministers of finance. Both of these assessments would be borne out not just by the manner in which the EMS was created, but also by the launching of the single currency in the latter part of the 1980s and the first half of the 1990s.

BEFORE BRUSSELS

Roy Jenkins was born in south Wales, the son of a coal miner, trade-union official, and later Labour MP. His roots were thus in a strong working-class

Labour heartland, but he also had close ties to the upper reaches of the Labour Party from childhood. Clement Attlee, then deputy prime minister, was for instance a close friend of his father and would be witness at Jenkins' wedding in 1945. And this privileged, almost patrician, aspect of his background was reinforced by an educational trajectory that took him from a local Welsh secondary school to Balliol College, Oxford, where he was a contemporary of Denis Healey and Tony Crosland, and a year or so below Edward Heath. At Oxford he read PPE—Politics, Philosophy, and Economics—this last being taught, at Balliol, by Thomas Balogh, later an adviser to the Labour governments of the 1960s in which Jenkins would serve and an energetic opponent of Jenkins on the question of EEC membership in particular. From his memoir account, a huge amount of Jenkins' time at university was spent in student politics: in the Oxford Union, in the University Labour Club, and then in the Oxford University Democratic Socialist Club which he helped to found. But despite or perhaps because of this he was able enough to emerge with one of the four Firsts (out of the fifty or so taking the subject) in PPE awarded in his graduation year. This underlying ability was then confirmed by Jenkins' military service during the Second World War where, after a brief interlude serving in an artillery battery on the home front, he was selected as a cryptographer for work at Bletchley Park rather than seeing the type of active service on the front line experienced by Heath and Healey (Jenkins 1991: 3–58).

After the war Jenkins embarked on a career in politics. He stood unsuccessfully for election in 1945; made a fruitless bid to be selected as the Labour Party candidate for the seat formerly held by his father in 1946; and in 1948 was successfully elected as MP for Southwark, a London constituency, becoming in the process the 'baby' of the House of Commons—i.e. the youngest MP. With the Southwark seat destined to disappear in a round of electoral reform, he was able to secure the Labour nomination to Stechford, in Birmingham, a seat that he won in the 1950 general election and was then to hold until 1977 when he became president of the European Commission. A lengthy and distinguished career in British politics had begun (Campbell 2014: 94–123).

Within the Labour Party, Jenkins was at first close to Attlee, and later emerged as a member of the inner circle of Hugh Gaitskell, the party leader from 1955 until his unexpected death in 1963. As a Gaitskellite, Jenkins was involved with a succession of major tussles with the left of the party, notably over unilateral disarmament in 1960 and 1961. He was also a member of the Campaign for Democratic Socialism, a pro-Gaitskell grouping that would involve many of Jenkins' later allies in the formation of the Social Democratic Party (SDP) in the early 1980s (Campbell 2014: 111–242).

Between 1955 and 1957 he acquired his first taste of European politics, serving as a member of the Labour Party delegation to the Council of Europe during the very years that the Treaty of Rome establishing the EEC was being negotiated. Of this baptism in European politics he would later write 'I have no doubt that these experiences sowed the seeds of my subsequently persistent [European] conviction' (Jenkins 1991: 104). In parallel to his political activities, he was also able to become an acclaimed and successful biographer, publishing well-received and commercially lucrative studies of Herbert Asquith, Charles Dilkes, and Stanley Baldwin (Cannadine 2004).

Labour's victory in the 1964 general election, ending thirteen years in opposition, made possible a first taste of ministerial responsibility for Jenkins, despite his somewhat problematical relationship with Harold Wilson, the new prime minister. His first post was as Minister for Aviation, a job in which he took a number of controversial decisions firmly and efficiently (Campbell 2014: 243–58). Then in 1965 he became Home Secretary, entering the Cabinet for the first time, and quickly acquiring a formidable reputation as a liberal-minded reformer. During his three years at the Home Office, Jenkins helped oversee a relaxation of the divorce laws, the abolition of theatre censorship, and the legalization of homosexuality and that of abortion (Allen 2004).

In late 1967 he replaced James Callaghan as Chancellor of the Exchequer, charged with restoring Britain's economic position after repeated sterling crises and the November 1967 devaluation which General de Gaulle had used as a pretext for blocking the United Kingdom's second application for EEC membership (Parr 2006). In this role too he was widely regarded as a major success. His first two budgets in particular were seen as playing a major role in stabilizing the pound sterling and helping to restore British economic fortunes after the woes of 1966 and 1967. And the manner in which he defended his actions, both in Parliament and in the press, marked him out as one of the most effective speakers and debaters of his generation (Taverne 2004). As the 1970 general election approached, a contest Labour was widely expected to win, Jenkins was earmarked for the post of foreign secretary and also seemed heir-apparent to the party leadership. Being leader-in-waiting was all the more important, given that Wilson had already let it be known to his inner circle that he intended to step down at some point well before the end of the next government (Campbell 2014: 357). Number 10 Downing Street was tantalizingly close.

This ministerial trajectory was important for the EMU story in at least two respects. The first was that it gave Jenkins direct experience of how ruinous exchange-rate crises could prove and of the imperfections of international monetary arrangements. No Cabinet minister under Wilson in the 1960s could fail to realize how many of Labour's ambitious plans had fallen victim to the perennial weakness of sterling. Britain's balance of payments and the vulnerability of its currency would prove the Achilles heel of the United Kingdom throughout the 1960s but never more than in the middle of the decade (Tomlinson 2004).

Furthermore, as Chancellor, Jenkins became a participant not just in the battle to save the pound from further decline, but also in the fraught international discussions about monetary arrangements in the early stages of what would turn out to be the terminal decline of the Bretton Woods system. He took part, for instance, in the November 1968 meeting in Bonn which is widely regarded as the moment when Germany's position as the most financially sound of the Western powers was internationally recognized (Jenkins 1991: 265–9). Hence he had a painful awareness of how much difficulty such German strength could cause countries whose finances were less healthy. Both the realization of German centrality, and a sensitivity to the problems that this very centrality could cause for others, would later mark Jenkins' approach to EMU.

The second consequence of Jenkins' ministerial service in the Wilson governments of the 1960s was to convince him still further both of the importance of European integration, and the necessity of Britain playing a full part in this process. Such views predated his ministerial career. As early as 1961 Jenkins had emerged as one of the most articulate Labour advocates of British EEC membership, a stance that put him at odds with his party leader and mentor Hugh Gaitskell (Young 1999: 150–1, 161–4). Jenkins had thus been unhappy with Labour's 1962 decision to qualify its support for British membership with a series of preconditions deliberately intended to be unobtainable. But, in the mid-to-latter stages of the Wilson governments, he had had the gratifying spectacle of seeing opinion in the Cabinet, if not necessarily in the wider party, swing decisively back in his direction. Jenkins had thus been able to lend an important and powerful voice to the pro-European cause in the crucial Cabinet debates that were to decide on Labour's 1967 membership application (Wall 2012: 187–200).

This forceful pro-European stance would, however, do much to contribute to Jenkins' downfall as a Labour politician once the party unexpectedly lost the 1970 general election to Edward Heath's Conservative Party. For in opposition, the bulk of the party including the former prime minister, Wilson, and Jenkins' greatest rival, James Callaghan, turned against an EEC application that the Wilson government had initiated and which a new Wilson government would undoubtedly have pursued had the electoral outcome been different, leaving Jenkins and those others who remained consistent in their pro-European stance increasingly vulnerable to attack (Kitzinger 1973: 276–330). In October 1971 this led to the unusual spectacle of Jenkins as Labour Party deputy leader, heading a group of sixty-nine rebels, who defied a party three-line whip to vote in favour of the government's European Economic Community Bill, the legislation accepting the membership terms negotiated by Heath's government—a rebellion without which the legislation would not have passed (Kitzinger 1973: 371–4). By 1972 Jenkins had resigned the deputy leadership, in protest against his party's decision to promise a referendum on British membership (Jenkins 1991: 338–49). And in 1975 Jenkins would serve as the leader of the 'yes' campaign in the eventual referendum, working much more closely with opposition politicians like Heath, Willie Whitelaw, and Jo Grimond than he did with Wilson who was now back as prime minister but who had decided to play a semi-detached role in the referendum campaign (Jenkins 1991: 399–418).

Hence disillusionment with Labour's European policy played a key role in Jenkins' progressive detachment from his party, ruining any residual hopes of becoming party leader, but also making him feel less and less committed to its fortunes and ever more out of step with its priorities (Campbell 2014: 397–419). It was this state of semi-detachment—despite having returned to the government and resumed his former role of Home Secretary—that helps explain Jenkins' 1976 decision to accept the offer of becoming European Commission president. As he later explained, his initial reaction when the possibility was mentioned by Wilson was to refuse.

> Over the next few days I became increasingly doubtful of the wisdom of this reply. Brussels would certainly be an escape from the nutshell of British politics. It would be an opportunity to do something quite new for me and in which I believed much more strongly than in the economic policy of Mr Healey, the trade union policy of Mr Foot, or even the foreign policy of Mr Callaghan. There might also be the chance to help Europe regain the momentum which it had signally lost since the oil shock at the end of 1973. (Jenkins 1989: 4)

Jenkins put his hat into the ring in the battle to succeed Wilson (Campbell 2014: 457–62). But, when he did poorly in the party leadership ballot, trailing both Michael Foot and Callaghan, the eventual winner, he was able to turn away from British politics and embark upon a new European career.

CHOOSING EMU

There is absolutely no evidence to suggest that Jenkins arrived in Brussels having identified EMU as a key priority. European monetary integration was not a subject on which he had much of a track record. He had, it was true, briefly discussed EMU in his final months as Chancellor of the Exchequer, travelling in February 1970 to Paris, where he assured his then French counterpart, Valéry Giscard d'Estaing, that once inside the EEC Britain would be willing to play its part in any monetary Europe that was created (Wall 2012: 348). The loss of office in the summer of that year had removed any need to follow up on this pledge.

It was also the case that, as chair of the Labour Committee for Europe, he had endorsed a 1971 report on the Werner proposals prepared by one of those who had served with him at the Treasury in the late 1960s, Dick Taverne (Taverne 1971). In welcoming its publication, Jenkins described the study to *The Guardian* as 'the first serious attempt by any serious politician in this country to evaluate the implications of the Werner proposals especially in relations to sterling and its reserve role' (*The Guardian*, 16 April 1971). Press reports also confirm the international reputation for financial acumen that Jenkins had acquired as Chancellor, suggesting that he was the preferred candidate of several countries, including the Federal Republic of Germany, for the position of International Monetary Fund (IMF) managing director when this became vacant in 1973—an offer he turned down (*The Guardian*, 21 May 1973).

But there is little sign of Jenkins having intervened any further on the subject of EMU during the early or mid-1970s. Indeed a search through the press records and the collection of his speeches preserved amongst his personal papers unearths only two public speeches on monetary themes made by Jenkins in the years between 1970 and his arrival in Brussels, both in 1973. In March of that year he told the Manchester branch of the United Europe Association of 'the urgent search for a new world monetary system'; two months later he underlined to a conference in Washington, DC on US–European relations the need to develop a new international monetary system based on a reserve currency that was neither the US dollar nor any European currency (*The Guardian*, 17 March 1973 and 27 May 1973). Direct remarks about Europe's struggle to create its own monetary system are, by contrast, notable by their absence.

Nor does the paperwork accumulated during the months prior to his arrival in the Berlaymont suggest any particular interest in monetary matters. Jenkins was the first Commission president to be appointed a full six months before taking up office, and therefore had longer to prepare for the job than any of his predecessors. The fact that one of his first actions on accepting the job was to recruit an extremely efficient British diplomat, Crispin Tickell, to run his private office (and later to become his *chef de cabinet*), also means that historians have a very thorough record of Jenkins' activities during these preparatory months, now preserved at All Souls College, Oxford.[1] But references to EMU are few and far between. There was a sub-folder labelled 'Economic and Monetary Union' which momentarily aroused my expectations. It turned out, however, to contain a single letter from the British Treasury to Jenkins' private secretary in the Home Office, referring to a call on Jenkins made by a Treasury official to outline British thinking on the subject, and enclosing a copy of a Treasury report.[2] There was nothing else in the file to suggest that any follow-up action had been taken, nor any indication

[1] Tickell papers, All Souls College, Oxford, Box 1.

[2] Tickell papers, Box 1, 'Economic and Monetary Union', Baker to Phillips, 20 July 1976.

that the views of other Member States had been canvassed. The other records from this preliminary period, with one exception, were equally mute on the subject. The vast majority of the conversations that Jenkins and his team had, both with Member State governments and with multiple Brussels officials, appear to have centred on who should be appointed to the Commission, what portfolios they should hold, and how, if at all, the Commission might be reorganized and strengthened. To the extent that actual policy priorities were discussed at all—and they were very much the exception rather than the rule—this tended to take the form of Member State governments mentioning their preferences to Jenkins, rather than the president-designate testing out his possible options. So the Danish, Dutch, and Irish governments did briefly allude to monetary integration, but Jenkins seems to have done no more than acknowledge their interest.[3]

The only occasion on which discussion moved a little bit further was when the future Commission president met the French prime minister, Raymond Barre. But here too it appears to have been Barre who raised the subject rather than Jenkins. The record of the meeting reads:

> M. Barre said that he had no immediate hope of economic and monetary union, but agreed with Mr Jenkins that it should be retained as a target. He still hoped for growing convergence of the economies of the member states of the Community. At the time of the Paris Summit of 1972 he had looked forward to the achievement of economic and monetary union relatively soon. But afterwards only the Germans had accepted the monetary disciplines that had been agreed by the Ministers of Finance among themselves at the same time. Since then the French economy had been very weak, and things had got out of hand in the run up to the last elections. Things had got worse since.[4]

A little later in their talk the conversation returned to monetary issues, with a brief discussion of the problem of sterling balances and Barre's observation that a solution to this issue was only likely be found when the economic outlook improved. 'Mr Jenkins thought that the Community should be central to any such solution, and M. Barre agreed. It was vital that the Community countries should together align their currencies against the dollar. He agreed when Mr Jenkins said that he thought it was a mistake to float currencies.'[5]

This solitary exchange offers little reason to alter the basic assessment that Jenkins did not arrive in Brussels with any concrete plans to make EMU a

[3] Tickell papers, Box 1, 'Netherlands. Visit to The Hague, 16–17 September', Note for the Record, 21 September 1976; 'Visit to Dublin, 23 September 1976', Note for the Record, Conversation with Mr Nally and Mr Keating, 24 September 1978; 'Denmark', Note of a meeting with Ivar Norgaard, Minister for Foreign Economic Affairs, and others, undated.

[4] Tickell papers, Box 1, 'France', Record of a meeting between Mr Jenkins and the French Prime Minister, 1 November 1976.

[5] Tickell papers, Box 1, 'France', Record of a meeting between Mr Jenkins and the French Prime Minister, 1 November 1976.

priority. On the contrary, the fact that he was ready to give to François-Xavier Ortoli, the outgoing Commission president, who most unusually had agreed to stay on in Brussels, this time in a vice-presidential capacity, the portfolio for economic and monetary affairs suggests that Jenkins at this point in time had no intention of acting on this issue. After all, no politician as canny as Jenkins would have placed his single strongest rival within the Commission in charge of a policy area that he planned to make his own. The distribution of jobs in the new Commission thus confirms the basic message of the preliminary paperwork: Jenkins took office in January 1977 with few clear priorities beyond the reform of the institution he had been placed in charge of, and most certainly with no blueprint or action programme in the economic and monetary field.

The archival record would therefore appear to confirm Jenkins' own account of the timing of his turn towards EMU, namely that this occurred in the last two weeks of July 1977 (Jenkins 1991: 463). The new Commission president did not regard his first half year in office as having been particularly successful. His main achievement, gaining access as of right to G7 meetings, had been achieved at the cost of serious damage to his relationship with French President Valéry Giscard d'Estaing, one of the sponsors of his appointment and a figure the Commission president could ill-afford to alienate (Garavini 2006). It was also hard immediately to gauge the importance of a victory that could still be called into question. There was no immediate sense of satisfaction, moreover, given the outcomes of the Downing Street summit and the petty humiliations to which the Commission president was subjected while there. As Jenkins noted dryly in his memoirs: 'Extracting an invitation by stubborn complaint is rarely a recipe for enjoying the party' (Jenkins 1991: 460).

In addition, he had struggled to adapt to both the way in which the Commission itself functioned and the working of other European institutions, particularly the European Parliament (Jenkins 1989: 63). More seriously perhaps, he had found the departure from British politics more disruptive than expected, confessing to one colleague that he still dreamt of Westminster every night.[6] And the state of European politics and of the Community in general was dispiriting, with little sign of progress or European commitment in evidence amongst the Member States. As he told the members of his *cabinet* as they assembled for a study day in early August at the president's house in Oxfordshire:

> the first seven months in office had not been wholly satisfactory, though he felt that the achievements should not be minimised . . . But he thought that he had underestimated the complexities of Commission organisation and had not

[6] Interview with David Marquand, 7 June 2011.

> therefore fully worked out a 'style of operation'. He said that the British Presidency of the Council had not helped (although its effects should not be exaggerated), and that although this situation would now be a little easier, most of the major difficulties would still remain, because not one of the four major powers was really prepared consistently to support the Community. What support there was came in varying degrees from Italy, and the five small countries. Certainly it was unlikely that the British would go into a very pro-Europe gear for the moment. Furthermore, no European statesman was prepared to 'stick his neck out' over Europe. The role of the President as simply an intermediary between governments was unsatisfactory, the Commission as a whole needed to set out a new and more 'decisive policy'.[7]

The campaign for European monetary union was thus to serve as Jenkins' 'decisive policy' and the issue on which he would 'stick his neck out over Europe', in a fashion that other European leaders were not prepared to do. EMU was in other words to perform an analogous function to the single European market programme under Jacques Delors, albeit with the important difference that, whereas Jenkins turned to his galvanizing policy only several months after he had arrived in Brussels, Delors had seemingly identified which option to pursue before he assumed office and had used his preliminary consultations in the six months prior to arrival to canvas Member State views on the subject (Grant 1994: 66).

Why though did Jenkins decide to use EMU as his big new idea rather than some other area of Community policy? There is virtually nothing in the archival record that I have seen to challenge the threefold explanation advanced by Peter Ludlow over thirty years ago. He suggested that Jenkins' motivations were, first, a belief that a debate about EMU would help Europe arrive at a strategy to address the problems of unemployment, inflation, and economic divergence; second, a sense that monetary integration, if properly pitched, might tempt Germany into action; and, third, an awareness that a growing number of the Member States, including the Belgians who were next to hold the Council presidency, might be receptive to a monetary initiative (Ludlow 1982: 43–4).

The first point is confirmed by the records of meetings such as that with Barre cited earlier, and by a second meeting with the French prime minister in February 1977. Jenkins had little patience with the monetary status quo.[8] Furthermore, it is quite clear from the text of the Florence speech in which Jenkins would make public his ideas on monetary integration, and that of a follow-up speech delivered in Bonn, that the Commission president saw EMU

[7] Tickell papers, File 16, 'Records of Conversations and Meetings, Sept 1976 to 1977', Record of a meeting at East Hendred, 2 August 1977.

[8] For the second meeting, see Tickell papers, File 16, 'Records of Conversations and Meetings, Sept 1976 to 1977', Discussion between Mr Jenkins and M. Barre at the Hotel Matignon, 28 February 1977.

as a major step forward in the fight against both unemployment and inflation as well as, more obviously, a measure that would encourage economic convergence between the Member States.[9] The same point about EMU being compatible with—and indeed supportive of—the fight against European unemployment had earlier been made by David Marquand at the East Hendred meeting in August. It was reiterated, at some length and with greater force, in the paper written by Michael Emerson and presented by Jenkins to the special Commission meeting at La Roche-en-Ardenne in September.[10]

And it was also a point Jenkins argued strongly at the December 1977 European Council meeting in Brussels, seeking to persuade Europe's assembled leaders that a renewed push towards monetary union could be an important part of their response to the ongoing economic crisis.[11] In making this case, which may look surprising in an era when monetary union has come to be widely associated with higher rather than lower unemployment, Jenkins and his advisers laid particular emphasis on the inefficacy of national macro-economic policies in 1970s Europe, and the corresponding prospect of much more effective macro-economic policy being exercised at a Community level. This last would aid the fight against inflation, increase stability, and encourage business to invest, thereby creating new jobs.[12]

The second idea, namely that Germany could be tempted to act, is harder to back up in the archival record. Certainly neither of Jenkins' two bilateral conversations with Schmidt in the first half of 1977, nor that with Hans Apel, the German minister of finance, provided much indication of the Federal Republic's openness to a relaunch of monetary integration.[13] But the archival record does demonstrate that Jenkins had taken note of the Franco-German statement of February 1977 when Giscard and Schmidt had reaffirmed their belief in the desirability of progress towards EMU, since he specifically raised the subject with Barre.[14]

Furthermore the whole text of the Bonn speech delivered in December was evidently designed to appeal to a German audience, with multiple allusions to

[9] The Florence speech of October 27, 1977 is available electronically through the archive of European integration hosted by Pittsburgh University at <http://aei.pitt.edu/10983/>; that delivered in Bonn, at <http://aei.pitt.edu/10986/>.

[10] Tickell papers, File 16, 'Records of Conversations and Meetings, Sept 1976 to 1977', Record of a meeting at East Hendred, 2 August 1977; the Emerson/Jenkins paper is European Commission Archives (ECA), SEC (77) 3125/2, 16 September 1977.

[11] <http://aei.pitt.edu/11005/>.

[12] ECA, SEC (77) 3125/2, 16 September 1977.

[13] Tickell papers, File 16, 'Records of Conversations and Meetings, Sept 1976 to 1977', Summary record of a conversation between President Jenkins and Chancellor Schmidt: Chancellor's Office, Bonn, 18 March 1977; Call by the President of the European Commission on the Federal German Chancellor, Chancellery, 12 May 1977; Call by the President of the European Commission on the Federal German Minister of Finance: Bonn, 12 May 1977.

[14] Tickell papers, File 16, 'Records of Conversations and Meetings, Sept 1976 to 1977', Discussion between Mr Jenkins and M. Barre at the Hotel Matignon, 28 February 1977.

both the amount that the Federal Republic's own experience and approach to economic governance could contribute to any European debate about EMU, and to the way in which an export-orientated large economy like Germany could benefit from tighter monetary union.[15] Jenkins was also very aware of Schmidt's profound dissatisfaction with the manner in which Carter was steering US macro-economic policy. The Bonn speech thus went rather further than Jenkins' previous statements about monetary union in highlighting the extent to which greater European monetary integration would lessen the global dominance of the US dollar and allow Europe to play 'a major and perhaps decisive role in the restoration of order to the international monetary system'.[16] And finally it is clear from the East Hendred record, that Jenkins originally envisaged this Bonn speech as the launch pad for his monetary ideas, again highlighting the centrality of Germany in his thinking.[17]

The third claim, namely the likelihood of an EMU proposal gaining greater support from the Member States than would have been the case prior to 1977, is rather easier to document. As noted previously, several states, including the Netherlands, Denmark, and Ireland, had raised the issue in the course of Jenkins' tour of the Member State capitals in the autumn of 1976, without much initial response from the Commission president-designate. The Dutch and the Irish both returned to the question when Jenkins visited once more in the spring of 1977, this time eliciting much more obvious interest and engagement from the president of the Commission.[18] The Franco-German declaration of February has already been noted, as has Jenkins' conversation with Barre shortly afterwards. And the Belgians, who were the next Member State to hold the EEC presidency, were widely known to be preparing to launch their own ideas to revivify EMU (Ludlow 1982: 44–5; Mourlon-Druol 2012: 132–4). The annex to the Jenkins/Emerson paper presented at Roche-en-Ardenne, outlining Member States' views on EMU, could thus afford to be cautiously optimistic.[19] Only the British and the German Bundesbank were expected to be wholly against. Launching a major Commission initiative in this field would still be a gamble, but it would be one on which the odds were not massively discouraging.

There is, however, one additional reason that Peter Ludlow overlooked and which was barely picked up in the much more recent Mourlon-Druol (2012) study, namely the link between EMU and EEC enlargement. As Commission president, Jenkins was deeply committed to the expansion of Community

[15] <http://aei.pitt.edu/10986/>. [16] <http://aei.pitt.edu/10986/>.

[17] Tickell papers, File 16, 'Records of Conversations and Meetings, Sept 1976 to 1977', Record of a meeting at East Hendred, 2 August 1977.

[18] Tickell papers, File 16, 'Records of Conversations and Meetings, Sept 1976 to 1977', Discussion between Mr Jenkins and members of the Dutch Government at The Hague, 21 March 1977 and Visit of the President of the Commission to Dublin, 19–20 May 1977.

[19] SEC (77) 3125/2, 16 September 1977.

membership to include Greece, Spain, and Portugal (Karamouzi 2014). To have done otherwise, he believed, would be to betray the new southern democracies at a point in their transition processes when each remained highly fragile. But he was also highly conscious of the difficulties that EEC enlargement might entail and of the way in which many feared that the incorporation of three much poorer new Member States might paralyse the Community and thwart all prospects of forward movement. Flanking enlargement with a bold policy initiative like EMU would hence serve to send a decisive signal to all involved in the European integration process that widening and deepening could be pursued in parallel; that to allow the three applicant states to enter would not be to renounce all hopes of further integration. Furthermore, Jenkins insisted, a Community strengthened by a bold bid for monetary integration would be better equipped to cope with the stresses and strains that the entry of three new Member States would inevitably bring. As the Commission president put it in another of his colourful metaphors, this time used both in bilateral conversations with Raymond Barre and James Callaghan and in his European Council statement, moving decisively towards EMU would provide the Community with the stronger bones and sinews that it would need to bear the weight of three additional and highly needy Member States.[20]

AN ORIGINAL CONTRIBUTION?

The extent to which Member State views on the subject could already be mapped out well before the Jenkins initiative had been formally launched, only serves as a reminder of how much discussion there had already been about EMU (Mourlon-Druol 2012). In choosing European monetary integration as his 'big idea', the Commission president was in a sense being profoundly unoriginal. Just as would later be the case with Delors and his single market proposals, this repackaging of an old idea was in most respects a major advantage. Nobody could really criticize the European Commission for re-proclaiming an objective to which all EEC Member States had been committed since the early 1970s. Furthermore those like Michael Emerson who drafted Jenkins' speeches could draw upon an extensive pre-existing range of expert and political commentary on the theme. And there was a ready-made coalition

[20] Tickell Papers, File 16, 'Meetings and Conversations, Sept 1976 to 1977', Record of a conversation between the President of the European Commission and the French Prime Minister at the Hôtel Matignon, Paris, 19 November 1977 and Record of a conversation between the President of the European Commission and the British Prime Minister, No. 10 Downing Street, London, 25 November 1977; <http://aei.pitt.edu/11005/>.

of enthusiasts likely to rally to the cause, even if there were also long-established enemies well dug into fortified positions of hostility. But it is also important to ask what, if anything, was new and distinctive about Jenkins' ideas. Did the Commission president add to the ongoing monetary debate, or was he merely rehashing old ideas, extensively discussed beforehand?

In terms of economic substance there was relatively little that was wholly new about Jenkins' ideas. Indeed, neither of his major speeches on the subject, in Florence and in Bonn, constitutes a clear set of proposals. Instead they simply rehearse the arguments, economic and political, in favour of a rapid advance towards monetary union. Nowhere in either is there a clear roadmap to get to EMU; nor does either outline in any kind of detail what exactly a monetarily integrated EEC would look like. Their purpose, as the Florence speech makes clear, was simply to 're-launch a major public debate about what monetary union has to offer'.[21] As such, a significant portion of each speech brought up to date a series of fairly well-known arguments in favour of monetary union and explained how EMU might prove an effective remedy for Europe's current woes. Given the pressing nature of the economic difficulties afflicting the region during the mid-to-late 1970s, this undeniably gave some potency and political relevance to the case advanced. It was clearly of importance to ask why Europe seemed to be showing fewer signs of recovery from the economic crisis than either the United States or Japan, and there was some plausibility in the suggested link between such comparative underperformance and Europe's fragmented economy. Furthermore, as one Commission official was later to observe, 'If monetary union is not presented in terms of current problems, politicians and public opinion will consider the subject as an obscure theological dispute, of interest to scholars but not to ordinary sinners' (Mourlon-Druol 2012: 160).

But adding topical relevance to the call for EMU did not really require the fundamental economic case to be altered significantly. Indeed the only area where a much greater degree of detail could be added—especially in the Emerson/Jenkins paper for La Roche rather than in the two public speeches—was in the estimates of how great a level of fiscal transfers a monetary union might require. Here Emerson was able to draw on the recent findings of the MacDougall Group with which he himself had worked (Commission of the European Communities 1977). The Florence speech did therefore include reference to the 5–7 per cent of Community gross national product (GNP) that the MacDougall Group had estimated would be required for fiscal transfers within a full working monetary union.[22]

Despite the relative unoriginality of its economic content, however, there are at least three more political features of the Jenkins approach that do

[21] <http://aei.pitt.edu/10983/>.

[22] <http://aei.pitt.edu/10983/>.

deserve to be highlighted. The first was the rejection of gradualism and the advocacy of a bold leap forward. Ever since the failure of the Werner Plan, Jenkins maintained, those in favour of monetary union had run scared of rapid advance.

> The concept of gradualism . . . has come to supplant more ambitious schemes. Some people seem to believe that we can back our way into monetary union; others that better coordination is all that is required. I am afraid that neither view is right. The last few years have seen a retreat rather than an advance. In any event, the idea of an antithesis between gradual evolution and dramatic advance is misconceived. Evolution is a process which once begun goes both gradually and in jumps. There is room for *tomorrow's* act of better coordination and for t*oday's* discussion of a more ambitious plan *for the day after tomorrow*. The process has to be seen as one.[23]

Thus the new debate that the Commission president called for had to include elements of ambition and boldness, in place of the previous all-pervasive caution.[24] As the paper presented to the Commission at La Roche-en-Ardenne had put it, if advance towards EMU was to resume, 'a decision is basically required whether or not to jump in at the deep end'.[25]

Second, Jenkins insisted on the need to advance first on the monetary front rather than making any such progress conditional upon parallel steps towards other aspects of economic union. The importance of this aspect of Jenkins' plans can best be appreciated by comparing his ideas, as set out in the La Roche paper, with those presented to the same meeting by Ortoli. The French Commissioner's contribution also focused on EMU.[26] But, whereas the Emerson/Jenkins paper envisaged bold advance on a narrow (if highly controversial and far-reaching) front, Ortoli's draft presented a much more cautious set of steps in the monetary field: an extension of Community credit facilities, the greater use of the European unit of account, the maintenance and reform of the 'snake', possibly through the use of target zones, and the strengthening of the European Monetary Cooperation Fund (FECOM). Ortoli situated these steps within a five-year programme that would also comprise increased and more strictly policed economic convergence between Member States, the completion of the single market by 1982, a series of measures designed to stimulate investment and address Europe's energy needs, thereby enabling a return to growth, and the launch of a systematic European industrial policy. For Ortoli, advance would thus be less rapid, but over a much wider policy range.

Emile Noël, the Commission secretary-general, made a valiant attempt to minimize the divergence between the two sets of views, recording in the

[23] <http://aei.pitt.edu/10983/>.
[24] <http://aei.pitt.edu/10983/>, emphasis in the original.
[25] ECA, SEC (77) 3125/2, 16 September 1977.
[26] ECA, SEC (77) 3125, 15 September 1977.

minutes of the La Roche meeting that the ensuing discussion 'indicated a significant convergence of views and suggested wide possibilities for a synthesis of M. Ortoli and Mr Jenkins' ideas'.[27] But rather more accurate was a later passage of the same set of minutes which spoke of 'progress towards EMU (or to monetary union, if, as wished by some members of the Commission, this aspect was focused upon)'.[28] Unlike Ortoli, Jenkins was in other words suggesting a clear prioritization of the monetary over the economic aspects of EMU.

Third, Jenkins was absolutely clear in his own mind that the crucial level at which the debate that he desired on monetary integration was to take place was first and foremost that of the European Council. This did not mean of course that a wider public discussion was not also useful, hence his public speeches on the topic. Nor did the Commission president intend wholly to cut the ministers of finance and the Council of Finance Ministers (ECOFIN) out of the loop. A Commission paper on EMU, which tried to synthesize Jenkins' and Ortoli's approaches (although in reality rather closer to the latter than to the former), was duly submitted to ECOFIN in November 1977 (Mourlon-Druol 2012: 147). Jenkins also explained and defended his ideas at an informal meeting of European foreign ministers at Villiers-le-Temple in early October (Jenkins 1989: 152). But the audience that really mattered were Europe's most senior decision-makers who were next due to convene in Brussels in December 1977. In October, straight after delivering the Florence speech, Jenkins agreed with the Italian prime minister Giulio Andreotti that the European Council debate on the subject would be vital, adding 'what was important for the Council was not just what went into it but what came out of it'. In this respect he would like to see the Council conclusions 'take the debate beyond mere exhortation'.[29]

To Schmidt, two weeks later, he was rather more defensive:

> Mr Jenkins referred to the forthcoming European Council. He said he did not expect the Chancellor to endorse 'at a stroke' his Florence ideas on monetary union, but he hoped that he would give them a fair run. He hoped that there would be no pouring of cold water or stamping on them. Herr Schmidt said that the European Council was principally designed to present new perspectives. He was not against looking again at monetary union provided it was presented in reasonable as well as imaginative terms.[30]

[27] ECA, COM (77) PV 442, 2e partie (séance du 18 septembre 1977). My translation.

[28] ECA, COM (77) PV 442, 2e partie (séance du 18 septembre 1977). My translation.

[29] Tickell papers, File 16, 'Records of Conversations and Meetings, Sept 1976 to 1977', Meeting of President Jenkins with Prime Minister Andreotti, 28 October 1977 in Rome.

[30] Tickell papers, File 16, 'Records of Conversations and Meetings, Sept 1976 to 1977', Summary record of a conversation between the President of the Commission and the Federal Chancellor over lunch in the Chancellor's office, Bonn, 10 November 1977.

And with both Callaghan and Barre, the Commission president used the same phrase, hoping for 'a fair wind' behind his ideas at the Council meeting.[31]

Jenkins' statement to the Brussels European Council meeting in December 1977 was hence absolutely vital, since it was addressed to the nine men without whose majority support no advance towards EMU would be conceivable. In it Jenkins called for 'a new, non-utopian but more urgent and contemporary impulse to the old idea of economic and monetary union, particularly its monetary aspect'. This would be to the advantage of both the weaker and stronger economies within the EEC, he insisted. It could not be attained 'by an inevitability of gradualism in which everything happens painlessly, effortlessly, without any major act of political will'. Nor should it await total 'equality of economic performance' since this was unlikely to be attained in 'our lifetime or even our children's lifetime'.

> In this situation we need to look afresh at what monetary union would involve for the Community. I should emphasise at the outset that I do not foresee such a union as something for tomorrow, or even the day after tomorrow. But if we are to set ourselves an objective, it should be one within practical reach, something not over the horizon but at least on the horizon. After all, in the long run we are all dead. What I envisage in the short run is the setting of an objective and the reorientation of our existing policies in terms of it. Thus when we take, as we must, decisions on major economic and monetary issues, we should do so in the framework of policies which will eventually lead to monetary union. This is less than making for union in a straight line; but it is more than the coordination which is sometimes held up as sufficient for our current needs.[32]

It was true of course that not even these three political choices made by Jenkins were entirely original. The first and second—i.e. the plan to advance boldly, rather than gradually and to prioritize monetary over parallel economic measures—reprised the basic approach of the Werner Plan (Gros and Thygesen 1998: 12–15; see also Chapter 5 by Danescu). The Werner Plan had also been to some degree a child of summitry, the original call for monetary union having been issued at the Hague Summit of December 1969 (Hiepel 2003). And the strategy of appealing to the still new European Council had been anticipated by the Commission's April 1976 paper on EMU, which was addressed directly to the Community's most senior decision-making body (Mourlon-Druol 2012: 93).

[31] Tickell papers, File 16, 'Records of Conversations and Meetings, Sept 1976 to 1977', Record of a conversation between the President of the European Commission and the French Prime Minister at the Hotel Matignon, Paris, 19 November 1977 and Record of a conversation between the President of the Commission and the British Prime Minister, No. 10 Downing Street, London, 25 November 1977.

[32] <http://aei.pitt.edu/11005/>.

But the timing of Jenkins' initiative, the switch in tactics it represented from the gradualist approach championed by Ortoli, and the manner in which the Commission president was able to trail it in public, seek a degree of support bilaterally, and then sell it in a multilateral setting like the Council did make an important difference. Apart from anything else, it was received in a positive, if non-committal fashion by most of Europe's leaders in December 1977. Jenkins recalled the Council giving 'a fair if not tremendously enthusiastic wind behind our monetary union proposals'. They helped demonstrate to Schmidt and Giscard that the circumstances might be favourable, were they to decide, independently of Jenkins and for their own reasons, to set sail for the same destination (Jenkins 1989: 183).

Similarly the relatively undefined nature of Jenkins' ideas, both economically and institutionally, was an asset not a disadvantage, since it allowed the German and French leaders to make the ideas their own, without having to fundamentally denature them. Jenkins did therefore perform a vital service to the duo of European political leaders who would eventually do most to create the EMS.

Once Schmidt decided to act in February 1978, Jenkins quickly lost any control over the discussion that he had helped to revitalize (Ludlow 1982: 63ff.; Mourlon-Druol 2012: 151ff.). It was flattering of course that the German Chancellor should choose to tell Jenkins of his monetary plans before any other international interlocutor.[33] Given Schmidt's notorious impatience with the European Commission, the gesture of inviting Jenkins to Bonn and letting the Commission president know his determination to press ahead with monetary integration was both generous and revealing about the usefulness of Jenkins' prior reconnaissance of the terrain.

But from the February meeting onwards, and still more from the Copenhagen Council in April in the aftermath of which the trilateral Schulmann–Clappier–Couzens discussions commenced and the details of the EMS began to be fleshed out, the Commission president became a supporting actor in a drama primarily carried forward by others, and played out on stages where he was not present. He continued to be highly active of course, giving further speeches about EMU, intervening on the subject both bilaterally and at the Copenhagen, Bremen, and Brussels European Council meetings in 1978, and at the G7 meeting in Bonn (Jenkins 1989: 244–9, 286–90, 292–5, 348–53). He also circulated a letter to all of the European leaders on the eve of the Copenhagen meeting, outlining the key tasks ahead, and reiterating the need for monetary advance.[34] And in Bremen he may also have played a useful role

[33] Tickell papers, File 17, 'Records of Conversations and Meetings, 1978 to March 1979', Record of a conversation between the President of the European Commission and the Federal German Chancellor, Bonn, 28 February 1978.

[34] Tickell papers, File 15, 'European Councils', Jenkins' Memorandum for the Copenhagen European Council, 5 April 1978.

in blunting Callaghan's hostile questioning about the need for economic and monetary advance to proceed in parallel, supposedly largely by dint of reciting a strange piece of British doggerel (Jenkins 1991: 480). But even those who had worked closely with the Commission president on the issue would acknowledge that, from the spring of 1978 onwards, Jenkins no longer had much control over the monetary union dossier.[35] Revealingly perhaps, his principal interest in the 'concurrent studies' that accompanied the latter stages of the EMS talks and which were designed to make it easier for countries with weaker economies to participate in the planned system, was not as a partial implementation of the ideas for fiscal stabilization that he had raised in his Florence speech, but instead as a political gesture which might increase the chances of Ireland and Italy joining the EMS (Ludlow 1982: 170ff.).

ASSESSING JENKINS' CONTRIBUTION AND LEGACY

So how important overall had Jenkins' role been in the birth of the EMS? And do his ideas have any relevance in the longer-term story of how the EC/EU was to opt for the euro? The answer to these questions depends very much on whether the main criterion is path-breaking economic analysis or political savvy.

In terms of the former, Jenkins' contribution was very slight. As noted earlier, he was not an out-and-out economist, even though by the standard of his day he was more economically educated than most of his political peers, in the United Kingdom at least. Thanks partly to the collaboration of Michael Emerson, who drafted most of the La Roche paper, and the bulk of the Florence speech, Jenkins was able to become a convincing and articulate spokesman for a relaunch of monetary integration. But his plans were deliberately lacking in specifics, re-proclaiming the goal, rather than mapping out the precise steps needed to get there. As far as precise economic content is concerned, therefore, neither Schmidt's initiative in the spring of 1978, nor the eventual EMS as it emerged in 1979, and still less EMU as it was constructed in the 1990s, could trace much of their DNA to Jenkins' or Emerson's views.

Indeed it is perhaps revealing that in the area in which Jenkins (thanks to Emerson) went furthest in outlining a specific view of how monetary union should work, namely on the question of what sort of central budgetary redistribution might be required, his ideas were so totally disregarded. Later, the absence of a large-scale redistributive mechanism was seen by many as one of the major flaws in the design of the euro project. This neglect of the fiscal element began during the EMS negotiations themselves, where the 'concurrent

[35] Interview with Michael Emerson, 10 July 2013.

studies' fell far short of initial hopes and expectations. It went further in the early 1990s, when the 1993 'Stable Money—Sound Finances' report scaled down the degree of fiscal stabilization that MacDougall had foreseen. The implementation of monetary union downplayed this fiscal aspect of EMU even more than the 1993 report (European Commission 1993).

If EMU is analysed as a political process, however, rather than simply as an economic objective, several of Jenkins' insights seem much more relevant with hindsight. The former Commission president seems to have been correct to regard EMU instrumentally, and to perceive it as a mechanism by which to push European integration forward more generally, every bit as much as it was a worthwhile goal in its own right. As such, Jenkins' views accurately foreshadowed those of leaders like Helmut Kohl or François Mitterrand, who were directly associated with the birth of the euro. They too, to put it flippantly, were more interested in 'a Europe made of money' than specifically in 'money made by Europe'. And instrumental thinking of a similar sort helps explain the evident belief of later European leaders during the post-2008 Euro Area crises that to protect the euro during its difficulties was also to protect the whole process of European integration.

Equally prescient was Jenkins' emphasis on the idea of a qualitative leap, of the big idea, rather than that of cautious and gradualist advance. To be sure, the leap made in 1978 or 1979 was not nearly as large nor as far-reaching as the Commission president might have wished, hence Mourlon-Druol's conclusion that Jenkins' hope for a qualitative leap forward had 'already virtually faded away' by November 1977 (Mourlon-Druol 2012: 160). Similarly, it can be argued that the EMS as it eventually came into being bore more than a passing resemblance to the 'snake' that it ostensibly replaced, albeit with a crucial difference in terms of its membership. This too might suggest the triumph of Ortoli's gradualist inclinations rather than Jenkins' bolder aspirations.

But viewed politically, such criticisms rather miss the point, since the purpose of proclaiming a bold leap was not necessarily to bring this about straight away but rather to revitalize a debate that was in danger of becoming either ritualistic or confined to academic experts. A cautious manifesto would not have had the same effect. It was therefore vital that both Jenkins' public speeches and his advocacy of monetary union at European Council meetings were pitched in a fashion that excited interest and enthusiasm, not bored lip-service. And on this too there are important similarities between the manner in which Jenkins aimed to gain attention, by outlining an ambitious and bold target, and Jacques Delors' *modus operandi*, first on the single market and subsequently on monetary union (see Chapter 10 by Hodson).

Jenkins' third, and perhaps most important, insight was his identification of the European Council as the crucial forum within which the case for monetary advance needed to be made. Had the debate about EMU in the 1970s remained primarily confined to the level of ECOFIN and the EEC Monetary Committee—the levels at which Ortoli most naturally operated—it is safe to say that precisely nothing of significance would have resulted. Both the ministers of finance and the central bank governors had held multiple previous discussions on these topics with little concrete result, and it is difficult to see why the situation would have been any different in 1977–8. But by raising the campaign to European Council level Jenkins helped encourage bigger players, like Schmidt and Giscard, to seize the initiative. In the process he largely sidelined the many ministry of finance and central bank officials who harboured substantial doubts about monetary integration.

Again this has contemporary echoes. German federal finance minister Wolfgang Schäuble commented in 2010 that the survival of the euro was *Chefsache*, that is something on which the EU heads of state and government rather than their ministers of finance would have the final word (Ludlow 2010: 16). One of Jenkins' great merits was to recognize this aspect of monetary integration as early as 1977 and to place this realization at the very heart of his strategy to revitalize the European Community.

7

Hans Tietmeyer, Ethical Ordo-Liberalism, and the Architecture of EMU

Getting the Fundamentals Right

Kenneth Dyson

Hans Tietmeyer's claim to be an architect of the euro remains contested, on two main grounds. It can be argued that he was not as innovative a thinker as his early intellectual mentor, Professor Alfred Müller-Armack, founder of the Cologne School of the social market economy; and that he was hostile to European monetary union.

The first of these arguments is more plausible than the second. As State Secretary for European Affairs from 1958 to 1963, Müller-Armack had led the way in developing new thinking about a 'second phase of the social market economy'. His thinking was a response to the impending exhaustion of reconstruction as an engine of economic growth and to the challenge of how to design a more ambitious structure of European economic governance within the new European Economic Community (EEC). He argued that the Treaty of Rome of 1957, during the negotiation of which he had been a prominent member of the German team, had not gone far enough in devising an EEC structure of policy coordination and liquidity provision that could cope with the implications of an integrating European economy. Müller-Armack proposed a new EEC counter-cyclical stabilization mechanism, covering fiscal, monetary, and credit policies and based on an agreed code of good behaviour. This mechanism involved creating new institutional arrangements and financial instruments for providing coordinated fiscal stimulus when appropriate, in particular by large-scale infrastructure investment. Müller-Armack could claim credit as an architect of the European Investment Bank (EIB). However, the lack of support from more fundamentalist Ordo-liberals in his Federal Economic Ministry, from his minister Ludwig Erhard, and from the Federal Finance Ministry meant that these ideas were soon jettisoned.

Even the European Commission proved reluctant to pursue them (for details see Dyson forthcoming).

Tietmeyer's intellectual journey was one away from the Cologne School of the social market economy and the more flexible thinking of his early mentor. From the 1970s, under the influence of the broader shift in the international economics mainstream towards the monetarist paradigm, he shifted towards the stricter Ordo-liberal approach of Walter Eucken and the Freiburg School. This approach rested on the advocacy of the primacy of the economic order, founded on firm constitutive and regulative principles for safeguarding a competitive market order. This strict form of Ordo-liberalism regarded ideas of European fiscal stimulus and liquidity provision with great suspicion. It placed its faith in a rule-based competitive market order.

In addition, Tietmeyer's claim to be an architect could be questioned by those who believed that his emphasis on a long-term and strict approach concealed hostility to European monetary union. He was seen by many as a potential saboteur. The political decision to go ahead with a stage three of Economic and Monetary Union (EMU) with eleven Member States in 1998–9 was one he confronted with a sense of resignation, not of enthusiasm. Tietmeyer believed that a hasty, politically driven approach would lead to an unsustainable monetary union that would soon inflict major political as well as economic damage on European integration. He saw himself not as a saboteur but as the 'better European', his fears about the dangers as confirmed as the Euro Area crisis gathered momentum in 2010–12.

TIETMEYER AS AN ARCHITECT OF THE EURO

If not an intellectual innovator, Tietmeyer's claim to be an architect of the euro can be justified in three ways. First, he was the longest-serving German official in the making of EMU, the consummate 'Bonn insider', and a reference point for younger German officials in the EMU process. Tietmeyer was more or less continuously involved: from the writing of the two Schiller Plans on EMU in 1969–70 and working in the Werner Group in 1970–1 to his retirement from the presidency of the Bundesbank in August 1999. His personal imprint was clearest in four official documents: the Stoltenberg memorandum of March 1988 during the German EC presidency; the Bundesbank statements of October 1990 and November 1991 before and close to the end of the Intergovernmental Conference (IGC) on EMU that helped prepare the Maastricht Treaty; and the Bundesbank statement of February 1992 in the wake of the agreement of the Maastricht Treaty (for details see Dyson and Quaglia 2010a: 369–71, 443–7, 490–1). Such was his reputation that the eminent French sociologist

Pierre Bourdieu (1996) condemned German emphasis on a strict interpretation of the convergence criteria for entry into European monetary union as 'the Tietmeyer idea'. In the previous month, the highly respected former Federal Chancellor Helmut Schmidt (1996) singled Tietmeyer out for personal attack for his lack of strategic acumen over EMU.

At the same time, in assessing Tietmeyer's contribution, two qualifications are in order. First, his career path as a federal government official from 1962 to 1989 meant that his chief contribution related to the economic and fiscal pillar of EMU. With respect to the monetary pillar, Bundesbank officials—above all Karl-Otto Pöhl and the chief economist Helmut Schlesinger—were much more important. Schlesinger was the key intellectual in the Bundesbank and central in the drafting of the Pöhl Paper that was presented to the Delors Committee in 1988 (see Chapter 8 by Harold James). Nevertheless, their contributions were essentially complementary, making Tietmeyer's move to the Bundesbank in 1990 relatively seamless. This complementarity derived from shared belief in Eucken's principles of the primacy of monetary policy and of enforcing liability and the argument that the role of fiscal and supply-side policies was to flank monetary policy in creating and safeguarding a competitive economic order (Eucken 1952: 255–64).

Moreover, the fact that Tietmeyer was by far the longest-serving German official involved with EMU should not disguise the intensive engagement of other officials at different times. Johann Baptiste Schöllhorn, his superior as State Secretary in the Federal Economics Ministry under Karl Schiller, played a pivotal part in the Werner Group negotiations in 1970–1. Horst Köhler, State Secretary in the Federal Finance Ministry after Tietmeyer, was the lead German negotiator in the IGC on EMU in 1990–1; Jürgen Stark, State Secretary in the Federal Finance Ministry, was the lead negotiator over the Stability and Growth Pact (SGP) in 1996–7; whilst Otmar Issing, chief economist of the Bundesbank, played the lead role in helping to shape the design of the ECB monetary policy strategy in the late 1990s. Their own particular contributions were substantial.

Tietmeyer's second claim to be an architect rests on his tireless advocacy of getting the economic and political foundations of EMU right at the outset. From 1970–1, Tietmeyer retained a deep personal attachment to the Werner Report's principle of 'effective parallelism' in the economic and the monetary pillars of EMU. This principle was for him second best to the 'coronation' theory, in which monetary union would be the final stage in European political union. However, though falling short, insistence on 'effective parallelism' erected a convenient negotiating hurdle for the French government. It had to show that it was prepared to cede fiscal sovereignty, alongside the shift of monetary sovereignty to the Community level. Tietmeyer's attachment to 'effective parallelism' made him an arch-opponent of the 'monetarist' school of EMU. For Tietmeyer, adherence to this principle was the minimum condition for moving ahead with EMU. This condition was not honoured in the Maastricht Treaty provisions on EMU, a factor at the root of his scepticism about the chosen path to the single currency.

Fundamentally, Tietmeyer believed that European monetary union required a comprehensive political union, if it was to be durable. For this reason, unlike some of his German peers, Tietmeyer recognized that 'economic government' was essential within EMU. A sustainable monetary union could not be achieved in isolation from political union as a 'stand-alone' project. Tietmeyer (1988) spelt out the implications: the single currency 'will lead to member nations transferring their sovereignty over financial and wage policies, losing gradually their autonomy over taxation policies'. At the same time he remained faithful to his Ordo-liberal principles. 'Economic government' had to go along with safeguards for central bank independence in the pursuit of price stability; speedy and effective enforcement of strict fiscal rules to ensure domestic discipline; and institutions strong enough to ensure an open, competitive market order.

Getting right the economic constitution of EMU mattered because, as he argued, the path to EMU was a one-way street. As a good Ordo-liberal in the Eucken tradition, he rejected as too risky the view of EMU as an experimental process of 'learning by doing'. The *process* should be subordinate to ensuring the proper terms for a competitive economic *order* in the European Union (EU). As Tietmeyer (1999: 136) put it: 'once the "genie is out of the bottle", it is very difficult to get it back in'. His approach was grounded in the metaphor of architecture (Tietmeyer 1994). In line with Ordo-liberal principles, EMU had to be founded on a durable 'stability-orientation' (*dauerhafte Stabilitätsorientierung*), enforcement of the principle of liability (*Haftung*) on Member State fiscal and economic policies, and an institutional framework that would ensure long-term coherence and consistency in economic and monetary policies.

Tietmeyer's thinking about the foundations of EMU was linked to his personal and family religious background. The theological basis of Ordo-liberalism is traditionally attributed to newly popular Lutheran social ethics in the 1940s (cf. Manow 2001). However, in Tietmeyer's case, it was the early study of Catholic theology in Münster that gave him an abiding interest in the ethical foundations of economic policies. It informed his sense that those economists who make public statements bear a particularly heavy political and moral responsibility (Tietmeyer 1999: 127–36; Tietmeyer 2002).

Like other Ordo-liberals, Tietmeyer had an ambivalent relationship to Catholic social teaching. On the one hand, he was averse to its neo-corporatist thinking and residual *Ständestaat* thinking. He saw the emphasis on cooperation amongst powerful social groups as likely to encourage rent-seeking behaviour that would subvert market principles. On the other hand, Tietmeyer endorsed the Roman Catholic principle of subsidiarity as compatible with

Ordo-liberalism, above all understood as a moral injunction to exercise personal responsibility. Social Catholicism helped to reinforce Tietmeyer's commitment to a principle-based approach to economics. It also gave a pronounced ethical and didactic quality to his approach to economic policy.

However, the substance of Tietmeyer's approach was grounded, above all, in his reading of Ludwig Erhard (1964) and Eucken (1952)—both Lutherans—as well as his years in the 1950s as a student under Müller-Armack in Cologne. At this time Müller-Armack worked closely with the Federal Economics Ministry under Erhard. He became head of its key economic policy division in 1952 and later the second State Secretary with responsibility for European affairs (Löffler 2003). Tietmeyer was recruited to Müller-Armack's former economic policy division (*Grundsatzabteilung*) in 1962. His arrival coincided with the European Commission's Action Programme for the Second Stage and its rejection as *dirigiste* by leading Ordo-liberal officials in his new division. Tietmeyer retained a deep distrust of the European Commission's motives in trying to carve out an enhanced role through EMU.

In the post-Erhard period Tietmeyer saw himself as the conscience of the principles of the social market economy within the ministry. He followed Müller-Armack's strong engagement with issues of institutional integration in the EEC. In this, like his mentor, he differed from Erhard's narrower functional conception of European integration. However, in line with the stricter Ordo-liberalism represented by the Freiburg School, Tietmeyer was more tenacious than Müller-Armack had been in resisting the notion of EEC policy coordination for counter-cyclical purposes.

Tietmeyer inherited Erhard's intense distrust of the European Commission and his scepticism that the social market economy could be exported to the rest of the EEC (Kowitz 1998; Löffler 2003). He regarded the European Commission as too open to French *dirigiste* economic ideas and as too focused on seeking short-term political consensus, based on synthesizing economic and monetary plans. This approach made the Commission an advocate of policies that would lead to an EMU based on harmonization of policies and progressive detailed intervention in the economic process. Tietmeyer advocated the design of EMU on the model of best performance, defined in terms of global competitiveness and the transfer of the monitoring and surveillance functions of the Commission to a new politically independent authority. This last proposal found an echo in the Federal Finance Ministry's abortive proposal for a European Monetary Fund in February–March 2010 and in the Bundesbank's plan for EMU reform in 2015.

Erhard had a highly conditional and reserved approach to European integration, influenced by Ordo-liberals like Wilhelm Röpke. In the 1950s this approach was evident in his advocacy of a toughening of credit conditions within the European Payments Union (EPU); his rejection of the notion that surplus states like Germany should share in the burden of adjustment to external imbalances; and his belief that free convertibility of currencies was far more important than loyalty to the EPU (Dyson 2014; Kaplan and Schleiminger 1989; Löffler 2003). Erhard came into sharp conflicts with Federal Chancellor Konrad Adenauer over the EPU; over the negotiation of the Treaty of Rome in 1955–7; and later over the Franco-German Elysée Treaty in 1962–3 (Laitenberger 1986; Schwarz 1997). Tietmeyer (1999: 11) quoted approvingly from Erhard's memo to Adenauer in 1956: 'economic science and conscience' should not 'automatically be sacrificed to tactical considerations'. This dictum deeply conditioned his attitude to EMU.

These conflicts in the 1950s and early 1960s foreshadowed the difficulties that Tietmeyer would later experience with Chancellor Helmut Kohl, who saw himself as heir to the Adenauer tradition of prioritizing European integration (Dyson and Featherstone 1999). Tietmeyer feared that building European integration on a basis that defied sound economic principles of global competitiveness and monetary stability would lead to illusion, hubris, and complacency. He was never free of this fear, which he saw as confirmed as the Euro Area crises gathered momentum from 2007–8. Hence, as a senior civil servant, Tietmeyer devoted much time and energy to shadowing and seeking to control the Federal Chancellor at times when the European Council was discussing EMU matters. He succeeded in 1985 at the Luxembourg European Council's final negotiation of the Single European Act. However, Tietmeyer failed twice: in 1988 at the Hanover European Council over the creation of the Delors Committee; and in 1991 at the Maastricht European Council over the transition to stage three of EMU and the final date.

In the last analysis, Tietmeyer remained the loyal civil servant. He never forgot the constraints that were represented by the foundations of political legitimacy on which the Federal Republic rested. As a good Ordo-liberal, Tietmeyer thought politicians often ill-informed, short-sighted, and myopic. Nevertheless, his sense of loyalty took precedence over the desire to fully speak his mind, above all as president of the Bundesbank when the final date for stage three of EMU approached and the political pressures from Bonn intensified.

The third basis for Tietmeyer's claim to be an architect of the euro rests on his larger-than-life persona. The significance of his contribution was bound up with his distinctively didactic and combative style. For reasons of historical background, German negotiating style is typically presented as that of the reluctant hegemonic power in Europe. This style was expressed in a preference for a multilateral approach of accommodating and balancing interests in the EU. It meant letting other Member States, like the Netherlands, take the lead in confrontational arguments, above all with France (Dyson and Featherstone 1999). Post-war German national interest was defined in terms of dissociating Germany from historic images of bullying authoritarianism and imperialism and ensuring that Germany never again became isolated in Europe.

For this reason many other negotiators, German included, often felt uncomfortable with Tietmeyer's tough negotiating style. Tietmeyer's style reflected his belief that convergence under EMU must follow the standards of the 'best performer' in terms of global competitiveness rather than harmonization around average performance. It led him to be impatient with the tendency of heads of state and government, of economics and finance ministers, and of European Commissioners to agree political compromises that sacrificed sound economic fundamentals.

Tietmeyer favoured 'truth-telling to power' by experts who were independent and possessed intellectual understanding (*Sachverstand*). In his view, the European Commission was too focused on achieving consensus to play this role. This scepticism about the European Commission and impatience with the outcomes of voting in the Council of Ministers meant that he retained an acute awareness of the design weaknesses of the Maastricht Treaty and of the SGP in surveillance and monitoring fiscal rules on deficits and debt. His preference was for removing this surveillance and monitoring function from the Commission and giving it to an independent body.

Tietmeyer was highly respected by both his ministerial and Bundesbank colleagues and by his European negotiating partners. He demonstrated an enormous capacity for hard work; he possessed a detailed technical mastery of policy briefs and negotiations; and his expositions in meetings were models of intellectual clarity. Many who worked with Tietmeyer found him an awe-inspiring, larger-than-life character. At the same time, Tietmeyer was often judged an uncomfortable partner. His belief was that negotiations should be about searching for the best solution, consistent with a stability-oriented EMU and using the best performer as the standard.

Even as a young official in the Werner Group, Tietmeyer was prepared to make his disagreements known, along with his dissatisfaction with negotiations that sought just to establish a short-term consensus. To some, Tietmeyer came to represent the 'intelligent egoism' of German power. He was seen as lacking larger strategic acumen and as risking German isolation through a too abrasive and narrowly focused assertion of German negotiating positions (Schmidt 1996). His legacy could be attacked as paving the way for a form of European integration which in style and substance could be represented as a 'Teutonic EMU'.

BACKGROUND AND INFLUENCES

Tietmeyer was born in 1931 in Westphalia, in the Münsterland, and was raised and educated in a strongly Roman Catholic milieu. In 1952–3 he studied Catholic theology and philosophy at the University of Münster, where he came under the influence of Joseph Höffner, holder of the chair of Christian social teaching. Höffner was an unusual figure in having a doctorate in economics (supervised by Eucken) as well as in theology. He argued for an approach to economics rooted in ethical principles. The state's responsibility was to foster personal responsibility and to respect the principle of subsidiarity (Tietmeyer 2002: 26–7). From Höffner, Tietmeyer drew justification for his view that social justice was not primarily about the state correcting the market through policies of redistribution. Primary importance attached to *iustitia commutativa* (exchange justice). Social justice was best served by a state that promotes the market, breaks up monopolistic privileges, rewards performance, and confines itself to restitution for 'unjustified' enrichment (Tietmeyer 1999: 133–4). Tietmeyer (1999: 128) quoted with approval the future Pope, Cardinal Josef Ratzinger:

> A morality that believes it can leave out objective economic knowledge is not morality, but rather moralism, which is the opposite of morality. And objectivity that believes that it can manage without ethics fails to appreciate human reality, and thus lacks objectivity.

Cardinals Höffner and Ratzinger could be drawn on as Christian justification for strict adherence to the Ordo-liberal principles of liability and subsidiarity in thinking about social policy and, by extension, about European integration.

However, beyond the subsidiarity principle, the study of Catholic social teaching offered Tietmeyer little in the way of substantive understanding of macro-economics. Tietmeyer pursued his interest in economics at the University of Cologne, under Müller-Armack. There he became immersed in the literature on the social market economy (Tietmeyer 1999: 5–13). Strikingly, Tietmeyer's diploma was on 'The Ordo Concept in Catholic Social Teaching'. The intellectual challenge of marrying this economics literature with Catholic social teaching was made easier by the efforts of Müller-Armack and of Eucken to ground their economic analysis in a theological framework. Tietmeyer saw the 'social' in the social market economy as the bridge that would introduce a greater economic realism into Catholic social teaching and rid it of neo-corporatist elements. The bridge was provided by the moral principle of encouraging personal responsibility.

Tietmeyer's thinking about responsibility can be criticized for neglecting the question of capability. As Nussbaum and Sen (1993) argue, the state—and, by extension, European integration—has a vital role in enabling people to exercise their responsibility effectively by providing appropriate supportive economic and social conditions. In this way of thinking, the promotion of economic and social cohesion would be central to the sustainability of the EMU project. It would require, at a minimum, policy instruments to help compensate individuals and communities for the heavy costs of fiscal and structural reforms to help speed economic adjustment in a monetary union.

Tietmeyer's intellectual development in macro-economic theory took place within the context of the post-war German 'economic miracle' during the 1950s and early 1960s and the popular attribution of this miracle to the social market economy (but cf. Abelshauser 1983). It led him to a strong and abiding identification with Erhard as the so-called father of the economic miracle. Tietmeyer believed that later problems in German economic development could be traced to the way in which powerful vested economic and, above all, political interests and ideologies had subverted the social market economy. The prime culprits were seen as excessive faith in counter-cyclical economic policies and as excessive expansion of welfare-state entitlements. Tietmeyer (1999: 15–34, 101–10) was later to criticize Müller-Armack for unwittingly encouraging these developments. Their outcome was, he argued, excessive public debt. From the 1970s Tietmeyer's Ordo-liberal critique gained new intellectual support from US monetarist ideas and from new Anglo-American economic theories of rational expectations. The language of long-term inflation expectations and of market credibility was used to justify his Ordo-liberal emphasis on strict rules and compliance.

Tietmeyer's diagnosis of the problems of German and European economic policies was reflected in his highly controversial role as State Secretary in the Federal Economics Ministry, in particular in authoring the so-called Lambsdorff Paper in 1982. Its call for faster and deeper fiscal consolidation ushered the collapse of Chancellor Schmidt's Social Democrat/Free Democrat (SPD/FDP) federal government. This episode poisoned his long-term relations with the SPD. Tietmeyer's hand could also be traced in the Bundesbank convergence report of March 1998. Reference was made to 'significant doubts about the long-term sustainability of the public finances' of both Belgium and Italy. In fact, Tietmeyer and others in the Bundesbank had more serious reservations about the size, heterogeneity, and thus sustainability of the Euro Area that was established in 1998–9.

On his retirement Tietmeyer became actively involved with the New Social Market Initiative as its chair. In this capacity he returned to the theme that had been central to the work of the Cologne School: the principle that economic and social policies should be measured for their conformity with market principles, including price stability.

Müller-Armack remained a central influence on Tietmeyer as the academic who coined the term 'social market economy' in 1946 and as a close collaborator of Erhard. For Tietmeyer he was a role model, less as an originator of Ordo-liberal thought and more as a disseminator of its key ideas and their adaptation to post-war economic and political circumstances. However, Tietmeyer recognized that the 'social' in social market economy had offered a hostage to fortune. He believed that, in his search for a 'social irenic', Müller-Armack had conceded too great a role to anti-cyclical and social policies, offering opportunities for the development of vested interests that subverted structural reforms. The Cologne School had attempted to combine the principle of freedom in the market with that of social balance and peace through operational rules derived from the principle of conformity with the market (Müller-Armack 1956).

Over the longer term, Eucken, a founding figure of the Freiburg School, remained more foundational for Tietmeyer's understanding of Ordo-liberalism. Crucially for Eucken, and relevant for Tietmeyer's future understanding of EMU, a functioning market economy depends on a foundational political decision. It requires the creation through transformational leadership of a comprehensive and robust institutional framework to secure a competitive economic order. In contrast to laissez-faire thinking, the 'strong' state is vital in constituting markets and establishing a coherent 'economic constitution' (Eucken 1952: 254–304). For Tietmeyer, Erhard offered living evidence for the importance of transformational leadership in constructing an economic order, in taking the necessary decisions, and in shaping how economic policy evolves. The high risk with the establishment of EMU in the Maastricht Treaty was that it would lack this type of transformational leadership at the European level. However, in his biography, Hentschel (1996) raised serious doubts about the transformational nature of Erhard's leadership.

With respect to EMU, Tietmeyer took from Eucken the idea that it was vital to codify the constitutive and regulatory principles in order to secure a robust institutional framework that would safeguard the 'competitive order' of Europe. As outlined by Eucken (1952: 254ff.), the constitutive principles were the primacy of monetary policy and an 'automatic monetary stabilizer' (however, not central bank independence); a systematic policy of free and open markets; security of property rights; liability for one's commitments and actions; and stability and consistency in economic policies. Eucken (1952: 356–60) had feared a 'competition to prevent competition' (*Behinderungswettbewerb*). The regulative principle most relevant to the design of an EU fiscal-policy regime was the avoidance of negative externalities. An EMU that was consistent with Ordo-liberal principles would have strong and resolute central institutions, a test not met by the Council or by the European Commission. It would also have constitutionally limited functions, above all in ensuring compliance. EMU would be rule-based, not output-oriented, and 'market-conformable' in its actions (Tietmeyer 1999: 16–22). Above all, it would not lose sight of the insight of Erhard (1964: 15): 'the social market economy is inconceivable without a consistent policy of price stability'.

TIETMEYER AND THE PROBLEM OF PARTISAN ENGAGEMENT

> Men of science, by virtue of their profession and position being independent of economic interests, are the only objective, independent advisers capable of providing true insight into the intricate inter-relationships of economic activity, and therefore also providing the basis upon which economic judgments can be made.[1]

Tietmeyer's thinking mirrored the Ordo Manifesto of 1936. He inherited from Eucken, and from Ordo-liberalism more generally, a deeply felt faith in the intelligence of experts and in non-majoritarian institutions. This faith was accompanied by a detached and critical attitude to mass democracy and to political pluralism. Tietmeyer's strongly elitist approach was grounded in confidence in expert judgement. He believed that it was the function of economic theory to understand and see through popular opinions and the ideologies of vested interests and to speak truth to power (cf. Eucken 1950: 321). Respect for expertise (*Sachverstand*) was the basis for sustainable social cooperation. Tietmeyer's emphasis on the need for expert and objective analysis was linked to his belief that interest-group and partisan interests too easily subvert the common good. They generate rent-seeking activity and myopic and short-sighted economic policies. For this reason, he emphasized the importance of subjecting EMU, and economic policy more generally, to expert domestic scrutiny by non-majoritarian bodies: the German Council of Economic Experts, the advisory councils of federal ministries, the German economic research institutes, and, above all, the Bundesbank (Tietmeyer 1999: 132–3).

However, accusations of authoritarian, anti-democratic thinking, echoing national conservative thinking in the late Weimar Republic, miss the mark. Tietmeyer was no disciple of Carl Schmitt. Ordo-liberal thinkers—at least from the end of the 1930s—differed from Schmitt in stressing the mutual interdependence of the competitive economic order with a liberal legal system and a liberal political system. Their foundational beliefs placed liberalism before democracy and before European integration. Ordo-liberal beliefs provided the platform for radical critiques of European integration. This critical distance could lead to accusations that Ordo-liberals like Tietmeyer were extremists who pushed their arguments to the limits and failed to recognize that European integration must rest on the principle of reciprocity and respect for democratic political processes.

[1] F. Böhm, W. Eucken, and H. Grossman-Doerth, 'The Ordo Manifesto of 1936', reproduced in Peacock and Willgerodt (1989: 15).

As a German civil servant, Tietmeyer sought to avoid partisan association by emphasizing his attachment to economic logic. He did so in terms of the Ordo-liberal belief in the importance of an independent public sphere that could help correct the malfunctioning of democracies. Tietmeyer was motivated by a strict, traditional German conception of the role of the civil servant. Nevertheless, despite its self-image, it could be credibly claimed that Ordo-liberalism was one of many kinds of ideological engagement: its 'truth-telling' concealing its own vested interests. It was more closely linked programmatically and discursively to the Christian Democratic Union (CDU) and its Bavarian sister-party, the Christian Social Union (CSU), and even more strikingly to the liberal FDP. Its chief mouthpiece in the press was the conservative *Frankfurter Allgemeine Zeitung*. Tietmeyer's background in Christian social ethics was also suggestive of proximity to the CDU/CSU. Later Tietmeyer was to become more actively associated with the CDU, making his membership public.

For these reasons, Tietmeyer was very distrusted within the SPD and within the German Trade Union Federation (DGB). The SPD and the DGB were more attracted to Keynesian ideas, to social partnership in managing processes of economic change, and to the conception of social justice through fiscal redistribution. SPD politicians had also not forgotten the association of Tietmeyer with the Lambsdorff Paper and the fall of the SPD/FDP coalition government after thirteen years in power. The Bundesbank publication that honoured Tietmeyer's contribution to EMU indicates an asymmetry in his public engagements. They included presentations to the CDU Economic Council (*Wirtschaftsrat*), to the Konrad Adenauer Foundation of the CDU, to a working group of the FDP parliamentary party, and to various financial and business associations. The SPD and the DGB did not feature (Der Zentralbankrat der Deutschen Bundesbank 1996). This asymmetry may of course reflect the lack of demand rather than Tietmeyer's unwillingness to supply his views to the SPD and the DGB.

Perhaps most tellingly, former SPD Federal Chancellor Schmidt (1996) took aim at Tietmeyer in an 'open letter', labelling him 'the most important opponent of monetary union'. He claimed that Tietmeyer lacked strategic insight. Tietmeyer threatened to isolate Germany through advocacy of an excessively strict interpretation of the convergence criteria for euro entry and of the need for excessively rigid fiscal rules within the monetary union. For Schmidt the problem lay in the gap between Tietmeyer's public profession of commitment to European integration and his deep personal scepticism evident in the elaboration of necessary conditions. In cataloguing Tietmeyer's previous errors of policy judgement, Schmidt included the role of the Lambsdorff Paper in bringing down his own federal coalition government.

THE BONN YEARS: APPLYING ORDO-LIBERALISM TO THE CHALLENGE OF EMU

The challenge that Tietmeyer faced as a working official was to apply the general principles of Ordo-liberalism to the changing political and economic realities of European economic and monetary integration. However, confronting this challenge was made difficult by three areas of intellectual neglect in Ordo-liberalism. This neglect was evident not just in the 1950s and 1960s, the formative years in Tietmeyer's intellectual development. It continued into the 1980s and 1990s.

Judging by the contents of the ORDO Yearbook, their main publishing outlet, Ordo-liberals paid relatively little attention to fiscal policy and public finances; to the experiences in other European states; and to issues of institution building in European economic governance (cf. Bönker et al. 2001: 171–3). The founders of Ordo-liberalism had been notably vague on the desirable institutional arrangements for European economic governance. Either they wrote before the process of European integration began in earnest (Eucken died in 1950), or like Röpke they saw European integration in limited functional terms and as a potentially dangerous diversion from the larger gains associated with international economic and financial liberalization. There was a gap to be filled in applying Ordo-liberalism to European integration. In doing so, Müller-Armack's contribution in 1958–9 was overlooked.

European integration had proved very much a second-order engagement in Ordo-liberal theory building, with the exception of the practical involvement of Müller-Armack in institution building. However, even he regarded the social market economy in historical-cultural terms as essentially a German model that would be difficult to export (Kowitz 1998). The preference of Ordo-liberals continued to be to embed the social market economy in a competitive order at the global level, based on freedom of trade and of capital movement (Tietmeyer 1999: 11). They feared that 'little' Europe would evolve into a protectionist framework, discriminating against third countries and slowing down structural changes. This fear focused on the alternative French economic model of *dirigisme*, which Erhard and Müller-Armack saw as a major threat within the post-1958 EEC. Their opposition to the Action Programme for the Second Stage of 1962 focused on the European Commission's proposal for strengthening economic policy coordination through medium-term economic programmes and for pursuing expansionary and inflationary policies at Community level. The beginning of Tietmeyer's career in the Federal Economics Ministry began in the context of this conflict. It intensified in 1963 with Erhard's opposition to the bilateralism of the Franco-German Elysée Treaty and to the French veto of British membership of the EEC. Erhard succeeded in ensuring that economic and monetary policies were not included in the Elysée Treaty.

Tietmeyer's introduction to the challenge of applying Ordo-liberal principles to the practical problems of European integration began in 1968–9, by which time he was head of the Federal Economics Ministry's economic policy division. The central problem within the EEC was external imbalances, which were grounded in differential development of unit labour costs. They had given rise to clear exchange-rate misalignments and tensions, above all between France and Germany. Two conclusions were drawn within the German federal government. First, deep resentment had been caused, above all in Paris, by the refusal of the German Grand Coalition government of CDU/CSU/SPD to countenance a change in the D-Mark parity in November 1968. The Foreign Ministry under SPD chair Willy Brandt feared German isolation, creating an opening for him to promote new ideas on EMU. Second, the Bretton Woods system of stable but adjustable exchange rates appeared as a less robust guarantor of the public good of economic stability for the EEC. It was increasingly seen as part of the problems of, rather than part of the solution to the problems of, European integration. There was a need to reflect on a possible post-Bretton Woods world.

This evolving context helped foster new German intellectual support for tighter EEC and international coordination of both exchange rates and wider economic policies to underpin domestic non-inflationary policies. An early indication of this new type of thinking was the proposal in the 1966–7 Annual Report of the German Council of Economic Experts for a 'hardened currency standard', though one not limited to the EEC. It was followed in November 1967 by the Advisory Council of the Federal Economics Ministry, which advocated 'embarking on negotiations towards forming a community of stability (*Stabilitätsgemeinschaft*) as soon as possible and to extending it beyond the European Economic Community to other leading countries in world trade' (Tietmeyer 1999: 179). However, Tietmeyer reacted cautiously. Reasoning from an Ordo-liberal perspective, his preference was for Herbert Giersch's earlier proposal in 1965 for flexible exchange rates—under either a free-float or under a crawling peg system. For Tietmeyer (1999: 183–4), its advantage was that Member States could retain maximum economic policy autonomy and optimize trade and output within an integrating Europe.

The September 1969 federal elections initiated a major change of German political drive on European integration and a rapid learning process for Tietmeyer and his colleagues. Brandt's first post-war SPD-led federal government was intent on flanking its new and bold Eastern policy (*Ostpolitik*) of easing Cold War tensions in Europe, as well as support for future EEC enlargement, with a new political impetus to European integration. The aim was to reassure anxious opinion, above all in Paris, about German motives. In this context Tietmeyer worked with others on the first Federal Economics and Finance Ministry Plan for the Realization of EMU in Stages in October 1969. The so-called Schiller Plan was the first official German plan to deal with the institutional arrangements for EMU (for full details see Dyson and Quaglia 2010a: 162–5). It bore the imprint of Federal Economics Minister Karl Schiller's commitment to a Keynesian-style new 'enlightened' social market economy, having a more explicit counter-cyclical component and pursuing coordination to achieve a set of four interrelated economic policy goals, including price stability.

At the core of the Schiller Plan was the message that the creation of EMU could not 'be an isolated economic process but must be accompanied by a further development of broad political cooperation between the partner states' (Dyson and Quaglia 2010a: 164). The first stages of EMU were to be a 'probationary period', in which no 'hard' decisions are taken. It was made clear that the precondition for progress between stages was the demonstration of the political will to transfer sovereign rights in economic policy and to tolerate the 'considerable pain' that some Member States would face in the transition. This aspect of the Schiller Plan reflected Tietmeyer's thinking. However, the Schiller Plan did not wholly reflect Tietmeyer's preferences. It did not endorse flexible exchange rates during the transition. Instead, the Schiller Plan provided for a pooling of foreign-exchange reserves. It also laid considerable stress on Community counter-cyclical mechanisms rather than fiscal rules.

The steepness of the learning curve in EMU increased after the Hague Summit of December 1969. Tietmeyer was appointed the representative of his State Secretary, Schöllhorn, in the Werner Group. Schöllhorn was very much an enthusiast of the new neo-Keynesian thinking associated with Schiller. Tietmeyer was moved to head the division on the EEC. Brandt had used the Hague Summit to send a clear political signal that it was in Germany's strategic interest to give new impetus to European integration through EMU (for full details see Dyson and Quaglia 2010a: 166–8). However, despite Brandt's backing for a European Reserve Fund (ERF), the main drive from the Federal Chancellor's office was on the foreign and strategic aspects of EMU rather than on institutional and policy issues. Despite pressures from Jean Monnet's Action Committee and from other heads of government, Brandt did not actively push the idea of the ERF on Schiller.

The second Schiller Plan of February 1970 provided more detailed guidelines on the 'economic and political prerequisites' for moving forward with EMU (for full details see Dyson and Quaglia 2010a: 198–201). They included progress in reducing economic imbalances; liberalization of money and capital markets; conditionality attached to the transition from one stage to another; transfer of competences, including to the European Parliament; and treaty amendment to legitimate this transfer. This second Schiller Plan provided Tietmeyer with his negotiating mandate.

Tietmeyer was identified with the so-called 'economist' coalition within the Werner negotiations. He focused on ensuring that the Werner Report gave priority to the institutional and political implications of EMU, in particular prior harmonization of economic policies and transfer of sovereignty over fiscal and economic policies. The outcome was a compromise based on the principle of 'effective parallelism' in developing the economic and the monetary pillars. This principle included strengthening the European Commission and the European Parliament and moving to majority voting in Council. The key safeguard was provided by acceptance that there would be no automaticity in the transition from one stage to the next and that treaty change would be required. A political decision was required based on results achieved in the previous stage. The challenge was summed up in the Werner Report's statement that the first stage only makes sense if the Member States are in principle willing to enter the final stage. In this way the seriousness of French intentions to transfer sovereignty could be tested. However, Tietmeyer was less successful in pushing the agenda of firm and automatic rules in fiscal and in monetary policies (Tietmeyer 1999: 188). He also had no negotiating mandate for flexible exchange rates in the transition.

Within two months it became clear that, subjected to harsh Gaullist criticisms in the National Assembly, the French government was unwilling to accept the institutional and political prerequisites laid down in the Werner Report. In order to avert an internal EEC crisis, and save something, Schiller reacted by proposing a 'let-out' clause, which was accepted by the Council of Finance Ministers (ECOFIN). Stage one's monetary measures, including the later 'snake' exchange-rate system, would be launched but with a fixed time limit. They would expire if, after four/five years, it became apparent that no agreement had been reached on the succeeding stages. Tietmeyer held to the conviction that the EEC could not proceed with EMU in the absence of a fundamental debate and hard decisions about its economic and political structures.

Tietmeyer's engagement with the negotiations on the European Monetary System (EMS) in 1978 was much narrower and primarily in his capacity as chair of the EEC Economic Policy Committee. In the wake of the Bremen European Council, this Committee was charged with the task of conducting the concurrent studies. Their aim was to clarify what type of resource transfer might be needed to induce the British, Irish, and Italian governments to lend their support to the new EMS and to facilitate economic convergence to enable their participation. Though this approach was akin to the parallelism envisaged in the Werner Report, it differed in crucial respects. The three Member State governments were not agreed on the kind of resource transfer that they sought. They also saw a new Community resource-transfer mechanism as a way of reducing constraints on their policies rather than as part of Community institution building. In particular, Tietmeyer was aware that Federal Chancellor Helmut Schmidt had, at best, only a very limited conception of what this mechanism might entail. Against this background, above all the lack of political drive in Bonn, Tietmeyer was happy to preside over discussions that produced no significant outcome (Mourlon-Druol 2012: 219–24).

Tietmeyer's scepticism about the willingness and the capacity of Member State governments to bind themselves supranationally in EMU was reinforced by his experience with the Werner Report, with the snake exchange-rate system, and later with the fraught negotiations on the establishment of the EMS. In his view, EMU was not a self-contained project. It was an instrument in the service of European integration, requiring prior agreement on its institutional and political preconditions. On this point Tietmeyer was in agreement with Commission President Roy Jenkins' Florence speech of September 1977. For Tietmeyer, European integration boiled down to the core political question 'national political sovereignty—yes or no?' (Der Zentralbankrat der deutschen Bundesbank 1996: 161). It also had to be compatible with economic logic, understood by him in terms of the principles of Ordo-liberal theory.

From 1982 to 1989 Tietmeyer's engagement with EMU was as State Secretary in the Federal Finance Ministry during the federal government of Chancellor Kohl. Accordingly, he became a key player in the EC Monetary Committee. This role brought him into closer contact with Bundesbank officials, with whom he shared a common Ordo-liberal approach to EMU. Tietmeyer relied on mobilizing the Bundesbank, wider Ordo-liberal economic opinion, and Bundestag support. Before and after the 1983 Exchange Rate Mechanism (ERM) crisis, and French Finance Minister Jacques Delors' appointment as European Commission President, Tietmeyer strongly resisted fresh attempts to put EMU back on the agenda before the economic and political preconditions were in place. He set out to mobilize against 'creeping' EMU via secretive agreements behind closed doors. Central to this strategy was closely shadowing Federal Chancellor Kohl at European Council meetings to avoid political deviation from the Ordo-liberal line that EMU was a very long-term issue. Containment of Foreign Minister Hans-Dietrich Genscher was a key part of the strategy.

Tietmeyer's most decisive engagement was before and during the Luxembourg European Council in December 1985, when he conducted hard-line opposition to the attempt by Delors to insert a treaty commitment to EMU in the last stages of negotiating the Single European Act (for full details see Dyson and Featherstone 1999: 316–20). The crucial issue was whether this commitment to treaty change would take the form of Article 235, which required decisions just by Council, or—as Tietmeyer insisted—under Article 236, which would involve national parliaments and referendums and include consultations with the EC Monetary Committee and the Committee of Central Bank Governors. Tietmeyer was successful. Delors failed to get formal competence for the EEC in monetary affairs as a complement to the single market and a new role for the European Commission in this area. This clearing of 'EMU bugs' from the Treaty represented a temporary victory for

Tietmeyer's conception of EMU. For Tietmeyer the key phrase in the new Article 102a was that, in furthering cooperation in economic and monetary policy, Member States 'shall respect existing powers in the field'. It was code for safeguarding the independence of the Bundesbank (Dyson and Featherstone 1999: 319).

However, resistance to 'creeping' EMU became more difficult as external and internal pressures mounted in the wake of the Single European Act, especially during the German EC Presidency in the first half of 1988. As part of the 25th-anniversary celebrations of the Franco-German Treaty, Chancellor Kohl and President Mitterrand proposed a new Franco-German Economic Council, which was to include the president of the Bundesbank as well as the Economics and Finance ministers. Tietmeyer leapt to the defence of the independence of the Bundesbank, stressing successfully that the new body was purely consultative (Dyson and Featherstone 1999: 323–5). He also used the EC Monetary Committee to block the French Balladur Memorandum of January 1988, which sought to put a European Central Bank (ECB) on the agenda (for full details see Dyson and Quaglia 2010a: 361–3). The argument began to revolve around whether EMU was part of the logic of the new single market, as well as necessary to correct the asymmetry in the functioning of the EMS. This functional economic logic put the Ordo-liberal approach to EMU on the defensive. In particular, rapid progress in agreeing freedom of capital movement in May 1988 suggested that one key Ordo-liberal precondition had been met.

More ominous still for Tietmeyer, the Balladur Memorandum was followed in February 1988 by the Genscher Memorandum for the Creation of a European Currency Area and a European Central Bank. The two initiatives provoked the Stoltenberg Memorandum of March 1988, which was presented to ECOFIN. This document represents perhaps the single clearest official statement of Tietmeyer's views (for details see Dyson and Featherstone 1999: 332–4; Dyson and Quaglia 2010a: 369–71). It referred back to the Werner Report for inspiration. 'Without a . . . comprehensive transfer of competences, a common currency would not be safeguarded against possible tensions, which could arise out of the different economic and monetary policy decisions of the Member States.' It noted continuing lack of economic convergence, notably in fiscal deficits. It also specified as a precondition that all Member States establish independent central banks with a clear mandate of price stability. EMU remained 'a longer-term goal'.

Tietmeyer's sense of marginalization was accentuated before and during the Hanover European Council in June 1988. The groundwork had been prepared in close collusion between Kohl, Delors, and French President François Mitterrand (for details see Dyson and Featherstone 1999: 334–9). Tietmeyer was not able to replicate his Sherpa role at the 1985 Luxembourg European Council. The establishment of the Delors Committee cut him out of the negotiating process, because it was constituted on a very different basis from the Werner Group. Tietmeyer was reassured to an extent by the presence of the Bundesbank president, Karl-Otto Pöhl, in the Delors Committee and his respect for the central bank's Ordo-liberal credentials. However, this time he was an outsider in the negotiating process. On the German side the Bundesbank became the key player. This outcome was seen as a victory for Delors, Kohl, and Mitterrand. It raised the prospect that the economic and fiscal foundations of EMU would be neglected in favour of an approach too narrowly focused on the monetary foundations.

Hence, in contrast to the Werner Group, Tietmeyer played a background role during the Delors Committee. He was reassured by Bundesbank reports that the Delors Report would contain no fixed dates for stages two and three of EMU. Pöhl claimed that the process would take a very long time and, like the Werner Report, become mired in countless political and economic difficulties. Nevertheless, measured against the Werner Report, Tietmeyer (2003) judged the final Delors Report to be cognitively flawed. It failed to provide for 'effective parallelism' in the economic and monetary pillars. This failure reflected the composition of the Committee. He saw it as the task of the Federal Finance Ministry to correct this failure, above all by ensuring strong mechanisms for fiscal discipline in the transition period. After the Delors Report, Tietmeyer sought to re-establish the link of EMU to political union. His efforts to do so were bolstered in April 1989 by a cabinet reshuffle that led to the replacement of a politically embattled Stoltenberg by the chair of the CSU, Theo Waigel, as Federal Finance Minister.

However, Tietmeyer was not to be the key figure in the process of Finance Ministry intellectual reflection on EMU in the wake of the Delors Report. He was replaced as State Secretary by Horst Köhler in January 1990 and appointed a director of the Bundesbank. Until July he was preoccupied as leader of the negotiations on the state treaty on inner-German economic, monetary, and social union. Tietmeyer quickly recognized that German unification in 1989–90 had radically changed the political parameters of EMU. At the same time, he did not change his view that precedence should be given to putting in place the foundations of a sustainable EMU, including economic convergence and political union, before any commitment to monetary union. This view meant that he had considerable reservations towards Chancellor Kohl's revival of the Adenauer dictum that German unification and European unification were two sides of the same coin.

Although Tietmeyer was observer rather than participant in the early phase of the post-Delors Report discussions in Bonn, he was able to become closely involved in the early work on the European System of Central Banks (ESCB) statute in the Committee of EC Central Bank Governors and, above all, its alternates' meeting. From July 1990 he actively re-entered EMU negotiations through his responsibility for international affairs in the Bundesbank directorate and membership of the EC Monetary Committee. Tietmeyer was a powerful advocate of central bank independence and the principle of the indivisibility of monetary policy against French attempts to weaken the governance of the Eurosystem by the ECB and to retain national central bank prerogatives. In this way he contributed much to laying down the foundations for a strong ECB, which later evolved as the main effective supranational institution in managing the post-2007 crisis.

Tietmeyer immediately attempted to regain the initiative by taking the lead in authoring a Bundesbank statement of October 1990 on EMU (for full details see Dyson and Quaglia 2010a: 443–7). As a seasoned Bonn insider, he was aware that the negotiating strategy of the federal government rested on ensuring the support of domestic public opinion by 'binding-in' the Bundesbank at every stage. This political requirement of the federal government offered Tietmeyer an opportunity to gain Bundesbank support for a list of 'indispensable, and not optional, requirements' (Bundesbank statement, October 1990: 446). Strikingly, all of the later convergence criteria were listed in the Bundesbank statement, including that 'inflation is largely stamped out in all the countries' (445). Also: 'The contractual arrangements (including binding rules and sanctions) for effective budgetary discipline in all member states must be agreed at Community level' (446). The Bundesbank statement expressly endorsed a tough German negotiating position in the impending IGC on EMU and warned against compromises. In particular, it noted that 'the transition to another stage must not be linked to deadlines fixed in advance' (446). It 'must be made dependent solely on the fulfilment of previously defined economic and economic policy conditions' (446).

Tietmeyer was frustrated by the subsequent treaty negotiations. He was active in the EC Monetary Committee and in the Committee of EC Central Bank Governors. However, he was at a distance from the IGC on EMU. The treaty negotiations involved a division of labour. Tietmeyer and the Bundesbank focused on stage three and on monetary issues, especially the statutes of the European Monetary Institute (EMI) and of the ECB in the Committee of Central Bank Governors. Here Tietmeyer was essentially negotiating on behalf of Bundesbank positions that had been defined previous to his appointment.

Nevertheless, Tietmeyer made two notable contributions. He ensured that Germany retained a veto in Council on any formal agreements on an exchange-rate system for the single currency. By this means he sought to protect the external flank of the ECB price stability mandate (Dyson and Featherstone 1999: 425–6, 445–6). In addition, Tietmeyer ensured a German veto in Council on any decision to confer on the ECB tasks in prudential supervision of banks. This contribution was of particular note in the light of later post-2012 moves to European banking union with an ECB-based Single Supervisory Mechanism. Tietmeyer's stated aim was to avert moral hazard that might result from any Treaty provision that might imply a role for the ECB in rescuing individual banks. The ECB was denied a lender-of-last-resort role (James 2012: 291–2, 313–17). Tietmeyer was keen to limit the ECB to a narrow function of price stability rather than a larger function in financial stability.

Köhler and the Finance Ministry dealt with fiscal and economic convergence issues. During the EC Monetary Committee negotiations Tietmeyer showed some impatience with what he saw as the more conciliatory approach of Köhler to the politics of EMU. He also viewed with suspicion the more conciliatory approach of some Bundesbank officials in the IGC (Dyson and Featherstone 1999: 436). His concerns about the IGC were reflected in the Bundesbank statement of 7 November 1991, one month before the Maastricht European Council (for details see Dyson and Featherstone 1999: 435–6).

Tietmeyer viewed the Maastricht Treaty negotiations as an Ordo-liberal failure. It involved a failure by the Federal Chancellor's Office and the Foreign Ministry to gain agreement on the future structure of political union in which EMU should be embedded. Tietmeyer also saw the negotiations as a Finance Ministry failure in several respects. In the IGC Köhler had conceded too much in agreeing that the EMI should have an externally appointed president and that the EMI should have its own capital. Tietmeyer was later to be intensely suspicious of the new EMI and a thorn in the side of its president and senior officials. In addition, the convergence criteria were not defined in sufficient detail and enabled too much discretion. Also, the provisions on fiscal discipline in stage three were too weak to ensure a sustainable monetary union. More seriously, Tietmeyer saw as disastrous the absence of technical-level agreement on a clear procedure for entry into stage three. The politically motivated insertion of a final date for stage three at the Maastricht European Council in December 1991 created the danger of a lack of rigour in applying the convergence criteria for entry.

Tietmeyer ensured that all these failures were highlighted in the statement of the Bundesbank council on the Maastricht decisions in February 1992 (for full details see Dyson and Quaglia 2010a: 490–1). In particular, it noted that: 'The fulfilment of the entry criteria or the convergence conditions must not be impaired by any dates set' (Bundesbank Council, February 1992: 491). Tietmeyer's imprint was clear in the criticism of the lack of agreement 'on the required parallelism with monetary union' (491). It reiterated the message that: 'Future developments in the field of political union will be of key importance for the permanent success of the monetary union' (491).

Because of their official positions, neither Tietmeyer and the Bundesbank nor the Federal Economics Ministry could lend their support to the open letter of 11 June 1992, which was signed by sixty-two German economists and published in the *Frankfurter Allgemeine Zeitung* (for details see Dyson and Quaglia 2010a: 493–4). The letter criticized the Maastricht Treaty for, amongst other things, the 'lax' convergence criteria and the 'overhasty' introduction of European monetary union. Like other officials, Tietmeyer was disposed to be defensive of a treaty in whose negotiation he had been closely involved. Nevertheless, he shared the serious concerns that were expressed in the letter.

TIETMEYER AS PRESIDENT OF THE BUNDESBANK

On 1 August 1991 Tietmeyer became vice-president, and on 1 October 1993 president of the Bundesbank. Both in his dealings with Chancellor Kohl and Finance Minister Waigel and in his public statements Tietmeyer never ceased to make clear his views on what was still economically and politically necessary to make monetary union sustainable. His relations with Alexandre Lamfalussy as president of the EMI from 1 January 1994 were not good. Tietmeyer remained suspicious of his Keynesianism, his status as an outsider appointment to the EMI, his strong European convictions, and his access to the ear of Chancellor Kohl. The Bundesbank sought to counter Lamfalussy by ensuring that the new EMI, conveniently located in Frankfurt, was dependent on its own staff.

As the final date drew closer, Tietmeyer emphasized ever more strongly the need for a strict interpretation of the convergence criteria. Within the EMI Council he argued that the widening of the band of fluctuation within the ERM in 1993 had been valuable in reducing incentives for financial-market speculation against currencies and, above all, in underlining the responsibility of Member States for their own policies and credit ratings. However, he insisted that formal ERM participation was consistent with the terms and spirit of the Treaty and remained a key convergence criterion.

With respect to fulfilment of the convergence criteria Tietmeyer was confronted with the limits of his power. Chancellor Kohl had learnt from the problems that former Chancellor Schmidt had had in 1978 over the EMS the importance of keeping the Bundesbank on side. His strategy was one of carefully binding-in the Bundesbank at each stage. Correspondingly, in January 1998 Kohl asked the Bundesbank for an independent report on convergence before the final European Council decision on which Member States qualified. He pursued two aims: to underline to the Bundesbank the legal constraints within which it operated; and to reassure an anxious German public opinion just before federal elections in 1998. Kohl could count on a politically sensitive Bundesbank president, who was not keen to contribute to the unseating of a centre-right federal government. The federal government made clear that the final decision on who qualifies was political and subjected the Bundesbank to intense political pressure in writing its report. The Bundesbank could only offer independent expert advice. In offering this advice, Tietmeyer faced the additional problem that the Bundesbank was already bound up in agreeing the EMI convergence report, which was completed before that of the Bundesbank. It would be deeply problematic for the Bundesbank to break ranks with central bank colleagues in the EMI Council as well as with the federal government. The Bundesbank convergence report expressed serious reservations about the sustainability of public finances in Belgium and Italy. However, the report concealed the true state of deep scepticism inside the Bundesbank about the proposed size and heterogeneity of the Euro Area.

At the subsequent federal cabinet meeting to agree the German final position, Tietmeyer reiterated these concerns. He also added that Germany too was vulnerable because of its lack of labour-market flexibility and the contingent liabilities in its social welfare provision (Tietmeyer 2005: 254). This point reflected the way in which during the 1990s Tietmeyer had begun to justify EMU as a disciplinary device for a post-unification Germany which had suffered a double fiscal and competitiveness shock. He was deeply concerned about German unit labour costs and fiscal policy. Later, he was to praise the wage restraint of the German trade unions and the Agenda 2010 reforms of the centre-left government of Gerhard Schröder, as well as the German debt brake of 2009, for their acceptance of the economic realities of living in a currency union.

Once stage two was launched in 1994, Tietmeyer began to actively lobby for a tightening of the Treaty's Excessive Deficit Procedure (EDP). He feared that, unless the German federal government took the initiative, the European Commission would act. The outcome would be negotiation around a text that took a lax approach to fiscal discipline. Tietmeyer advocated a rule-based approach to medium-term fiscal consolidation, with quasi-automatic sanctions. However, the Bundesbank could not assume responsibility. The negotiation of the SGP in 1995–6 was a Finance Ministry matter, though with close Bundesbank involvement (Heipertz and Verdun 2010). Tietmeyer viewed the outcome as too weak. He saw a Council regulation as inferior to a Schengen-type intergovernmental treaty, which would have given more authority to the fiscal rules. In this respect the fiscal compact treaty of 2012 was much closer to Tietmeyer's thinking. He also viewed the SGP as too dependent on political voting in Council and lacking automaticity in moving to sanctions. Later, after the SGP crisis of November 2003, when the German federal government used the Council to block the EDP, he called for an independent EU-level council of experts to name and shame governments. In 2015 the Bundesbank took up this idea once again as part of its proposal for a package of reforms to European economic governance. Tietmeyer continued to lack confidence in both the Council and the Commission.

In addition, Tietmeyer argued that delay on stage three was preferable to any indulgence of accounting tricks to qualify. He expressed severe reservations about Eurostat rulings, notably that on France Telecom, which cut the French fiscal deficit/gross domestic product (GDP) ratio by 0.5 per cent.

However, Tietmeyer's most direct engagement was a serious conflict with Kohl and Waigel in 1997. It was caused by Waigel's proposal that a revaluation of the Bundesbank's huge gold reserves should be used to reduce Germany's 1997 fiscal deficit/GDP ratio. Tietmeyer objected on the principle that the Bundesbank could not support an accounting trick to qualify for euro entry; on the basis that it would send a highly negative signal to other Member States; and on the basis that, according to the ESCB accounting rules which were being prepared by the EMI in 1997, all unrealized gains from the revaluation of gold and foreign-exchange reserves were to be credited to the revaluation account and not distributed. The Bundesbank council rejected the proposal as undermining its independence. The eventual outcome was agreement that the revaluation would not be applied to the 1997 deficit. In short, Germany would have to qualify without this accounting trick.

Tietmeyer's chief preoccupation with respect to the EMI was with its independence in the difficult technical task of preparing stage three and with ensuring that the Bundesbank legacy was firmly imprinted in the design of the ECB. Like the rest of the EMI Council, he reacted sharply to the attempt of the European Commission to take the lead in developing the changeover strategy from national currencies to the euro. Commission officials were attracted to the 'big bang' approach that was advocated by the expert group under Cees Maas in May 1995. Tietmeyer wished to keep the Commission distant from what he viewed as a technical central banking matter, stressed the need for the EMI to reassert its role in preparing stage three, and countered with the 'delayed big bang'. Eventually, the Commission deferred to the EMI changeover plan of November 1995. It envisaged a three-stage process over three years rather than the six months proposed in the Maas Report (Dyson and Quaglia 2010a: 545–51). The diplomatic skills of Lamfalussy were important in ensuring that the European Council backed the EMI.

With respect to the ECB monetary policy strategy and the Bundesbank legacy, Tietmeyer gave his backing to the ideas of the Bundesbank's chief economist, Otmar Issing. For reasons of both principle and pragmatism, it became clear that a two-pillar approach was sensible. Nevertheless, the Bundesbank placed great emphasis on retaining the monetary pillar as the 'first' pillar, alongside the economic pillar, and on rejecting formal inflation targeting (for full details see Dyson and Quaglia 2010b: 174–9). The objective was to counter the discretion built into the economic pillar of monetary policy strategy.

Tietmeyer was also active on issues that were highly symbolic for stability-orientation and that he judged as important investments of the Bundesbank in the future of the euro (Tietmeyer 2005: 263–4). He lobbied actively and successfully for the location of the ECB in Frankfurt; for the choice of its first president—Wim Duisenberg—to be determined by association with a small state with a strong historic reputation for central bank independence; and for

Issing to be appointed to the ECB directorate (Issing 2008: 29). Tietmeyer was behind the coup that led to the appointment of Duisenberg as EMI president from 1 July 1997, thus prejudging his appointment as ECB president in 1998.

However, Tietmeyer was to be disappointed by the negative signals from the European Council in May 1998 that finally launched the euro. The dispute revolved around the forceful French attempt to commit Duisenberg to a four-year rather than eight-year period of office, making way for a French candidate. At the Council, Tietmeyer objected in the strongest terms to this infringement of central bank independence as incompatible with relevant Treaty provisions. Though the attempt was formally rebuffed, Tietmeyer saw it as a signal from the very start that German vigilance would be required. This event adversely affected the position of the first ECB president, with the media interpreting it as a victory for the French government.

CONTRIBUTION AND LEGACY: DID TIETMEYER GET THE FOUNDATIONS RIGHT?

From Tietmeyer's Ordo-liberal perspective, the Maastricht architecture of EMU was very imperfect. The unfolding Euro Area crises from 2007 were testament to the prescience of Tietmeyer's diagnosis of the problems in the Maastricht construction of EMU. It lacked the supportive edifice of a comprehensive European political union, including a European economic government that had the requisite authority to strengthen global competitiveness and to ensure fiscal discipline. The Euro Area fiscal compact treaty of 2012 could be seen as a belated political recognition that Tietmeyer had been right. Similarly, the Franco-German proposal of May 2013 for new contractual arrangements in structural reforms and the Bundesbank proposal of 2015 for a new independent authority to take over the monitoring and surveillance functions of the European Commission were consistent with Tietmeyer's thinking. However, neither proposal made early headway. Above all, Tietmeyer seemed right in his view that lax treaty provisions and their lax interpretation had led to an over-large and heterogeneous Euro Area in terms of sheer numbers and sheer diversity of economic development, economic structures, and political cultures.

At the same time, key aspects of Euro Area crisis management sat uncomfortably alongside Tietmeyer's Ordo-liberal views. The problem of fit was most notable with respect to the ECB's commitment to interventions in the sovereign bond markets, through the Securities Markets Programme (SMP) in May 2010, the Outright Monetary Transactions (OMT) Programme in September 2012, and quantitative easing (QE) from early 2015. The OMT was designed to safeguard an appropriate monetary transmission and the singleness of the monetary policy in the Euro Area through the purchases of Euro Area government bonds in the secondary markets based on strict conditionality. However, for Ordo-liberals, it involved the blurring of the boundaries between monetary and fiscal policy. Moreover, through its non-standard monetary policy measures, especially in December 2011, the ECB had evolved a lender-of-last-resort role for the banking system. This development was in opposition to Tietmeyer's long-expressed fears of moral hazard (cf. James 2012: 313–17). For Ordo-liberals like Tietmeyer these monetary policy developments were a reminder of the need for eternal vigilance in protecting foundational principles of EMU. Adherence to these principles involved opposition to behind-the-scenes shifts towards a 'transfer union' and a mutual insurance union.

Overall, assessment of the success of Tietmeyer, and of the Ordo-liberalism that he espoused, needs to be contextualized and differentiated. In the first place, Tietmeyer was not an original Ordo liberal thinker like Müller-Armack. His contribution resided in applying established Ordo-liberal principles to EMU, not in 'modernizing' Ordo-liberalism in the framework of monetary union. His argumentative power derived from the logical coherence of this body of theory but, to Keynesian critics, remained narrowly focused.

Second, Tietmeyer was the beneficiary of favourable structural conditions. Aided by the 'stag-flation' of the 1970s, the combination of higher inflation with rising unemployment, Keynesian thinking had been displaced by monetarism and neo-classical theory. In short, mainstream international economics had moved closer towards German Ordo-liberal thinking. German arguments gained a greater international authority. In addition, Tietmeyer benefited from the most important bargaining resource of Germany: the indispensability of German involvement and support for the credibility of any agreement to move towards EMU. The combination of Germany's systemic significance with her creditworthiness, founded on her superior reputation for economic and monetary stability, ensured disproportionate influence for negotiators like Tietmeyer. Their capacity to retain influence over how Euro Area problems were defined and acted on depended on their association with the best performing economy in the EU and the Euro Area.

In other words, Ordo-liberalism's success and Tietmeyer's contribution and legacy were historically contingent on their fit with mainstream international economic thought and with the performance of the German economy. They were a function of this structural context of German semi-hegemonic power over economic and monetary thinking in Europe. Power rather than respect for the dictates of universal 'economic truth' proved decisive in resolving the problem of framing the Maastricht economic constitution.

Tietmeyer clearly recognized that a key foundation of a sustainable EMU was Germany's continuing status as the key EU performer. It required a combination of domestic economic reforms and tough EU-level negotiating to ensure that it remained the model. Above all, it meant ensuring that domestic German economic policy practice deviated as little as possible from Ordo-liberal principles. During the 1990s this insight led him to reframe EMU more positively as an essential disciplinary device for a Germany that itself required an overdue Ordo-liberal renaissance. It also led him to condemn the German violation of the SGP in November 2003 and the SGP reform of 2005 and, on retirement, to take on a senior position in the New Social Market Initiative.

Tietmeyer's contribution to the architecture of EMU reflected some internal and unresolved tensions within Ordo-liberalism. Part of the reason for Tietmeyer's status as an architect of the euro stemmed from the way in which Ordo-liberal principles provided coherence and rigour in his approach to EMU. He represented a powerful force of economic logic. However, at the heart of Ordo-liberalism was a tension between whether it was a culturally specific economic order, the product of German historical experience in the Weimar period and the Third Reich, or an ideal-type of economic order with universal validity. This tension had profound implications for whether the German model could be exported to the EU. Eucken (1950) had rejected the relativism of the German Historical School of economics, with its emphasis on 'stages' and 'styles' of economic development, in favour of an ideal-typical model. In contrast, Müller-Armack helped keep a strain of historical sociology alive in Ordo-liberal thinking with his emphasis on 'styles'. This tension had enormous implications for what German policy on EMU could hope to deliver. It was a tension that did not seem to be resolved in Tietmeyer's own thinking. Designing a sustainable EMU continued to be bedevilled by an acute problem of whether it would prove possible to overcome conflicting macroeconomic traditions and cultures and establish trust in a set of shared principles.

The post-2007 crises and this need for trust based on shared principles posed some fundamental questions about the limitations in Tietmeyer's approach. The Ordo-liberal stress on individual Member State responsibility overlooked questions of capability and the role of the EU and its Member States in helping to strengthen this capability. Seen in this way, solidarity could not just be limited to enforcing compliance with rules, especially if they risked locking a Member State into a vicious circle of depression. It required supportive measures to foster social and economic cohesion and ease the burden of fiscal and economic adjustment. Moreover, a preoccupation with 'order' neglected the importance of the political process in ensuring the values of inclusivity and mutual respect for differences in economic structures in the governance of the Euro Area. Neglecting this question risked isolating Germany as seeking to 'colonize' the EU rather than as a bridge-builder and reconciler.

Tietmeyer's emphasis on firm economic and political foundations for EMU begged two questions: which foundations, and how secure must they be?

Tietmeyer was correct in thinking that a single currency—critically on the back of the emerging single European market in financial services—would spur the integration of money and financial markets. However, he did not identify European banking union as a precondition or as part of the 'effective parallelism' that he espoused. In its statement of October 1990 on EMU, the Bundesbank made no reference to a single banking supervisory mechanism, let alone to a bank resolution mechanism. Equally, the insurance sector was overlooked. Indeed, Tietmeyer did everything he could to dilute the role of the Eurosystem in banking supervision and financial market stability when the Committee of EC Central Bank Governors drafted the ESCB Statute. The IGC diluted further the draft ESCB Statute provisions. In the subsequent consultation of the Committee of Governors, he did his best to ensure a weak and anodyne opinion.

This failure of architecture of the euro stemmed from a problem within Ordo-liberalism: the neglect of financial markets, their highly volatile and potentially destabilizing character, and their implications for financial and economic stability. Tietmeyer was less prescient than Lamfalussy in this regard. There was also a factor of institutional self-interest behind this failure. Once it was faced with loss of its classic monetary policy function, and attendant losses of both jobs and prestige, the Bundesbank jealously guarded, and sought to expand, its role in banking supervision. There had been a broad consensus within the Committee of EC Central Bank Governors that the Eurosystem needed to be able to act as lender-of-last-resort. At the same time, there was recognition of the need to avert a moral hazard problem.

In negotiations Tietmeyer focused on the moral hazard issue to resist the notion that the ECB should assume the traditional central bank function of safeguarding financial stability and acting as 'lender-of-last-resort' to the banking system (James 2012: 317). Tietmeyer successfully lobbied for a Treaty provision that limited the ECB to the 'task'—not the 'objective'—of contributing to the smooth conduct of policies pursued by the competent authorities relating to prudential supervision and the stability of the financial system. The outcome was the lack of precise language in the Treaty and the ESCB Statute. Neglect of this pillar in the foundational arrangements of EMU played a central role in the unfolding Euro Area crises. Fear of moral hazard triumphed over arming the ECB with the conventional weaponry of a central bank. For Tietmeyer, banking supervision was a responsibility of Member State finance ministries, not of central banks. However, it was difficult to conceal the role of vested interests in his argument, a role that Ordo-liberalism was supposed to critique.

Tietmeyer also gave little attention to the question of how best to ensure independence, professionalism, and integrity in European statistical services. Reliable data were fundamental to taking decisions about compliance with convergence criteria for euro entry and about compliance with the SGP. Italy and, above all, Greece suggested the naïvety of the assumption that such data were reliable.

Tietmeyer was more prescient on fiscal union, stressing the vital importance of a framework of firm, clear rules with quasi-automatic sanctions. However, in an interview in 2012 reflecting on the Euro Area crises, former Bundesbank president Helmut Schlesinger commented that in 1990–1 German negotiators had been naïve in assuming that commitments would be honoured and that state insolvency was not a possibility. Like other Ordo-liberals at the time, Tietmeyer failed to look beyond rules to questions of what the historical record revealed about state willingness and state capacity to comply (Dyson 2014). The tortured path of the Greek crisis from 2009 highlighted this failure.

In the case of state insolvency, Tietmeyer's views on debt restructuring—another instrument that was neglected in designing the foundation of EMU—can be inferred from his earlier extremely cautious and reserved position on debt forgiveness for highly indebted poor countries. He argued that it should be limited and conditional on the fulfilment of reform commitments. Reform efforts must be made in advance. He also cautioned that it was far from certain that debt forgiveness would actually benefit those most in need (Tietmeyer 1999: 111–26). This viewpoint was later mirrored in German views about the sequencing of any debt restructuring in dealing with the Greek crisis: it should follow the delivery of reforms. There should be 'prior actions' by the Greek government.

Tietmeyer was also prescient in emphasizing the importance of a fully functioning single European market to facilitate and speed economic adjustment. Again, however, greater dependence on cross-national financial markets and their implications for the institutional foundations of EMU had been ignored. Moreover, Germany proved slow to embrace a single European market in services. This mattered as services became more important within the economic structure, reducing the value of the single market which was more developed in product markets. The gap between Ordo-liberal theory and German domestic practice of economic policy continued to lay German negotiators open to charges of hypocrisy.

Equally, there were questions about the adequacy of both the convergence criteria and about the specificity of Tietmeyer's thinking about comprehensive political union. On political union, he could argue that the responsibility lay with the Federal Foreign Ministry and the Chancellor's Office. Any failures were theirs. On the convergence criteria, Tietmeyer could argue that ultimately their interpretation and application was a matter for the political authorities. Nevertheless, the question remains whether the technical-level negotiations on the convergence criteria produced a framework that could be used to effectively assess sustainability. The European Commission and the EMI were asked only to 'take account' of external imbalances and of the development of unit labour costs. The timeframe of assessment was a mere two years. Convergence could prove contingent, fragile, and reversible. The outcome was a much larger Euro Area membership of eleven Member States in 1999 than the five/six that Tietmeyer had expected. It was followed by the highly problematic Greek entry, which post-dated his presidency of the Bundesbank.

EU enlargement and the enlarging Euro Area membership were further sources of problems for Tietmeyer's approach. The Werner Report had been negotiated in an EEC of six Member States; the Delors Report in an EC of twelve Member States; and the euro launched in an EU of fifteen. By 2015 the EU had twenty-eight Member States and more Member States in the Euro Area (nineteen) than in the EU as a whole when it was launched. EU enlargement, above all in 2004, and the greater diversity in economic development and economic structure raised the question of whether Tietmeyer's earlier belief in European political union remained feasible. The implication that he drew was that the Euro Area had to rely on a combination of tough fiscal controls and the more careful selection of Member States. However, the question was whether—as Tietmeyer had feared—the 'genie was already out of the bottle', not least because of the past lack of careful selection of Member States. Another question that he did not address was whether a sustainable monetary union would have to diminish in size to a smaller, more homogeneous 'core' Euro Area and whether this was feasible in an orderly manner.

From 2008, banking and sovereign debt crisis management drew attention to the limits to the power of the Ordo-liberal economic expert. It exposed the discomfort of others with this power, with how it was used, and with its implications for attitudes to Germany. Germany risked negative stereotyping as arrogant and bullying and subsequent isolation. Its policy-makers were confronted with the fundamental historical tension between the sense of German moral responsibility for fostering peace and prosperity in Europe through widening and deepening integration and the protection of the tried-and-tested Ordo-liberal principles of economic 'good' governance. By 2012 this tension had spilled over into a domestic 'war' of economic manifestos between 'fundamentalist' Ordo-liberals and other academic economists over the ECB's operations and over European banking union (on which see Dyson forthcoming). Notably, Tietmeyer, ever the good public servant, remained aloof from this new domestic divide about German Ordo-liberalism.

Fast-evolving Euro Area crises reopened debates that Tietmeyer had hoped to close in negotiating EMU. They revealed the lack of consensus at EU expert as well as political levels about various issues and the continuing resilience of neo-Keynesian critiques of the Maastricht design of EMU. At their heart were different assessments of the benefits and costs of ceding sovereignty, above all in fiscal and economic policies, and about the purpose for which sovereignty should be used. There was a lack of consensus about the relative value of top-down fiscal rules and of endowing Member State governments with fiscal discretion, above all to cope with painful structural reforms and to safeguard social nets of support. Crisis management also brought back onto the agenda other issues, like the proper functions of the ECB, above all in financial stability, and building a European-level anti-cyclical fiscal capacity.

In particular, Euro Area crisis exposed the problematic relationship of Ordo-liberal thought to economic growth. It stressed the long-term requirements for sustainable economic growth and the risk that emphasis on short-term cyclical stabilization would deter structural change. Keynesians argued that the combination of fiscal contraction with structural reforms could inflict massive long-term political as well as economic damage on market economies. Ordo-liberalism also contrasted with earlier German theorists of historical and institutional economics, like Lorenz von Stein and Adolph Wagner, who had espoused the value of the developmental or entrepreneurial state in harnessing fundamental science-based innovation that is too uncertain and long-term for private capital (Dyson 2014). In short, public debt to finance infrastructure investment could be a force for good in contexts of high state capacity and sound public-sector management.

Moreover, Ordo-liberalism could be criticized for ignoring Keynesian insights into the importance of managing aggregate demand in the Euro Area by reference to the overall fiscal stance and of shared adjustment of creditor and debtor states to excessive financial and trade imbalances. There was a serious danger that the institutional arrangements and policies of the Euro Area could tip Europe into long-term stagnation or even outright deflation, exacerbating unemployment, debt burdens, and fiscal problems. National elections, the European Parliament elections of 2014, and the progress of the Greek crisis suggested that Euro Area policies were contributing to a lessening of trust in European integration and dangers of destabilizing political contagion across borders. The risk of a major contradiction and clash between what Ordo-liberals deemed desirable and necessary for Europe and what publics would accept had grown. It threatened a disorderly unravelling of the Euro Area, with untold consequences for Europe and the wider world.

In the final analysis, Tietmeyer did not consider the question of whether the Euro Area needed an independent executive capacity for discretionary action in supreme emergency when its coherence and integrity was threatened (Dyson 2012). Logically, as an exponent of the no-bail-out principle, he could not be expected to do so. The Euro Area membership should adjust to the governing principles and policies of the Maastricht Treaty, not the reverse. Nevertheless, the question remains of whether the principle of irreversibility in creating monetary union, which had been enshrined in the Maastricht Treaty, should also apply in safeguarding its coherence and integrity. The OMT programme and QE were moves in this direction and suggested a departure from founding Ordo-liberal principles, notably the separation of fiscal and monetary policies. In contrast, Ordo-liberals emphasized either the tougher application of the rules (like Tietmeyer) or reliance on the capacity of financial markets to sanction states and hasten overdue structural reforms (like Issing). Issing (2013) stressed the importance of promoting institutional competition as opposed to policy centralization in the EU and the Euro Area.

Creating a supreme emergency capacity stood in sharp contrast to the kind of Ordo-liberalism represented by Tietmeyer. However, there were huge economic and political risks in enabling financial markets to test the Euro Area to destruction. Former US Treasury Secretary Tim Geithner (2014) argued that the 'fundamentalist Ayatollahs of moral hazard' risked the destruction of economic and financial stability.

The fundamental question was whether EMU could survive and prosper on the basis of Ordo-liberal economic logic. Helmut Schmidt (1996) had singled out for criticism Tietmeyer's lack of strategic acumen and the risk that pursuit of his logic would drive Germany into isolation. Notably, Issing (2013) concluded that the greatest danger facing the Euro Area was political: the spreading belief across Member States that they were suffering under a 'Teutonic yoke'. This fear was to lead Chancellor Angela Merkel to give priority to managing Euro Area crises, above all the Greek crisis, so as to avert this danger of German isolation and political stereotyping. Above all, every effort must be made to ensure that Germany did not take the blame for any euro exit.

8

Karl-Otto Pöhl

The Pole Position

Harold James

It may seem strange to include someone who often articulated fierce criticism of the project of establishing the single currency in a book on 'architects of the euro': but that is the perverse way history often works. Karl-Otto Pöhl played an important role in designing and creating the euro, even though he was never really enthusiastic about the single currency, and indeed in the last phase of his public-sector career became harshly critical. His most obvious contributions lie simply in his agreement to the Delors Committee report (ensuring that the report was unanimous), and then in the design of a European Central Bank (ECB) in which the primary mandate was the price stability that was at the heart of German monetary thought.

The fact that the currency was decisively designed by a non-believer is telling. On the one hand, the monetary union could not simply have been conceived and designed and implemented by federalist visionaries such as Jacques Delors, because there was never any significant popular or political support that would allow federalism to be translated into a realistic programme. On the other hand, the project could not really have been devised by a true believer in German Ordo-liberalism, as there were too many irregularities to subsume in a world of strict rules. Pöhl saw the process in which he and his fellow central bankers were engaged as fundamentally an extension or intensification of the normal mechanisms of central bank cooperation. In short, he lived in the world of messy compromises.

The decisive but also often indirect ways in which Pöhl shaped the process illustrate the Hegelian principle of the 'cunning of reason' (*List der Vernunft*). In the first place, it was Pöhl's aggressive and non-cooperative monetary policy-making stance at the Bundesbank that convinced other—in particular French—European central bankers that they needed to find an institutional mechanism to control Germany's capacity for an independent monetary policy that ignored the policy needs of its neighbours. This interpretation was sketched out by the British Chancellor of the Exchequer, Nigel Lawson, who saw the Bundesbank president as playing a decisive role in provoking a bitter and fateful backlash against German monetary hegemony: 'It was the way in which Pöhl openly revelled in his role, via the EMS, of the ruler of Europe's monetary affairs and arbiter of its destiny...that the French... found so intolerable that they were prepared to sacrifice their own national independence in order to see the Bundesbank abolished' (Lawson 1992: 662–3).

But there were also deeper, more structural reasons, intrinsic to the workings of the European Exchange Rate Mechanism (ERM), that ensured that in the 1980s debate increasingly centred around the role of the Bundesbank. Most fundamentally, Pöhl was the head of what was obviously the most successful, and the most independent, central bank in the world, and one which was increasingly seen as a model for emulation elsewhere (including, and especially, in France, where the issue of central bank independence was highly controversial politically). In the negotiations about monetary union, he successfully set out a vision of a purist Bundesbank-style central bank that would not pollute its primary commitment to monetary stability by embarking on financial supervision; and he insisted on the indivisibility of monetary policy in the transitional stage two of the move to monetary union. A mixture of German monetary policy intransigence and German institutional success thus set the stage for the institutional shape of the new ECB.

Second, the critical document that laid out the blueprint for monetary union was the 1989 Delors Report, and Pöhl played a decisive role in the work of the committee that crafted it. He was a firm proponent of the need for a budgetary rule to accompany monetary union, and indeed was the first in the discussions around the committee to assert the 3 per cent deficit criterion that became such an important and controversial part of the Maastricht convergence criteria and then of the Stability and Growth Pact (SGP). The estimate of the 3 per cent came from the experience of France in the early 1980s, when Jacques Delors had fought as Finance Minister to keep France in the European Monetary System (EMS) and in the European Community. It was important that this was a unanimously endorsed document, and that the UK representative, Bank of England Governor Robert ('Robin') Leigh-Pemberton could sign. When the Delors Committee was established, Margaret Thatcher believed that it would never produce an endorsement of Delors' vision, as Pöhl (whom she found a much more intellectually sympathetic figure than Chancellor Helmut Kohl) could be relied on to block agreement. She told Leigh-Pemberton that he could endorse anything that the Bundesbank president agreed to—and she was quite furious when he took her at her word.

Later, Pöhl seemed to backpedal and complained that the report was 'a confused piece of work. There were some wild ideas in it' (Marsh 2009: 123).

But—and here is another decisive contribution—he still worked hard at implementing the committee's programme in practice, and produced an institutionally viable solution which deliberately reproduced at the European level many of the features of the Bundesbank.

Pöhl was not an easy man to deal with, and was prone to volcanic outbursts, especially in international negotiations. In Chapter 7, Kenneth Dyson refers to Hans Tietmeyer (another president of the Bundesbank) as having a 'distinctively combative style' in negotiations. Both Pöhl and Tietmeyer were outsiders to the Bundesbank, and their personalities were indeed different from those of many Bundesbank insiders. Pöhl had grown up intellectually under the influence of Karl Schiller and Helmut Schmidt, both of whom had a strong sense of superiority that often was interpreted as arrogance. Two other long-serving and influential Bundesbank officials, Otmar Emminger and Helmut Schlesinger, were much more fundamentally polite, and Schlesinger in particular had an exquisitely gentlemanly quality. But that did not make them easy negotiators either, and in fact Emminger and Schlesinger were both more dogmatic and less flexible as negotiators. Pöhl's flexibility and his occasionally powerful intellect gave him enormous tactical advantages, which he used to make sure that the Bundesbank kept winning battle after battle in the European negotiations. But his was fundamentally the lazy intellect of a permanently tanned *bon viveur*—not the honed mind of a Bundesbank insider. The tactical superiority did not amount to an overall strategy, and under Pöhl the Bundesbank in the end won the battles but lost the war over Europe's money.

CONSTRUCTING THE EMS

Pöhl was not an obvious central banker. Born on 1 December 1929, just months after the world's most famous stock market crash, he had studied economics at Göttingen, had worked at the Munich economic think-tank Information und Forschung (Ifo) from 1957 to 1961 and then in a variety of journalistic positions and for a brief time in 1968–9 with the Bundesverband deutscher Banken, a bank pressure lobby, until Karl Schiller brought him into government as a press adviser in 1970. At the age of nineteen, he had joined the Social Democratic Party (SPD), and seemed an ideal figure to represent the new German centre-left government after 1969.

There was something intellectually incoherent about his position—he referred to his two models for *Ordnungspolitik* (the ordering of the institutional framework) as John Maynard Keynes and the economically liberal (and politically Christian Democratic) German economist and minister Ludwig Erhard. But incoherence was exactly the impression of adding a little Anglo-Saxon left-liberal touch to the German tradition of the 'economic miracle' (*Wirtschaftswunder*) that the federal government under Chancellor Willy Brandt wished to convey. Most German economists and policy-makers interpreted the Keynesian tradition as antithetic to the old Ordo-liberalism: the German view of economics upheld a principle of individual responsibility and liability that would limit state activism, while the French and the Keynesians wanted an active state. Where Ordo-liberalism emphasized rules, the Keynesian tradition saw policy possibilities.

When in July 1972 Helmut Schmidt took over Schiller's 'superministry' portfolio at the Finance and Economics Ministry, Pöhl stayed on, and was promoted to the senior position in the Finance Ministry, State Secretary. Subsequently, in 1977, Pöhl had been appointed vice-president of the Bundesbank by Schmidt (now the Federal Chancellor) as a future replacement for the veteran Bundesbank insider Otmar Emminger, who was due to retire in 1980. Like previous German chancellors, Schmidt had found dealing with the independent Bundesbank frustrating, and wanted to have someone who thought along his lines as a sympathetic presence in Frankfurt. Who would be more suitable than his clever and loquacious former press spokesman and then state secretary in the Finance Ministry and the German Sherpa for the G5 summits? Schmidt believed that, unlike the Bundesbank traditionalists, Pöhl would fully understand the international framework within which German monetary action needed to occur. According to Schmidt, Pöhl 'had a broader framework than Emminger and Schlesinger [the chief economist of the Bundesbank]. He had one great advantage over these people: he came from the outside, and that means his yardsticks, his standards had not been set by the wallpaper within the Bundesbank' (Marsh 2009: 78). Schmidt did not want to channel his schemes through the deeply sceptical Bundesbank; and he preferred to present the Bundesbank with a fait accompli. In Schmidt's thinking, the best approach for the federal government was to make an end run around the technocrats. First, he tried to avoid discussing his plans with the Bundesbank; and then he had his own man as the number-two person in the Frankfurt bank.

In practice, however, the appointment of Pöhl soon seemed to recall the famous story of the English King Henry II who appointed his friend and minister, Thomas à Becket, as Archbishop of Canterbury when he was locked in a conflict with the English church. Like Becket, Pöhl very quickly reproduced the priorities of his new institution. As he put it, 'Schmidt may have had the view that, once I was on the Bundesbank Council, I would serve him by being respectful of the Government. That turned out not to be the case' (Marsh 2009: 78). Or, as he noted in relation to Chancellor Kohl's deliberations over economic union with the German Democratic Republic (GDR), 'I always advise politicians to consult the Bundesbank first' (*Die Zeit* 1992). On one occasion, he talked about the Bundesbank as 'a kind of state within the state—an economic policy counterweight to the government' (*Die Zeit* 1992). He had a rather condescending attitude to Kohl, as a provincial figure who might well be a master of the art of party political intrigue, but who failed to understand economic logic.

Pöhl had always had a rather ambiguous relationship to efforts at European monetary integration. The tension was evident in his first years as a central banker, when he had to think about the implications of the joint initiative of Helmut Schmidt and French President Valéry Giscard d'Estaing to create a scaled-down version of the Bretton Woods system in the European context: the EMS. He quickly wrote to Schmidt to inform him that the Bundesbank's directorate had discussed the question of a 'European contribution to solve the problem of the dollar', but that 'the views of my colleagues are known to you. They continue to be sceptical and critical of such an initiative.'[1] Within the Bundesbank, Pöhl circulated a memorandum on European currency integration, summarizing the current state of play. According to this account, the newly proposed coordination of central banks did not correspond to the European Economic Community (EEC) Council decision of 22 March 1971, which had laid out the institutional basis for European central bank cooperation. The new initiatives being discussed were aimed at making the existing European Unit of Account (EUA) into a new international reserve currency (and renaming it as the ECU, or European Currency Unit, a name that recalled an ancient French coin), as well as at providing financing for currency interventions by non-'snake' members. The Bundesbank paper argued that these suggestions were not 'well thought out' as there were no existing attractive instruments for the holding of EUAs; but also that an attractive ECU would provide competition for the dollar and might embarrass Europeans by producing a further decline in the dollar exchange rate; and, if another scenario should materialize, a weak ECU would necessarily focus even more unwelcome attention on the D-Mark as an investment currency.[2]

The Schmidt–Giscard European initiative was the focus of the Bundesbank Council meeting of 13 July 1978, when Emminger reported on his participation in the previous day's federal government cabinet discussion. Emminger stated that—like the political leaders—he wanted a durable solution that would not produce new currency crises every few years. He worried about the risk that some members of the new currency arrangement would maintain unrealistic and damaging exchange rates that would set off speculative movements and might also pose an inflationary danger; about the quantity of international credit that would be required to make the scheme work; and

[1] Historisches Archiv der Deutschen Bundesbank (HADB), N2/264, Pöhl to Schmidt, 21 March 1978.

[2] HADB, N2/K26 (13), 14 April 1978, Karl-Otto Pöhl to members of Central Bank Council, with memorandum by Peter Christian Schlüter.

about a possible undermining of the Bundesbank's monetary policy through commitments to interventions. In the discussion of the report, Pöhl was critical of the implications posed by a system based on exchange rates fixed against a unit of account. In the final summing up, Emminger reasserted that 'the final responsibility in currency issues lies with the Federal Government, but the law gives the Bundesbank the duty to advise in the determination of policy'.[3]

Pöhl also criticized the basket system as a means of forcing the Bundesbank to make large-scale interventions. The Bundesbank council then voted a resolution emphasizing the risk of including high-inflation countries in any new scheme; criticizing the basket system as reflecting average inflation rates and hence pushing up Community expectations of inflation; and emphasizing the danger that the Bundesbank would lose monetary control.[4]

The criticism before the EMS started up was straightforward compared to Pöhl's campaign, once he was number one at the Bundesbank, to eviscerate the EMS by removing the main institutional element that differentiated it from the European currency snake arrangement of the 1970s, in which France had participated but which it had been forced to leave twice. That innovation had been the proposal for a European Monetary Fund (EMF), analogous to the International Monetary Fund (IMF) on the global stage that had been a product of the fundamental monetary redesign at the 1944 Bretton Woods conference. The absence of an EMF limited the extent of the financial contributions of members; but also—as it proved—made it much harder to handle severe crises as in 1992–3 (Buiter et al. 1998).

In January 1980, Pöhl participated for the first time in the Committee of EEC Central Bank Governors in his new function as president of the Bundesbank. He immediately took a much more critical and confrontational tone than was customary in the conventionally rather polite climate of the central bankers' meeting. He was impatient about the discussion of the 'evolutionary' development of an EMF, and suggested that the present system of the EMS was working adequately, and that the best way of improving it was to secure the participation of those countries that were presently outside the EMS. He also emphatically reasserted the German position that any legal framework that permitted the Council to give instructions to the EMF would be incompatible with German law and would require a revision of the Bundesbank law. Pöhl also made very clear his belief that it would be impossible to submit all monetary policy decisions to a preliminary discussion in the Committee of Governors. In the case of the Bundesbank, he emphasized that the president

[3] HADB, B330/14740, 512 meeting of Zentralbankrat (Central Bank Council: henceforth ZBR), 13 July 1978.

[4] HADB, ZBR 515, 7 September 1978: Stellungnahme des Zentralbankrats der Deutschen Bundesbank zu den Vorschlägen für ein europäisches Währungssystem.

could not commit the central bank council to a particular course of action.[5] The EMF in particular would require, in his view, parliamentary approval, a point that had already been made by Emminger in the setting of the Bundesbank council in November 1979. For Pöhl, there were three possibilities: what he termed a 'minimal solution' of keeping existing institutions and simply renaming the European Monetary Cooperation Fund (EMCF) as the EMF; a regional fund as a governmental institution which would control medium-term financial resources within the EEC; and third, the development of the EMCF into a common central banking system. He sometimes expressed a preference for the third, and most radical of these solutions, as he claimed it corresponded most precisely with the Bremen and Brussels European Council decisions. But this seemed more of an academic argument than a policy proposal. It was not the first or last time a theoretically convincing case for an ambitious programme was put forward as a way of blocking practical and realizable small-scale steps. After discussion in the Bundesbank council, Pöhl came to the conclusion that the functioning of the system did not really require the invention of a special new fund.[6]

Pöhl had thus succeeded in standing the original EMS concept—as he put it—'on its head' (*Die Zeit* 1992). The strongest European currency, the D-Mark, became the undisputed standard of the system; and there was no automatic or quasi-automatic equivalent to the IMF that could enforce from a position of superior authority the rules of the monetary order.

CORNER SOLUTIONS

Intellectually, the EMS was a partial, and perhaps an incoherent, solution to the currency coordination issue. Margaret Thatcher's adviser Sir Alan Walters later referred to it as 'half-baked'. The theory of exchange rates on which this comment was based became known as the 'corner' theory later in the 1990s: the extreme solutions of completely and freely floating currencies or a permanently locked currency in the form of a monetary union are more robust and hence preferable as institutional design: they alone were not vulnerable to speculative attack from the increasingly large capital markets.

The vulnerability became clear in the early 1980s, after the victory of the socialist candidate, François Mitterrand, in the French presidential election. It was not only that Mitterrand's fiscal policy was incompatible with EMS membership; it also seemed that his commitment to the system which he

[5] EEC Committee of Central Bank Governors, Meeting 141, Basel, 8 January 1980.
[6] HADB, ZBR of 17 January 1980.

viewed as the intellectual construct of his rival and predecessor as president, Giscard d'Estaing, was weak.

The European Commission worried that François Mitterrand's left-wing government would reject the EMS. Something in consequence needed to be done in order to appeal to French socialists. As a result, the Commission developed a series of initiatives for strengthening the system, involving in particular a greater use of the ECU, but also a new surveillance process that would use 'a set of comparative indicators' and would determine objectives by 'common agreement'.[7] The technical changes were designed in part as a political manoeuvre to win over the new French government, though there had been some Commission discussion of ways of making the ECU into a regional version of the IMF Special Drawing Rights (SDR) even before the French elections.[8] The proposals for greater use of the ECU inevitably attracted criticism from the Bundesbank. In the Bundesbank council, critics of the 1978–9 agreements took a much tougher line, arguing that the aims of the EMS had not been achieved and were endangering the stability policy of the Bundesbank, and that the European system was plagued by a fundamental lack of consensus on basic assumptions and priorities.[9] In consequence, in the lead-up to the Council of Finance Ministers (ECOFIN) meeting at which the EMS was to be discussed, Pöhl wrote to Chancellor Schmidt to argue that the Commission's proposals would weaken discipline in the system.[10]

In the wake of the debate between the Commission and the Bundesbank, a surprising idea was floated. When the Italian economist and director-general of Economic and Financial Affairs at the Commission, Tommaso Padoa-Schioppa, visited Pöhl in his Frankfurt office on 1 March 1982, the Bundesbank president not only explained his opposition to further institutionalization of the EMS, but also laid out his position (that he had also explained in the Bundesbank council) that intellectually the better solution would be a complete monetary union. Earlier, Padoa-Schioppa had explained in a letter to Pöhl that: 'To couple the defence of monetary orthodoxy with that of the institutional status quo may lead to defeat in terms of both monetary stability and independence. Your "monetary constitution" has been too successful on the fight for stability. It will now either become the monetary constitution for Europe or be contaminated by the sins of the others. That is, by the way, a very "deutsches Schicksal" [German fate].'[11] The germ of the idea of a new push for monetary union thus

[7] HADB, B330/26942, 23 February 1982, Tommaso Padoa-Schioppa to members of EC Monetary Committee, 'EMS Non-Paper'.

[8] HADB, B330/14554, 4 December 980: Betr. Fortsetzung der EWS-Diskussion; 1 December 1980 Commission papers: Fundamental Questions in Connection with the Institutional Phases of the EMS.

[9] HADB, ZBR 592, 5 November 1981.

[10] HADB, N4/51, 9 March 1982, Pöhl to Schmidt.

[11] HADB, B330/26941, 27 May 1981, Tommaso Padoa-Schioppa to Pöhl.

lay in the very unsatisfactory early experience of the EMS. The embrace of what was a completely coherent corner solution was thus hinted at, at the very early moment when Mitterrand had pushed the EMS into its first major political as well as financial crisis.

THE DELORS COMMITTEE

The Bundesbank always worried that any new wave of European integration might be driven unilaterally from the monetary side, without any economic convergence. The 1986 Single European Act contained no new initiatives in non-monetary areas, but pushed the capital liberalization issue, and also included an odd subheading in Article 20 which referred explicitly (but without any follow-up in the text) to economic and monetary union. The oddity of a subheading that stood on its own was attributed by some to the machinations of German Foreign Minister Hans-Dieter Genscher. Later Delors proudly referred to this reference as a 'little white pebble' which he had carefully and deliberately thrown on the ground, like Petit Poucet in the fairy story, in order to show a way out of the maze (Delors 2004: 221; Grant 1994: 74).

The most decisive push for a European solution came as a result of failures to tackle a global coordination problem. When the dollar was soaring in the mid-1980s, when American manufacturing was threatened and when there appeared to be the possibility of a protectionist backlash, the finance ministers of the major industrial countries pushed for an exchange-rate agreement. The target zone discussion had proceeded largely without central banks, and only the powerful chair of the Federal Reserve System, Paul Volcker, had been informed in advance of the 1985 Plaza meeting (Boughton 2001: 206–9). At the Plaza there was no discussion of interest-rate policy or of monetary policy: in fact, as Barry Eichengreen (1996: 151) points out, there was a complete lack of 'the web of interlocking agreements needed to lock in policy adjustments'. At the G7 finance ministers Louvre meeting in 1987 they agreed to lock their exchange rates into a system of target zones.

The Bundesbank was deeply suspicious of the whole exercise. Pöhl explained that it would be a mistake to fix exchange-rate targets, as such targets would need to be defended.[12] In 1985 Pöhl had described the notion of target zones, which was relentlessly advocated in Washington by the Institute of International Economics, as 'twenty years too late'. Pöhl did not believe that there had been any agreement on target zones or pegging.[13] At the Louvre meeting, he had simply said: 'Let's leave everything open and wait and see how

[12] HADB, ZBR 686, 26 September 1985.
[13] HADB, ZBR 737, 5 November 1987.

the market responds' (Funabashi 1988: 183; Henning 1994). The Bundesbank believed that Treasury Secretary James Baker had consulted too much with the German Finance Minister, Gerhard Stoltenberg, and with his State Secretary, Hans Tietmeyer, and had ignored the legally guaranteed position of the German central bank. But Pöhl did agree to participate in the interventions to bring down the dollar, while insisting that other central banks should take the lead in such interventions.

In January 1987, at the Committee of EC Central Bank Governors, Pöhl brought back an old idea that had already been floated two years earlier of regularly conducting small (3 per cent) parity changes in order to 'de-dramatize' the exchange-rate issue, and to take the political heat away from the Bundesbank. Here was a push in the direction of the other corner to monetary union—greater exchange-rate flexibility. This was a proposal that many central bankers felt that they could endorse. The process of building allies in Europe for the Bundesbank now began.

Pöhl needed to embark on some currency diplomacy, since the coordination exercise seemed to raise very tough political issues in the crucial Franco-German relationship, relating to French interest rates which were higher as a result of the need to defend the franc parity in the EMS. On 22 October 1987, Pöhl told the Bundesbank council that the opinion of the federal government urging the Bundesbank to play a greater role in international cooperation was intelligible and should be respected.[14] This wish translated directly into the formulation of policy on interest rates. Chancellor Kohl telephoned Pöhl to emphasize the political importance of easing rates. Pöhl explained to a quite tumultuous meeting of the Bundesbank council on 3 December that a half-point cut on the eve of a European Council meeting and of a G7 meeting would be a way of demonstrating that the Federal Republic was cooperative, and he reminded the council that, apart from its legal obligation of defending the currency, the Bundesbank also had the duty of supporting the economic policy of the government. The council correspondingly cut the central policy rate (discount) to 2.5 per cent.[15]

Pöhl was fighting against an alternative proposed by France's Finance Minister Édouard Balladur, the man who had developed the international or global target zone plan discussed at the Louvre meeting. After the failure of the global plan, Balladur turned to Europe and proposed a series of initiatives, first in terms of a strengthening of the EMS and then a bold plan in January 1988 which included the notion that the liberalization of capital markets established a logic for creating a zone with a single currency, managed by a common central bank and federal banks in all the member countries (Dyson and Featherstone 1999: 164–6).

[14] HADB, ZBR, 22 October 1987.

[15] HADB, Bundesbank ZBR 739 meeting, 3 December 1987.

In private, Pöhl was seething, arguing that Balladur was talking 'verbiage' and that his 'confused ideas' 'made no sense'. He felt that any discussion of further development of the EMS risked putting Germany in the position of the permanent naysayer.[16] In a press conference, he explained carefully that European monetary union would be a failure if it were not accompanied by convergence in economic, financial, regional, and social policy; that the EMS needed to be more inclusive (in other words, the United Kingdom should join); that there should be a full liberalization of capital movements; that cooperation in the Committee of Governors should be intensified; and finally that a European central bank would need to be built on a federal basis with a firm commitment to price stability (*Frankfurter Allgemeine Zeitung* 1988; *Wall Street Journal* 1988).

But the German reaction to Balladur was positive, and Foreign Minister Genscher responded with a 'Memorandum for the Creation of a European Currency Area and a European Central Bank'. The apparent Franco-German agreement on monetary integration was realized at the Hanover European Council (27–28 June 1988), when it was agreed that Commission president Jacques Delors should institute a study group on the realization of monetary union.

On the eve of Hanover, Pöhl was in an explosive mood. He told the Bundesbank council that the establishment of a Franco-German Economic Council had confirmed the Bundesbank's worst fears, and that the central bank governors were being degraded into the role of assistants to the finance ministers; he also complained of the confused ideas of the new French finance minister Pierre Bérégovoy (a socialist) who had announced on television that the central banks would reduce interest rates.[17] But Pöhl also reported on the discussions he had held on 26 May with the government in Bonn, in which he had pleaded with Chancellor Kohl not to make commitments in Hanover that would affect the activities of the central bank while Genscher had pushed on with the idea of a committee of wise men. Pöhl had claimed to Kohl that Bérégovoy was not really interested in a European central bank, but rather in pressuring the Bundesbank in the current spat over monetary policy.[18] Immediately after the 1 June meeting of the Bundesbank council, Pöhl wrote to Kohl to explain that too early an abandonment of the possibility of altering parities would require a considerable transfer of resources; that an economic and monetary union could only develop over a substantial period of time; and that a parallel currency developing out of the ECU would be a harmful initiative. He thought that the best option lay in the European governments

[16] HADB, B330/17837, 1 May 1988 report.

[17] HADB ZBR, 751, 1 June 1988, verbatim protocol, HADB, B330/17837.

[18] HADB, N4/49, 1 June 1988, Bitterlich to Pöhl with transcript of 26 May 1988 Ministergespräch.

calling on the Committee of EC Central Bank Governors to develop an investigation of currency union as the endpoint of a process of economic integration: that would be a way of disposing of the Balladur–Genscher initiative. He also stated—once more—the importance of central bank independence and a commitment to price stability.[19]

The Hanover European Council meeting of June 1988, which endorsed the idea of setting up a committee of wise men, produced one big surprise: that Delors himself would chair this committee. Pöhl was extremely irritated. He conducted an angry telephone call with Kohl in the middle of the Hanover Council (Dyson and Featherstone 1999: 340–2; Delors 2004: 334). He claimed that the EC Monetary Committee would have been a more appropriate forum for the discussion of monetary union. In the presence of Finance Minister Stoltenberg on 30 June 1988, Pöhl told the Bundesbank council that the choice of chair and the character of the secretariat guaranteed that the European Commission would dominate the work of the committee and that what he termed 'Latin' monetary views would prevail at the expense of German commitment to the culture of stability.[20]

It was extremely hard for the German political authorities to pacify Pöhl. Chancellor Kohl felt obliged to make an appearance before the Bundesbank council, where he underlined his strong political commitment to the independence of the Bundesbank. But the tone of the Chancellor's remarks was much more critical than that of Helmut Schmidt in the celebrated November 1978 meeting. Kohl began by providing a striking and far-sighted account of the importance of the EC, explaining that it was likely that Austria and the Nordic countries would apply to join, and that there was also 'great interest' in the EC in Eastern Europe (a remarkable statement *before* November 1989!). But above all, Kohl stressed the importance of Franco-German relations which 'went beyond the economic'. The Bundesbank should not be so fussy. 'It was not a question of principle whether the interests of the central bank were referred to in an additional clause of the ratifying law or in the preamble.' In reply, Pöhl simply reminded the Chancellor that international commitments, both in the G7 and in Europe, were increasingly placing tight limits on the independence of the central bank.[21]

On 4 July 1988, Pöhl called his British colleague Leigh-Pemberton and other governors, starting by saying 'how unhappy he was about the formation of the Committee and the fact that Delors was chairman', and stating that the appointment of Padoa-Schioppa as secretary would mean 'that the report would immediately get a strong bias in the wrong direction'.[22]

[19] HADB, N4/51, 1 June 1988, Pöhl to Kohl.
[20] HADB Bundesbank ZBR 753, 30 June 1988.
[21] HADB Bundesbank ZBR 754, 14 July 1988.
[22] BoE, 8A/250/1, 4 July 1988, J. R. E. Footman: Delors Committee.

During the Committee's deliberations, Pöhl was often deliberately difficult. But there were obvious limits. Delors realized quite well that Pöhl had political instructions, from the German government, to be cooperative, and that he could not block agreement: after all the independence of the central bank was really limited to the determination of monetary policy, and not general lines of foreign policy. On the other hand, he also appreciated that Pohl would do anything that was needed to get a result which looked like a Bundesbank-type central bank. It was this basic compromise that produced the eventual institutional design of the ECB. Pöhl also worked in a quite detached way, and deliberately sidelined the international division of the Bundesbank. In contrast, the British and French central bank governors on the Delors Committee worked very closely with their staffs, and a great deal of the report, which was in the English language, was done by Bank of England officials. Dyson and Featherstone (1999: 344–6) rightly noted that Pöhl was preoccupied with avoiding 'being simply a prisoner of the Bundesbank'.

His approach in fact reflected a particular style of policy-making: we might call it 'lazy'. He liked a notice that he put on display in the Bundesbank, which stated that: 'In this country you must give the impression you are overworked in order to be taken seriously' (Engelen 2014: 59). His approach—a deliberate undermining of the dominant German national approach to a work ethic—had its German adherents too: a statement attributed to the anti-Nazi General Kurt von Hammerstein-Equord (but sometimes also attributed to the elder Helmut Moltke) divided officers into lazy, hard-working, stupid, and intelligent categories (Enzensberger 2009: 87). The lazy and stupid constituted 90 per cent of the officers, and were useful; the hard-working and stupid were very dangerous and needed to be removed; the intelligent and hard-working were the staff officers (i.e. the staff of the Bundesbank); while the intelligent and lazy were the commanders—in other words, Pöhl.

The Bundesbank staff had tried to anchor Pöhl by setting out the Bundesbank position in a carefully argued paper that bore the intellectual imprint of the major theorist of the Bundesbank, vice-president Helmut Schlesinger. Schlesinger, intelligent and hard-working, conformed to the model of the good staff officer: but the commander ignored him, and became de-anchored. Sometimes frustrated Bundesbank officials tried to find allies in Germany's small neighbours to argue the case, officials from Denmark, Luxembourg, and the Netherlands; and in fact, the fundamental Bundesbank position was set out more consistently by the Netherlands and by its central banker, Wim Duisenberg (also a fundamentally lazy person, but an agreeable personality who listened to his staff and worked with them). The final part of the personal chemistry of the Delors Committee lay in the suavity of Pöhl's counterparts and opponents. Both the French governor, Jacques de Larosière, and the Bank of England's Leigh-Pemberton were (unlike Pöhl) highly courteous figures who could craft a diplomatic consensus.

At the end of the first meeting of the Delors Committee, Pöhl spoke quite bluntly and pleaded for a rejection of the utopian solutions of a hard currency union:

> Maybe we can save a lot of time if we concentrate on that, but we should tell the Heads of State and governments that we are of the opinion and we have agreed that for the time being there is no realistic chance for monetary union in the sense of the Werner Report. We should be honest and we should say that and we should stop all this talk by people like Helmut Schmidt and Giscard, etc. If we are all of this opinion, if we all agree on that that would be a very strong statement, I would subscribe it [sic] immediately. (ECB 1988a)

Pöhl also rejected any notion of the Committee making a political gesture in favour of monetary union. He was visibly chafing against the political masters.

> Who can give the political signal? The politicians, the governments. What can be the political signal? Of course, they could say that we decided today that we will start to negotiate a Treaty for EMU, but I will not propose that because I think we fool ourselves. Firstly, we all know that several governments in Europe are not prepared to start such negotiations at this stage, that is for sure, neither the British Government and I think also the German Government. The German Government has said in its Annual Report they have made a warning against premature institutional changes, so I don't think they will accept that. So two governments at least, I don't know about Denmark, Holland, other countries, I don't know about France, I don't know whether governments in Europe are really prepared at this stage to negotiate a Treaty which would imply far-reaching transfers of sovereignty rights. (ECB 1988a)

He continued his tirade by pointing out how few countries satisfied any notion of economic convergence.

> As long as almost half of the membership of the EEC is either not able or not willing to fulfil the rules which are already there—the EMS is there and it is clearly defined and it works—as long as 5 countries, if I am not mistaken, are either not able (in some cases) or not willing (in the case of Britain or in the case of Italy, which is also unfortunately after 10 years only half a member—and it seems to me, if I may say so as a footnote, a little bizarre that the Prime Ministers of Spain and Italy, I read, are the ones who ask for monetary union. Two countries which are obviously not in a position to fulfil the given rules. As long as that is the case I don't think it makes much sense to negotiate a Treaty. (ECB 1988a)

Talking about negotiations for a Treaty would thus be highly 'unrealistic'.

By the third meeting (8 November 1988), he had developed a precise proposal for transforming or 'upgrading' the Committee of Governors into a Bundesbank-like system:

> Call it a European Central Bank Council, you have a Chairman who would be elected not only for one year but for three years and who could attend the

> meetings in Brussels, could get a little more profile, etc. and then this Council could give recommendations, let us say on monetary policy in the respective member countries of the EC, on economic and fiscal policy even, if it affects the exchange rate stability, price stability in the EEC. (ECB 1988b)

He also added: 'That means, by definition, that gradualism is hardly conceivable.' In particular, he thought that the Committee of Governors might even develop a competence in the setting of exchange rates:

> We could suggest that at least we examine whether the exchange rate pattern is reasonable, appropriate, I think there is no better institution than the Council of Central Bank Governors to come to an objective judgement and if we would come to such a conclusion that would be very rare of course and wouldn't happen very often, but let us assume we would say with these surpluses in Germany the best thing to do is to have a little realignment. (ECB 1988b)

The Bundesbank model remained with the Committee as a constant point of reference. In particular, it was the experience of the Bundesbank council, with regional representation of the state central banks (*Landeszentralbanken*) but no attempt to have weighted voting (in relation to population or economic size), that gave the strongest basis for arguing against a more political version of a European central bank.

In December 1988 Pöhl and Duisenberg severely criticized the focus on institutional engineering. The minutes of the meeting recorded an opinion that: 'It was generally felt that the skeleton went too far in considering the transition to a single currency as essential to a monetary union. A single monetary policy had to be considered more important than a common currency.'[23]

Pöhl wanted a slower institutionalization, in part because the changes he foresaw required the framework of a treaty; and in part because (in the tradition of German policy on integration that went back to Karl Schiller—see Chapter 7 by Kenneth Dyson) he wanted convergence to be demonstrated before the institutional 'coronation' occurred. In consequence, a large part of the final sessions were devoted to the consideration of how many new commitments should be made in the initial stage of the monetary union. Pöhl at this point embarked on an extraordinary series of reflections about how the American model might be more suited to European needs than would be the example of the Bundesbank: indeed he often complained about the provinciality of the Bundesbank system, which subjected the president to votes on the Bundesbank council in which powerful and cantankerous 'barons' appointed by state (*Länder*) governments held sway. 'On the contrary, I think an ESCB [European System of Central Banks] should be constructed

[23] ECB, Delors Committee, Fourth meeting, 13 December 1998, minutes.

in my view very similarly to, let us say, the American system more than the German system. I would not advocate the German system as a model for many reasons which we can discuss when we come to that point. I am not convinced, frankly speaking, that the German system is the most optimal system, I think that the American system is much better than ours' (ECB 1989). Perhaps he thought that the position of the Federal Reserve chair was more eminent and dignified than that of the Bundesbank president, who was only *primus inter pares* on the central bank council.

Pöhl's reflection on the charms of the Federal Reserve was really just a prelude to the real point of his statement—namely, that institutions mattered less than the adoption of appropriate rules for shaping national policies within the European context.

> I don't think we need major institutional changes, for instance, in order to avoid a crisis in the EMS if it would happen. We don't need a Reserve Fund, for instance, which wouldn't help to get a crisis under control. The most important thing is that we should aim for, you called it a set of rules and I think that maybe we should call it a set of principles or a set of rules, but what is meant is that we are aiming for more convergence in economic performance. If we would recommend to the Council that all member states of the Community would commit themselves to a policy which would lead to inflation rates, let us say below 3% as an example, and to reduce their budget deficit to levels, let us say below 3% of GDP, very concrete steps which wouldn't need any institutional change but would be a very very major and substantial step in the direction of a monetary and economic union. These are the kind of recommendations we should not forget in our Report. Talking about the first step I think we have to mention at some occasion that as long as divergences exist to the extent that we have them, realignments and changes in exchange rates have to be a legitimate instrument for the adjustment process. (ECB 1989)

This is the first statement in European discussions of the 3 per cent budget figure that later was to form a crucial (and highly controversial) part of the Maastricht Treaty and of the SGP, which was intended to give a fiscal anchor to the single currency. The 3 per cent figure in fact surprised most of the economists who had participated in the discussions of the late 1980s and had not been willing to give any precise figure as to what might be an appropriate fiscal stance.

Pöhl's achievement in the Delors Committee lay in inserting the fiscal rule. It also lay in getting an agreement at all. At the outset Margaret Thatcher had told Robin Leigh-Pemberton explicitly: 'I have confidence in Karl-Otto Pöhl. If he is proposing something, you can accept it.' Chancellor of the Exchequer Nigel Lawson formulated a distinct sabotage plan: 'It was clear to us, too, that Robin's tactics should be to assemble the widest possible opposition within the Committee both to any early treaty amendment required to achieve the full EMU objective espoused by Delors, and to anything that smacked of a recommendation to take any particular course of action.' But that plan was frustrated, he believed, largely because of the inconstancy of Pöhl who 'proved a broken reed [who...] made a number of sceptical interventions in the Committee's deliberations, but he never really engaged himself' (Lawson 1992: 908). Pöhl had in fact engaged himself enormously; but was also aware—from the outset of the discussions—that there was no real political alternative to the Franco-German path of cooperation.

The Bundesbank responded directly to the Delors Report. Internally, it welcomed the report as an 'optimal' solution from its viewpoint, with a federal central banking system, a commitment to price stability, and a rejection of the idea of a parallel currency. Members of the Bundesbank council recorded their surprise that 'astonishingly all the committee members agreed with the German position'.[24] Subsequently a major discussion developed about whether under the new mechanism the Committee of EC Central Bank Governors could commit the Bundesbank to action, which would be a violation of the autonomy provisions of Bundesbank law.

In a letter to Chancellor Kohl, the Bundesbank set out its institutional opinion very directly: 'our views' were expressed, in the descriptive and analytical parts of the report, as well as in the fundamental recommendations. The letter then focused on Paragraph 7 of the report, with its reference to the Committee of Governors, and focused on the Council decision to define more extensively the competence and tasks of the Committee of Governors. 'If in the course of time our capacity to act is reduced, this can only be accepted if the political commitment to an economic and currency union is at the same time affirmed and not set in doubt once again.'[25]

The subsequent Madrid European Council was followed by some more sceptical commentary from Frankfurt. In an interview with the *Financial Times*, Pöhl seemed to cast doubts on the later stages of the integration programme and in particular on the need for 'an EC bank'. British journalists interpreted the interview as implying that 'the West German government is underplaying the difficulties of establishing such an institution', and implied that Pöhl was 'echoing the arguments of Mrs Margaret Thatcher'. In the interview, Pöhl argued that it would take 'many years' before there was satisfactory economic convergence. 'He believes the basic issue over the European central bank proposals—the transfer of monetary sovereignty away from the present national institutions—has been grasped by relatively few people, one of whom is Mrs Thatcher. There is some doubt whether this has been understood by Chancellor Helmut Kohl.' Then he added: 'If the idea spread and the (German) population understood what it is about—namely that it centres on their money, and that decisions on it would be taken not by

[24] HADB Bundesbank ZBR 772, 20 April 1989.
[25] HADB B330/22720, Pöhl and Gleske to Chancellor Helmut Kohl, 16 June 1989.

the Bundesbank but by a new institution—then I would imagine that considerable resistance might arise.' He also stated that the issue of the site of a future central bank was a question of 'absolute importance' but that the debate was 'an indication of the political problems in setting up such an institution' (*Financial Times* 1989).

A few days after the interview, Pöhl wrote a further letter to German Federal Finance Minister Theo Waigel, arguing against drawing the EC central bank governors formally into meetings of ECOFIN. The Bundesbank case was that the EC Treaty gave strong powers to the Commission, but not in the question of 'currency political issues'. Pöhl reminded Waigel about the phrase in the Single European Act about the 'responsibility of central banks' (*Eigenverantwortung der Notenbanken*).[26]

IMPLEMENTING THE DELORS REPORT

Pöhl's next tactical campaign was to mould the shape of the future European monetary institution. The decisive vehicle for that campaign was the Committee of EC Central Bank Governors, which was now converted into the embryo of a central bank. The ECOFIN Council decision of 13 November 1989 gave the Committee a higher profile. Pöhl now had a radically altered view of the Committee: previously, he had declined to take the chair when it should have devolved on him by rotation and seniority, and he seemed to have a rather low view of the Committee's significance and relevance. By contrast, now he wanted to be chair for a two- or three-year term, so that he could preside over the work of the Committee while it was engaged in the fundamental task of drawing up the statutes for a future European central bank.

There were other signs of institutional change. In an extensive list of proposals to other EC central bank governors, Pöhl suggested language about independence, the use of money stock as an intermediate target for policy, as well as innovations in institutional design, including an alteration of seating arrangements to restrict participation at the round table to the governors themselves, a representative of the Commission (as a guest), the chair of the committee of alternates, the secretary-general of the Committee of Governors, and a rapporteur. The chair would represent the Committee to ECOFIN. Pöhl's initiative reflected more than simply personal proclivities. The major issue was the one that had been at the heart of every discussion of the Bundesbank, namely central bank independence. The idea of a well-designed central bank seemed to be fundamentally a question of taking over

[26] HADB, B330/22720, Pöhl to Waigel, 6 July 1989.

a German model that was already functioning well (Dyson and Featherstone 1999: 386).

The future ECB thus came to look more and more like an internationalized version of the Bundesbank. From the German standpoint, it was especially important that there be no joint meetings of the EC central bank governors with ECOFIN, as that might be held to diminish the Committee's independence. The secretary-general would 'receive his instructions from the Chairman'. There would be a research component to the work of the secretariat. The chair of the committee of alternates, who would be elected by the Committee of Governors, would cooperate closely with the chair of the EC Monetary Committee.[27]

The Committee of EC Central Bank Governors began to run with the ball on institutional design of the new central banking system, and it was a very German ball. In April 1990, Pöhl made a proposal at the Committee of Governors for draft statutes on the objectives, organization, functions, instruments, and voting system of a new bank (van den Berg 2004: 6). The governors were resistant to any hint of political supervision, and believed that any measure of political control would in practice mean pressure to inflate. They also largely wanted to escape from any obligation to accept quantitative inflation targets—a view which was beginning to have a strong impact among policy-oriented academic economists (Bernanke et al. 1999). Pöhl stated emphatically that:

> A press communique should never contain normative price increases; this would give the impression that a certain rate of inflation was being aimed at, whereas the objective was in fact to reduce it. It was perhaps essentially a question of presentation. For example, when the Bundesbank published its monetary targets, it explained that they had been calculated taking account of the potential growth rate (or assumed real growth) and the unavoidable inflation rate.[28]

Pöhl presented this outcome to the ECOFIN on 8 September 1990, making clear the high importance that price stability would have for the new regime:

> Starting with the objective, we want to underline the unequivocal statement in the Delors Report that the primary objective of the system must be to preserve price stability. But, of course, giving primacy to this objective must not be misinterpreted as an invitation to act in a single-minded manner and without due regard to other economic policy objectives. There is full recognition that monetary policy is not conducted in a vacuum and the new System shall, without prejudice to the objective of price stability, support the general economic policy of the Community. This will be explicitly stated in the draft Statute. However, there should be no misunderstanding: in the event of a conflict between price stability

[27] Committee of Governors, 30 November 1989, letter of Pöhl to central bank governors.
[28] Committee of Governors, Meeting 245, 15 May 1990, Basel.

> and other economic objectives, the governing bodies of the System will have no choice but to give priority to its primary objective. There can be no compromise in this respect.[29]

This was the solution eventually adopted in the enumeration of ECB tasks in Article 2 of the Statute, and it seemed to strengthen the emphasis on price stability in comparison to the US system, where the concept only appeared in 1977 and was qualified by a dual mandate which also referred to high employment.

Pöhl also insisted on the ECB not being categorized as an EC institution:

> Our unanimous support of an independent System should not be interpreted as an attempt to escape from democratic accountability or as a claim of exclusive competence to conduct a stability-oriented monetary policy. But we are convinced, based on actual experience in our countries, that the success of pursuing a monetary policy in accordance with the primary objective hinges critically on safeguards against political pressures. Even more than in some of our countries this is likely to be true in a large Community, given the different traditions and experiences with inflation.[30]

The odd result, that the ECB's institutional position in the European Union had no political anchor, was only resolved by the Treaty of Lisbon (in article 1 (14) producing the new Article 9). It was thus only on 1 December 2009, in consequence, that the ECB became an EU institution—to the dismay of the Bundesbank, at exactly the moment that ECB decisions were becoming highly politicized in the wake of the global financial crisis. But the ECB was also sceptical, and its then president, Jean-Claude Trichet, was quoted as arguing: 'Because of its specific institutional features, the ECB needs to be differentiated from the union's institutions.' He implied that governments were trying to impose a political control on the ECB.[31]

In the Committee of EC Central Bank Governors, Pöhl was sceptical about the desirability of including references to exchange-rate intervention. He emphatically stated that: 'The exchange rate policies and operations of the System should never conflict with the priority of price stability.' He therefore suggested deleting the sentence in square brackets and including an additional phrase to the effect that 'the commitment to exchange rate policies should not be in contradiction to the task of maintaining price stability'. He said that 'the System should not be obliged to intervene in the foreign exchange markets

[29] Committee of EC Central Bank Governors, 8 September 1990, Statement by President Pöhl on the Statute of the System.

[30] Committee of EC Central Bank Governors, 8 September 1990, Statement by President Pöhl on the Statute of the System.

[31] Tobias Buck, 'Central bank chief urges change to EU treaty', *Financial Times*, 11 August 2007, <http://www.ft.com/intl/cms/s/0/80a871b6-47a2-11dc-9096-0000779fd2ac.html?ft_site=falcon&desktop=true#axzz3zJWJ45rd>.

when such action would be incompatible or interfere with the monetary policy objectives of the System.'[32]

The Bundesbank's response to the remaining uncertainties was to press for all monetary policy-making to be concentrated in the executive board,[33] rather than in the governing council of the ECB. That would have in effect excluded the council members—the representatives of the national central banks—from voting on monetary policy, but this was too controversial and too German to stand any chance of acceptance. Article 12 of the ECB statute made the governing council central, but that was just the position of the Bundesbank's own council.

CONTRIBUTION AND LEGACY

In many vital areas, then, the ECB looked as if it was a replica of the Bundesbank: the primacy of price stability; the institutional guarantee of independence; as well as the provision that the national central banks (NCBs) should also be independent (Article 14 of the ECB statute). It even looked as if the relationship between the ECB and the NCBs was a mirror of that between the Bundesbank and the state central banks in Germany.

At the time, in the early 1990s, some influential figures in the Bundesbank, such as Helmut Schlesinger, liked to make the argument that a treaty was a stronger embodiment of the principle of independence than a simple national law, like the Bundesbank law, which could always be easily reversed by a parliamentary vote. Was it really that easy? The Bundesbank had often emphasized the way that it was backed not just by law but by a strong, almost immutable, public sentiment about 'stability culture' (*Stabilitätskultur*): my late colleague, Peter Kenen, loved to say that this term sounded much better in German than in an English translation. The 'stability culture' that was the underpinning of Pöhl's mental world—and of his strength in international negotiations—did not really quite exist in a European form. And, as the Lisbon Treaty showed, treaties could be renegotiated and supplanted by other treaties.

One reflection of the 'stability culture' thinking was the question of how central banks reached decisions. On occasion, Pöhl expressed criticism of his dependence on the voting of the Bundesbank directorate, which contrasted with the Banque de France or the Bank of England where the governor was *the* authority. But it was a substantial advantage in international negotiations: the Bundesbank president could never commit his colleagues. Pöhl and his Bundesbank colleagues assumed that the mindset of the Bundesbank would

[32] Committee of Governors, Meeting 249, 13 November 1990, Basel.

[33] Committee of Governors, 9 September 1990, Stellungnahme zum Draft Statute.

simply transfer to the ECB, and that decisions would be made on the basis of a consensus-forming process rather than after politically justified votes. Pöhl's assumption that the Bundesbank logic would simply win by consensus was perhaps in the face of the fact that he—unlike some of the other architects examined in this volume—was not really a consensus manager, a teamwork player, or a builder of European networks. The politician he impressed most, and who was consequently most disappointed in him, was Margaret Thatcher, who was also not a builder of European networks. In fact, the consensus model did originally function within the ECB, but this was not really Pöhl's achievement, and the triumph did not last. At the first ECB Council meeting, Pöhl's successor at the Bundesbank, Hans Tietmeyer, successfully rearranged the seating so that Council members would sit in the alphabetical order of their names, not of the names of the Member States from which they came. But, after 2009, discussions and voting in the ECB became increasingly polarized along national lines.

On 16 May 1991, Pöhl abruptly announced his resignation as Bundesbank president for 'personal reasons'. He sincerely felt that the security precautions that surrounded the head of the Bundesbank imposed a heavy burden on his young family. In the wake of the collapse of the GDR, the left-wing extremists of the 'Rote Armee Fraktion' had unleashed a final wave of terror against prominent representatives of the Federal Republic's economic elite, killing the head of Deutsche Bank Alfred Herrhausen and the director of the Treuhand-Anstalt that was winding up East German state companies, Detlef Rohwedder. His second wife, Ulrike, was a political scientist who had written about the RAF and its milieu, and longed to be able to do simple things such as go to restaurants or take children to play dates. But it was easy for commentators to interpret the move as a political gesture, an outcome of a deteriorating personal relationship with Chancellor Helmut Kohl, and especially of Pöhl's frustrations about German fiscal policy in the wake of German unification (Marsh 1992: 26–31). He had pressed for tax increases to pay for the cost of unification, but had been put down by Finance Minister Theo Waigel. The events of 1991 were an early signal of how—in the final decision, in the midst of a political crisis—politics would trump economics.

There were also in 1991 differing visions of Europe in Frankfurt and Bonn. Pöhl applied some of the lessons from the experience of German unity to the European debate. Did not the German currency union show the dangers of a politically desired union without a fundamental economic convergence? The phrase that had outraged the German federal government was Pöhl's use of the English word 'disaster' in appearing before the Economic Affairs Committee of the European Parliament on 19 March 1991, when he had mentioned in an aside that the GDR had been poorly prepared for the currency union.

With surprising rapidity, the most charismatic and voluble—as well as volatile—central banker in European politics stepped off the stage. Looking back on his career, as the Maastricht Treaty negotiations were finalized, he tried to present himself as someone who had been trying to prevent 'disaster' in Europe. In August 1991, he stated: 'For eighteen months, I talked myself crazy. I was ignored. If I had had the feeling that I could have stopped this [Maastricht] I would not have left [the Bundesbank]' (*Die Zeit* 1992). In 1992, in the prestigious Per Jacobsson lecture at the annual IMF meetings, he emphasized that 'only a multi-speed approach has a chance to be realized'. That meant that 'participation [in the monetary union] should be strictly limited to members which fulfill a number of stringent conditions' (Engelen 2014: 59).

Pöhl's resignation set what became a pattern, when other presidents of the Bundesbank—notably the powerful Axel Weber, like Pöhl an outsider to the Bundesbank but like him a powerful advocate of its traditions—noticed that they could not turn the European tide. Weber's resignation followed the same dynamic: a conflict over Europe leading to a clash with the German Federal Chancellor of such magnitude that the Bundesbank president's position was no longer sustainable.

It is tempting to depict Pöhl as the clear-minded and visionary thinker who had correctly diagnosed and anticipated the imperfections and problems of the monetary union. But the reality is otherwise: it was under Pöhl's leadership that the Bundesbank had taken the decisive steps that meant that it no longer had the veto power in European and international monetary affairs that had so frustrated Chancellor Schmidt in the late 1970s. Pöhl had wanted to defend the Bundesbank, and he built an ECB largely on the Bundesbank model. But the framework on which he worked in the end left the Bundesbank politically weakened and practically obsolete in the setting of Europe's monetary policy. During the Euro Area crisis, after 2010, the German federal government did not always follow the line of the Bundesbank, notably in the aftermath of the 26 July 2012 Mario Draghi speech, committing the ECB to do 'whatever it takes' to safeguard the euro, and of the subsequent announcement of the Outright Monetary Transactions (OMT) programme. Unlike the US Federal Reserve Open Markets Committee, where the New York Fed always has a vote, the Bundesbank had no guaranteed vote in the large ECB governing council (after its expansion to nineteen NCBs when Lithuania joined the Euro Area in January 2015). Pöhl died on 9 December 2014, just three weeks before the Bundesbank's marginalization was made legally apparent.

9

Tommaso Padoa-Schioppa

EMU as the Anchor Stone for Building a Federal Europe

Fabio Masini

The institutional rhetoric about European integration highlights its successes. Among them, a prominent place is occupied by the foundation of the single currency: the euro. Nevertheless, as the post-2008 asymmetric shocks and the subsequent Euro Area financial, economic, and sovereign debt crisis has shown, it is hardly possible to label the euro as an unqualified success.

Masini (2009a, 2009b: 138, 2014) has suggested that a different theory of the historical evolution of European integration should be provided. European integration has been built, usually with full awareness by some of its protagonists, as a series of increasing contradictions. These contradictions were to provide the critical framework necessary to agree on the next step.

When the European Economic Community (EEC) was founded in 1957, it was clear that its institutional architecture had several shortcomings. In particular, it was clear that the system of economic governance would never be able to survive the end of the US dollar-exchange standard. Flexible exchange rates would create increasing pressure to make quick, legitimate, and effective collective choices. The outcome was the foundation of the European Monetary System (EMS) and the first elections of the European Parliament with direct voting in 1979.

When, in the 1980s, the European heads of state and government decided to liberalize capital movements and to create the single market, it became manifest that the EMS would not survive financial speculation without a strong political commitment to a European monetary union. Similarly, the euro was created as a tool to challenge national sovereignty while waiting for some kind of political union.

Tommaso Padoa-Schioppa (often referred to, especially in the mass media, as TPS, an acronym that he also used in his writings) was not only perfectly aware of the value of contradictions in driving European integration. Also, he tried to guide this process.

This chapter examines TPS's contribution to European monetary integration, in order to understand what drove him in his efforts to give strong credibility to the project of the euro and how he struggled for its success. It deals only with his commitment for monetary integration before the launch of the euro. It leaves out important parts of TPS's story—such as his role as central banker in the executive board of the European Central Bank (ECB); as an architect of national and international financial supervision; and his commitment to a radical reform of the international monetary system. Unfortunately, TPS's archives are only available until 1984 (the thirty-years rule in Italian law), whereas his most important contributions to European monetary integration are in the late 1980s and 1990s. Hence the chapter relies mainly on his official writings and a few interviews with some of his colleagues, friends, and relatives.

The first section examines the intellectual foundations of his pro-European attitude and stresses his most important ideological roots. The second section looks at his main theoretical and policy contribution to the creation and evolution of the EMS. The next two sections explore his attitude towards EMU before and after the approval of the Delors Report. Finally, the chapter outlines his most important legacy.

TPS's INTELLECTUAL BACKGROUND AND EUROPEAN INTEGRATION

Born in Belluno in 1940, after attending the high school (*Liceo Classico*), TPS worked for two years for an insurance company in Bremen and entered the faculty of economics of the private University Luigi Bocconi, in Milan, where he graduated *cum laude* in 1966. In 1966, just married, he moved to Germany to work for the retailer C&A Brenninkmeyer, an international chain of clothing stores, where he stayed until 1968, when he started to collaborate with the Banca d'Italia. Thanks to a Bonaldo Stringher Fellowship, he had the opportunity to go to the Massachusetts Institute of Technology, where in 1970 he obtained a Master of Science in Economics. In that period, TPS started a collaboration and a robust friendship with Franco Modigliani, one of the 'moderate Keynesian' economists—according to Ciocca (2004: 592) together with Hicks, Samuelson, Klein, and Tobin—with whom the Banca d'Italia had established close contacts (Maes 2013b).

In 1970 TPS returned to Italy and was hired as an economist in the research department of the Banca d'Italia in Milan. From 1975 to 1979 he was head of the money market department of the Banca d'Italia and, from March 1978 to June 1979, he was seconded as economic adviser to the Ministry of the Treasury under Filippo Maria Pandolfi. His main interests in this period were domestic, concentrated on the modernization of the management of national monetary policy.[1]

It seems that TPS was rather sceptical about the effectiveness of international cooperation and about serving in international economic organizations.[2] He was not at all confident that any progress in European monetary integration would be possible in 1977. TPS recalled this scepticism when he was asked by Alberto Majocchi and Alfonso Jozzo, on behalf of Mario Albertini, to support initiatives 'in the monetary field to re-launch the process of European integration' (Padoa-Schioppa 2002: 190) just before the speech by Roy Jenkins in Florence on 27 October 1977.

The year 1979 marked a turning point in TPS's career. According to Saccomanni,[3] the troubles facing the Banca d'Italia due to the arrest of its director general, Mario Sarcinelli, and the resignation of its governor, Paolo Baffi, suggested that the most brilliant men in the Bank should be seconded abroad. Thanks to a diplomatic effort by Giulio Andreotti, Carlo Azeglio Ciampi, and Pandolfi, in June 1979 TPS became director general for economic and financial affairs (DG II) in the European Commission. Here he prioritized the strengthening of its analytical capacity, playing a crucial role in the professionalization of economics at the European Commission (Maes 2013b: 40). During his service in Brussels TPS came into close contact with François-Xavier Ortoli, then European Commissioner at DG II, and Jacques Delors, then minister of finance in France, later president of the European Commission. They were to become important figures in his professional life. In 1979 he was also asked to join the Group of Thirty, a small but very influential think-tank which advised on global economic and financial governance.

In 1983 TPS returned to the Banca d'Italia as general director for economic research. Thanks to the experience and contacts acquired in DG II, and with the help of Carli and a personal request from Delors, he joined the Delors Committee for the Study of Economic and Monetary Union. Here he played a key role as one of the two rapporteurs, working closely with Delors. This period also illustrated the distrust of TPS in German official circles, notably the Bundesbank, as too close to Commission thinking. The Bundesbank insisted that Gunter Baer of the Bank for International Settlements share

[1] Interview F. Saccomanni transcript, 2015.
[2] Interview F. Saccomanni transcript, 2015.
[3] Interview F. Saccomanni transcript, 2015.

this role with him. Again, TPS sought to engage policy-makers in the academic debates about monetary union and the steps to be taken.

The year 1993 was another crucial one in TPS's career. As Saccomanni recalls, when Ciampi resigned as governor of the Banca d'Italia to become prime minister, he favoured TPS as his successor. However, the president of the Italian Republic, Oscar Luigi Scalfaro, opposed TPS—as too laic—and preferred Antonio Fazio.[4] Again, TPS had to look outside the Banca d'Italia. From 1993 to 1998 he became a leading figure in international financial supervision, first as president of the Basel Committee on Banking Supervision (until 1997), and later as president of Consob, Italy's stock-market supervision agency.

From 1998 to 2005, TPS was a member of the executive board of the ECB. In October 2005 he became president of the Paris-based think-tank Notre Europe (until his death) and, from May 2006 to May 2008, was minister of economy and finances in the Italian government.

The question arises of what were the leading intellectual sources and who were the main people who influenced TPS during his career. With respect to his economic thought, Bini Smaghi (2012) suggests his major references were Robert Mundell, Robert Triffin, and the so-called 'monetarist' approach to European monetary integration as opposed to the 'economist' approach (see Chapter 2 by Maes on Triffin and Chapter 7 by Dyson on Tietmeyer). The 'economist' approach considers monetary integration as the final result of a macro-economic convergence process; the 'monetarist' approach sees monetary integration as driving economic convergence. As this chapter shows later, TPS is not to be labelled as belonging to either of the two groups.

Saccomanni emphasizes how, in addition to Modigliani, TPS had been influenced by Paul Samuelson and Robert M. Solow.[5] In Italy he had developed strong links with Beniamino Andreatta and a very close relationship with Carlo Azeglio Ciampi.

With respect to his commitment for European integration, in his book *Europe, a Civil Power* (*Europa, forza gentile*), TPS wrote that the most important contributions Italy gave to the creation of Europe were provided by 'Einaudi, Spinelli and Albertini' (Padoa-Schioppa 2001: 102). Luigi Einaudi (1874–1961) was one of the most renowned Italian intellectuals of the twentieth century, well known for his pro-European commitment (Vigo 1986; Morelli 1990; Cressati 1992; Sarcinelli 2004; Forte 2007; Masini 2012a) as well as an economist, politician, governor of the Banca d'Italia, and president of the Italian Republic.

Altiero Spinelli (1907–86) is perhaps less well known—not only abroad but also in Italy—although he is one of the officially recognized 'founding fathers'

[4] Interview F. Saccomanni transcript, 2015.
[5] Interview F. Saccomanni transcript, 2015.

of the European Union. In 1941 he wrote—together with Ernesto Rossi and the help of Eugenio Colorni—the Ventotene *Manifesto for a Free and United Europe*. TPS wrote the introduction to a reprint of the *Manifesto* in 2006, published by Mondadori. This manifesto inspired belief in the integration process and the birth in 1943 of the European Federalist Movement (MFE), an organization that aimed to achieve a European federation. Spinelli served for several years in key positions within European institutions, fighting for higher levels of political integration. He was also the father of TPS's last partner, Barbara Spinelli, after he divorced from his wife Fiorella Kostoris in 2000.

In contrast, Mario Albertini (1919–97) is completely unknown to the public. He was Professor of Philosophy of Politics at the University of Pavia and the intellectual leader and the president of the MFE in Italy from the 1960s to the early 1990s. Albertini provided both the theoretical seeds for, and the organizational support to, Spinelli in his activities within European institutions, although they were often in disagreement about strategies. With respect to Albertini's 'strong and far-reaching influence', Padoa-Schioppa (2002: 190) claims that 'many people, like myself, feel that the course of their active life and their careers in European affairs would not have been the same without this important influence'.

What united Einaudi, Spinelli, and Albertini was the strong belief that only by surrendering part of their national sovereignty to a federal constitutional structure could European states become credible subjects on the world scene. Following the US experience, European federalism would provide an efficient allocation of collective decision-making between national and supranational institutions. It allows a better provision of public goods, from the local to the regional, national, and European dimensions.

TPS shared most of this view. In the introduction to one of his books he suggested that what Europe needed was to overcome the dogma of exclusive sovereignties, citing Kant's *Perpetual Peace* and Einaudi as precursor of this idea (Padoa-Schioppa 1992a: ix). Federalism, as a constitutional system of multilayer government, was one of the most powerful intellectual sources of TPS's commitment to European integration. Correspondingly, he thought of economic and monetary integration as only a step towards greater political integration, although, as becomes clear later in this chapter, he did not always make this connection explicit.

Strikingly, TPS used to give friends (Saccomanni 2005), as presents, the *mémoires* of Jean Monnet and of Spinelli (Saccomanni 2005). This strong commitment to a federal Europe went along with his pragmatism, as a supporter of a step-by-step approach to the goal of a federal Europe (Padoa-Schioppa 2002: 191).

According to his brother Antonio (henceforth APS), TPS's first contact with the idea of European integration was at Trieste, between 1956 and 1959, when he was at high school, thanks to the enthusiasm which his brother transmitted to all the family. TPS confirms this account (Padoa-Schioppa 2002: 190), referring to his reading of the *History of Europe in the Nineteenth Century* (*Storia di Europa nel secolo decimonono*) by the Italian philosopher Benedetto Croce, where in the last page the author dreams of a united Europe in which national identities would nevertheless not be cancelled.[6]

After TPS moved to the Bocconi university in Milan in 1959, he came to know, again through APS who was studying law at the prestigious College Ghislieri of Pavia, the group of federalists gathering around Mario Albertini (first of all Francesco Rossolillo, Alberto and Luigi Vittorio Majocchi) and the MFE group from Turin (mainly Alfonso Iozzo, who was to become one of his best personal friends, and Lucio Levi). He would only later meet personally both Mario Albertini and Altiero Spinelli.[7] TPS's contacts with the federalist culture are also well documented in his archives. From the 1970s, there are plenty of letters (TPS Archives, folder 281) with some of the most representative figures of the MFE in Italy, namely Alberto Majocchi, Dario Velo, Giovanni Vigo, Alfonso Iozzo, and Mario Albertini himself. It is not clear whether TPS was ever was a member of the MFE—according to Saccomanni (2005) he joined already when a student at Bocconi. However, he participated in some of its activities until his death.

It is more complex to assess the way this intellectual background forged his commitment to greater integration in Europe. It seemed to evolve in time. Thus APS suggests that TPS's 'filo-European attitude would gradually become "federalist" in the proper sense'.[8] It was influenced by the opportunities that arose for him to play a part in key decision-making processes in European monetary integration, as the next sections show.

LAUNCHING EUROPEAN MONETARY INTEGRATION: THE EMS

During the 1970s, TPS gained a higher profile in Italy following a paper that he wrote with Franco Modigliani on 'Economic Policy in an Economy with Wages Linked to Inflation at 100% and More' (Modigliani and Padoa-Schioppa 1977). Its influence extended beyond academia into political and journalistic debates. They claimed that there is only one level of aggregate (national) income coherent with price stability and that this level may not be consistent with full employment. Higher indirect taxes and greater social costs

[6] Interview Antonio Padoa-Schioppa transcript, 2014.
[7] Interview Antonio Padoa-Schioppa transcript, 2014.
[8] Interview Antonio Padoa-Schioppa transcript, 2014.

reduced the level of income compatible with price stability, implying the need to dramatically reduce production in order to reduce inflation.

As a consequence, expansionary monetary policies are ineffective in the real economy and can only boost inflation. The solution does not lie in an import-substitution policy because this would be ineffective in Italy's open economy and would raise the price of imports, thereby boosting inflation. The key policy contribution was that the only way to have external balance was to constrain wages to a level compatible with productivity, which should be increased thanks to new investments made possible by higher profit margins. Stag-flation was the result of unfettered wage demands. Hence action to constrain wages was to be considered a top priority for recovery.

With this model in mind, TPS gave support to the creation of the EMS. Notwithstanding his scepticism before Jenkins' speech (see Chapter 6 by Ludlow), his role in the Italian decision to participate in the EMS from the beginning was important. He worked in two stages. First, TPS radically changed the initial draft of the Pandolfi Plan in 1978 (the multiannual planning document of the Ministry of Treasury) so that it was not only compatible with the external constraint but also actually needed this constraint. Participation in the EMS would mean a bigger market for Italian products, which would force firms to raise productivity in order to survive international competition. It would also lead to the loss of monetary policy discretion, which would in turn make clear that only a general wage reduction could positively impact on competitiveness.

Second, TPS agreed with his friend Modigliani a strategy of communication that might facilitate a change of attitude by the Banca d'Italia, which had opposed the entry of the lira into the EMS (Masini 2004: 49). They wrote an article published in *Il Corriere della Sera*, signed only by Modigliani (1978), because the rules of the Banca d'Italia made it ethically incorrect for TPS, one of its employees, to sign. This article exerted considerable influence on the way that Baffi, the governor of the Banca d'Italia, talked to the government of Andreotti about the conditions for joining the EMS, *de facto* paving the way for Italian participation.

Nevertheless, TPS's attitude in favour of the EMS was not only due to the virtues of 'tying one's hands' in economic policy. He also thought that the EMS was a starting point for a more profound and forward-looking process of European unification, from which Italy could not stay outside. The global challenges should be faced by a strong European-wide strategy. Staying out of the EMS would mean not being part of these decision-making processes.

TPS's views were made clear in a letter of 6 November 1980 to Alfredo Recanatesi, who had published an article in *La Repubblica* expressing doubts about the success of the EMS. He defended the choice of Italy to enter the EMS with the following arguments: participation in the EMS is a commitment to a policy of stability; and the EMS is necessary to defend the Customs Union and the Common Agricultural Policy from the volatility of exchange rates after the collapse of the Bretton Woods system. He writes: 'I personally think that the "defensive" component of the initiative of Giscard and Schmidt of 1978 was even more important than the "constructive" one' (TPS Archives, folder 525). In the same letter he also expresses the fear that the only alternative would be a Franco-German agreement where Italy could be left outside. In that case, although benefiting from the possibility to depreciate the currency, Italy would gain no serious advantage and would actually be kept out of the most relevant strategic changes in European policy. In 2008 TPS made this point again, quoting from Robert Cooper's (2003: 44) claim that 'for the post-modern state, sovereignty is a seat at the table'. The increasing interdependence in the world cannot imply an attempt (bound to fail) to defend national sovereignty, but only an attempt to be part of a greater decision-making process.

THE INCONSISTENT QUARTET: A PROBLEM OF COLLECTIVE ACTION

Describing the world system in 1965, Warren Smith wrote: '1) there is complete freedom in the international movement of goods and capital, 2) exchange rates are fixed, and 3) individual countries are free to use monetary and fiscal policy—primarily the former—to attain their domestic price and employment goals. And the system is subject to the constraint that each country possesses a limited supply of reserves with which to cover deficits in its balance of payments.' And he adds: 'The trouble with this system is that it is basically inconsistent' (Smith 1965: 210).

This argument forms the basis for the trilemma of economic policy, popularized later in macro-economic textbooks. The Fleming (1962) and Mundell (1963) model, which describes the macro-economic constraints in a context of perfect international capital mobility, predicts that an autonomous monetary policy can be effective only under flexible exchange rates. In this latter case, a reduction of the interest rate can be left free to be reflected in a devaluation of the currency, thus increasing competitiveness, exports, and therefore the aggregate demand and the overall level of equilibrium income. Conversely, as nominal interest-rate differentials tend to reflect exchange-rate differentials, under fixed exchange rates domestic interest rates will tend to follow the prevailing international ones so that no autonomous monetary policy is effective.

Building on this theoretical apparatus, TPS coined the concept of the 'inconsistent quartet' (Padoa-Schioppa 1982). Policy cannot achieve simultaneously free movement of production factors (labour and capital); free movement of final outputs (goods and services); fixed exchange rates; and autonomous national monetary policies. This theoretical tool became key to TPS's policy views and proposals during the 1980s, as is manifest from his writings of those years, later collected in a volume (Padoa-Schioppa 1992b). Although the idea of the inconsistent quartet was not a theoretical innovation, it exerted a great influence on the policy debates that characterized European monetary integration since then. It was not by chance that the three elements of the 'trilemma' became a 'quartet'. They represented exactly the roadmap that TPS had in mind for the process of European monetary integration on which he worked in the following years. And its steps reflect exactly those of European integration between the mid-1980s and the early 1990s.

During the 1980s TPS acted on two stages. During the first period, as director general of DG II in Brussels, he committed himself to transform the directorate general into a robust analytical service, where macro-economic, policy-oriented analysis was to become a fundamental prerequisite 'in preparing the European Commission for the important role it would play in the EMU process' (Maes 2013b: 22).

In the second period, when he had left Brussels, TPS contributed to both academic and policy-oriented debates on the pros and cons of a single currency and to helping politicians, especially Delors, president of the European Commission from January 1985 to January 1995. He became economic and financial adviser and close friend to Delors (see Chapter 10 by Hodson on Delors). His advice centred on following the logic of the inconsistent quartet, with full awareness that it could be used to justify the move to European monetary union—and later the surrender of part of national sovereignty—as politically necessary. TPS played a major role in instilling in Karl-Otto Pöhl the idea of a monetary union as a radical solution to the stabilization of European exchange rates (see Chapter 8 by James on Pöhl).

TPS had also already hinted at this approach in a European Commission document of 1987 (known as the Padoa-Schioppa Report) on *Efficieny, Stability and Equity* (European Commission 1987). The report suggested that the allocation functions of the market should be accompanied by active stabilizing and redistributive actions from a coordinated system of national and European institutions. According to the report: 'in a quite fundamental way, capital mobility and exchange-rate fixity together leave no room for independent monetary policies' (European Commission 1987: 4). At the same time, market liberalization is recognized to carry risks of regional imbalances, requiring 'accompanying measures . . . to speed adjustment in the structurally weak regions and countries'. The report was also explicit on the institutional side, requiring an increase of the European budget financed by 'own resources' (European Commission 1987: 11).

The Single European Act of 1986 officially set the process in motion. The decision to agree on a strict time schedule for the completion of the European single market (1992), where goods and services are supposed to circulate freely with the enforcement of European law by the European Court of Justice (ECJ), matched the second point of the quartet. In 1988 the final stage of full capital mobility in Europe was agreed, thanks to a strong political commitment of the European Commission. The most important contribution to the first point of the quartet was liberalized. When the EMU project was launched, with the Delors Report in 1989, the inconsistent quartet became suddenly manifest. Exchange rates were to become irrevocably fixed, while national policies had to accelerate macro-economic convergence. It was not by chance that in 1992 and 1993 speculation bets against the ERM and the transition to EMU followed. They were the result of the expectations that had been generated by the evolution of these intrinsic inconsistencies.

There are several examples of TPS being perfectly well aware of this process. He knew that capital mobility would raise the general degree of economic interdependence and ignite financial speculation against some of the ERM currencies (Padoa-Schioppa 1987c: 118, 2001, 2004a, 2004b). For this very reason, he thought the only correct response in the short run was to increase the degree of cooperation among central banks. This cooperation should take the form of providing liquidity denominated in the appreciating currencies and reducing the liquidity of currencies under attack, so that speculative attacks might be discouraged. He knew that 'cooperation did not progress at the same phenomenal pace at which interdependence did' (Padoa-Schioppa 2008: 213) and that this gap should be filled.

TPS was asked to draft the Delors Report, as co-rapporteur of the Committee with Gunter Baer, a collaborator of Lamfalussy (see Chapter 11 by Maes on Lamfalussy). This provided him with the opportunity to make the logic of the inconsistent quartet a fundamental part of the report's analysis. The Delors Report acknowledged the intrinsic instability of the commitment towards the single market:

> By greatly strengthening economic interdependence between member countries, the single market will reduce the room for independent policy manoeuvre and amplify the cross-border effects of developments originating in each member country. It will, therefore, necessitate a more effective coordination of policy between separate national authorities. (Delors 1989d: 10)

Also, the Delors Report clearly understood that free capital movement was a critical point that would oblige national monetary authorities to give up their autonomy:

> Well before the decision to fix exchange rates permanently, the full liberalization of capital movements and financial market integration would have created a situation in which the coordination of monetary policy would have to be strengthened progressively. (Delors 1989d: 16)

Summing up, the Delors Report referred to the importance of the consistency of fiscal policies:

> Economic and monetary integration in Europe would imply complete freedom of movement for persons, goods, services and capital, as well as irrevocably fixed exchange rates between national currencies and, finally, a single currency. This, in turn, would imply a common monetary policy and require a high degree of compatibility of economic policies and consistency in a number of other policy areas, particularly in the fiscal field. (Delors 1989d: 13)

The Delors Report and the early documents that circulated in the Intergovernmental Conference (IGC) on EMU in early 1991 testify to the great intellectual influence that TPS exerted on the way in which the strategy for European monetary integration was set in motion. Maes (2013b: 39) synthesized TPS's role in the early days of this process as follows: 'In this way, he [TPS] had a very influential role . . . The Delors Report came to assume a crucial role as a reference and anchor point in further discussions and negotiations on EMU. It would become the broad basis for the chapters on EMU in the Maastricht Treaty.'

MONETARY UNION AND POLITICAL UNION

One crucial and recurrent question in the debates on European monetary integration concerns the link between economic and political union (Hodson 2009). This question was central to TPS's struggle for European integration. For TPS the question took the following form: can higher degrees of monetary integration be sustainable in the long run when no collective decision-making process is given constitutional form with respect to choices affecting the credibility of the other macro-economic variables? In short: can a single market and a single currency survive without a single government?

The inconsistent quartet thesis had nothing to say on this question, specifying only that national monetary sovereignty should be surrendered to ensure the general consistency of economic integration. TPS's federalist world-view suggests a negative view about the sustainability of monetary union without a single government. However, in practice he adopted a more differentiated view, probably due to the need to build diplomatic consensus in specific circumstances. Also, TPS had a different idea of federation from the one held by most of its advocates.

According to Francesco Papadia (2015), TPS 'believed that moves towards political union, including fiscal union, but without reaching a fully-fledged federal set-up, were sufficient to support monetary union'. This interpretation is probably correct in some phases of his life. However, it seems that in the later period he firmly believed that the final goal of a European federation was the only way to make European economic governance credible and effective both within and outside its boundaries. The key point is to understand what TPS considered a suitable model of federal constitution for Europe.

Before his role as co-rapporteur for the Delors Committee and during the early negotiations in the two IGCs on EMU and on political union, convened before the Maastricht European Council of December 1991, TPS spoke about the need to overcome national economic policies. At the same time, he explicitly argued against the need to assist this process through specific measures of political integration. In October 1987, TPS wrote that a monetary union cannot be considered just a technical decision (Padoa-Schioppa 1987c: 127–8). At the same time, he denied that 'without a political union there can be no monetary union'. Yet, the Padoa-Schioppa Report of 1987 presented several possible forms for a federal European budget, depending on the quantity of public goods to be provided at the supranational level (European Commission 1987: 150ff.). One possibility was an autonomous fiscal and borrowing capacity for the European Community. Nevertheless, the report did not come down in favour of any specific solution.

A similarly cautious attitude was evident in the Delors Report, as Hodson (2009: 508) underlines. It seems that this attitude reflected a tactical choice, agreed between TPS and Delors, in order to reduce the prospect of negative reactions to the transfer of monetary authority to a European central bank. During the negotiations of the Maastricht Treaty, it was essential to create as much consensus as possible, avoiding the fear that the transfer of monetary sovereignty would *necessarily* imply the transfer of larger parts of national sovereignty to European institutions.

From this point of view, TPS was very skilful in helping to forge consensus embracing the Germans and the British, the most dangerous opponents of EMU. He did so in two ways. He supported the idea of a politically independent central bank, in line with German thinking. He also showed early sympathy for the British proposal for a parallel currency (HM Treasury 1989). On the first point, TPS could draw on the vast literature of the late 1970s and 1980s on the crucial role of credibility, and therefore of political independence, in central banking. TPS was convinced that a central bank should be independent of political power, above all in order to stabilize expectations about the commitment to price stability. From this point of view, the proposal of the Delors Report for a 'federal' monetary authority, combined with national economic policies, could be the best architecture to safeguard such independence.

As we have seen, TPS was fully aware that such structure was unstable in the long run. However, he avoided stressing this point until the political decision to fix the roadmap towards the euro was secured. As he wrote later: 'Any delicate negotiation involves a degree of ambiguity, whether we like it or not'

(Padoa-Schioppa 2010a). Earlier, he had claimed that it had often been necessary to further European integration with a 'masked face' (Padoa-Schioppa 2002). The rationale was to avoid public discussions and pressures on the choices of enlightened European political elites.

The second aspect of TPS's consensus-seeking was more controversial, given the explicit intellectual paternity that the British Treasury attributed to Hayek in drafting its proposal. In 1976 Hayek had published *Denationalization of Money*, in which he argued that money is not a good requiring public monopoly but something that can be provided privately in a competitive market (Hayek 1976b). In such a situation, one or more currencies will eventually emerge as more stable and credible, thus progressively substituting the bad ones in monetary circulation. The proposals for a parallel currency in Europe, already advanced in the debates about the EMS, aimed at issuing a currency in addition to the existing national ones. The European Currency Unit (ECU) itself, after all, was a sort of parallel currency. And TPS had actively struggled to increase the private market of the ECU, as a way to raise its desirability on the market.

The British proposal for a hard ECU was offered as an alternative to the single-currency proposal of the Delors Report. It suggested a market-driven, competitive, and bottom-up process of monetary integration rather than an institutional, political, and top-down process (Masini 2010). In August 1990 TPS opposed the competitive currency solution à la Hayek, entrusted by the British government, but only if it was meant as an alternative solution to the final goal of the Delors Report (Padoa-Schioppa 1990: 188–9). On the other hand, the competitive currency plan was considered positively if it was meant as a contribution to the design of the transition phase that would lead to the single currency (Padoa-Schioppa 1990: 193).

This attitude might be attributed to the influence of Triffin, who had been very optimistic that a 'wider use of a parallel currency would pave the way for a monetary union' (see Chapter 2 by Maes and Bussière on Triffin). TPS took a more cautious approach to this question (Padoa-Schioppa 1991d). He was also aware of its risks. His argument was that a parallel currency might help to solve the problem of the change-over. However, a strong political commitment to the final goal of the single currency was necessary if the project was to be credibly implemented.

A crucial aspect of TPS's approach to monetary integration was the attitude that he showed towards the 'domestic house-in-order' strategy that was supported by the Germans. In line with the 'economist' approach of the 1960s–70s, the Germans always tried to negotiate monetary integration as the final result of a convergence process, devoted to a sound economic policy at home, thus decreasing the potential tensions to which a single currency could be subjected. TPS was always radically opposed to this strategy. He referred to 'the fallacy of the "house in order" precept as an adequate rule to deal with the policy issues raised by economic interdependence' (Padoa-Schioppa 2008: 211). International public goods cannot be efficiently provided by national governments. They require a collective system of rules and institutions that enforce cooperative results. Pursuing the goal of supranational integration only through a strategy of 'each having their own house in order' is wrong. A wider framework of economic policy is a fundamental prerequisite to achieve the goals of balanced growth. Also TPS firmly believed that collective problems require collective choices (Padoa-Schioppa 2008: 212ff.).

This belief did not contradict his strong commitment to a rigorous economic policy in Italy. On the contrary, TPS was aware that only by acquiring credibility by pursuing economic policies that were not detrimental to the collective needs could a country participate actively in the process of collective choices. Hence, while believing that the management of the European economy needed a European government, he struggled to make sure that Italy could not be deemed to be an obstacle to building a collective European will.

This twofold attitude is not contradictory. It shows that progress must be achieved on both levels of action. Correspondingly, any attempt to label TPS as a 'monetarist' or as an 'economist' is ill-suited. He certainly was not an 'economist', although he recognized the crucial role of macro-economic soundness at the domestic level to support the monetary union. And he was not even a 'monetarist' like those who expected an endogenous dynamic to emerge as concerns currency optimality: he never thought that a monetary union would spontaneously create the conditions for a subsequent economic convergence. The latter had to be the result of rigorous economic policies at the national level and a complex system of collective institutions to tackle problems of asymmetry in exogenous shocks. He struggled for the euro because he thought that monetary union was the crucial point on which advancement in the European integration process could be realized at the time and that therefore all efforts should be made to assist this choice by action to further macro-economic convergence.

Another central feature in the way in which TPS communicated his idea of the relationship between economic and political integration in the late 1980s and early 1990s was the stress he put on the different role of *institutions* from that of *politics*. The strengthening of public institutions is necessary to provide the constitutional framework that guarantees the enforcement of the rules that allow a smooth operation of the market and help to stabilize expectations. As he always made clear in his works on financial regulation and supervision, the activities of public authorities are crucial in order to ensure that market competition does not degenerate into volatility and chaos (Padoa-Schioppa 2000b; Papadia 2014: 1).

The political dimension is implied in this emphasis on institutional architecture, but TPS rarely referred to it explicitly. Only later did TPS clarify his thinking, claiming: 'the economic order implies a political order'

(Padoa-Schioppa 2007: 5). The reason for this change in his attitude towards the vital importance of transparency about European integration goals is provided in an earlier source. TPS claimed that with the euro it was no longer possible to proceed further with a 'masked face'. A clear vision of Europe's institutional order had to be provided if public opinion was to accept the next steps (Padoa-Schioppa 2002).

The question arises about the nature of this political order. As suggested earlier, the constitutional framework that TPS had in mind was a multilayered federal system, founded on the principle of subsidiarity (Padoa-Schioppa 2007). Functions were to be allocated as close as possible to individual citizens. However, when justified and required in terms of efficiency, it was essential to allocate crucial functions to higher government levels, from regional through national and supranational to global.

One possible reason why TPS often stressed the concept of subsidiarity in the early 1990s was that he was afraid of losing credibility with respect to British representatives, who were usually considered radically anti-federalist in their approach to Europe. Hence he emphasized the idea of subsidiarity in his proposal for federalism (Padoa-Schioppa 1995: 154). In this way he cast light on the decentralizing—rather than on the centralizing—aspect of federalism. Nevertheless, this concern never prevented TPS from expressing and defending his fundamental thoughts. He actually firmly believed that subsidiarity and a soft federation model would best suit Europe, much more than a rather centralized federal system like that of the United States. From this point of view, TPS was a classical liberal in the mould of Einaudi and Lionel Robbins (Masini 2012b). They supported a supranational federation as the best guarantee to have a system of economic and political governance that would defend freedom without degenerating into anarchy at the international level, with a very few but crucial competences allocated to the federal level.

TPS's LEGACY: A ROADMAP FOR EUROPE

In February 2010, just after the Greek crisis had broken out but had not yet become a wider crisis affecting the Euro Area as a whole, TPS engaged in a public disagreement with Otmar Issing. Both had been founder members of the executive board of the ECB. The first interesting point in TPS's arguments related to the nature of financial markets and the role of politics. There are times, TPS claimed, when markets cannot be left to work spontaneously, as Issing argued, because the results would be economically inefficient.

> In a climate of fear, markets can become as blind and destructive as a natural catastrophe and fail to distinguish between the errant and the irreproachable,

> between Greece and the outside. A point could soon be reached where not to act would invite disaster upon all. We are now so close to such a point that the EU leaders' statement was a wise step. Through inaction, virtuous but myopic countries could deal a blow to their own prosperity and stability. What is needed is not altruism, only enlightened self-interest. (Padoa-Schioppa 2010a)

In such a case, public authorities should intervene to restore trust. TPS was well aware that the ECB alone cannot avoid disasters, if there is no coherent political will to support the euro project. This insight is the first legacy of TPS: markets may fail in times of crisis due to the lack of credible political commitment to the existence, effectiveness, and legitimacy of a political decision-making system like the Euro Area.

The second aspect of his legacy is connected: what kind of political decisions are required to save the euro from speculative attacks? The answer lies in the completion of the euro project with the achievement of a political union:

> True, monetary union came before political union. But it did not come with a promise that there would never be such a union. Quite to the contrary: the founding fathers wanted the euro primarily as a step towards political union, knowing little of the overriding technical arguments in its favour. Those who argued against it then on the grounds that 'there can be no monetary union without political union' are precisely those who should welcome political union now that it finally knocks at the door claiming its rights. (Padoa-Schioppa 2010a)

This extract offers a sort of historiographical interpretation of the ideas that supported the foundation of the euro. Despite scepticism about his true attitude, one can hardly question that, at least towards the end of his life, TPS was very clear on political union. The final goal of the European integration process, whose monetary aspect is an important step, is a political union. It was to be a union based on very simple principles, such as the use of majority voting (instead of unanimity and veto power) and the use of supranational instead of intergovernmental decision-making systems not only in the monetary field but also in the other two pillars of the EU: foreign policy and justice (Padoa-Schioppa 2002).

While engaged in the early process towards monetary integration, TPS was aware of the need to be cautious in recognizing publicly the full implications of monetary integration, i.e. the transfer of small but fundamental parts of national sovereignty to a supranational system of economic and political governance. Otherwise, he feared losing credibility as a negotiator, weakening the prospects of implementation of his goals. But once the project was launched, TPS struggled to make the monetary construction sounder and more stable, until later he called for a political union in order to create the institutional framework and the democratic legitimacy to defend the monetary project from various attacks. This is TPS's second legacy: no monetary union can survive without political union in the long run.

The difficulty is in understanding, and this is the third point, how to achieve the political union that TPS had in mind. From this point of view, we should recall first the importance that TPS attached to gradualism, a method he derived from his admiration for Jean Monnet. Gradualism does not mean waiting for Godot; it means struggling to make advancements, step by step, but with a precise direction in mind:

> To have a roadmap we need to know where we want to go. Among the mistakes that we pay today there is the fact that we have not solved clearly enough the question of where we want to go . . . In my opinion, the goal is twofold: to give up the principle of unanimity and the availability of budgetary resources to implement the decisions taken. (TPS in Rotondo 2007)

It is not by chance that well before the Euro Area crisis TPS had tried to push the accelerator on a banking union, as a prerequisite for further integration steps. When he became Minister of the Treasury in Italy, he tried to convince the other Euro Area Member States that a single rule book for banking supervision was necessary—without receiving any support.

The roadmap of the four presidents in 2012, *Towards a Genuine Economic and Monetary Union* (Van Rompuy 2012), seems to have taken up TPS's challenge. What this document lacks is a precise and irreversible time schedule. Here we find another important suggestion that TPS left to European policy-makers. TPS stressed the importance of a highest-level political agreement for the adoption of a precise time schedule for the three stages of European monetary integration. He saw this as vital for the success of the whole process. Nowadays, if European leaders want to give credibility to the roadmap for a genuine EMU, they should adopt a precise and binding time schedule, no matter how far in time, for the four unions—banking, fiscal, economic, and political.

The final legacy of TPS was the notion of gradualism with a precise goal, together with a binding time schedule for a roadmap towards political union. He saw this method as perfectly fitted to pursue an ambitious goal like sustainable European integration.

CONCLUSION

It is tricky to single out direct relationships between economic theorizing and policy-making. The way these two systems of human action interact is often complex and hardly visible. One of the most intriguing aspects of the relationships between economic analysis and policy is the key individuals who happen to connect the two realms, especially when they belong to both. This connection was apparent in the case of TPS with respect to the birth of the euro. His strongly pro-European intellectual background, combined with a rigorous analytical knowledge of economics, connected to political practice through the several institutional roles that he played in his life. His economic background and position cannot be easily subsumed within a standard academic category. Similarly, his attitude towards economic integration in Europe cannot be simply identified with either the standard categories of monetarists and economists. He was a pragmatist, who believed in the need to compromise between market and public institutions (Visco 2011: 4), between rules and discretion (Masini 2015). And he was a genuine classical liberal; so genuine that he probably felt constrained in an unfriendly political climate at home where the values of liberalism could be defended and pursued only with difficulty.

TPS had a robust theoretical knowledge of monetary macro-economics, combined with a strong belief in the historical necessity of uniting Europe, both economically and politically. He also had extraordinary capabilities of communicating with individuals in key institutional positions, thus bringing his ideas within policy-making. These capabilities were demonstrated in the negotiations to decide whether the lira should join the EMS from the beginning, in the Delors Committee, and at many other crucial moments when he provided advice to Carli, Andreotti, Delors, and others. His relationship and friendship with Delors was probably the single most important one in his network on EMU, as also testified by the fact that he was appointed president of Delors' think-tank Notre Europe.

TPS exerted a very important influence in academic and professional meetings. He forged the way in which DG II of the EU Commission became a governmental service in managing the transition to the single currency. He co-drafted crucial policy proposals such as the Delors Report. He managed some of the most important institutions for financial-market supervision and later for monetary policy, above all as a founding member of the ECB executive board. Successfully, as far as he was concerned, he supported the soundness of macro-economic stances in Italy, despite his aversion towards the 'domestic house-in-order' approach, as a way to acquire credibility in pushing for more solidarity at the European level. This influenced his views on the emerging Greek crisis in 2010. For more than thirty years, he pushed European monetary integration forward. At the same time, he recognized that this progress could not be sustained without a strong political commitment to change the institutional architecture of European governance so that the problems of collective action could be solved without blockage by veto-players.

In short, TPS was a smart adviser to policy-makers, uniting high-level professional skills in monetary macro-economics with a precise (although evolving) goal in mind, and able to adapt strategies and tactical moves towards its achievement. From this point of view, he not only played an important role as an architect of the euro. He was also a great engineer of EMU, thanks to his strong awareness of the need to found the euro process within a multilayered framework of public institutions, both at national and supranational level, in a logic of subsidiarity and a federal constitution. This view of institutional design embodied the guiding principles for a stable governance of the European economy. TPS did not seek a federation like the United States or Germany, where most powers and competences are allocated to the federal government. He looked to a softer federation, where only the fundamental questions are left to the federal government, above all the three pillars of EMU, foreign policy, and justice; a federation in which the federal power works as a proper unitary collective body, not as an intergovernmental one. According to TPS, monetary integration should serve as a point of reference for the extension and completion of European integration in the other two pillars, making it an original but true federal system.

10

Jacques Delors

Vision, Revisionism, and the Design of EMU

Dermot Hodson

Few individuals are more closely associated with the project of European Economic Monetary Union (EMU) than Jacques Delors. As French finance minister between 1981 and 1984, Delors played a decisive role in *le tournant de la rigueur*, the economic U-turn that saw President François Mitterrand abandon expansionary policies in favour of fiscal consolidation, market reforms, and continued membership of the European Monetary System (EMS). This move not only paved the way for France's recommitment to EMU, it also propelled Delors to the presidency of the European Commission, a post that he held between 1984 and 1995.

The Community made major strides towards EMU during Delors' time in Brussels. The signing of the Single European Act in 1986 ended the *de facto* moratorium on EMU by recalling the EEC heads of state and government's commitment at Paris in 1972 to 'the progressive realization of economic and monetary union' (Heads of State and Government 1972). This set the scene for the European Council's decision at Hanover in June 1988 to convene a high-level committee led by Delors to study and propose 'concrete stages towards this union' (Council of the European Union 1988). The Delors Report, as it came to be known, served as a rough blueprint for the first stage of EMU, which was launched by the European Council in June 1989. This led to a firm commitment to a single currency, alongside looser plans for political union in the Maastricht Treaty, which envisaged two further stages to EMU, the first of which began in January 1994 as Delors entered the final twelve months of his presidency.

Whether Delors was an architect of EMU or more of a draughtsman is a matter of debate within the scholarly literature. For Moravcsik (1998: 435–6),

Delors did little more beyond his time as French finance minister than lend his name to a committee in which the preferences of national policy-makers dominated. The Commission president drafted much of the final report. But, Moravcsik argues, it was left to the national central bank governors who made up the majority of this committee to make substantive proposals on the possible design of EMU. Dyson and Featherstone (1999: 717), in contrast, see Delors' approach as a calculated one designed to mollify Bundesbank president Karl Otto Pöhl, while relying on the other central bank governors present to put forward proposals with which the Commission president was sympathetic. Either way, Delors handled his brief well and can claim credit for encouraging consensus within a committee comprised of what Harold James (2012: 237) describes as 'a combination of skeptics and enthusiasts'.

This chapter is less interested in Delors' political influence on, than in his personal vision of, EMU. It seeks, in particular, to understand what Delors' idea of EMU was, how it evolved over time, and what its legacy is for contemporary debates about the single currency. In so doing, it tries to reconcile some of the contradictions concerning Delors' reputation as a consummate technocrat with a strong ideological commitment to the European project, as an economist with a passion for theology, and as an enthusiastic proponent of the euro who later admitted to fundamental flaws in EMU's design and execution.

The central argument is that Delors' vision of EMU was a blurred one. Although the Frenchman's public support for the project can be traced back to the early 1960s, he remained vague about the precise meaning and purpose of monetary union until the Delors Committee concluded its work. Even then, the Commission president remained guarded about his plans for European economic governance and remained so after he left the Commission in 1995. Ambiguity is an important part of a diplomat's toolkit (Jönsson and Hall 2003). However, this chapter sees Delors' opacity as more than just a negotiating device. Delors' blurred vision of EMU, it suggests, is indicative of his lived experience as an economist, political activist, and politician en route from Paris to Brussels and back again. Much is made in the literature of Delors' Catholicism and his commitment to European integration (Grant 1994; Dyson and Featherstone 1999; Rollat 1993). Such accounts overstate the ideational importance of Delors' religion for EMU, however, while understating both his reluctance to align himself with any one mainstream macro-economic theory and his unease with European federalism.

Delors' economic eclecticism helps to explain why he did not begin with a fixed definition of EMU and how he was able to build an alliance with the more Keynesian-minded members of the Delors Committee, while making concessions to the Ordo-liberals who sought greater emphasis on price stability, central bank independence, and fiscal discipline. Delors' views on European federalism are also important since they shed light on the Commission president's determination to follow Member States' political lead on EMU and his initial reluctance about championing a centralized approach to monetary policy. They also account for Delors' frustrations regarding debates about political union at Maastricht.

Seen in these terms, Delors' long-term legacy in relation to EMU is a divided one. On the one hand, Delors succeeded where his predecessors as Commission president had failed by keeping an open mind about EMU's design and taking his political cues from the Member States. On the other hand, such pragmatism raises the question of whether Delors thought through the full implications of creating a single currency and whether he could and should have done more to address his concerns over European economic governance.

INSIGHT

Born in Paris in 1925, Jacques Delors was an early and enthusiastic proponent of European monetary cooperation. Having founded the periodical *Citoyens 1960, cahiers d'éducation politique, économique et sociale* in 1960 and served as its first editor, Delors lent his support to the European Commission's Action Programme for the Second Stage of the Community, which suggested that monetary union could go hand in hand with the completion of the single market (see Grant 1994: 24; see also Chapter 3 by Seidel). As a Member of the European Parliament (MEP) from 1979 to 1981, Delors produced a positive assessment of the EMS in his capacity as chair of the Economic and Monetary Affairs Committee (Grant 1994: 44). As French finance minister from 1981 to 1984, Delors faced down calls from within François Mitterrand's circle of advisers to leave the EMS. This defence of European monetary cooperation helped to cement Delors' reputation at home and abroad and so aided his rise to the presidency of the European Commission. For François Mitterrand, the Berlaymont was a useful place to send one of his more belligerent cabinet members (Delors 2004: 209). Delors' reputation as an economic reformer, meanwhile, endeared him to UK Prime Minister Margaret Thatcher, albeit briefly (Thatcher 2011: 548).

In the months before he took office as Commission president in January 1985, Delors toured national capitals to take soundings from the EEC heads of state and government on EMU, among other ideas for relaunching European integration (Delors 1994: 220). Although national leaders remained circumspect about EMU at this juncture, Delors still made the case for 'increased monetary integration' in his maiden speech to the European Parliament as Commission president (Delors 1985a). What he meant by 'increased monetary integration' at this time was not easy to discern. In a speech to the Confederation of British Industry in October 1985, the Commission President called for 'a genuine European monetary area', but he did not say what such an area would entail other than alluding to the fact that it would go beyond the EMS in its current form (Delors 1985b).

At the Intergovernmental Conference (IGC) on the Single European Act in October and November of that year, Delors was more forthcoming in his call for a full incorporation of the EMS into the new treaty alongside a clause for the creation of a European Monetary Fund, but such proposals failed to win the support of all Member States (Grant 1994: 73). More successful was Delors' support for including a general reference to EMU in the Single European Act, the final text of which recalled EEC heads of states' commitment to EMU in Paris in 1972 and included a new chapter on economic and monetary policy coordination. For Moravcsik (1998: 21) these provisions amounted to no more than a 'rhetorical commitment', but Delors (2004: 280) saw them as providing an impetus for subsequent discussions of EMU.

The heads of state and government signed the Single European Act in February 1986. Thereafter Delors said more about his vision of EMU but still not that much. Appearing before the European Parliament at this time, Delors acknowledged that the time was 'not yet ripe' for radical reform of the EMS and argued, instead, that the free movement of capital was a key stumbling block in this regard (European Commission 1986a). In May 1986, the Commission outlined its 'Programme for the Liberalization of Capital Movements in the Community'. In this Communication it was recognized that free movement would entail 'greater uniformity within the Community of the techniques of monetary control', but it did not say how (European Commission 1986b). Instead, this question was left to a 'forward study' on the implications of financial integration for monetary cooperation, led by Tomasso Padoa-Schioppa, a former director general for economic and financial affairs at the European Commission and someone who would exercise a major intellectual influence on Delors (see Chapter 9 by Masini).

The Padoa-Schioppa Report, which was published in April 1987, weighed its words carefully. It did not call outright for EMU but concluded rather that 'the elimination of exchange-rate controls, coupled with the requirements of exchange-rate stability...will require moving closer to the unification of monetary policies' (Padoa-Schioppa 1987: 3–4). It was not so much this policy conclusion that attracted attention as the economic reasoning that underpinned it. Member States faced an inconsistent quartet, Padoa-Schioppa memorably argued, between completing the single market, facilitating the free movement of capital, ensuring exchange-rate stability, and maintaining autonomy in monetary policy. Having embarked on the single market project, in other words, Member States faced a choice between national monetary policies and EMU.

Delors' reading of Padoa-Schioppa's report was a curious one. Although the Commission president needed no convincing that capital market liberalization would serve as a catalyst for European monetary cooperation, he paid little heed in public to Padoa-Schioppa's implicit critique of the EMS as a half-way house between national autonomy in macro-economic matters and no autonomy at all. Instead, Delors continued to champion the EMS as a successful exchange-rate regime that would encourage stability in Europe and in the international monetary system more generally (e.g. Delors 1987).

Political tactics were clearly at play here, but so too were economic convictions. This tension in the Commission president's thinking came to a head during the Exchange Rate Mechanism (ERM) crises of 1992–3. Speaking to the European Parliament in the aftermath of 'Black Wednesday', when the United Kingdom exited the ERM, Delors acknowledged that EMU had 'presupposed a medium-term economic strategy, based on gradual convergence of our economies, underpinned by the consolidation and the successes of the European Monetary System' (Delors 1993). Padoa-Schioppa laboured under no such illusion. The inconsistent quartet, he would later write, meant that 'it would have been Utopian to consider an adjustable peg such as the EMS as being indefinitely sustainable [since]...the only sustainable solution indeed was the single currency' (Padoa-Schioppa 2000b: 2).

Although Delors maintained his mantra in public on strengthening of the EMS, he stepped up his campaign for EMU behind closed doors. At the European Council in Copenhagen in December 1987 Delors canvassed EC leaders about convening a 'wise-persons' group on EMU but said nothing about this issue in public (Delors 1994: 420). Whereas German foreign minister Hans-Dietrich Genscher and French finance minister Édouard Balladur put forward bold plans in early 1988 for a European central bank with a single currency, Delors struck a conservative tone at this time. The EC should not abandon the 'pragmatic approach that has served us well' he told MEPs in January 1988, while indicating that continued efforts to promote the European Currency Unit (ECU) as a private currency and overhaul the European Monetary Cooperation Fund would suffice for the time being (Delors 1988). Such public caution did not, however, prevent Delors from holding a series of bilateral behind the scenes meetings with German Chancellor Helmut Kohl on EMU in the months ahead. It was on the basis of these meetings that Kohl arrived at the idea of a high-level committee on EMU, chaired by Delors, a decision that was ratified by the European Council in Hanover in June 1988 (Dyson and Featherstone 1999: 712).

Delors brought his considerable political talents to bear in the Committee for the Study of Economic and Monetary Union. The twelve central bank governors and three external participants who made up the Delors Committee may have shared causal beliefs about the importance of low inflation and stable exchange rates and a normative commitment to European monetary cooperation (Verdun 1999). But they came to the forum with disparate views about EMU and varying degrees of good will. Bundesbank President Karl Otto Pöhl cast himself as leader of the awkward squad, and it took a concerted effort from Delors to keep the German central banker engaged in the work of the committee (see Dyson and Featherstone 1999: 342–8). What Delors did not bring to the committee was a clear and compelling vision of EMU. For the most part, the Commission president was content to let other committee members take the floor (Dyson and Featherstone 1999: 714). He also allowed Tomasso Padoa-Schioppa, as co-rapporteur, to shape the terms of discussion through position papers and a skeleton draft of the final report (James 2012: 246–8).

To suggest that Delors was agnostic about EMU's design would be misleading. Initially, as Dyson and Featherstone (1999: 717) note, Delors favoured a European Monetary Fund tasked with coordinating Member States' monetary policy in keeping with the French tradition on EMU. He was not wedded to this approach, however, and left open the door to the idea of a European central bank with centralized control of monetary policy even before the committee had met (Delors 1988). Delors was less guarded on the fiscal dimension of EMU, arguing against binding fiscal rules on government borrowing on the grounds that financial market discipline would keep Member States in check (James 2012: 252).

For all his reticence about national fiscal rules, Delors was reluctant to leave fiscal policy to the discretion of Member States. Here he made the case for a political counterweight to the ECB that could facilitate 'an EC countercyclical policy' (Dyson and Featherstone 1999: 718). To this end, he called for an increase in the Community budget from 1.2 to 3.0 per cent by the year 2000 (James 2012: 253). This idea was not backed in the final report, which considered a number of arguments in favour of a supranational budgetary authority (Thygesen 1989: 639–40), while accepting that 'the centrally managed Community budget [was] likely to remain a very small part of total public sector spending' (Committee for the Study of Economic and Monetary Union 1989: 19–20).

In addition to his role as chair, Delors presented two background papers to the Committee for the Study of Economic and Monetary Union. The first was a short note, more political than economic in character (Delors 1989a). On the surface this note offered a descriptive overview of the key stages in European monetary cooperation since the Werner Report. This chronology was punctuated, however, by a cautionary tale about the 'creeping paralysis' that results when Member States reject the Community method, an approach to policy-making that emphasizes the 'progressive and limited transfer of powers to common institutions possessing a real power to make decisions' (Delors 1989b: 64).

The second paper was richer in economic analysis. In this piece, Delors focused on the risks of regional imbalances in EMU and policy options available in the absence of national exchange-rate policy. Delors covered familiar ground here by arguing that the experience of more mature monetary unions, although by no means uniform, pointed towards 'a substantial development of the budgetary function of the EC in the case of monetary union' (Delors 1989b: 82). More innovative were his thoughts on the possible functions of such a budgetary instrument, with the schemes 'designed to compensate for institutional rigidities in factor or price mobility' or 'sustain income and demand in the regions...that may be economically weakened' rejected in favour of 'decentralized supply-side regional policies' focused on 'subsidized investments in physical infrastructure and human capital' (Delors 1989b).

It is in regional policy that Delors' imprint on the committee's final report is most discernible. Although the report steered clear of explicitly recommending a centralized budgetary instrument, it acknowledged concerns over regional imbalances in EMU and underlined the need for 'common policies aimed at structural change and regional development' (Committee for the Study of Economic and Monetary Union 1989: 16).

Having given a cautious welcome to the Delors Report at the European Council in Madrid in June 1989, EC heads of state and government decided in December of that year to convene an IGC on EMU. In approaching this conference, Delors stood by the conclusions of his eponymous committee for the most part, even on those points on which the central bank governors had overruled him. In a note circulated to EC finance ministers in March 1990, the Commission president agreed that EMU would be based on a common monetary policy controlled by an independent central bank, something which he had initially resisted in the Delors Committee, and 'in the budgetary policy field, a system of coordination and voluntary constraints designed to guarantee both consistency with the stability-oriented monetary policy and a satisfactory overall policy-mix' (European Commission 1990a).

Having previously rejected the need for binding rules on government borrowing, the Commission president now argued that 'the convergence of budgetary policies can...be sought more appropriately through procedures to which all Member States would be bound' (European Commission 1990a). No mention was made here of the pecuniary sanctions that would be provided for under the Maastricht Treaty's Excessive Deficit Procedure (EDP). Delors was not against a rules-based approach per se but argued for the incorporation of 'budgetary rules or guidelines into national law' and a 'graduated response' to profligate Member States, beginning with recommendations and ending with 'the withdrawal of conditional Community budgetary assistance' (European Commission 1990a).

If Delors presented an essentially conservative view of EMU's architecture, he could not resist a few embellishments. Noticeable in this regard was a reprisal of arguments for strengthening regional funds for EMU, including a centralized budgetary instrument to provide a 'shock-absorber mechanism capable of reacting promptly in the event of unexpected economic shocks' (European Commission 1990a). The aforementioned reference to conditional assistance was also significant since it hinted at the need for a fiscal crisis-resolution mechanism. On this point Delors was adamant that a no-bail-out clause did 'not exclude conditional assistance' (European Commission 1990a).

Aside from an agreement by Member States to establish a new EU regional policy instrument, the Cohesion Fund, the IGC on EMU offered Delors few of these additional desiderata. Still, such negotiations were plain-sailing for the Commission president compared to the IGC on political union, agreed in April 1990. Although it turned out to have little to do with EMU, Member States agreed instead to instigate intergovernmental cooperation in the domains of foreign and security policy and justice and home affairs. In their letter to the Irish presidency of the EC in April 1990, Kohl and Mitterrand, the two driving forces behind political union, called for an acceleration of 'the political construction of the Europe of the Twelve' not only because of 'far-reaching changes in Europe' but also in view of 'the realisation of economic and monetary union' (Kohl and Mitterrand 1990).

If Delors was primed for a debate on EMU in 1988, he was less keen to have one on political union two years later. Having failed to convince Kohl and Mitterrand to convene a high-level committee to explore the concept of political union, he made little attempt to disguise his unease with the project (Dyson and Featherstone 1999: 722). Speaking in Ireland in April 1990, the Commission president asked: 'Why has the question of the political and institutional future of the Community become topical?' (Delors 1990a). His answer, on this occasion, touched on Germany's concern that German unification should take place within a European context, the perceived discord between economic and political integration, and the need for greater democratic and political accountability as part of moves towards EMU. Relevant though these issues were, Delors struggled to weave them together into a coherent narrative and in so doing demonstrated just how speculative his thinking on political union was at this juncture.

The following months brought more rather than less confusion for Delors. Having intended to publish a plan on political union in April 1990, the Commission delayed doing so until October of that year (Grant 1994). This text was a motley collection of proposals on foreign policy cooperation, democratic legitimacy, and institutional questions, all very much in keeping with the subject matter of the IGC but no less lacking in coherence for that.

These proposals divided Member States to varying degrees, as did draft treaties circulated by the Luxembourg and Dutch EC presidencies. Having railed against the Luxembourg draft for its failure to uphold the Community method, Delors tried but failed to secure support for the Dutch draft, only to see Member States switch back to the Luxembourg draft. As a result of this reversal, Delors found himself marginalized in the IGC on political union and sorely disappointed with the final text (Wester 1992: 212). The Commission president's doubts about the Maastricht Treaty, he would later admit, were one reason why he remained aloof from France's close-run referendum campaign in 1992 (Delors 1994: 275).

In January 1993, Delors agreed to serve a third truncated term as Commission president, so as to allow the European Parliament to exercise its new consultative role in appointing the College of Commissioners from January 1995. Speaking to MEPs in the midst of the ERM crisis and a yet-to-be-resolved political emergency over Denmark's rejection of the Maastricht Treaty in 1992, Delors cut a disconsolate figure. 'The economy is in crisis', he told MEPs, 'society is in crisis, democracy is foundering...[t]he very idea of a united Europe is in peril' (Delors 1993).

Amid this doom and gloom, Delors' growing preoccupation with the competitiveness of the European economy became apparent. It was this issue rather than EMU that came to define his final two years in office. Key in this respect was the Commission's 1993 White Paper on Growth, Competitiveness and Employment, a detailed policy plan designed to 'foster debate and to assist decision-making at decentralized national or Community level—so as to lay the foundations for the sustainable development of the European economies, thereby enabling them to withstand international competition while creating the millions of jobs that are needed' (European Commission 1993). This White Paper was long on economic ideas, short on specific proposals, and shorter still in its ambition for the Community to take centre stage in relation to economic and social policies. Mention was made of EMU, most noticeably in the White Paper's calls for closer economic policy coordination and a more balanced macro-economic policy mix, but it was vague on how best to achieve these ends. Striking in this regard was the Commission's reticence about the Broad Economic Policy Guidelines (BEPGs), a set of non-binding guidelines on economic policy provided by the Maastricht Treaty, which would later come to be seen as central to the EU's efforts at macro-economic policy coordination (see Deroose et al. 2008). Here the report hinted at a lack of consensus when it noted that 'all Member States' accept the case for 'a stable framework for macroeconomic policy', while acknowledging that only 'a number of Member States advocate the use of guidelines provided for in the Treaty' to this end (European Commission 1993). Either way, the White Paper produced few tangible policy outputs during Delors' remaining months as

Commission president, which after a decade of policy activism ended with a whimper rather than a bang.

Many expected Jacques Delors to return to a high-level position in French politics after his time as Commission president. By late 1994 he was seen by some as the candidate best placed to lead the Left to victory in the following year's presidential election (Tudor 1994). In the end, however, Delors refused to stand, leaving the question of what impact he would have had as French president as one of the great 'what if' questions about EMU. Having ruled out a run for the Elysée, Delors returned to Paris to found the think-tank Notre Europe in 1996.

Through his activities at Notre Europe Delors emerged as and remained a prolific commentator on European affairs, particularly during periods of perceived crisis for the European project. The reform of EMU is a recurring theme in such commentary, with Delors championing the success of the single currency while calling for greater emphasis on economic growth relative to fiscal discipline and for an 'economic government' (*gouvernement économique*) to serve as a counterweight to the European Central Bank (ECB). Here again Delors' precise vision of EMU is difficult to discern. Among his more concrete recommendations in this regard is a pact for economic policy coordination (*pacte pour la coordination des politiques économique*). However, even this proposal, which was put forward in 1997 to counter negotiations over the Stability and Growth Pact (SGP), is couched in generalities about cooperation in areas such as budgetary policy and structural reform (Delors 1997).

The Euro Area crisis, it would seem, has had only a limited impact on Delors' thinking about EMU. True, the former Commission president became blunter in his assessment of the single currency's shortcomings and more critical of EU and national policy-makers as the Euro Area's sovereign debt crisis worsened. But, in so doing, he offered a familiar vision of the functioning of EMU.[1] In December 2011, Delors hit the headlines when he admitted that the euro suffered from 'a fault in execution' (Moore 2011). Far from being a mea culpa, what Delors meant by this remark was not that the Delors Report or the IGC on EMU had been mistaken but that Member States had failed to heed his warnings in the early years of EMU about the need for a more comprehensive coordination of economic policies.

As the crisis worsened, Delors went further in his calls for a *fonds de régulation conjoncturelle* (Delors 2013). This fund, it would seem, was a return to Delors' earlier idea of the need for a centralized budgetary instrument. But, as always, such proposals were sketched with a broad brush rather than in fine detail, leaving his precise vision of EMU a matter of interpretation.

[1] Euractiv, 'Delors points the finger at Europe's "killers"', 29 March 2012. Full text available at: <http://www.euractiv.com/future-eu/delors-denounces-killers-europe-news-511850>.

HINDSIGHT

Having described Delors' particular vision of EMU, this chapter moves on to explore the political and intellectual context in which his views arose. It is important to note that he had a personal connection to the world of central banking. His father, Louis Delors, was a messenger boy at the Banque de France. Louis was not entirely satisfied with this position at the bank, but he put pressure on his son to apply for a traineeship there. Delors, who had planned to go to film school, reluctantly agreed, passed the entrance exam and joined the Banque de France in October 1945 (Grant 1994: 9).

Biographers say little about Delors' time at the central bank, but it was here that the future Commission president spent 17 years learning about the fundamentals of economic policy. Grant (1994: 11), for example, concludes that 'neither the nature of the work nor the bank's culture inspired' Delors. Milesi (1995) mentions Delors' time at the central bank only in passing and focuses instead on his fledgling political activities in the 1950s and 1960s. Although Delors' first five years at the Banque de France were spent in an essentially managerial role—he ran a team responsible for processing securities transactions—his later role in the cabinet of the director general for stocks and money markets ensured an education in the functioning of financial markets, exchange rates, and public finances (Delors 2004: 38–9). This was also a period of intensive academic study for Delors, who took a three-year diploma from the Centre d'études supérieures de banque, during which time he attended classes on economics, finance, and banking (Delors 2004: 37).

Delors quit the Banque de France in 1962 to join the French Planning Commission (Commissariat général du Plan), but a sense that he saw unfinished business in the world of central banking is discernible at different stages of his subsequent career. In 1972 Delors was appointed by Valéry Giscard d'Estaing to the general council of the Banque de France. Later Delors said of this move that he was delighted to be back at the central bank and to have an opportunity to enrich his knowledge of economic and monetary affairs (Delors 2004: 135). In 1981 Delors became French finance minister and hence a key actor in relation to monetary policy. He was not a free agent here, however, as evidenced by his frustration in autumn 1982 over the government's decision to cancel a proposed interest-rate cut on state savings accounts. When François Mitterrand later offered him the post of prime minister, Delors made it a condition that he would assume control of monetary policy (Delors 2004: 210). Mitterrand was unwilling to accept such terms, however, and Delors remained as finance minister, albeit with an enlarged portfolio and a higher rank in cabinet.

Another instance of Delors' enduring interest in central banking was his decision as president of the European Commission to attend monthly meetings of the Committee of EC Central Bank Governors. This was not a standard operating procedure for a Commission president but a deliberate attempt by Delors to gain access to the 'enclosed world of central banking' (Dyson and Featherstone 1999: 708).

If this account gives a sense of Delors' personal connection to the world of central banking, it does not tell us where his intellectual influences came from and how they shaped his vision of EMU. Scholars seeking to understand Delors' motivations as a political actor have placed great emphasis on his Catholic faith (see, for example, Grant 1994: 236–9; Drake 2000: 30). The interplay between politics and religion certainly seems to have been important for the young Delors, who joined the international movement La Jeunesse ouvrière chrétienne and developed an interest in social Catholicism through his involvement in the trade union La Confédération Française des Travailleurs Chrétiens. Ross places particular emphasis on Delors' Jansenism, a strain of Catholic thought comparable to Calvinism (Ross 1995: 176). Dyson and Featherstone go further by arguing that Jansenism endowed Delors with a moral seriousness, a frugality, an individualistic streak, a tendency towards pedagogy and didacticism, and a concern for solidarity, all of which made their mark on his approach to EMU negotiations (Dyson and Featherstone 1999: 695–6). It is not difficult to recognize Delors in some of these character traits, but Jansenism is a broad collection of beliefs that can be reconciled with a variety of personality types and political philosophies (see, for example, McLendon 2006).

Scholars seeking to understand Delors' Catholicism have also attached great importance to his interest in Emmanuel Mounier, a French Catholic philosopher who in the 1930s developed a 'personalist' critique of 'bourgeois civilization' that called for greater emphasis on individualism and communitarianism (e.g. Grant 1994: 12–15; Ross 1995: 17). Personalism is arguably a better philosophical fit for Delors than Jansenism for two reasons. First, Delors has made little public comment about his Jansensism but, in contrast, has rarely missed an opportunity to talk about Mounier. A case in point is Delors' speech to the College of Europe in October 1989 in which he stated his position 'as an advocate of personalism also, and as a disciple of Emmanuel Mounier whose influence will, I am sure, become once again very important as Europeans will notably become aware of the impasses resulting from wholesale individualism' (Delors 1989c). Second, rarefied though these ideas are, there is an intellectual link between personalism as a political philosophy and the idea of European integration. As Loughlin (1993: 1) notes, a sense of frustration with the nation-state is a recurring theme for those personalists who believed in the 'bypassing of the nation-state by a double movement or rather one movement with two aspects: "returning to the sources"; and building a federal Europe'. Although there is some overlap between Delors' and Mounier's thinking on international issues, personalism finds clearer expression in Delors' involvement in the 1950s and 1960s in La Vie nouvelle, a Social Catholic movement inspired by Mounier's teaching (Delors 1975: 38–9).

How important Delors' Catholicism was for his presidency of the European Commission is a matter of debate. He was certainly not a politician who was comfortable talking about his faith, describing himself in an interview long after he left Brussels as a 'secular catholic' who was critical of public figures who wore their religion on their sleeves (Delors 2004: 311–13). As Commission president, Delors emphasized dialogues with all faiths as well as with non-believers (Delors 2004: 330), and his vision of European society was one that encompassed several religions as well as the Continent's secular and intellectual traditions. Meanwhile, Delors' relations with Pope John Paul II were strained, the pontiff being wary of the Commission president's social Catholicism (Grant 1994: 83).

Some scholars see Delors as using his faith to strategic advantage in his dealings with another Catholic politician, Chancellor Helmut Kohl (Hutton 2008). While it is true that the French Socialist and the Germany Christian Democrat had a rapport, it had as much to do with their shared beliefs in this world than in the next. Delors was very much a man of the French Left, but his politics were more complicated than this label suggests. After the Second World War, he joined not the French section of the Workers' International (Section Française de l'Internationale Ouvrière, SFOI) but Charles de Gaulle's Popular Republican Movement (Mouvement républicain populaire, MRP), based on the belief that the latter was closer to his social Catholicism (Delors 1975: 27). Delors left the MRP after a matter of months, but he did not completely cut ties with the Right. This can be seen, for example, in Delors' willingness to serve as an adviser to Gaullist prime minister Jacques Chaban-Delmas between 1969 and 1972 (Ludlow forthcoming) and in his association with the politically mercurial Pierre Mendes France (Delors 2004: 86). Delors eventually joined the French Socialist Party in 1974 but he would retain, Wolfram Kaiser (2007: 325) suggests, a Christian Democratic side to his political character. This fact could explain Delors' close working relationship with Germany's Kohl, with Luxembourg's Jacques Santer and Jean-Claude Juncker (Delors 2004: 274), and with Belgium's Phillipe Maystadt (Dyson and Featherstone 1999: 707), as well as with other members of what Karl Magnus Johansson (2002) calls the Christian Democrat coalition on EMU.

One issue on which Delors' Catholicism is said to have shaped his Commission presidency concerns his championing of the idea of subsidiarity (Burgess 2000). Subsidiarity, the principle whereby 'the Union shall act only if and in so far as the objectives of the proposed action cannot be sufficiently achieved by the Member States' (Article 5, Treaty on European Union) is referenced in the Delors Report (Committee on Economic and Monetary Union 1989: 18) and associated with the Catholic tradition (Follesdal 1998: 207). Care must be exercised, however, before jumping between Delors' religious and political beliefs and his wider intellectual influence on EMU. For one thing, there is significant slippage between Delors' usage of the term subsidiarity and that of Catholic theologians (Spicker 1991). Nor is subsidiarity a concept that Delors can claim copyright on, the European Parliament having done much to popularize the term in the 1970s (Peterson 1994). The United Kingdom was another early champion of subsidiarity, even if it did not use the term, and helped to ensure that the Community's embryonic environmental policy included a principle about the concentration of Community activity on areas where it was likely to be most effective (Golub 1996: 688). This principle was codified in the Single European Act's provisions on environmental policy—the first reference to subsidiarity in the Treaties—under protest from Delors, who described the language agreed by Member States on environmental policy as 'window dressing' (Golub 1996: 690).

The fact that EU scholars have paid so much attention to Delors' religious beliefs is, in one sense, testament to just how difficult it is to discern the influence of one or more mainstream macro-economic policy paradigms on his thinking. Take, for example, Margaret Thatcher's conversion to monetarism in the 1970s, the subject of a classic case study by Peter Hall. In this account, Hall (1993) acknowledges the importance of political philosophy for Thatcher's approach: *The Road to Serfdom* by Hayek is cited as a key influence in this regard. But he suggests that it was Milton Friedman's monetarism that ultimately informed her rejection of the post-war Keynesian consensus. This is more than supposition on Hall's part who can point towards the influence on Thatcher of think-tanks with an interest in monetarist economics and the appointment of monetarist-minded advisers, including Friedman himself, after the Conservatives won the 1979 general election. It is difficult to tell a similar story about Delors, who has variously been described as monetarist and neo-Keynesian but who remained reluctant to break with Keynesianism, even if he was critical at times of its application. This can be seen, for example, in Delors' refusal to see the embrace of rigour (*le tournant de la rigueu*) as a paradigm shift from Keynesianism to monetarism. 'I prefer the expression stable money rather than strong money', he would later say of his policies during this period, 'because the latter has taken on a monetarist connotation' (Delors 1994: 160). Although Thatcher may have been a grudging admirer of French economic policy under Delors, the feeling was not mutual (Thatcher 2011: 81). The policies of Thatcher, he suggested, were not without reason, but they were excessively laissez-faire and neo-liberal for his tastes (Delors 1994: 80).

For Maes (2004), Delors is a part of the 'orthodox' triptych in the French economic policy-making tradition, alongside Jacques Rueff, a noted economic adviser to President Charles de Gaulle, and Raymond Barre, who served as prime minister of France (see Chapter 4 by Howarth). Rueff, Barre, and Delors showed a preference for rigour during periods of high crisis for the French economy that was at odds with what Maes (2004) calls 'pragmatic Keynesians and left-wing economists' of the day. And yet, there were important differences between Rueff and Barre on the one hand and Delors on the other. Rueff and Barre were members of the economic establishment. Rueff, for example, debated James Tobin in the *Quarterly Journal of Economics* over Keynesian theory (Rueff 1947, 1948); while Barre (1966) introduced generations of students to economic theory with his two-volume textbook *Économie politique*. Delors made no such contribution to the mainstream economics literature and was, by comparison, altogether more heterodox in his approach to the discipline.

Evidence of Delors' eclectic economic thought can be found in his work as an academic economist. In 1973 he quit his role at the Interministerial Committee for Professional Training, which he had taken up after Chaban-Delmas lost the premiership twelve months earlier, to take up a post as visiting professor at Université Paris-Dauphine. At this institution, Delors taught a course on the comparative political economy of employment and industrial relations and established a research centre entitled 'Travail et Sociétés' (Delors 2004: 137). It was at this time that Delors, by his own admission, developed his thinking on the problem of inflation. This can be seen, for example, in his 1975 book, *Changer*, which devotes a chapter to inflation (Delors 1975: chapter 18). Here Delors makes the intellectual case for what would later become his policy of rigour by criticizing the government for trying to inflate their way out of downturns and social partners for their irresponsible wage demands (Delors 1975: 305). There is also hint of monetarism in Delors' criticism of central banks for pursuing lax monetary policy alongside a call for closer cooperation between national monetary authorities. There is no reference to the macro-economic rationale for such coordination, however, with Delors concentrating instead on the need for an international approach to prudential supervision (Delors 1975: 298). If a large multinational bank were unable to meet its obligations, then the inability of policy-makers to intervene in the way the Banque de France can in relation to French banks, he warns, would result in a 'gigantic international crash' (Delors 1975: 298).

Changer also goes beyond mainstream macro-economic theory by offering a twist on the classic problem of demand–push inflation. Excessive demand is a key source of inflationary pressures, Delors speculates, in part because of the advertising industry's encouragement of 'false needs' (Delors 1975: 301). He would develop this line of argument in a background paper for a European Parliament study on the 'problem of inflation' (Delors 1976). In this paper, which Delors later said did much to develop his interest in inflation, he took aim at the problem of ostentatious and wasteful consumption as key drivers of rising prices. Noticeable by their absence here are detailed references to monetary and fiscal policy and the role of social partnership. Instead, Delors looks to the state's role in managing the demand for scarce resources, inter alia, by investing in public transport, encouraging the production of durable goods and after-sales services, and promoting recycling (Delors 1976: 40), recommendations that recall his time at the French Planning Commission between 1962 and 1979.

These writings on inflation in the 1970s offer only a glimpse of Delors' thinking, but they do point towards an economic eclecticism that is important for understanding his subsequent views on EMU. First, they suggest a practical concern for real-world policy problems, such as inflation, rather than a theoretical predilection for specific policy solutions. Seen in these terms, it is not surprising that Delors championed France's continued membership of the EMS during his time as French finance minister, while seeking to reform European monetary cooperation during his tenure as Commission president. Similarly, it is not surprising that he advocated fiscal discipline for France while resisting binding fiscal rules for EMU and that he continued to champion the EMS until the exchange-rate crisis of 1992–3. In these cases, Delors' policy advice was tailored to prevailing economic conditions and challenges rather than a commitment to a particular policy paradigm.

Second, Delors' search for policy solutions to such challenges reveals a basic affinity with Keynesianism but an openness to the insights of monetarism and policy planning. Such eclecticism helps to understand how Delors started out with a more or less Keynesian conception of EMU before backing an institutional design that owed more to German Ordo-liberalism with its emphasis on stability-oriented monetary policies, central bank independence, and fiscal discipline.

If Delors' economic eclecticism shaped his blurred vision of EMU, then so too did his particular views on European integration. Delors is sometimes described as a federalist (Ross 1995: 47). However, such claims overlook the Frenchman's ambivalence about European federalism. Although Delors would occasionally use the F-word (Delors 1990b), he neither joined the Union of European Federalists nor found common cause with federalist founding fathers such as Altiero Spinelli before or during his time as Commission president (Drake 2000: 18). There was no shortage of opportunities for such alignment since Spinelli and Delors were both elected to the European Parliament in 1979, but the two men clearly had different political priorities in mind. Whereas Spinelli brought federalist MEPs together in the Crocodile Club, Delors founded the Amigo Club to encourage an informal exchange of views between social democratic MEPs. Nor did Delors, as Commission president, show much enthusiasm in public for Spinelli's Draft Treaty Establishing the European Union, which was published in 1984 and which included among its aims 'the progressive achievement of full monetary union'.[2]

[2] 'Draft Treaty Establishing the European Union', Official Journal of the European Communities, No. C 77/33, 14 February 1984.

There are at least three reasons why Delors was reluctant to throw in his lot with the European federalists and all three are relevant for understanding his blurred vision of EMU. First, federalism's inherent idealism rested uneasily with Delors' commitment to the art of the politically possible. Federalists such as Spinelli sought new competences for the Community across a wide range of policy areas with little apparent regard for their feasibility, but Delors preferred a minimalist approach based on identifying specific integrationist initiatives that enjoyed the support of key Member States. EMU did not initially enjoy such support, as Delors found out when he toured national capitals in 1984. This was one reason why he stuck to comparatively vague language about the reform of the EMS until signs of support for EMU started to emerge from France and Germany (Delors 1994: 220). It may also explain why Delors, having made the case for a centralized budgetary instrument in negotiations over the Maastricht Treaty, did not push harder on this issue after the Treaty was ratified.

Second, the fact that European federalism came to be associated with the centralization of powers at the supranational level jarred with Delors' long-standing interest in the decentralization of power (Drake 2000: 17–18). Although this interest found its clearest expression in Delors' support for subsidiarity, it can also be seen in his initial reluctance to countenance a supranational monetary authority and a single currency.

A third and final tension centres on the issue of a *finalité politique*. Whereas federalists such as Spinelli had in mind 'the definitive abolition of the division of Europe into national sovereign States', Delors preferred to talk of a 'European federation of nation states' a term that seeks to accommodate national and European ambitions while remaining vague as to the precise nature of such accommodation.

Seen in this light, Delors' unease with the link between EMU and political union at Maastricht is not hard to understand. Whereas federalists such as Spinelli were only too willing to sketch out their plans for political union, Delors saw projects such as the single market and EMU as decisive steps towards political union but did not offer a clear sense of where they might lead to. Such hesitancy can be seen, for example, in 'Europe's Ambitions', an essay published by Delors on the eve of the IGC on political union (Delors 1990b). In this publication, Delors offered a thoughtful overview of the challenges facing the EU in the post-Cold War period, ranging from the Community's need to take the lead on issues such as democracy promotion and the proliferation of weapons of mass destruction to environmental policy. What Delors did not do here is say how the Community should address such challenges. It was not until the IGC was underway, indeed, that Delors made his first speech on the modalities of European security cooperation and even then his thoughts were tentative (Delors 1991).

FORESIGHT: CONTRIBUTION AND LEGACY

So much for the origins of Delors' vision of EMU. What about its relevance in light of the single currency's successful launch in 1999 and its subsequent difficulties after the global financial crisis struck in 2007? Viewed through a long-angle lens, Delors can claim credit for succeeding where his predecessors at the European Commission fell short. Although he benefited from economic and political headwinds that the likes of Roy Jenkins and Robert Marjolin did not enjoy, Delors showed himself to be a more accomplished navigator. Both Marjolin, as Commissioner for economic and monetary affairs in the early 1960s, and Jenkins, as Commission president in the late 1970s, put forward grand visions for EMU that fell foul of the central bank governors and/or national governments (see Chapter 3 by Seidel and Chapter 6 by Ludlow).

Delors, in contrast, began with a blurred vision of EMU that remained in the background until signs of political support within key Member States emerged and came into clearer focus only after national governments had agreed on a blueprint for EMU. Moravcsik (1998) is correct in saying that national policy-makers determined the final draft of the Delors Report, but this conclusion downplays Delors' agnosticism about EMU's design and his ability as chair to bridge the divide between Keynesian and non-Keynesian conceptions of European monetary cooperation. Whether Jenkins, a more ardent Keynesian (see Jenkins 1978), or Marjolin, to whom the central bank governors did not warm (James 2012: 60), would have managed this feat is debatable. Nor is it certain that Karl Otto Pöhl, who would presumably have chaired the Committee on the Study of EMU in Delors' absence (Dyson and Featherstone 1999: 712), could have produced a workable blueprint for monetary union, given the Bundesbank president's initial scepticism about the project and cavalier approach to the committee.

Delors' blurred vision may have been a strategic advantage in negotiations about EMU, but, seen through the rear-view mirror, it raises the question of whether he put politics before economics in his pursuit of a single currency. Although the preceding discussion challenges the conception of Delors as a European federalist, he did see EMU as a means to further the cause of European integration. Pursuing integration for integration's sake is a recipe for impetuous policy-making, and Delors, for his part, may have been guilty of undue haste in his pursuit of EMU. During his time as Commission president, there was scope for a more rigorous assessment of the economics of EMU. True, the Padoa-Schioppa Report, which Delors commissioned, helped to highlight the risks to fixed exchange-rate regimes from capital mobility. But, as noted previously, the Commission president's reading of this report was a selective one, which downplayed Padoa-Schioppa's warnings over the EMS and reworked his choice between full and flexible exchange rates into a gradualist argument for EMU.

This reticence about understanding EMU from first principles can be seen in the Delors Report, which at Delors' insistence stuck to its task of analysing the how of EMU rather than the why (Dyson and Featherstone 1999: 715–16) and in the Commission's cost–benefit analysis of EMU, 'One Market, One Money' (European Commission 1990b). Detailed though the latter was, it was published only after stage one of EMU was underway. The report's dismissive approach to optimum currency area theory as being 'a too narrow and somewhat outdated framework of analysis' (European Commission 1990b: 31) was also symptomatic of Delors' reluctance to engage with so-called Anglo-Saxon economists, whom he saw as having an anti-EU agenda (see Moore 2011). Imperfect though optimum currency area theory may be, it would have helped to focus Delors' mind on the need to reduce exposure to asymmetric shocks and enable adjustment mechanisms in the absence of nominal exchange rates.

Slavish devotion to one economic theory can produce tunnel vision, but an eclectic approach that jumps between theories can lead to inconsistent analysis. Delors' vision of EMU, it could be argued, suffered from two key inconsistencies. The first was its lack of regard for the problem of cross-border financial supervision in EMU. Although this charge could be levelled at a long list of economists, Delors himself seemed well aware in the mid-1970s that the international financial system was ill-prepared to deal with troubled multinational banks (Delors 1975: 298). Yet he said little about this issue when it came to debates on EMU in the 1980s and 1990s, even though the Padoa-Schioppa Report explicitly called for a coordinated approach to financial supervision (Padoa-Schioppa 1987: 47).

The second more glaring inconsistency in Delors' vision concerns his analysis of the fiscal dimension of EMU. During debates about EMU's design Delors argued against binding fiscal rules at the EU level, which he saw as unworkable, and for a modest increase in the EU budget to allow for cyclical stabilization (James 2012: 252–3). Having found himself on the losing side of both arguments, it is then puzzling why Delors did not push harder for a reconfiguration of EMU's fiscal dimension after the Maastricht negotiations concluded. Political pragmatism may explain Delors' reticence. The Commission did undertake a major study on public finances in EMU, but its publication was delayed, according to Charles Goodhart, an economist who contributed to the report, so as not to jeopardize negotiations over the EU budget at Edinburgh in 1992 (Goodhart 2006: 247). A degree of economic myopia in Delors' vision of EMU was also discernible. Always self-critical on such matters, Delors suggested in a lecture to mark the fiftieth anniversary of the *Journal of Common Market Studies* that he may have placed too much faith in EU regional policy to promote convergence between Member States (Delors 2013).

If Delors' vision of EMU fell short in these and other respects it also remains highly salient in others. Although his faith in the ability of market mechanisms to keep public finances in check is difficult to defend, given the low long-term interest rates enjoyed by high-debt Member States such as Belgium, Italy, and Greece during the first ten years of EMU, the Commission president was right to foresee political difficulties in the implementation of fiscal deficit and public debt criteria of the SGP. Whether Delors' proposal for a corresponding *pacte pour la coordination des politiques économique* would have made much difference here is difficult to say. But it can be seen as a forerunner to the Macroeconomic Imbalance Procedure launched in 2011 to address the kind of cross-country growth and inflation differences that marred the first decade of the euro. Also prescient here was Delors' call in March 1990 for the incorporation of 'budgetary rules or guidelines into national law', an idea that would be later codified in the Fiscal Compact, an intergovernmental treaty designed to promote closer economic policy coordination in light of the global financial crisis and that entered into force in January 2012.

Delors will also see his legacy in *Towards a Genuine Economic and Monetary Union*, a high-level report presented by the president of the European Council Herman Van Rompuy in December 2012 (Van Rompuy 2012). Not only does the title of this report echo Delors' call in 1985 for 'a genuine European monetary area' (Delors 1985b), it also owes an intellectual debt to the former Commission president's proposal for financial inducements for supply-side reforms and a centralized budgetary mechanism for EMU. Whether the political-economy obstacles to such proposals are any more surmountable than they were in the 1980s and 1990s is a moot point, but what is clear is that Delors vision of EMU, however blurred, remains relevant.

In conclusion, Delors was without doubt a highly visible player in the founding of EMU, even if scholars disagree as to whether his role was a leading or supporting one. This chapter has sought to understand Delors' intellectual contribution to the project by exploring how and why he came to support the idea of EMU before considering his legacy in light of the single currency's ups and downs. Delors' vision of EMU is a blurred one, it was argued, insofar as he has been unwavering in his support of the project since the early 1960s but wilfully obscure at times about what sort of EMU he was in favour of. Prior to joining the European Commission in 1985, Delors' enthusiasm for EMU was a long-standing matter of record, but his thinking on whether it would involve closer macro-economic policy coordination or the ceding of policy-making powers to the supranational level was not. Upon assuming the role of Commission president, Delors weighed his words carefully about the merits and modalities of monetary union until his work as chair of the Committee on the Study of Economic and Monetary Union was done. He said even less about EMU's institutional design after the Maastricht Treaty was signed. Since leaving the Commission in 1995, Delors has been consistently critical of Member States for failing to embrace some form of European economic government, but his remarks on this matter leave open the question of precisely what he has in mind.

This blurred vision of EMU reflected Delors' economic eclecticism as well as his ambivalent relationship with European federalism. On the first of these points, Delors was seen to have a more or less Keynesian outlook, but his criticisms of Keynesian economic policies in France and his openness to alternative approaches, be it monetarism, policy planning, or heterodox economics, suggested a reluctance to align himself with any one mainstream macro-economic theory. This helps to understand Delors' reluctance to define EMU in strict terms and his willingness to look beyond Keynesian conceptions of economic and monetary policy during EMU negotiations.

On the second point, Delors saw EMU as a means to further the cause of European integration, but his pragmatic and philosophical objections to European federalism help to explain his reticence at various points towards centralized approaches to decision-making in the embryonic Euro Area. It also places Delors' evident unease when it came to discussions of political union at Maastricht within its proper intellectual context.

Turning to Delors' legacy in relation to the euro, EMU may ultimately be the product of a political process in which Member States chose to cede control over monetary policy to the supranational level. But Delors helped to facilitate this process through his adroit approach to the project and his adept chairing of the Committee on the Study of Economic and Monetary Union. Here Delors' economic eclecticism and equivocal views on European federalism were a strategic asset since they sensibly encouraged him to hold fire on EMU until signs of support from key Member States emerged and, thereafter, to build bridges between policy-makers with Keynesian and Ordo-liberal conceptions of EMU, not to mention varying degrees of commitment to the European project.

All of this raises the question, however, of whether Delors put politics before economics in his pursuit of EMU and whether a more candid approach to the constraints of a one-size-fits-all monetary policy would have encouraged more prudent economic policies by Euro Area members in the run-up to the global financial crisis. Key inconsistencies in Delors' vision of EMU included his failure to follow up on initial concerns about international prudential banking supervision and his reluctance to press the case for strengthening EMU's fiscal dimension. That said, Delors can claim to have been ahead of the curve in predicting problems with the implementation of the SGP, even if his proposals for an alternative approach to economic policy coordination remained vague. Delors' vision of EMU can also be seen to a certain degree in reforms to EMU enacted or proposed in the light of the global financial crisis, including the codification of national fiscal rules under the Fiscal Compact and plans to offer financial inducements for supply-side reforms and to develop a fiscal capacity. In this sense, though Delors may not be the visionary that he is sometimes said to be, his vision of EMU remains an illuminating one.[3]

[3] Earlier versions of this chapter were presented at the British Academy in October 2013 and at the National Bank of Belgium in March 2015. Thanks to the participants at these conference and, in particular, Kenneth Dyson, Piers Ludlow, Ivo Maes, and Niels Thygesen for useful comments. The usual disclaimer applies.

11

Alexandre Lamfalussy

A Cassandra about Financial Stability

Ivo Maes

There are three main reasons to consider Alexandre Lamfalussy (1929–2015) as an architect of the euro. First, he was the founding president of the European Monetary Institute (EMI), the precursor of the European Central Bank (ECB), in whose construction he played a crucial part. The introduction of the euro, a major logistical operation without precedence in history, happened flawlessly. Moreover, the ECB, a central bank without a state, became the pre-eminent institution in an asymmetric Economic and Monetary Union (EMU). There is a broad consensus that the ECB fulfilled its mandate and had a key role during the financial crisis that erupted in 2007, as shown by the extension of its tasks into financial supervision.

Second, as chair of the Committee of Wise Men (2000–1), Lamfalussy had a key role in the revision of the regulatory framework governing Europe's financial industry through what became known as the 'Lamfalussy procedure'. In the wake of the financial crisis, the new so-called 'Level 3 Committees' became the basis for the EU's later supervisory authorities—the European Banking Authority (EBA), the European Securities and Markets Authority (ESMA), and the European Insurance and Occupational Pensions Authority (EIOPA).

Third, at the Bank for International Settlements (BIS) and as a member of the Delors Committee, Lamfalussy played a leading intellectual role in Europe's central banking community. He was especially influential as a Cassandra about financial stability. This concern stemmed from a distrust of the functioning of financial markets. It was an important factor in Lamfalussy favouring a symmetric EMU, with a strong economic pole. It also made him an early Cassandra, warning of the dangers of financial crisis, and a clear advocate of the thesis that central banks should also consider financial stability as an objective. Moreover, he was an early advocate of giving the ECB a role in the supervision of systemically important financial institutions, a key element of the European banking union that was set up from 2012 onwards.

Lamfalussy's work on European monetary integration reflects his three-pronged career: as a commercial banker, as a central banker, and as an academic.

LAMFALUSSY'S FORMATIVE YEARS

Lamfalussy was born on 26 April 1929 in Kapuvar, Hungary. He began his economics studies at the Budapest Polytechnic before, in 1949, fleeing to Belgium, where he continued his studies at the Catholic University of Louvain. At that time, Louvain was one of the leading centres for economics in the francophone world.

The dominant figure at Louvain in the 1950s was Léon-H. Dupriez, a leading scholar of business cycle analysis, in its broad sense: namely, the interaction of economic growth with different types of economic cycle. Two elements were typical of Dupriez's approach to economics (Maes 2008). First, he based his analysis on extensive empirical investigations. Second, he was not in favour of new schools of economic thought, like Keynesian economics. Lamfalussy became Dupriez's assistant and also took part in the monthly meetings with industrialists. Dupriez's approach of basing economic analysis on empirical material was to become a hallmark of Lamfalussy's style of economics.

Lamfalussy did his PhD in Oxford. The theme was investment and growth in post-war Belgium, with Philip Andrews as supervisor and Sir John Hicks as the main examiner. Later, under the influence of Robert Triffin, he went to Yale, which gave him an American experience. He also met James Tobin, who was already critical about the functioning of the financial system.

In *Investment and Growth in Mature Economies: The Case of Belgium*, Lamfalussy (1961) focused on growth and investment theory. At that time, he was intrigued by the issue of reconciling macro- and micro-economics and especially by imperfect competition theory. For Lamfalussy, this preoccupation was strongly pragmatic. He had seen that other countries were developing new industries, which were notoriously absent in Belgium. Later, in *The United Kingdom and the Six: An Essay on Economic Growth in Western Europe* (1963), Lamfalussy emphasized virtuous (as well as vicious) circles, in which stronger export growth promotes higher investment, which in turn strengthens productivity, further reinforcing exports. Broadly speaking, Lamfalussy's analyses fitted into the Keynesian tradition. His emphasis on vicious and virtuous circles clearly showed that the free market economy was not stable and self-adjusting. Much later, Lamfalussy was still considered as one of the main protagonists of the Keynesian approach of export-led growth (Crafts and Toniolo 1996: 12).

Lamfalussy was always a convinced pro-European. In *The United Kingdom and the Six*, he clearly admits this 'value judgment': 'I do believe that the Common Market is a good thing, that 1st January, 1958, is a turning point in Western European history' (Lamfalussy 1963: ix). During his student days in Louvain, along with several friends, Lamfalussy was active in the 'Cercle Européen' and the 'Nouvelles équipes internationales' (the European Christian Democratic movement). For them, European integration was a very profound conviction. It had a special dimension for Lamfalussy, as he had just escaped from Hungary (Lamfalussy et al. 2014). They were asking the practical question: what can we do? Their answer reflected their conviction that it was necessary to break down the barriers that divided Europe. In their view, European integration should be a stimulus to lift the economy out of its stagnation. There was also a clear cultural dimension: a sense of belonging to a common cultural heritage.

Lamfalussy attended a meeting of the 'Nouvelles équipes internationales' in Saarbrücken, a symbolic city on the Franco-German border. The meeting was a clear expression of the participants' conscious attempt to involve Germany in European integration. Kaiser (2007: 302) argued that the Christian Democrats' fundamental aim was to create a 'tamed Europeanized nation-state embedded in a supranational constitutional system'. Their ideas drew on their shared religious and regional identities and their opposition to the 'centralized liberal and socialist nation-state'.

In particular, Lamfalussy was influenced by his teacher Dupriez, who was involved in research work for the High Authority of the European Coal and Steel Community (ECSC). Dupriez was also a member of the 'Groupe de Recherches sur les Conditions et les Conséquences sociales du Progrès technique', which was chaired by Jean Fourastié (Dupriez 1960). This group undertook several studies on the coal and steel industries. As Dupriez's assistant, Lamfalussy became professionally involved in European economic integration studies.

THE EARLY CAREER OF LAMFALUSSY AS A COMMERCIAL BANKER

After returning from Oxford in the summer of 1955, Lamfalussy began working at the Banque de Bruxelles, Belgium's second commercial bank. He started as an economist in its economic studies department, becoming the bank's economic adviser in 1962. From 1965 to 1970, he served as an executive director and, from 1971 to 1975, as chair of the executive board.

His experience as a commercial banker led Lamfalussy to develop a keen awareness of the financial markets, which became a constant feature of his analysis. However, in 1974, during Lamfalussy's period as chair of the Banque de Bruxelles, some traders took large, open foreign-exchange positions which caused significant losses (Moitroux 1995: 217). At the end of 1975 Lamfalussy resigned from the bank.

During his time at the Banque de Bruxelles, Lamfalussy's research interests shifted to monetary and financial issues (Maes 2011b). Partly under the influence of Triffin (see Chapter 2 by Maes and Bussière), he became interested in international and European monetary issues. Initially, he advocated an increase in international liquidity and the creation of an international central bank. In the 1963–5 period, he was a member of the Segré Committee, which was appointed by the European Commission to investigate capital market integration in the EEC (CEC 1966). He also took part in meetings of several groups on the reform of the international monetary system. One of the most famous was the Bellagio Group with, among others, Roy Harrod, Harry Johnson, Peter Kenen, Fritz Machlup, Robert Mundell, Jacques Rueff, Robert Triffin, Tibor Scitovsky, and Pierre Uri.

In *The United Kingdom and the Six*, Lamfalussy argued that the EEC had transformed the macro-economic policy framework in the countries of the Community. He was optimistic about the future of the EEC and believed that it might be easier to deal with balance of payments imbalances within the Community, thanks to the new EEC institutional framework. Lamfalussy argued that an asymmetric adjustment to payments imbalances might be avoided:

> If the surplus countries can be persuaded to expand their home demand at the same time as the deficit countries deflate their own economy, the balance can be restored without undue damage to the rate of growth of the Community as a whole. We do not know what will be the *degree* of success achieved by the Community authorities in their co-ordinating activity; but it is certain that the existence of an administrative machinery and of an institutional framework (already successful in other fields) will improve the ability of the area to deal with such problems. (Lamfalussy 1963: 131)

It turned out to be a rather optimistic assessment. Asymmetric adjustment and the fair sharing of the burden of adjustment were to become key themes in European monetary integration debates in the following decades, and resurfaced with a vengeance in the post-2008 crisis. However, Lamfalussy's optimistic assessment was in line with some of the prevailing ideas of the time.

Lamfalussy was in favour of strengthening monetary integration, very much in line with Triffin's plea for a European Reserve Fund: '*A fortiori*, the organization of common monetary institutions could be of great help in coping with possible balance of payments problems of the Community. For instance, the pooling of gold and foreign exchange reserves would greatly strengthen the E.E.C.'s resilience to export-induced recessions' (Lamfalussy 1963: 131–2). However, Lamfalussy took a more balanced position than Triffin, emphasizing also policy coordination: 'the prerequisite to a successful pooling of reserves is the effective co-ordination of economic policies'. This advocacy of symmetry between the monetary and the economic dimension would become a constant feature in Lamfalussy's work.

At the Hague Summit in December 1969, EMU became an official objective of the EEC. The October 1970 Werner Report provided the first blueprint for EMU. But, with the turbulence in the international monetary system and the oil shocks, not much progress was made in the ensuing decade. During this period Lamfalussy continued to wrestle with the question of how to advance European monetary integration.

In September 1971 he gave a presentation for the Belgian Financial Forum on the topic of European monetary integration. Arguing his case on the basis of his banker's instincts (*sentiments de banquier*), he rejected a system of floating exchange rates, mainly because it created incentives for lax economic policies and caused uncertainty. Foreshadowing the 'impossible triangle' thesis, Lamfalussy argued that monetary integration was embedded in the logic of the European integration process.

> At the same time, economic integration also requires complete freedom of financial movements. And the coexistence of the two elements: fixed and rigid exchange rates (with no margin or only a very small margin) alongside capital movements would be practically tantamount to monetary integration. *Consequently, we must adopt as a basic postulate the establishment of a system of fixed exchange rates within the Community.* (Lamfalussy 1971: 15, original italics)

Lamfalussy was well aware that the international environment, with greater exchange-rate instability and a stronger emphasis by governments on their own national policy objectives, was unfavourable to European monetary integration. Moreover, he was convinced that a monetary union was only viable with profound changes in the economic policy framework, implying a centralized European economic government and thus massive transfers of sovereignty: 'It is not enough just to harmonize cyclical policy, nor is it enough to harmonize taxation—and these are very important things, but it is not enough. There is a need to create a single financial market, set up a central government with standardized fiscal levies and social security expenditure' (Lamfalussy 1971: 20). In response to a question, Lamfalussy mentioned that his views were quite close to those set out in the Werner Report:

> I think that the Werner Plan is a plan that does not say entirely what it means. And perhaps it is better like that. But I believe that the gradual establishment of a certain degree of exchange rate fixing is nevertheless one of the Werner Plan's ideas. What isn't, if you like, are the fundamental consequences in institutional

terms. And I think . . . that it was perhaps a good thing not to say it out loud like that. But it seems to me that there is no really striking difference between the Werner Plan's angle and mine. (Lamfalussy 1971: 23–4)

So, Lamfalussy was convinced that monetary integration should go hand in hand with progress in economic policy coordination, a fairly balanced position in the 'monetarist' versus 'economist' debate. However, in his conclusion, Lamfalussy took a rather 'forward-flight' (*fuite en avant*) approach, favouring a 'monetarist' approach:

> Starting monetary integration . . . exchange rates will have to become more and more stable, the margins will have to start narrowing, and there you are, we will be entering into the process. And that is the moment when it will be necessary to make the institutional changes. Why? Because it is at this stage that we will literally be condemned to succeed, forced to carry through these changes. (Lamfalussy 1971: 22)

The crucial factor is that Lamfalussy cannot accept the status quo. He wanted to go forward with the process of European integration, which was for him a very profound conviction: 'I don't accept the status quo . . . I think it is in Europe's destiny to be unified, and that it will be a good thing for Europeans and also for the rest of the world. It is a fact that is hard to prove, but in any case, it is an act of faith on my part' (Lamfalussy 1971: 21).

In August 1974, Lamfalussy presented the introductory paper in the session on monetary and fiscal integration at the congress of the International Economic Association in Budapest. These were dire times for European monetary integration. With his background as a commercial banker, Lamfalussy was critical of the European exchange-rate agreement, the so-called 'snake-in-the-tunnel':

> Personally, I have always thought that such an agreement was somewhat spurious, in that it gave all market parties an illusion of stability. The purpose, of course, was to achieve real stability, but this cannot be expected from an arrangement setting a limit to *continuous* exchange rate movements while leaving the way open for *discontinuous*, and possibly large, parity changes. If I have left myself without forward cover and incur an exchange loss because the Deutschmark central rate is revalued against the Belgian franc, it is small consolation to me that this revaluation has in fact not infringed the rules of the Community 'snake'. (Lamfalussy 1976: 219)

The core of the paper was a discussion of whether the EEC constituted an optimum currency area or not. Lamfalussy had to admit that several conditions for the creation of an optimum currency area were not fulfilled: 'This applies, in the first place, to intra-Community mobility of factors of production and, hence, to the formation of factor prices compatible with the existence of a currency area' (Lamfalussy 1976: 223). A second condition, that its

Member States should have a fairly similar 'inflation propensity', was not met: 'In this there are very wide divergences among European countries and these divergences matter all the more as inflation gathers pace throughout the world' (Lamfalussy 1976: 224). However, in Lamfalussy's opinion, there were arguments that were 'weighty enough to win the day'. His first argument was that foreign-trade integration among the EEC Member States had expanded rapidly, which had raised the degree of openness of the EEC countries. Second, there was the question whether the Customs Union had any chance of survival without monetary union: 'My instinct is to say no' (Lamfalussy 1976: 224). Third, there were the negative effects of intra-Community exchange-rate fluctuations. Fourth, Lamfalussy argued that the international monetary crisis constituted an argument in favour of 'transforming the EEC into a currency area' (Lamfalussy 1976: 226).

Notwithstanding all his arguments, Lamfalussy admitted that, because of the turbulence in the world economy and the absence of political will, it was not the right moment to stick to the exchange-rate mechanism:

> In these circumstances, I regard the open and free floating of European currencies against each other as the lesser evil compared with the efforts to keep the diminished snake alive, because (a) if the snake survives, it will tend to create a Deutschmark zone, which would have serious political drawbacks; and (b) if the snake perishes, in spite of all efforts to keep it alive, then the idea of a concerted policy of central banks, which even now is open to a good many doubts, will be discredited forever. (Lamfalussy 1976: 227)

He argued in favour of structural reforms in order to create the conditions for the establishment of a currency area. It is noteworthy that Lamfalussy did not like a parallel currency approach, like the 'Europa' proposal of Triffin, an approach which was quite influential in the 1970s, not only in the academic world, but also at the European Commission.[1]

LAMFALUSSY AT THE BANK FOR INTERNATIONAL SETTLEMENTS

In January 1976 Lamfalussy joined the BIS in Basel as economic adviser and head of the monetary and economics department. He was general manager from May 1985 until the end of 1993. The BIS was set up in 1930 to administer the German war reparation payments and as a forum for central bank cooperation (Toniolo 2005). It provided central bankers with three main services: research on issues relevant to international payments and prudential

[1] Letter to Magnifico, 30 June 1976, BISA 7, 18(15) LAM 7/Fo 18.

supervision; a venue for regular and discreet meetings; and a financial arm, which was particularly important in the gold market. In the post-war period, Basel was one of the main centres of international monetary cooperation, contributing to the longevity and success of the Bretton Woods system.

At the BIS, Lamfalussy was in a first-rate position to observe the international and European monetary system. He took part in the meetings of the G10 governors, including the informal dinners. It was at these dinners that the most open and confidential discussions took place between the world's central bank governors. Moreover, throughout the process of European monetary integration, the BIS provided services to the central banks of the European Community. Lamfalussy was also invited to attend the meetings of the Committee of EEC Central Bank Governors. With the support of the monetary and economics department of the BIS, he presented analyses of the economic and monetary situation, typically placing current developments in a broader analytical framework (Maes 2011b).

During Lamfalussy's time at the BIS, three topics dominated the agenda: exchange rates, inflation, and the Latin American debt crisis. The strong appreciation of the US dollar, due to differences in the policy mix between Europe and the United States in the early 1980s, left a profound mark on him. He felt that this was a clear indication that flexible exchange rates could not be relied on to avoid serious exchange-rate misalignments. Moreover, the period showed the dangers of exchange-rate misalignments, especially the strengthening of protectionist threats.

The mid-1970s was the time of the 'great inflation', and, amongst central bankers, monetary targets became a major issue of discussion. Lamfalussy (1985) took a balanced approach, favouring 'rules applied with a pragmatic sense of discretion'. He rejected a monetary policy based on mechanical rules: 'It is difficult to define such rules; it is sometimes impossible to apply them; and it would often be irresponsible to stick to them.' For Lamfalussy, notwithstanding thorough research, monetary policy remained an art, not a science.

Financial stability became an important topic for Lamfalussy. As early as the mid-1970s, he was warning about the debt build-up in Latin America (Maes 2011a). Moreover, he stressed the interrelationship with loose US monetary policies and the US balance of payments deficit. In 1976 he proposed the creation of a 'risk office' at the BIS in order to collect crucial information on a limited number of systemic banks. In 1979–80 a working party which he chaired advanced a 'macro-prudential' approach. Later, in the 1980s, Lamfalussy played a significant role in the management of the Latin American debt crisis.

Lamfalussy took a cautious attitude towards financial innovations, an increasingly important topic (Maes 2009b). In a certain sense, he always kept a 'Keynesian' *Weltanschauung*, with a certain scepticism about the functioning of financial markets. Lamfalussy (1984) argued in favour of a research programme in the field of 'normative financial economics', referring to Tobin's Hirsch memorial lecture, which raised questions about the efficiency of the financial system (Tobin 1984).

At the end of December 1984, Lamfalussy was a speaker at the American Economic Association meeting. He focused closely on the accelerating speed of financial innovation, which was leading to a flow of new financial instruments and techniques, as well as the blurring of dividing lines between institutions and between markets. After discussing the implications for monetary policy, Lamfalussy turned to the prudential implications. His fundamental question concerned the effects on financial stability of the redistribution of risk by these new instruments.

> You may argue that when risk-averse market participants shift risks associated with unexpected interest and exchange rate developments onto willing risk takers, everybody is going to be better off. This may well be the case, but increased collective happiness does not necessarily mean greater systemic stability. Or does it? (Lamfalussy 1985: 411)

Lamfalussy greatly contributed to the creation of a 'BIS atmosphere', namely that one should be attentive to imbalances, debt build-ups, and bubbles, which sow the seeds of financial crises. He became an early advocate of the BIS 'macro-prudential' approach to financial stability, with its focus on the financial system as a whole.

By taking part in the meetings of the Committee of EEC Central Bank Governors, Lamfalussy followed the discussions on European monetary integration very closely. He and his staff were also involved in the preparations for the new European Monetary System (EMS). In Lamfalussy's view, there were close interrelations between the international monetary system and the process of European monetary integration. He was therefore at pains to stress the interaction between movements of the US dollar and European exchange-rate troubles:

> If we look at the history of attempts at monetary integration in the Community, it can be seen that the weakness of the dollar has regularly played a destructive role. The failures of these attempts are certainly due to divergences between the Member States, but these divergences have been exacerbated by the weakness of the dollar which has differing effects on the European economies.[2]

Initially, Lamfalussy was relatively sceptical about the impact of setting up the EMS. In a paper on the consequences of the EMS for the international monetary system, prepared for the Trilateral Commission, he wrote that he feared that the role of the European Currency Unit (ECU) would remain limited. In his view, its use would only take off if the European Monetary

[2] Minutes of the 120th Meeting of the Committee of Governors, 11/04/1978, NBBA.

Fund, planned for the second stage of the EMS, 'were to play the role of a genuine European central bank' (Lamfalussy 1979: 7).

Over time, Lamfalussy became more optimistic about the EMS. He observed that the realignments were transforming the EMS into a 'crawling peg', but that this was not necessarily 'a failure for the EMS'. 'Indeed, in so far as this confirms inflation differentials and maintains real exchange rates between participating currencies, it avoids the major problem of the system of generalized floating rates, namely the very wide gaps in comparison with changes in purchasing power parities that can be observed in the case of the dollar and the yen, for example.'[3]

At a conference held in honour of Robert Triffin in the early 1990s, Lamfalussy argued that the EMS had shown a judicious balance between exchange-rate constraint and exchange-rate flexibility:

> There has been enough flexibility to avoid real exchange rate movements of a duration and magnitude that could have led to the collapse of the System. On the other hand, the mere existence of a declared and unambiguous exchange rate commitment has exerted a lot of pressure on the behaviour of labour market participants as well as on domestic policies, as a result of which changes in nominal exchange rates have been limited. (Lamfalussy 1993: 41)

Moreover, he argued that the 'effectiveness of monetary policy action undertaken to counter pressure on the exchange rate is greater, and the costs involved in such policy action are smaller under a regime of fixed but adjustable pegs than under a system of floating rates'. The crucial reason, for Lamfalussy, was the way that exchange-rate expectations are formed: 'the absence of any anchor in a floating rate system allows expectations to run wild. We have learned the hard way that the moderating influence of stabilizing speculation by market participants is wishful thinking' (Lamfalussy 1993: 42).

However, shortly after the conference, a major crisis broke out in the EMS. In September 1992, Italy and the United Kingdom had to leave the exchange-rate mechanism (ERM). For both countries, the fixed exchange rate had led to losses of competitiveness and balance of payments imbalances, given their higher inflation and rising costs. Sir Alan Walters, Margaret Thatcher's economic adviser, had already argued that there was an inherent tendency towards instability in the EMS. Countries with higher inflation rates would have lower real interest rates (as joining the ERM would lead to a lowering of nominal interest rates), in turn leading to more inflation and competitiveness losses. The same process would contribute to the Euro Area crisis in the twenty-first century.

[3] Minutes of the 175th Meeting of the Committee of Governors, 12/04/1983, NBBA.

In the Committee of EC Central Bank Governors, Lamfalussy defended the promotion of the international role of the ECU:

> The international monetary system will probably not come back under total domination by the dollar (even though it may periodically reassert its position) or by gold again. Consequently, the multiple reserve currency system should remain in place, and even develop further, an issue on which the member countries of the EEC have taken varying stances over the years . . . The Community approach to these problems could consist of promoting the international use of the ECU, an approach that has so far not yet been debated in any depth.[4]

However, the issue was not taken up in the work of the Committee. A major factor was that the Bundesbank was not only cautious about the ECU; also, it even resisted an international role for the D-Mark.

Lamfalussy was also a member of the Delors Committee. As the meetings took place at the BIS in Basel, after the meetings of the EEC Committee of Governors, Lamfalussy was *de facto* its host. One of his colleagues, Gunter Baer, was a Committee rapporteur, together with Tommaso Padoa-Schioppa (see Chapter 9 by Masini). The BIS also provided several services, such as a secretariat, for the Delors Committee.

Lamfalussy was not one of the political heavyweights in the Delors Committee, like Jacques Delors or Karl-Otto Pöhl (see Chapter 10 by Hodson and Chapter 8 by James). Nevertheless, he played an intellectually stimulating role, in line with the work he had provided for the EEC Committee of Governors. He contributed three background studies, with the help of collaborators at the BIS. The first one was a more descriptive paper on the functioning of the ECU banking market (Lamfalussy 1988). The other two studies concerned the coordination of fiscal policy and monetary policy operations in the second stage. He also tried to raise the issue of banking supervision, but it was not taken up in the work of the Committee (Coene 2014).

For Lamfalussy, the coordination of budgetary policy was a crucial issue in the construction of EMU. In the second meeting of the Committee, in December 1998, marked by his experience of the Latin American debt build-up, he questioned whether market forces were enough to ensure fiscal discipline. He argued that 'the idea, not shared by him, that market discipline was sufficient to bring about fiscal convergence should be considered in the report' (James 2012: 248). In a later note for the Committee, Lamfalussy went further into the issue, in terms that were to prove extraordinarily prescient:

> With widely divergent 'propensities to run deficits' prevailing in the various European countries, I doubt whether we could count in the foreseeable future on a convergence within a European EMU similar to that observed in most contemporary federal systems. Nor do I believe that it would be wise to rely

[4] Minutes of the 162th Meeting of the Committee of Governors, 12/01/1982, NBBA.

> principally on the free functioning of financial markets to iron out the differences in fiscal behavior between member countries: (a) the interest premium to be paid by a high-deficit member country would be unlikely to be very large, since market participants would tend to act on the assumption that the EMU solidarity would prevent the 'bankruptcy' of the deficit country; and (b) to the extent that there was a premium, I doubt whether it would be large enough to reduce significantly the deficit country's propensity to borrow. There is, therefore, a serious risk that, in the absence of constraining policy coordination, major difference in fiscal behavior would persist within a European EMU. (Quoted in James 2012: 249)

Lamfalussy's conclusion was in favour of an EMU with a significant economic pillar: 'In short, it would seem to me very strange if we did not insist on the need to make appropriate arrangements that would allow the gradual emergence, and the full operation once the EMU is completed, of a Community-wide macroeconomic fiscal policy which would be the natural complement to the common monetary policy of the Community' (quoted in James 2012: 249).

In his published paper, Lamfalussy argued that fiscal policy coordination 'appears to be a vital component of a European EMU' (Lamfalussy 1989a: 93). He put forward two main reasons. The first one closely reflected his preoccupations with the policy mix on the international monetary scene: 'the determination of a global fiscal policy in a way that is sufficiently responsive to evolving domestic and international requirements'. The second reason foreshadowed the 'binding rules on budgetary policy' in the Delors Report itself, namely, the need 'to avoid tensions arising from excessive differences between public sector borrowing requirements of individual member countries'.

The paper had an extensive annex, discussing the experience of federal states and the EEC. It singled out the particularity of the EEC, with a much smaller-sized Community budget. For Lamfalussy, this had far-reaching consequences:

> The combination of a small Community budget with large, independently determined national budgets leads to the conclusion that, in the absence of fiscal coordination, the global fiscal policy of the EMU would be the accidental outcome of decisions taken by Member States...As a result, the only global macroeconomic tool available within the EMU would be the common monetary policy implemented by the European central banking system. (Lamfalussy 1989a: 101)

For Lamfalussy, there were two unpalatable implications:

> Even within a closed economy, this would be an unappealing prospect as it would imply the serious danger of an inappropriate fiscal/monetary policy mix and pressures tending to divert monetary policy from the longer-run objective of preserving price stability. But such a situation would appear even less tolerable once the EMU was regarded as part and parcel of the world economy, with a clear obligation to cooperate with the United States and Japan in an attempt to

> preserve (or restore) an acceptable pattern of external balances and to achieve exchange rate stabilization. (Lamfalussy 1989a: 101)

While the paper put more emphasis on the external dimension than most central bank analyses, it was well received by the central bank governors, not least because it was in line with the consensus view that constraints on fiscal policy were necessary for a truly independent monetary policy. This theme was taken up by Coeuré (2015: 1), an executive director of the ECB, who argued that Lamfalussy had been 'right': 'A monetary union creates complex interactions which have to be governed by a strong and comprehensive framework. Many of these interactions we have only really understood due to the crisis.'

The third paper by Lamfalussy concerned a proposal for stage two, under which monetary policy operations would be centralized. His idea was that EC central banks should set up a joint subsidiary and use it for carrying out monetary policy operations in the financial markets. However, national central banks would remain responsible for monetary policy-making. As Lamfalussy emphasized: 'Although their operations would be performed through common facilities, and hence be completely transparent to their partners, individual member central banks would retain ultimate responsibility for the deployment of their national foreign exchange reserves, and for the supply of domestic bank reserves' (Lamfalussy 1989b: 214).

Lamfalussy admitted that the scheme could impinge on national sovereignty, as Member State central banks would no longer be able to hide the content of their domestic and foreign monetary operations from their EC partners. He also admitted that there could be a tendency, over the long run, for money markets to migrate to the country in which the 'subsidiary' was located. This proposal was much less enthusiastically received by the central banks, especially the Bundesbank, which adhered firmly to the view of the indivisibility of monetary policy.

LAMFALUSSY AS FOUNDING PRESIDENT OF THE EUROPEAN MONETARY INSTITUTE

On 1 January 1994, at the time nearly 65 years old, Lamfalussy became the first president of the newly created EMI. These were turbulent times for the EMU process, with the financial markets still in turmoil after the 1992–3 EMS crises and with the difficult ratification of the Maastricht Treaty (Maes 2002). However, the second stage of EMU started on 1 January 1994, and the EMI was set up on schedule. Lamfalussy remained its president until 30 June 1997.

The establishment of the EMI was a milestone in the process of European monetary integration. The main preoccupation of European central bankers became the preparation of a single monetary policy for the countries of the future Euro Area. This contrasted with their earlier focus on exchange-rate stability in the framework of European monetary arrangements, like the 'snake' and the EMS. The tasks of the EMI fell into two broad categories: strengthening coordination of EU Member States' monetary policies and organizing preparations for the final stage of EMU, especially the conduct of the single monetary policy and the introduction of the single currency. Internally, the EMI council adopted a master plan as early as autumn 1994, including a timetable for all the main decisions to be made by the governing council in order to meet the deadline (Raymond 2014).

One of the main unresolved issues at the time concerned the precise scenario for the changeover to the single currency. This issue was very complex and delicate, as it affected the banking system, financial markets, enterprises, and the public at large. The European Commission issued a Green Paper in May 1995 and, in so doing, brought the issue to the fore. The EMI published its scenario for the changeover in November 1995 (EMI 1995). These two documents formed the basis for the scenario that was finally adopted by the European Council in Madrid in December 1995. The Madrid Summit took some very important decisions: it confirmed the date of 1 January 1999 as the starting date of the third stage; it decided on the name 'euro' for the future single currency; and it endorsed the scenario for the switch-over to the single currency.

A crucial issue at the time was that the banking system was still very hesitant about EMU and reluctant to undertake the very heavy investment needed. Lamfalussy described the sentiment in banking circles as follows:

> up until mid-1995, i.e. a year and a half after I took up my position, there was still profound pessimism in the markets and the banks. I had telephone conversations with 40 leading bankers and told them, 'You need to get to work, we'll send someone over to explain how to do it.' 'Oh, but this kind of thing is terribly expensive', came the response. (Lamfalussy et al. 2014: 145)

The EMI and the European Commission decided then that 'the only way of convincing the banks—and, moreover, the participating central banks—was to pull out all the stops on the IT front and to have a precise timetable of what was going to happen as of 1 January 1999' (Lamfalussy et al. 2014: 145).

The proposed changeover scenario outlined three separate periods. The first period would start when the European Council decided on which countries satisfied the convergence criteria. Crucial in this phase was the creation of the ECB. The second period would start on 1 January 1999 when the euro became the official currency, while national currencies became non-decimal subdivisions of the euro. It ended when euro notes and coins were introduced. From the start of this period onwards, exchange rates between the participating countries would be irrevocably fixed and the ECB would conduct the single monetary policy in euros. Furthermore, the participating countries would issue all new debt in euros. The aim of these decisions was to create a 'critical mass' so that the financial markets would shift towards the euro. The third period would start on the day that euro notes and coins were introduced.

The decisions made at the Madrid European Council strengthened confidence in the EMU process. They also marked the moment from which the international financial community started to take the EMU process seriously. In this way, Lamfalussy and the EMI played an important role in calming down the financial markets after the EMS crisis.

Meanwhile, the EMI was also working on preparations for the single monetary policy in phase three of EMU. However, as the Maastricht Treaty stipulated that the single monetary policy was to be the ECB's responsibility, official decisions could only be taken in the second half of 1998. So, for the conduct of the single monetary policy, the EMI prepared the strategy as well as the monetary policy instruments (Scheller 2014). A regulatory, organizational, and logistical framework was set up as well. This task was not only technically difficult. It was also politically sensitive, as it affected the competitive positions of different financial markets and institutions. The EMI also started work on the euro banknote production process.

In several speeches and articles, Lamfalussy discussed the benefits and costs of EMU. Here he was responding to the explicit demand of Chancellor Helmut Kohl, which was evidence of the interrelationship between the architects of the euro and Europe's political leaders. As Lamfalussy wrote:

> Kohl was explicit with me, he said, 'I know that you have a lot to do, but please go and speak to the Germans. Explain the facts in different places, and especially in Bavaria. Don't worry about the big banks—the big banks will accept it, but the people need to hear how it's going to work.' I followed his advice and I got the shock of my life. I arrived one day at a meeting of the Bavarian association of the savings banks, the mortgage loan banks. I explained what was being done—this was right at the beginning of my visit—and then I asked if there were any questions. A fairly elderly man got up and said, 'Mr Lamfalussy, you give the impression of being an honest man, so please tell us what percentage of our financial wealth is going to disappear as a result of the introduction of the euro?' The Germans had had two currency reforms, one in the 1920s and one after the Second World War. Both reforms had entailed a considerable loss of financial wealth . . . Above all, it brought home to me how fundamentally reluctant these people were. Helmut Kohl heard about the meeting, and he called me and said, 'You really won over those Bavarians, and they are a difficult lot.' (Lamfalussy et al. 2014: 147)

In Lamfalussy's view, EMU would lead to major benefits, although there were also costs. He emphasized that, in order to ensure these 'large and lasting net benefits', countries had to enter EMU in a state of sustainable macroeconomic convergence and had to improve the working of their labour markets.

In line with his earlier views on exchange rates, Lamfalussy argued that a crucial benefit of EMU would be to remove the risk of serious real exchange-rate misalignments. In his view, well before the Euro Area debt crises, EMU would stabilize real exchange rates as 'the fixity of nominal exchange rates would be accompanied by an equalisation of inflation rates: a single monetary policy in a single market means that major inflation differentials between "regions" are simply not sustainable. Wage increases can, of course, differ—but only to the extent that they are warranted by differences in the rates of increase of productivity. Otherwise, the inflation-prone region would simply price itself out of the single market' (Lamfalussy 1998: 36).

Lamfalussy's optimistic conclusion was based on his belief in the new policy framework of EMU as well as on the working of market forces:

> I believe that the hard discipline of a stability oriented single monetary policy will gradually steer our governments towards the required degree of co-operation—just as it will alter the behaviour of labour market participants and the pricing policies of our enterprises. The freedom of choice of all of us will be substantially constrained—in particular, the freedom to pursue irresponsible policies at all levels. Not by decree, but by market forces operating within an environment of monetary stability. (Lamfalussy 1998: 41)

With hindsight, however, not enough attention was paid, including by Lamfalussy, to balance of payments imbalances and competitiveness issues in the EMU economic governance framework. The boom–bust cycle to which EMU gave rise in Member States like Spain is a reminder one of the earlier cycle theories on which the 'young Lamfalussy' had worked.

Lamfalussy emphasized that significant policy adjustments were necessary for EMU to function. One area was budgetary policy:

> On the fiscal side, deficits in 1996 substantially overshot the benchmark laid down in the Treaty in most Member States, despite efforts aimed at consolidation. Debt ratios have continued to rise in the aggregate...the composition of consolidation continued to rely excessively on high revenue ratios and less than is desirable on expenditure restraint. Moreover, there were measures with a one-off effect, which cannot contribute to sustainable convergence. (Lamfalussy 1997: 5)

But he felt the greatest challenge was the labour market:

> I have already noted that wage and price flexibility is essential to facilitate economic adjustment to various kinds of shocks that may hit individual EU economies from time to time. With or without EMU, employment policies have to be in the forefront of attention of European policy-makers. The recent

> record of the Union in terms of job creation is dismal . . . This points to the crucial need for continued labour cost moderation and enhanced labour market reforms—including attention to tax and social security systems—across the EU...A cause for optimism in this respect is that the enhanced competition that EMU in combination with the Single Market will unleash will be fertile ground for those arguing in favour of measures of labour market deregulation and reform of bargaining structures. (Lamfalussy 1997: 5)

His successor Wim Duisenberg, in his address on the occasion of the farewell of Lamfalussy as president of the EMI, summed up Lamfalussy's contribution beautifully:

> One of your greatest assets is that you managed to combine this typical conservative and cautious nature of a central banker, always focused on substance, with your firm belief in European monetary integration . . . You have never believed that a true single market is in the long run compatible with a quasi-floating exchange rate system. Over the past three and a half years, you have acted as a devoted missionary of EMU and European integration in general. In this capacity, you have managed to convert at least some incredulous European central bankers. And like any good missionary, you have also spread the message of EMU to the outside world. (Duisenberg 1997: 2)

AN EARLY ADVOCATE OF EUROPEAN BANKING UNION

On retiring from the EMI, Lamfalussy took up an invitation from Yale University to deliver the 1998 Stimson Lectures. The theme, inspired by his BIS experience, was financial crisis in emerging markets (Lamfalussy 2000). Over the next few years, financial stability would increasingly become his main focus.

Lamfalussy was appointed chair of the Committee of Wise Men, which developed a new approach to the regulation of European financial markets. After the introduction of the euro in 1999, financial integration moved up the European agenda (Maes 2007). A key issue was the functioning of the securities markets, notably how to adapt the European regulatory framework to the continuously evolving financial markets. In July 2000, the Economics and Financial Affairs Council (ECOFIN) appointed an ad hoc Committee, chaired by Lamfalussy, to analyse 'practical arrangements for implementation of the Community rules' and 'propose various approaches to adjusting the practice of regulation and cooperation between regulators'.

The Committee of Wise Men was harsh in its analysis of the existing European regulatory framework: 'The committee notes that an almost consensual view has emerged that the European Union's current regulatory framework is too slow, too rigid, complex and ill-adapted to the pace of global financial market change' (Committee of Wise Men 2001: 7). It summarized the situation as follows: 'The challenges facing the creation of an integrated securities market in Europe are that the basic legislation is not in place; that there is still insufficient prioritization; and that the present system cannot produce quickly or flexibly enough the type of legislation that modern financial markets require; and that inconsistent implementation is severely handicapping the emergence of a pan-European market' (Committee of Wise Men 2001: 18).

In order to remedy these deficiencies, the Committee of Wise Men proposed a 'four-level' approach, making a clear distinction between key political decisions and technical implementation. The crucial aim was to speed up changes in regulation. Moreover, it significantly improved the transparency of the regulatory process and greatly extended private-sector consultation (Quaglia 2007). After the global financial crisis, the new governance structure that had been introduced by the Lamfalussy Committee was to become an important building block for Europe's new supervisory architecture with three European supervisory authorities: the EBA, the ESMA, and the EIOPA.

Significantly, the ECOFIN mandate for the Committee of Wise Men stipulated explicitly that the Committee would not deal with prudential supervision. So it could only raise the financial stability issue in the introduction, in a passage that Lamfalussy became fond of quoting:

> While the Committee strongly believes that large, deep, liquid and innovative financial markets will result in substantial efficiency gains and will therefore bring individual benefits to European citizens; it also believes that greater efficiency does not necessarily go hand in hand with enhanced stability. Increased integration entails more interconnection between financial intermediaries on a cross-border basis, increasing their exposure to common shocks. It is not within the remit of this Committee to evaluate such risks, and even less to make recommendations on how to deal with them. However, given the growing interlinkages between all segments of the securities markets and the full range of financial intermediaries, the Committee believes that there is an urgent need to strengthen cooperation at the European level between financial market regulators and the institutions in charge of micro and macro prudential supervision. The ECOFIN Council should ask the Economic and Financial Committee to report on the development of this cooperation. (Committee of Wise Men 2001: 17)

In his 2004 Pierre Werner Lecture in Luxembourg, Lamfalussy focused more closely on the organization of prudential supervision in the EU, which he described as a 'mind-boggling patchwork'. He stressed that central banks had a crucial role in the management of financial crises, especially in 'preventing a potential crisis from turning into a real one . . . In such a situation they should provide liquidity to the system, so as to avoid liquidity shortages pushing otherwise solvent banks into bankruptcy. They also have to care about the smooth functioning of the payments system.'

Lamfalussy further argued that the timely provision of liquidity was very much a matter of judgement, which implied that central banks had to be intimately familiar with financial institutions: 'They must possess direct information on banks' risk-assessment methods and capabilities, on their decision-making processes and control mechanisms and, not least, on their expertise and skills in using innovative financial instruments. Such information cannot be acquired by reading second-hand reports, however lucid and transparent such reports may be' (Lamfalussy 2004: 7).

In an early anticipation of the 2012 movement towards European banking union, Lamfalussy identified the crucial issue as whether one should give a responsibility to the ECB in the supervision of the large, systemically important, banks:

> I would start from the assumption that the group of financial intermediaries whose regulation and supervision deserves to be reconsidered are a limited number of very large banks which have become actors at the global level and are key players in the European interbank market. Their problems could have directly systemic consequences...Should one not consider exploring the desirability and the feasibility of entrusting the ECB with an operational responsibility in the supervision of this limited number of banks? (Lamfalussy 2004: 20)

One year before the start of the financial crisis, in his September 2006 Bank of Greece Zolotas Lecture, Lamfalussy turned to the threats that worldwide excess liquidity might pose. As in the 1980s, he was less concerned about potential inflationary dangers. He emphasized the 'genuine, although unquantifiable, danger' for the stability of the financial system. In his view, excess liquidity provided 'a favourable breeding ground for developing bubbles in markets for asset and commodity prices, it erodes risk awareness and therefore encourages careless risk taking' (Lamfalussy 2006).

The financial crisis induced Lamfalussy to adjust his opinions. In his dinner address to the Sixth ECB Central Banking Conference, he 'meditated' on his 1997 EMI farewell speech, in which he had argued not to 'overburden monetary policy' but to focus on price stability. He now argued that the financial crisis had 'confirmed something that was (or should have been) expected: that whether they like it or not, central banks are in the front line when it comes to keeping crisis manifestations under control' (Lamfalussy 2011: 170). Emphasizing the severity of the crisis, he said: 'What is *new* in the current experience is that central banks have had to carry out their liquidity-boosting operations in an environment where the liquidity shortage turned rather quickly into solvency problems of frightening dimensions—for which there has been no precedent since the 1930s. Nor has there been any precedent for the speed of contamination at the global level' (Lamfalussy 2011: 170).

Given the severity of the crisis, central banks reacted with a variety of 'non-standard' measures. This led not only to a spectacular expansion of their balance sheets, but also to a change in the composition of their assets. 'As a result, central banks have started navigating in uncharted waters, in terms of both operational techniques and their relations with governments.' Lamfalussy did not expect a quick end to the crisis. Consequently, financial stability should remain an objective for central banks, just like price stability, making life even more complex for central bankers.

CONTRIBUTION AND LEGACY

During his professional life, Lamfalussy lived through, and was actively involved in, the process of European monetary integration in the second half of the twentieth century. His early academic work was very much in the Keynesian tradition. Also later, Lamfalussy—like Keynes and Tobin—retained a certain scepticism about the functioning of the financial markets. At the BIS from 1976 to 1993, Lamfalussy was at the heart of central bank discussions on the international monetary system and European monetary integration. A fundamental experience during this period was the Latin American debt build-up and crisis. It reinforced Lamfalussy's view that financial markets functioned with moods of optimism and pessimism and that reliance could not always be placed on their assessments of debtors. He became an early advocate of the BIS macro-prudential approach to financial stability with a focus of the financial system as a whole and a Cassandra about financial stability. Lamfalussy's vision of the financial markets further permeated his view of the foreign-exchange markets, with a basic distrust of floating exchange rates.

Lamfalussy has always been an advocate of strengthening European monetary integration. In the early 1960s, he backed the creation of a European Reserve Fund, as proposed by Triffin. But, like the Werner Report, Lamfalussy favoured a symmetric EMU: not just a European system of central banks but also a European economic government, implying significant transfers of sovereignty. It would remain a constant element in Lamfalussy's vision of EMU, and also as a member of the Delors Committee, where he argued for a strong economic pillar of EMU. This also reflected his distrust of the capability of financial markets to generate the necessary fiscal discipline.

As president of the EMI he played a crucial role in preparations for the final stage of EMU, especially the conduct of the single monetary policy and the introduction of the single currency. The adoption of the scenario for the changeover to the single currency, in which the EMI and Lamfalussy himself had a key role, strengthened the credibility of the EMU process after the ERM crises in the first half of the 1990s. Lamfalussy was also a strong defender of EMU. With hindsight, however, like many other advocates of EMU, he had not given sufficient attention to potential economic imbalances, especially with regard to the balance of payments and competitiveness, to which EMU contributed.

As chair of the Committee of Wise Men in 2000–1, Lamfalussy was influential in developing a new approach to the regulation of European financial markets. After the financial crisis, the so-called 'Lamfalussy' committees became the basis for the EU's new supervisory authorities. In 2004, Lamfalussy discussed the organization of prudential supervision in the EU. He stressed that central banks had a crucial role in the management of financial crises and that one should give a responsibility to the ECB in the supervision of the large, systemically important, banks. He contributed early ideas for a European banking union that started to take shape only from 2012 onwards in the wake of the financial crisis.

Lamfalussy's advocacy of European monetary integration had its origin in two main sources: a profound European conviction, marked by the devastation of the Second World War and the Iron Curtain; and a fundamental distrust of floating exchange-rate systems. Lamfalussy's legacy for EMU can be considered from a double perspective: as a policy-maker, and in shaping the intellectual debates. As the top policy-maker at the EMI, he played a key role in the construction of the ECB. And, as chair of the Committee of Wise Men, he also contributed to laying the foundations for what would become the EU's new supervisory framework. In addition, Lamfalussy played a very important role in the intellectual debates about monetary union, especially, but not only, in the central banking community. He had a—more or less constant—concern for financial stability, based on a distrust of the way the financial markets worked, arguing instead for a strong economic pillar of EMU to ensure fiscal discipline. This led him to become an early Cassandra, warning of the dangers of financial crisis, and a clear advocate of the thesis that central banks should also consider financial stability as an objective. He was an early advocate of giving the ECB a role in the supervision of systemically important financial institutions, a key element of the European banking union.[5]

[5] The author would like to thank all those who contributed to this project, especially G. Baer, K. Dyson, C. Goodhart, M. di Matteo, A. Lamfalussy, F. Saccomanni, and participants of the STOREP (Gaeta), AISPE (Pisa), and UACES (Leeds) conferences, as well as all the participants in this project. The usual caveats apply.

12

Contributions, Legacies, and Lessons

Kenneth Dyson and Ivo Maes

This study of the history of European monetary integration has focused on what we have called the 'architects of the euro', intellectuals who had an active role in the process of designing the institutional arrangements of Economic and Monetary Union (EMU). They constitute a relatively neglected group of persons who were more than just 'technocratic' policy-makers. They also performed a critical liaison function between the political founders, who drove forward the EMU process and provided political legitimacy, and the ideational founders, essentially academic economists who provided intellectual ideas that fed into the work of the architects. The architects occupied this difficult middle ground. On the one hand, they operated within the constraints on sovereignty transfer, as well as the time constraints, that were set by the political leaders who commissioned their work. On the other, they were in contact with academics who were often critical of European monetary union—notably by reference to Optimum Currency Area (OCA) theory. Their contributions and legacies have to be assessed in this problematic and challenging context.

CONTRIBUTIONS AND LEGACIES

This study of architects of the euro has highlighted the very different types of thinking about the construction of European monetary union. The way in which the individual thinking of the architects developed reflected their very particular cultural, historical, and biographical backgrounds; the different timeframes of their engagement with the issues; structural changes in the ascendancy of economic ideas and theories; and, not least, the impact of the practical political and economic exigencies that they faced. These exigencies mattered. They variously favoured the adoption of particular schemes or led to their marginalization or their outright rejection. They induced differing moods of optimism or pessimism amongst the architects about progress with European monetary union. Hence the ideas of individual architects related in a very variable way with each other, with different sets of economic ideas like Keynesianism, monetarism and various forms of neo-liberalism, and with schemes that were put into practical effect.

As the architects were living in two worlds, that of the politically-minded governing elites and that of professional academics, it is appropriate, in assessing their contributions and legacies, to consider these two worlds before providing a more general assessment. They had to manage a world in which they were being assessed by two different peer groups.

The Architects as Policy-Makers

As policy-makers, the architects had to execute the mandate and deliver within the time deadlines which Europe's leaders, mostly at the highest political level, had given them. They depended on these leaders to provide them with the indispensable political legitimacy for their policy work. This level of political direction also accounted for the atmosphere of pressure, often countervailing pressure, which formed their working environment. It implied that they were bound up in the policy-making process and had to accept certain rules of conduct and certain political constraints, above all in relation to the sovereignty aspects of EMU. Reluctance of Member State governments to cede sovereignty, above all over fiscal and banking matters, and their political sensitivity over issues of labour markets, wage policy, and social policy, complicated their attempts to put flesh on the concept of 'union'.

However, the role of the architects was not limited to the execution of their political mandate. Their closeness to Europe's top politicians, combined with their technical expertise, also gave them opportunities to shape their mandate and the structure of EMU. An example is the role of European Commission president Jacques Delors, especially via his contacts with German Federal Chancellor Helmut Kohl, in shaping the mandate and composition of the Delors Committee, a crucial phase in the EMU process (for details see Dyson and Featherstone 1999). Other architects excelled in this role: not only politicians like Roy Jenkins and Pierre Werner but also more technocratic figures such as Robert Triffin and Tomasso Padoa-Schioppa. In the earlier pre-Maastricht period, contacts to Jean Monnet and his Action Committee for the United States of Europe were important for several of the architects, especially Robert Marjolin, Triffin, and Werner. They were very close to Monnet, who was often their intermediator with Europe's political leaders, particularly Federal Chancellor Willy Brandt before and during the work of the Werner Committee. Similarly, as a European Commissioner, Raymond

Barre placed great emphasis on his contacts to French President Georges Pompidou before the Hague Summit in December 1969, as well as to Brandt and Monnet. This volume shows the significance of Monnet in the patterns of networking by architects from the 1950s to the 1970s.

The launch of European monetary union in 1998–9 proved to be an almost flawless process, thanks to the detailed preparatory work, in which many of the architects played a key role, on the construction of the monetary pillar of EMU. The European Central Bank (ECB) quickly acquired credibility in anchoring inflation expectations to its price stability target (Issing 2008). Moreover, the operational framework of monetary policy proved flexible (Scheller 2014). Once the financial crisis struck, it was able to accommodate non-conventional measures without de-anchoring inflation expectations. In this respect the architects seemed to have been successful in designing a credible ECB.

The ECB emerged as the key player in the financial crisis. Beginning in 2007 it acted decisively to shore up the liquidity of the Euro Area banking system; in 2012, its president Mario Draghi convinced the markets that the ECB would do 'whatever it takes' to preserve the euro; and in 2015 it launched an ambitious programme of quantitative easing (QE), involving large-scale purchases of public-sector bonds. A clear indication of the trust of Europe's leaders in the ECB was that in 2014 the ECB became responsible for the Single Supervisory Mechanism (SSM), a crucial pillar of the new European banking union. The SSM was arguably the most important innovation since the Maastricht Treaty.

At the same time there was no unanimity of views amongst the architects about the role of the ECB and how it interpreted its mandate later. Lamfalussy and Padoa-Schioppa took a more pragmatic central banking view which stressed the pivotal role of the ECB in financial stability. However, German Ordo-liberals like Tietmeyer had mixed feelings about non-standard monetary policy measures. Such measures were seen as producing a big expansion of the Eurosystem balance sheet, involving a rapidly growing volume of public-sector bonds, and increasing risk exposure—despite a tightened risk control framework. In this view, the ECB was mixing monetary with fiscal policy and acting as lender-of-last-resort to sovereigns in difficulties, in breach of the Maastricht Treaty. The ECB risked neglecting its Treaty mandate of price stability in favour of financial stability and safeguarding the euro.

However, this study of the architects looks beyond the evolving Euro Area crisis. It locates the contributions and legacies of the architects of the euro in a longer historical perspective, starting from the European Payments Union (EPU) in the 1950s. The history of the architects shows that EMU is the result of a long process of gradual building on prior achievements. This process was repeatedly interrupted, owing to a diversity of economic and political difficulties. At the same time the realization of EMU was the result of all the experience gained over this period, including negative ones like the collapse of the Bretton Woods system in 1971–3 and the difficulties of constructing a system of managed exchange rates in a world of capital liberalization. It is undoubtedly greatly to the credit of Europe's political leaders that they were able to develop a visionary and forward-looking project, sometimes in the face of strong opposition and much scepticism. The architects played clearly a crucial role in the shaping and execution of the project.

Moreover, all of the architects were very aware of the faults in the design of EMU in the Maastricht Treaty, though they defined them in different ways and had different remedies. This awareness was not simply rooted in the benefit of hindsight, which only helped clarify the gaps in design. In fact, the architects showed considerable prescience.

It is possible to find intellectual antecedents of later reforms to European economic governance in the earlier contributions of architects. Thus Delors' proposal for an 'economic policy coordination pact' (*pacte pour la coordination des politiques économique*) can be seen as a precursor of some of the ideas in the Macro-Economic Imbalances Procedure (MIP). If conceived in a very different context, Triffin's proposal for a European Reserve Fund (ERF) was directed at similar problems to those that animated the European Stability Mechanism (ESM). The similarity was perhaps clearer in the case of Alfred Müller-Armack's proposal of 1958–9 for a European Counter-Cyclical Board, with a Stabilization Fund (see Chapter 7 by Dyson). Similarly, the Fiscal Compact treaty of 2012 links back to the ideas of two very different architects: Delors, who wanted to anchor fiscal rules in national law; and Hans Tietmeyer, who had wanted tighter treaty-based fiscal rules, in contrast to the Stability and Growth Pact (SGP) of 1997.

Financial stability, wages policy, and competitiveness are more problematic. Lamfalussy's concerns about the absence of prudential banking supervision at the European level can be seen as taken up in the European Systemic Risk Board (ESRB) as well as European banking union. Similarly, Padoa-Schioppa had been aware in 1987 of the importance of a coordinated cross-border approach to financial-market supervision. However, it took the deepening financial and economic crisis and its shift to systemically significant states like Italy and Spain to trigger the launch of European banking union in 2012–14. Not least, a Germanic line can be drawn between the idea of a European Concerted Action in the Schiller Plans of 1969–70, on which Tietmeyer had worked, and the Macro-Economic Dialogue, agreed at the Cologne European Council in 1999. The intellectual thread was about establishing a linkage between wage policy, macro-economic stability, and competitiveness. However, on the whole, financial stability, wages policy, and competiveness were neglected issues in the original design of EMU. For instance, the convergence criteria for euro entry required only that account be taken of 'the results of the integration of markets, the situation and development of the balance of payments on current account, and the development of unit labour costs'.

The Architects in the Academic Debates

Analysis and assessment of the role of individual architects of the euro highlights not just the scope and the richness but also the brittleness of the intellectual foundations of the project. As we showed in Chapter 1, this brittleness of the foundations of the euro was far from surprising. After all, the architects could not draw on a single authoritative theory of a sustainable monetary union. The project was extraordinarily complex both technically and in broader terms and, not least, could not be dissociated from fundamental political questions of legitimacy that went beyond the brief of the architects.

How was a sustainable monetary union to be constructed? Was a rule-based monetary union adequate, or did it require provision for aggressive debt restructuring of sovereigns and banks (Dyson 2014; Sandbu 2015)? Was economic convergence a precondition for sustainability? If so, in which aspects, and just how far, did states have to converge? Moreover, monetary union had inescapable cultural, moral, and political dimensions. What kind of Europe was being constructed? Did a sustainable monetary union require harmonization of Member State economic policies? Or, consistent with the treaty principle of subsidiarity that was enshrined at Maastricht, should its economic governance reflect and respect the diversity of economic structures and cultures by reflecting and exploiting differences of comparative institutional advantage? Did the diversity of Member State traditions of economic thought make possible living with a shared currency?

Did European monetary union accord with criteria not just of economic efficiency but also of social justice and political inclusivity? Was it designed to promote and sustain social solidarity? How were social justice and social solidarity to be understood? Could monetary union endure simply on the basis of reliance on rule compliance by Member States? Or did it also require either debt restructuring by Member States or the mutualization of debts and fiscal risk-sharing through a transfer mechanism? Could it survive without an independent basis of democratic political legitimacy to endow it with a fiscal capacity? Which Europe was being constructed? Who belonged in a more differentiated Europe? What was to be the relationship between euro 'ins' and 'outs'?

These many difficult and interrelated questions had not been adequately addressed by the architects, in part because they had not been asked to do so, and in part because they went beyond their technical competence—and beyond the technical competence of the academic economists on whom they relied for guiding ideas.

A key frame of reference was the academic literature on European monetary integration, which was very much dominated by optimum currency area (OCA) theory. On the one hand, OCA theory was far from a unified theory (Maes 1992). On the other, the thinking of the architects could not escape having to contend with the lessons of OCA theory. During the Delors period a clear example was the European Commission's main study on EMU, 'One Market, One Money' (European Commission 1990b). It dismissed OCA theory as 'too narrow and somewhat outdated' (European Commission 1990b: 31). In doing so, the report contributed to complacency about how to reduce exposure to asymmetric economic shocks in a currency union when neither nominal exchange-rate adjustment nor national interest-rate policy was available.

The starting point of OCA is that countries in a monetary union have to be able to manage 'asymmetric' shocks, shocks which do not affect all Member States in the same way. Naturally, also before EMU, countries faced policy constraints through their participation in the EMS; however, there was always the possibility of an exchange-rate realignment. Being in a monetary union implies that monetary and exchange-rate policies cannot be used in the adjustment process. OCA theory developed along two main research lines: (1) the analysis of asymmetric shocks in a monetary union; and (2) the adjustment mechanisms in case of asymmetric shocks.

Generally, the architects were working on the hypothesis of a rather small EMU, which would be relatively homogeneous and thus less prone to asymmetric shocks. This point applied particularly to the early architects. Until 1973 the European Economic Community (EEC) consisted of only six Member States. Also later, during the Maastricht process, the feeling was that EMU, certainly in a first phase, would be limited to a core group of Member States that had strong trading and financial links with Germany. This dominant view was reflected politically in the Schäuble and Lamers paper on 'Core Europe' of 1994. It envisaged a group of five to six Member States. However, the political dynamics led to the euro starting with eleven Member States, followed by several enlargements, beginning with Greece. The idea of a Euro Area of nineteen Member States (as from January 2015), with all its concomitant heterogeneity and proneness to asymmetric shocks, was far from the minds of the architects. It posed in a striking way the question of how economic policy coordination could be best adapted to a monetary union of much more diverse economic structures and cultures (cf. Abelshauser 2014).

OCA theory, which had its origins largely in the Anglo-American academic community, focused on asymmetric shocks that were exogenous and that had their origin in the private sector of the economy. However, asymmetric shocks can also be endogenous and self-inflicted, caused by growing internal imbalances, policy inertia, and weak institutional capacity. Not least, they can originate from the public sector. This risk was less evident in the United

States, where the budgets of state authorities are relatively limited and subject to several constraints. For European monetary union, the world was rather different. Budgetary and debt positions can be (and have been) important sources of asymmetric shocks, in part because of the size of national budgetary and debt positions in the monetary union, and in part because of the much larger autonomy of Member State governments. The need for a binding framework for Member State budgetary policies, in order to avoid 'asymmetric' budgetary policies, had been an important concern for many architects. This concern was forcefully expressed by the German Ordo-liberals, like Karl-Otto Pöhl and Hans Tietmeyer. However, it was also shared by other architects, like Raymond Barre, Jacques Delors, Alexandre Lamfalussy, and Pierre Werner. Several of these architects favoured a form of European 'economic government', for a mixture of reasons, some more narrowly economic and others federalist.

The OCA literature focused on three factors that were identified as key adjustment mechanisms in the case of asymmetric shocks in a monetary union: fiscal transfers, labour mobility (migration), and price and wage flexibility. The architects were very much aware that the effectiveness of fiscal transfers and labour mobility was limited in Europe, compared for instance to the United States and other federal states like Germany. This limitation was clearly evident with respect to labour mobility, given the important differences in languages and cultures between, and sometimes within, European Member States. At the same time labour mobility could prove a counterproductive adjustment process if skilled workers emigrate in times of high unemployment.

In the case of fiscal transfers, there was some optimism in the 1960s and early 1970s, evident in the chapters on Marjolin and on Werner, about constructing a symmetric EMU, including transfer mechanisms amongst Member States. However, the Maastricht compromise created an asymmetric EMU, with a transfer of sovereignty in monetary policy, but not in economic policy (Maes 2002). This design fault was the subject of criticism by some of the architects like Delors, who sought an increase, albeit modest, in the EU budget to permit cyclical stabilization. Even so, major proposals for fiscal risk-sharing were absent, not least because they were seen as Keynesian interventionism, going against the prevailing belief in market efficiency. Notably, the Maastricht Treaty contained in Article 104 the famous so-called 'no bail-out' clause, designed to set limits on mutual liability and to prevent moral hazard.

Given these limitations, the architects of the euro had focused on wage and price flexibility as the adjustment mechanism, whether out of a sense of realism (see Chapter 11 on Lamfalussy) of from principle (see Chapter 7 on Tietmeyer). However, reliance on this mechanism faced the problem of the 'stickiness' of wages in liberal democracies, a problem that John Maynard Keynes had identified as central. Karl Polanyi (1944) had argued that the reduction of labour to a 'commodity', as part of a self-regulating market, would prompt counter political mobilization. His argument pointed to the risk that the Euro Area could be caught up in a politically difficult 'double movement' between market liberalization and populist forces promoting social protection. This process seemed to unfold as the financial and economic crisis drew out.

Most of the OCA literature was a rather static type of analysis, comparing costs and benefits of joining a monetary union for a country. In the 1990s, a more dynamic variant of OCA became popular, analysing the dynamic effects of countries joining a currency union. The main argument of so-called endogenous OCA theory was that a monetary union would lead to greater trade integration, increasing over time the advantages for a country of joining the monetary union (Rose 2000). However, the European reality turned out to be very different. Baldwin (2006) suggested that the major trade gains from the euro were mainly restricted to the former D-Mark Zone (Member States of the ERM), all closely integrated into the German economy. Moreover, Paul Krugman suggested that EMU could lead to more specialization, making the Euro Area more prone to asymmetric shocks.

The subsequent post-2007 financial, economic, and sovereign debt crises within the Euro Area showed how the euro had led to growing trade, financial, and fiscal imbalances and competitiveness problems. Indeed the credibility of the monetary union had induced the financial markets to finance much larger external imbalances than in earlier periods (see Sapir 2014b for a comparison with the 1992–3 EMS crises).

In some Member States, such as Ireland and Spain, economic expansion—especially in the property sector—was initially bolstered by the convergence of nominal interest rates within the monetary union, as spreads with Germany more or less disappeared. This convergence was also due to increasing cross-border banking activity in a large Euro Area without exchange-rate risk. The ensuing boom further fuelled wage and price increases, which largely surpassed those in other countries like Germany, impairing the competitiveness of these Member States.

Notwithstanding these competitiveness losses, domestic demand further increased through the combined effects of strong wage increases and very low real interest rates (given the combination of low nominal rates with high inflation). This situation further added to the trade, financial, and fiscal imbalances, with excessive lending and debt, property market bubbles, and current account deficits.

These growing imbalances did not trigger a timely and determined economic policy response, because people bought into the illusion that real convergence was taking place. The final result was a severe asset-price boom and bust cycle and subsequent harsh and prolonged process of deleverage. This development was a reminder of the build-up of imbalances in the EMS in the late 1980s, foreseen by Sir Alan Walters, Margaret Thatcher's economic adviser (Dyson and Featherstone 1999: 547–9). Failure to identify this risk was probably the main weak spot of the architects of the euro. It had, not least, implications for budgetary policies and for wage coordination policies that had been neglected.

Notwithstanding important exceptions, like James Meade (1957), the OCA literature did not pay much attention to issues of financial integration and financial stability. Financial integration and stability would become the Achilles heel of Europe's monetary union. The global financial crisis, which had its origins in the US mortgage market, also hit Europe's banks seriously. When the property market bubbles in several EU Member States burst, their banking systems found themselves in serious trouble. The outcome in 2011–12 was a poisonous and potentially deadly mutual embrace between banks and sovereigns. The Euro Area faced the spectre of a vicious circle of bank balance sheet deleveraging, credit restrictions hampering economic activity, additional government intervention in the banking sector, further downgrades of sovereign debt, and sovereign debt restructuring hitting the balance sheets of banks.

The sovereign debt crisis clearly pointed up the flaws in the structure of EMU. It demonstrated that membership of a single currency in a single economic and financial market creates extremely strong and complex interdependencies. Of particular significance was the absence of institutions for prudential supervision and for handling a banking crisis at the European level, especially for systemic banks with cross-border operations. This gap mattered all the more because the Euro Area was a strongly bank-based financial system, compared to Britain and the United States. With some notable exceptions, like Lamfalussy and Padoa-Schioppa, most of the architects did not pay much attention to financial stability issues.

Towards a More General Assessment

A fundamental issue is how to assess the significance of an architect's contribution. Is it to be assessed by its intellectually challenging and innovative character? Or is it to be assessed by its proximity to final negotiated outcomes? Is the contribution to be assessed in the context of the political and intellectual space and time in which the architects operated? Or is it to be assessed from the perspective of the later achievements, risks, and failings of EMU?

Most of the architects favoured closer monetary policy cooperation before the final stage of EMU than emerged in the Maastricht Treaty. On this issue Pöhl and Tietmeyer were exceptions and were also closer to the agreed outcomes. Also, the majority of architects supported a more supranational organization of the Euro Area than emerged in the Maastricht Treaty. Here Barre was an exception. On this issue the thinking of Padoa-Schioppa, Triffin, and Werner was a less comfortable fit with the exigencies of power within the process of European monetary integration. Pöhl's and Tietmeyer's Ordo-liberal-inspired thinking was much closer to the fiscal policy outcomes negotiated not just in the Maastricht 'economic constitution' but also later in the SGP and then in the Fiscal Compact treaty. However, reflecting the complex nature of negotiating processes in the EU, neither Pöhl nor Tietmeyer was content with some of the key provisions of the Maastricht Treaty on the convergence criteria for entry and on the kind of supranational organization that was required for a sustainable monetary union.

This difference in success of architects in getting support for their thinking in negotiated outcomes stemmed from variation in the fit between their ideas about European monetary union, the ascendant economic thought and configuration of political power in Europe, and the opening—or closing—of a window of opportunity to make progress with EMU at a particular time. Architects varied in terms of whether they were structurally privileged or marginalized within the EU and by the fortunes or misfortunes of the timing of their interventions. EMU was eventually negotiated in the historical and structural context of the ascendancy of stability-oriented policies and of German economic power in Europe. In this particular sense Pöhl and Tietmeyer were structurally privileged. Monetary union was negotiated around the fundamental requirement of German participation for its credibility (Dyson and Featherstone 1999; Dyson 2014; Maes 2004).

However, assessment of success needs to look beyond getting one's ideas into the Maastricht Treaty and later add-ons to the treaty. Architects varied in their prescience in identifying the longer-term challenges that European monetary union would face. These challenges were revealed by the post-2007 financial, economic, and sovereign debt crisis. They suggested some serious gaps.

The challenge of fiscal union, in the sense of counter-cyclical stabilizers, was identified as crucial by Roy Jenkins. However, by 2015, there was not much evidence that the architecture of the Euro Area had evolved to provide him with belated success and recognition. With respect to fiscal policy, Pöhl and Tietmeyer could claim longer-term success. The reform of the SGP in 2011, and above all the Fiscal Compact treaty of 2012, moved the process of surveillance of Member State fiscal policies closer towards what they had favoured in the Maastricht Treaty and the negotiations that had led to the original design of the SGP. In the design of fiscal policy, domestic discipline triumphed over collective risk-sharing and insurance.

The crucial challenge of securing financial stability in monetary union was most clearly identified by Lamfalussy and by Padoa-Schioppa. Long before the Delors Committee, Lamfalussy had stressed financial stability risks and been an advocate of macro-prudential supervision. He was the closest to conceiving the need for European banking union. However, Pöhl and Tietmeyer, in the German Ordo-liberal tradition, focused on price stability, neglecting the implications of monetary union for financial integration and for financial stability. Delors was notably reluctant to press this issue.

Similarly, Delors, Marjolin, and above all Triffin identified the need for cross-national policy coordination to tackle the problem of trade and financial imbalances. In particular, Triffin stressed the importance of a European mechanism to provide financial assistance to Member States that faced financial-market difficulties. His proposal for the ERF offered a protective umbrella in cases of exchange-rate crises. The ESM, which was created in 2012, was designed to deal with a different problem: crisis in sovereign bond markets. Nevertheless, the thinking behind both was very much the same. It involved financial solidarity.

Another gap was in wage policy coordination (Sapir and Wolf 2015). As Polanyi (1944) had argued, the scope of market liberalization remains politically contentious, above all in relation to wages and labour markets. Wage policy coordination mattered in monetary union for two interdependent reasons: it was relevant to combating inflation and to prevent the build-up of imbalances as some Member States lost competitiveness through inflation differentials. The key was understood to be national and European mechanisms for productivity-oriented wage bargaining. Here German centre-Left thinkers were most active. Thus the Schiller paper of October 1969 (Dyson and Quaglia 2010a) proposed a European 'Concerted Action', on the German model, to coordinate wage bargaining with macro-economic stability. Later, the centre-Left federal government of Federal Chancellor Gerhard Schröder used its EU presidency to establish the Macro-Economic Dialogue, drawing the trade unions into an 'information sharing' process that included the ECB and Member State representatives. Occasionally, individual architects showed awareness of wage coordination issues. Thus Marjolin and Tietmeyer referred to it; the Bundesbank paper to the Delors Committee referred very briefly to the requirement for a differentiated wages policy in a monetary union. However, it remained a neglected issue. The Macro-Economic Dialogue proved to be strikingly invisible in macro-economic policy debates.

Another failure was in arriving at a settled consensus between the 'economist' and 'monetarist' conceptions of EMU. In an important sense the history of EMU was one in which the 'economists' claimed successes that turned out to be hollow. At the centre of their concern was the precondition of economic convergence before monetary union. However, the convergence criteria for euro entry, as enshrined in the Maastricht Treaty, proved weak. Though they stressed that convergence must be sustainable, they rested on only a two-year assessment period. Competitiveness was no more than a matter to take into account. It became clear that convergence could prove very fleeting. The convergence criteria encouraged opportunistic, and sometimes dubious, policy-making. More generally, the structural characteristics of the 'real' economy were neglected.

The economist/monetarist divide remained an unresolved tension at the heart of the EMU project. It was also linked to very different views about how economic adjustment to imbalances and stabilization were best achieved. On the one hand, some architects, notably Triffin, stressed the importance of the international and European systemic levels. The essential requirements were liquidity provision and economic policy coordination at these levels, based on the mutual obligations of creditor and debtor states to the system. On the other hand, Ordo-liberals like Tietmeyer emphasized the overriding importance of Member States taking individual responsibility for putting their own house in order. Otherwise moral hazard would infect states, European monetary union, and the international framework. Despite an initial design that was closer to the domestic 'house-in-order' approach, a settled consensus about the mechanisms for economic adjustment and stabilization continued to elude the architects.

LESSONS

Two principal issues arise with respect to the lessons to be drawn from this study of architects of the euro: the legitimacy of the EMU governance structure; and the future of EMU.

The Architects and the Legitimacy of the EMU Governance Structure

As the Euro Area financial, economic, and sovereign debt crises made clear, legitimacy is a core issue in a monetary union. It was also one on which the architects—and academic economists—were less qualified to speak. Moreover, legitimacy is a complex, multidimensional concept which is both extremely important and open to conflicting interpretations. It can be assessed in its input and its output dimensions (Scharpf 1999).

Output legitimacy rests on the ability to solve problems and deliver results, fostering at least tacit public consent. In the context of European integration it has been very much associated with the ability to deliver economic growth, higher employment, rising real incomes, and buoyant tax revenues—all strengthening the legitimacy of both Member States and the integration process. In its early phase, the integration process gained legitimacy from the economic growth of the 'golden sixties' through the formation of the Common Market. Later, in the 1980s, the single market programme was also able to serve as a source of output legitimacy. Monetary union was expected to build on this success by reducing business and financial transaction costs and fostering trade integration, investment, and growth. However, on a scale not seen before, even in the 1970s, the financial and economic crisis exposed the Euro Area, and the wider EU, to accusations of major policy failure and to the demise of the passive consensus about European integration. The EMU project was caught up in changing perceptions of the stabilizing character of financial markets and of the contribution of finance to economic growth. Clearly the reputation of the architects is bound up—perhaps not always fairly—with this widespread sense of failure and the growth of negative feelings towards a liberal, market-driven EMU project. Moreover, even before the crisis economic growth performance had been disappointing.

Conversely, input legitimacy relates to the participation of citizens, through the election of their representatives, the inclusiveness and the transparency of governance, and the capacity to hold elected representatives to account. However, European integration, and not least EMU, has been mostly an elite-driven project, susceptible to critique as disembedded from democratic politics. With the evolution towards a more critically engaged public on European matters, the issue of input legitimacy has increased in salience. Notwithstanding earlier debates and attempts to resolve the 'democratic deficit', and the difficult period of 'stag-flation' and exchange-rate instability in the 1970s, European integration had mostly benefited from a 'permissive' consensus as economic growth provided (output) legitimacy. However, once output legitimacy stalled, input legitimacy became a serious problem and concentrated on the 'austerity' policies attributed to the Euro Area policy elite. In short, EMU suffered from a double problem.

Most of the architects were convinced that the euro would contribute to a strengthening of Europe's economic performance, just as the single market project had done. In its famous study, 'One Market, One Money', the European Commission argued that:

> New economic theory and particular features of the Community's actual structure and situation add seven further arguments, all pointing to benefits for EMU in the Community. On these grounds the economic case becomes strongly advantageous. Political union objectives may further be added. But the case can stand powerfully on economic criteria alone. (European Commission 1990b: 29)

Reality would turn out to be different. During its first decade the euro witnessed a further integration of Europe's economies, especially the financial markets. Nevertheless, Europe's growth performance remained lacklustre. The financial crisis and the Euro Area debt crisis contributed to the Euro Area's worst economic performance since the Great Depression of the 1930s. Eurobarometer surveys, European Parliament election results, and national election results showed the scale of the damage to the output legitimacy of the euro project and the EU as a whole. This damage was especially evident in

Member States like France, Greece, Italy, and Spain, where protracted economic stagnation and high, especially youth, unemployment generated new challenges to traditional pro-European party systems. In addition, public opinion in the core creditor countries of the Euro Area, like Austria, Finland, Germany, and the Netherlands, was influenced by populist mobilization against an EMU that was becoming a 'transfer union' of a kind that was supposed to have been explicitly excluded in the Maastricht Treaty. It seemed that the earlier optimistic economic expectations of many of the architects had contributed to a sharpening of the 'output' legitimacy issue.

The Architects and the Future of EMU

The future of the construction of European monetary union poses questions about the strength and resilience of the shared understandings and economic policy beliefs, on the basis of which the euro was constructed—and which were examined in Chapter 1. These shared understandings included moral responsibility for fostering European integration that stems from the grim 'shadow of history', as well as the more practical advantages that flow from the Europeanization of economic and financial policies. Are they sufficient to help the Euro Area deal with potentially major asymmetric economic, social, and political shocks? Is there sufficient consensus about the normative basis of economic policy, as well as about the causal mechanisms at work in domestic and European economies, to sustain coordinated policies?

These questions are eminently political in nature and extend beyond the competence of the architects of the euro, at least as defined in this volume. They revolve around the discursive behaviour of Member State political elites in constructing and using historical memory to legitimate European monetary union and to promote inclusivity and domestic political ownership of the euro project. This discursive behaviour has ideological and cultural attributes, revealing attitudes to sovereignty and identity. In particular, the proper scope of market liberalization remains highly politically contentious. Does market liberalization have limits? Can it poison society by undermining solidarity and deepening inequality?

Debate about the normative basis of European integration brings out the interdependence between the economic, monetary, legal, social, and political orders, as well as their historically embedded character. It suggests that an 'optimum currency area' is more than a narrowly economic and technical matter. It is about Member States and the people of Europe wishing to live together because they share certain common values and about their elites retaining a commitment to fostering habits of mind that help them to learn to live together through practical cooperation.

In assessing the architects it is vital to remember that the most crucial decisions about EMU were taken by Europe's top political leaders. Two decisions stand out. First, the political commission to the architects implied an asymmetric EMU, in which sovereign powers over economic policies were essentially retained by Member States. Second, the decision to go ahead with a larger and more heterogeneous monetary union than the architects had initially envisaged had implications for vulnerability to asymmetric shocks and thus for robust institutional design to absorb these shocks. The unfolding crisis from 2007 led the European Council to agree significant changes to the structure of EMU governance, including stricter rules and surveillance on budgetary and other economic policies in the European Semester, the ESM, a banking union, and a projected capital markets union. Many of the architects had been advocating one or more of these elements. However, it took a brutal crisis before politicians acted belatedly.

Also, many of the architects favoured a political union. Here again Member State politicians proved reluctant to act. The failure of the European Constitutional Treaty in 2005, brought down by referenda in two Euro Area Member States, France and the Netherlands, and the subsequent difficulties in ratification of the Lisbon Treaty, deterred EU politicians from pursuing treaty revision. The loss of output legitimacy with the financial, economic, and sovereign debt crisis only acted as a further deterrent. By 2015 the Euro Area seemed to be locked into a long-term financial, economic, and political crisis of a kind and on a scale that its architects had not envisaged. It faced very slow economic growth or even stagnation; high unemployment, especially youth unemployment; and cuts to public services and social benefits for many. This context was more favourable to 'integration by stealth' than to bold institution building.

European monetary union had also gained a popular political association with 'austerity'. Reflecting this new political climate, eminent German social scientists like Fritz Scharpf and Wolfgang Streeck called for a return to the pre-1999 period when Member States retained ultimate sovereignty over their exchange rates, monetary policies, and fiscal policies. In their view, the opportunity for European political union had vanished. Democratic legitimacy could only be restored in the EU by abandoning monetary union. Otherwise, political extremism would flourish. This analysis overlooked the implications of the huge sunk costs of EU elites in the EMU project; the potential reputational risks to the EU as a whole from admission of defeat with monetary union; the risks to German trading interests from exchange-rate instability and appreciation; and the problems that had beset the old ERM.

This debate about political legitimacy took place in the realms of law, political science, and political theory, areas with which many of the architects were less familiar than they were with economics. Though highly normative and value-laden, it pointed to the way in which architects and their reputations become caught up in the sins of commission—and omission—of those who instruct them. From 2007 it became clear just how vulnerable the Euro Area was to asymmetric shocks. Moreover, these shocks were not just economic and financial. The Euro Area and the wider EU faced potentially contagious political shocks from populist extremism in the Member States. It also faced exposure of the naïvety of assuming Member State compliance with rules and programme commitments. Some Member States—Greece was an archetype—had not just problems of state capacity to deliver; they were problematic in the political will to comply and commit. These were hard and harsh lessons for the Euro Area and the EU. Ultimately, the Euro Area and the EU had to face up to the kind of fundamental questions about the nature of European integration as both a political project and a community of responsibility and solidarity that had been earlier evaded.

References

Abelshauser, W. (1983). *Wirtschaftsgeschichte der Bundesrepublik Deutschland 1945–1980*. Berlin: Suhrkamp.

Abelshauser, W. (2014). *Europa in Vielfalt einigen: Eine Denkschrift*. Universität Bielefeld.

Abraham, J. P. and Lemineur-Toumson, C. (1981). 'Les Choix monétaires européens 1950–1980', *Études Internationales*, 12(3): 499–512.

Aeschimann, E. and Riché, P. (1996). *La Guerre de sept ans: histoire secrète du franc fort, 1989–1996*. Paris: Calmann-Lévy.

Aglietta, M. and Baulant, C. (1993). 'Le franc: de l'instrument de croissance à la recherche de l'ancrage nominal', in M. Lévy-Leboyer et al. (eds.), *Du franc Poincaré à l'écu*. Paris: Ministère de l'Economie, Comité pour l'histoire économique et financière, pp. 503–53.

Albert, M. (2004). 'Robert Marjolin et la coordination des politiques économiques dans la CEE', in Institut de France, Académie des Sciences Morales et Politiques (ed.), *Colloque du mardi 9 décembre 2003 consacré à Robert Marjolin*. Paris: Palais de l'Institut, pp. 83–90.

Allen, P. (2004). 'A Young Home Secretary', in A. Adonis and K. Thomas (eds.), *Roy Jenkins: A Retrospective*. Oxford: Oxford University Press, pp. 61–82.

Amouroux, H. (1986). *Monsieur Barre*. Paris: Robert Laffont.

Badel, L. (2005). 'La direction économique extérieures (DREE): Origines, Cultures et Logique (1920–1970)', in L. Badel, S. Jeannesson, and N. P. Ludlow (eds.), *Les administrations nationales et la construction européenne*. Brussels: Peter Lang, pp. 169–206.

Baer, G. and Padoa-Schioppa, T. (1989). 'The Werner Report Revisited', in Committee for the Study of Economic and Monetary Union, *Report on Economic and Monetary Union in the European Community*. Luxembourg: Office des publications officielles des Communautés européennes, April, pp. 53–60.

Baffi, P. (1988). *Robert Triffin*. Turin: San Paolo.

Baldwin, R. (2006). 'The Euro's Trade Effects'. ECB Working Paper No. 594. Frankfurt am Main: European Central Bank.

Balladur, E. (1987). *Je crois en homme plus qu'en l'Etat*. Paris: Flammarion.

Balleix-Banerjee, C. (1999). *La France et la Banque Centrale Européenne*. Paris: Presses Universitaires de France.

Barre, R. (1966). *Economie politique*. Paris: Presses universitaires de France.

Barre, R. (1968). 'Les problèmes monétaires internationaux et la politique monétaire de la Communauté', *Bulletin des Communautés européennes*, 1(1): 17.

Barre, R. (1976). 'Déclaration de politique générale à L'Assemblée Nationale', 5 October.

Barre, R. (1981). *Une Politique pour l'avenir*. Paris: Plon.

Barre, R. (1984). *Réflexions pour demain*. Paris: Hachette.

Barre, R. (1987). *Au Tournant du siècle: Principes de politique étrangère*. Paris: Plon.

Barre, R. (1988a). 'Barre l'Européen: pragmatism et imagination', *Proposer et répondre*, numéro hors-série, 1st trimester.

Barre, R. (1988b). *Questions de confiance, Entretiens avec J.-M. Colombani*. Paris: Flammarion.

Barre, R. (1992). 'Raymond Barre: Les accords de Maastricht sont un succès et n'affectent en rien notre autonomie de décision', *Les Echos*, 10 January. <http://www.lesechos.fr/10/01/1992/LesEchos/16053-006-ECH_raymond-barre–les-accords-de-maastricht-sont-un-succes-et-n-affectent-en-rien-notre-autonomie-de-decision.htm#MOXhCHv4bmqtdaFp.99>.

Barre, R. (2000). 'Avant-Propos', in P. Dockès, L. Frobert, G. Klotz, J.-P. Potier, and A. Tiran (eds.), *Les traditions économiques française (1848–1939)*. Paris: CNRS Éditions, pp. 17–26.

Barre, R. (2004). 'Entretien avec Raymond Barre', in M.-T. Bitsch, E. Bussière, and G. Lavezzi, *CONSHIST.COM Histoire interne de la Commission européenne 1958–1973*, 20 February. Louvain-la-Neuve: Université catholique de Louvain. <http://archives.eui.eu/en/files/transcript/15160?d=inline>.

Barre, R. and Bothorel, J. (2007). *L'Expérience du pouvoir*. Paris: Fayard.

Barre, R. and Fontanel, J. (1991). *Principes de politiques economiques, l'economie en plus*. Grenoble: Presse Universitaires de Grenoble.

Beach, D. (2005). *The Dynamics of European Integration: Why and When EU Institutions Matter*. Basingstoke: Palgrave Macmillan.

Beck, U. (2013). *German Europe*. Cambridge: Polity Press.

Bernanke, B. S., Laubach, T., Mishkin, F. S., and Posen, A. S. (1999). *Inflation Targeting: Lessons from the International Experience*. Princeton, NJ: Princeton University Press.

Bini Smaghi, L. (2012). 'Padoa-Schioppa, Tommaso (1940–2010)', *The New Palgrave Dictionary of Economics*.<http://www.palgraveconnect.com/pc/doifinder/10.1057/9781137336583.1335>.

Bitsch, M.-T., Bussière, E., and Lavezzi, G. (2004). 'Entretien avec Raymond Barre'. Transcription. Paris, 20 February, in *Voix sur l'Europe: Histoire interne de la Commission européenne 1958–1973*. Available from David Howarth.

Bönker, F., Labrousse, A., and Weisz, J.-D. (2001). 'The Evolution of Ordoliberalism in the Light of the *Ordo* Yearbook: A Bibliometric Analysis', in A. Labrousse and J.-D. Weisz (eds.), *Institutional Economics in France and Germany: German Ordoliberalism and the French Regulation School*. Berlin: Springer, pp. 159–82.

Bossuat, G. (2012). *La France et la construction de l'unité européenne: de 1919 à nos jours*. Paris: Armand Colin.

Boughton, J. M. (2001). *Silent Revolution: The International Monetary Fund, 1979–89*. Washington, DC: International Monetary Fund.

Bourdieu, P. (1996). 'Wie Maos Rotes Buch', interview on the Bundesbank and neoliberalism, *Der Spiegel*, 50, 9 December.

Buiter, W., Corsetti, G., and Pesenti, P. (1998). *Financial Markets and European Monetary Integration: The Lessons of the 1992–1993 Exchange Rate Mechanism Crisis*. Cambridge: Cambridge University Press.

Burgess, M. (2000). *Federalism and European Union: The Building of Europe, 1950–2000*. London: Taylor & Francis.

Bussière, E. (2007). 'Moves towards an Economic and Monetary Policy', in M. Dumoulin (ed.), *The European Commission, 1958–72: History and Memories*. Luxembourg: Office for Official Publications, pp. 391–410.

Bussière, E. and Feiertag, O. (2012). 'Triffin et la construction monétaire européenne: Une contribution à la rénovation du système monétaire international', in J.-C. Koeune and A. Lamfalussy (eds.), *In Search of a New World Monetary Order*. Brussels: Peter Lang, pp. 73–96.

Campbell, J. (2014). *Roy Jenkins: A Well-Rounded Life*. London: Jonathan Cape.

Cannadine, D. (2004). 'Writer and Biographer', in A. Adonis and K. Thomas (eds.), *Roy Jenkins: A Retrospective*. Oxford: Oxford University Press, pp. 271–305.

Chalmers, D. (2013). 'European Restatements of Sovereignty'. LSE Law, Society and Economy Working Paper 10/2013.

Chélini, M.-P. (2001). 'Le plan de stabilisation Pinay-Rueff, 1958', *Revue d'histoire moderne et contemporaine*, 4(48–4): 102–23.

Ciocca, P. (2004).'Il contributo di via Nazionale', in G. Garofolo and A. Graziani (eds.), *La formazione degli economisti in Italia (1950–1975)*. Bologna: Il Mulino, pp. 579–600.

Coene, L. (2014). 'Introduction', in I. Maes and F. Moss (eds.), *Progress through Crisis? Proceedings of the Conference for the 20th Anniversary of the Establishment of the European Monetary Institute*. Frankfurt am Main: European Central Bank, pp. 13–16.

Coeuré, B. (2015). 'Lamfalussy was Right: Independence and Interdependence in a Monetary Union'. Lamfalussy Lecture. Budapest: Magyar Nemzeti Bank, 2 February.

Commission of the EEC (1958). Report on the Economic Situation in the Countries of the Community, September.

Commission of the EEC (1962a). Memorandum of the Commission on the Action Programme of the Community for the Second Stage, COM (62) 300 final, 24 October.

Commission of the EEC (1962b). Les perspectives de développement économique dans la C.E.E. de 1960 à 1970. Rapport d'un groupe d'experts.

Commission of the EEC (1963a). La coopération monétaire et financière au sein de la Communauté Économique Européenne (Communication de la Commission au Conseil), II/COM(63) 216 final, 19 June.

Commission of the EEC (1963b). Politique économique à moyen terme de la Communauté (Recommendation de la Commission au Conseil), II/COM(63) 271 final, 25 July.

Commission of the EEC (1964). Initiative 1964 for speeding up the implementation of the Common Market, Community Topics 15. European Community Information Service.

Commission of the European Communities (1966). *Le développement d'un marché européen des capitaux*, Rapport Segré. Brussels.

Commission of the European Communities (1975). Report of the Study Group 'Economic and Monetary Union 1980', 8 March.

Commission of the European Communities (1977). Report of the Study Group on the Role of Public Finance in European Integration.

Commission of the European Communities (1993). 'Stable Money—Sound Finances: Community Public Finance in the Perspective of EMU', *European Economy*, 53.

Committee for the Study of Economic and Monetary Union (1989). *Report on Economic and Monetary Union in the European Community*. Luxembourg: Office for the Official Publications of the European Community.

Committee of Wise Men (2001). *Final Report on the Regulation of European Securities Markets*, February.

Connolly, B. (1995). *The Rotten Heart of Europe*. London: Faber and Faber.

Cooper, R. (2003). *The Breaking of Nations: Order and Chaos in the Twenty-First Century*. London: Atlantic Books.

Council of the European Community (1988). *Presidency Conclusions*. Hanover European Council, 27 and 28 June, No. 2683/4/88.

Crafts, N. and Toniolo, G. (1996). 'Postwar Growth: An Overview', in N. Crafts and G. Toniolo (eds.), *Economic Growth in Europe since 1945*. Cambridge: Cambridge University Press, pp. 1–37.

Cressati, C. (1992). *L'Europa Necessaria: Il federalismo Liberale di Luigi Einaudi*. Turin: Giappichelli.

CVCE (2014–16). Oral history of European integration collection. Sanem: CVCE. <http://www.cvce.eu/en/oral-history>.

Danescu, E. (2011). 'Le comité Werner, nouvelles archives', *Histoire, économie et société*, 30(4): 29–38.

Danescu, E. (2012a). 'The First and Second Barre Plans', in *A Rereading of the Werner Report of 8 October 1970 in the Light of the Pierre Werner Family Archives*. Sanem: CVCE. <http://www.cvce.eu>.

Danescu, E. (2012b). *A Rereading of the Werner Report of 8 October 1970 in the Light of the Pierre Werner Family Archives*. Sanem: CVCE. <http://www.cvce.eu>.

Danescu, E. (2012c). 'Summary of the Werner Committee's Schedule and the Main Issues Addressed (6 March 1970–22 March 1971)', in *A Rereading of the Werner Report of 8 October 1970 in the Light of the Pierre Werner Family Archives*. Sanem: CVCE. <http://www.cvce.eu>.

Danescu, E. (2015). 'Pierre Werner: l'homme et son œuvre', in E. Danescu and S. Muñoz (eds.), *Pierre Werner, une vision pour l'Europe: pensée, action, enseignements/Pierre Werner and Europe: His Approach, Action and Legacy*. Brussels: Peter Lang, pp. 117–39.

Daniel, J.-M. (2008). 'Cinquante ans de finances publiques', *Sociétal*, 62, 4ème trimester: 31–43. <http://www.melchior.fr/fileadmin/fichiers/Revues/Societal/jmd_dossier_62.pdf>.

De Beckker, R. (1984). 'The EUA Sector', in M. Kerr (ed.), *A History of the Eurobond Market: The First 12 Years*. London: Euromoney Publications, pp. 128–9.

De Boissieu, C. (2010). 'L'économiste', in Académie des Sciences Morales et Politiques, FNSP, Aspen France, *Raymond Barre, Un homme singulier dans la politique française*. Paris: Éditions de Fallois, pp. 17–26.

De Ménil, G. (2010). *Raymond Barre, Un homme singulier dans la politique française*. Paris: Éditions de Fallois.

De Saint Périer, A. (2013). *La France, l'Allemagne et l'Europe Monétaire de 1974 à 1981*. Paris: Presses de la Fondation Nationale de Sciences Politiques.

De Tavernier, J. (2009). 'The Historical Roots of Personalism: From Renouvier's Le Personnalisme to Mounier's Manifeste', *Ethical Perspectives*, 16(3): 361–92.

Debré, M. (1988). *Trois Républiques pour une France. Tome 3: Gouverneur. Mémoires 1958–1962*. Paris: Albin Michel.

Dell'Amore, G. (1970). 'Pour un système monétaire européen', *Agence Europe*, 568, 12 March: 1.

Delors, J. (1975). *Changer: Conversations avec Claude Glayman*. Paris: Stock.

Delors, J. (1976). 'Problématique pour un autre développement', in European Commission, 'Report of the Study Group "Problems of Inflation"', Annexes. II/294/75. Brussels: DG Economic and Financial Affairs, pp. 33–52.

Delors, J. (1985a). 'Programme of the Commission for 1985: Statement by Jacques Delors, President of the Commission to the European Parliament and his Reply to the Ensuing Debate', Strasbourg, 12 March, Bulletin of the European Communities Supplement 4/85.

Delors, J. (1985b). 'Speech by Mr Delors to the Confederation of British Industries', 29 October, SPEECH/85/11. Brussels: European Commission.

Delors, J. (1987). 'Discours de M. Delors au Colloque du Centre de Promotion et de Recherche Pour la Monnaie Européenne sur "l'ECU demain"', Luxembourg, 6–7 November, SPEECH/87/73. Brussels: European Commission.

Delors, J. (1988). 'Programme of the Commission for 1988: Address by Jacques Delors, President of the European Commission to the European Parliament', Strasbourg, 20 January, Bulletin of the European Communities, Supplement 1/88.

Delors, J. (1989a). 'Economic and Monetary Union and Re-launching the Construction of Europe', in Committee for the Study of Economic and Monetary Union, *Report on Economic and Monetary Union in the European Community*. Luxembourg: Office for the Official Publications of the European Community, pp. 63–7.

Delors, J. (1989b). 'Regional Implications of Economic and Monetary Integration', in Committee for the Study of Economic and Monetary Union, *Report on Economic and Monetary Union in the European Community*. Luxembourg: Office for the Official Publications of the European Community, pp. 81–9.

Delors, J. (1989c). 'Speech by President Delors at the Opening Session of the 40th Academic Year of the College of Europe-Bruges', 17 October, SPEECH/89/73. Brussels: European Commission.

Delors, J. (1989d). *Report on Economic and Monetary Union in the European Community*. Committee on the Study of Economic and Monetary Union, 17 April.

Delors, J. (1990a). 'Press Conference by President Delors before the Informal Dublin European Council', 26 April, SPEECH/90/33. Brussels: European Commission.

Delors, J. (1990b). 'Europe's Ambitions', *Foreign Policy*, 80: 14–27.

Delors, J. (1991). 'Speech by President Delors at the International Institute for Strategic Studies', London, 7 March, SPEECH/91/22. Brussels: European Commission.

Delors, J. (1992). 'Monetary Cooperation in the Building of Europe: The 1992 Jean Monnet Lecture'. London: London School of Economics.

Delors, J. (1993). 'Address by Jacques Delors, President of the Commission, to the European Parliament on the Occasion of the Investiture Debate of the New Commission', Strasbourg, 10 February. Brussels: European Commission.

Delors, J. (1994). *L'unité d'un homme: entretiens avec Dominique Wolton*. Paris: Odile Jacob.

Delors, J. (1997). 'Pacte pour la coordination des politiques économiques'. Paris: Notre Europe, 6 August.

Delors, J. (2004). *Mémoires.* Paris: Plon.

Delors, J. (2013). 'Economic Governance in the European Union: Past, Present and Future', *Journal of Common Market Studies*, 51(2): 169–78.

Der Zentralbankrat der Deutschen Bundesbank (ed.) (1996). *Hans Tietmeyer: Währungsstabilität für Europa. Beiträge, Reden und Dokumente zur europäischen Währungsintegration aus vier Jahrzehnten.* Baden-Baden: Nomos Verlag.

Deroose, S., Hodson, D., and Kuhlmann, J. (2008). 'The Broad Economic Policy Guidelines: Before and After the Re-launch of the Lisbon Strategy', *Journal of Common Market Studies*, 46(4): 827–48.

Die Zeit (1992). 'Die Bundesbank, gefesselt von Europa', 40, 25 September.

Dierikx, M., Smits, M., Suijlekom, L. van, Clavert, F., Danescu, E., and Gabellini, M. (eds.) (2012). *Common Fate, Common Future: A Documentary History of Monetary and Financial Cooperation, 1947–1974.* The Hague: CVCE/Huygens ING.

Draghi, M. (2014). 'Financial integration and banking union', in I. Maes. and F. Moss (eds.), *Progress through Crisis? Proceedings of the Conference for the 20th Anniversary of the Establishment of the European Monetary Institute.* Frankfurt am Main: European Central Bank, pp. 151–9.

Drake, H. (2000). *Jacques Delors: Perspectives on a European Leader.* London: Routledge.

Duchêne, F. (1994). *Jean Monnet: The First Statesman of Interdependence.* New York: W. W. Norton.

Duisenberg, F. (1997). 'Farewell to a Central Banker'. Address on the Occasion of Baron A. Lamfalussy's Farewell as President of the European Monetary Institute, 30 June.

Dupriez, L. H. (1960). 'Préface', in C. Reuss, E. Koutny, and L. Tychon, *Le progrès économique en sidérurgie: Belgique, Luxembourg, Pays-Bas 1830–1955.* Louvain: Nauwelaerts.

Dyson, K. (1994). *Elusive Union.* London: Longman.

Dyson, K. (2000). *The Politics of the Euro Zone: Stability or Breakdown?* Oxford: Oxford University Press.

Dyson, K. (ed.) (2008). *The Euro at 10: Europeanization, Power and Convergence.* Oxford: Oxford University Press.

Dyson, K. (2012). 'Maastricht Plus: Managing the Logic of Inherent Imperfections', *Journal of European Integration*, 35, 2: 791–808.

Dyson, K. (2013). 'Sworn to Grim Necessity? Imperfections of European Economic Governance, Normative Political Theory, and Supreme Emergency', *Journal of European Integration*, 35(3): 207–22.

Dyson, K. (2014). *States, Debt and Power: 'Saints' and 'Sinners' in European History and Integration.* Oxford: Oxford University Press.

Dyson, K. (2015). 'Mastering Small-State Diplomacy: Pierre Werner in the History of European Monetary Union', in E. Danescu and S. Muñoz (eds.), *Pierre Werner, une vision pour l'Europe: pensée, action, enseignements/Pierre Werner and Europe: His Approach, Action and Legacy.* Brussels: Peter Lang, pp. 19–26.

Dyson, K. (forthcoming). *The Ordo-Liberal Tradition: Germany, Economic Crisis and European Integration.*

Dyson, K. and Featherstone, K. (1999). *The Road to Maastricht: Negotiating Economic and Monetary Union*. Oxford: Oxford University Press.

Dyson, K. and Quaglia, L. (2010a). *European Economic Governance and Policies. Volume 1: Commentary on Key Historical and Institutional Documents*. Oxford: Oxford University Press.

Dyson, K. and Quaglia, L. (2010b). *European Economic Governance and Policies. Volume 2: Commentary on Key Policy Documents*. Oxford: Oxford University Press.

EC (1969). Communiqué of the meeting of Heads of State or Government of the Member States at The Hague (1 and 2 December 1969), Bulletin of the European Communities, No. 1/1970: 12–15.

EC (1970a). Interim Report on the Establishment by Stages of Economic and Monetary Union, Document 9.504/II/70-D. Bulletin 7/1970, Supplement, Official Journal of the European Communities, No. C94 of 23 July. Luxembourg: OPOCE.

EC (1970b). Report to the Council and the Commission on the Realisation by Stages of Economic and Monetary Union in the Community (Werner Report). Luxembourg, 8 October. Bulletin 11/1970, Supplement, Official Journal of the European Communities of 8 October. Luxembourg: OPOCE.

EC Commission (1968). 'Memorandum on Community Action in the Monetary Sphere'.

EC Commission (1969). Mémorandum de la Commission au Conseil sur la coordination des politiques économiques et la coopération monétaire au sein de la Communauté, 12 February. Bulletin of the European Communities, Supplement no. 3/1969. Brussels.

EC Commission (1970). 'Communication from the Commission to the Council on the Development of a Plan by Stages for an Economic and Monetary Union'. Bulletin of the European Communities, Supplement no. 3/1970. Brussels.

Eichengreen, B. (1992). *Golden Fetters: The Gold Standard and the Great Depression, 1919–1939*. New York: Oxford University Press.

Eichengreen, B. (1993). *Reconstructing Europe's Trade and Payments: The European Payments Union*. Manchester: Manchester University Press.

Eichengreen, B. (1996). *Globalizing Capital: A History of the International Monetary System*. Princeton, NJ: Princeton University Press.

Eichengreen, B. (2011). *Exorbitant Privilege: The Rise and Fall of the Dollar*. Oxford: Oxford University Press.

Engelen, K. (2014). 'The Sadness of Karl Otto Pöhl's Legacy', *International Economy*, 29(1): 34–7 and 57–61.

Enzensberger, H. (2009). *The Silences of Hammerstein*. London: Seagull Books.

Erhard, L. (1964). *Wohlstand für Alle*, 8th edition. Düsseldorf: Econ Verlag.

Erhard, L. (1988). *Gedanken aus fünf Jahrzehnten: Reden und Schriften*, ed. Karl Hohmann. Düsseldorf: Econ Verlag.

Eucken, W. (1950). *The Foundations of Economics*. London: William Hodge.

Eucken, W. (1952). *Grundsätze der Wirtschaftspolitik*. Tübingen: J. C. B. Mohr.

European Central Bank (ECB) (1988a). First meeting of Delors Committee, 13 September, transcript.

European Central Bank (ECB) (1988b). Third meeting of Delors Committee, 8 November, transcript.

European Central Bank (ECB) (1989). Fifth meeting of Delors Committee, 10 January, transcript.

European Commission (1986a). 'President Delors Emphasizes the Importance of Closer Monetary Cooperation and more Growth and Employment', 21 February, IP/86/8. Brussels: European Commission.

European Commission (1986b). 'Programme for the Liberalisation of Capital Movements in the Community', 23 May, COM(86) 292 final. Brussels: European Commission.

European Commission (1987). *Efficiency, Stability and Equity: A Strategy for the Evolution of the Economic System of the European Community.* Report of the Study Group presided by T. Padoa-Schioppa, II/49/87, April.

European Commission (1990a). 'Economic and Monetary Union: The Economic Rationale and Design of the System', 20 March, IP/90/231. Brussels: European Commission.

European Commission (1990b). 'One Market, One Money', *European Economy*, 44. Brussels: European Commission.

European Commission (1993). 'Growth, Competitiveness, Employment: The Challenges and Ways Forward into the 21st Century', COM(93)700. Brussels: European Commission.

European Monetary Institute (1995). *The Changeover to the Single Currency.* Frankfurt: EMI, November.

Feldstein, M. (1992). 'Europe's Monetary Union: The Case against EMU', *The Economist*, 323(763), 13 June: 19–22.

Feldstein, M. (1997). 'EMU and International Conflict', *Foreign Affairs*, 76(6): 60–73.

Financial Times (1989). 'Pöhl Doubts Need for EC Bank', 1–2 July.

Fitoussi, J. P. (ed.) (1993). *Competitive Disinflation: The Mark and Budgetary Politics in Europe.* Oxford: Oxford University Press.

Fleming, J. M. (1962). 'Domestic Financial Policies under Fixed and Floating Exchange Rates', *IMF Staff Papers*, 9: 369–79.

Follesdal, A. (1998). 'Subsidiarity', *Journal of Political Philosophy*, 6(2): 231–59.

Forte, F. (2007). 'Economia dei Mercati Globali e Governo Sopranazionale secondo Luigi Einaudi', *Il Pensiero Economico Italiano*, 15(2): 21–49.

Frankfurter Allgemeine Zeitung (1988). 'Zeit noch nicht reif für europäische Notenbank', 6 May.

Friedman, M. (1997). 'Why Europe Can't Afford the Euro', *The Times*, 19 November.

Froment-Meurice, H. (1998). *Vu du Quai: Mémoires, 1945–1983.* Paris: Fayard.

Fuerxer, J. (2002a). *Raymond Barre à la loupe, Tome 1.* Paris: Le Manuscrit.

Fuerxer, J. (2002b). *Raymond Barre à la loupe, Tome 2.* Paris: Le Manuscrit.

Funabashi, Y. (1988). *Managing the Dollar: From the Plaza to the Louvre.* Washington, DC: Institute for International Economics.

Garavini, G. (2006). 'The Battle for the Participation of the Community in the G7 (1975–1977)', *Journal of European Integration History*, 12: 141–58.

Geithner, T. (2014). *Stress Test: Reflections on Financial Crises.* New York: Random House.

Ghymers, C. (2015). 'Une relecture du plan Werner par rapport à ses antécédents et ses successeurs', in E. Danescu and S. Muñoz (eds.), *Pierre Werner, une vision pour l'Europe: pensée, action, enseignements/Pierre Werner and Europe: His Approach, Action and Legacy*. Brussels: Peter Lang, pp. 183–201.

Giannini, M. (2010). 'Addio a Padoa-Schioppa, padre dell'euro', *La Repubblica*, 19 December. <http://www.tommasopadoaschioppa.eu/archivio/addio-a-padoa-schioppa-padre-delleuro>.

Giavazzi, F. and Pagano, M. (1988). 'The Advantage of Tying One's Hands: EMS Discipline and Central Bank Credibility', *European Economic Review*, 32(5): 1055–82.

Golub, J. (1996). 'Sovereignty and Subsidiarity in EU Environmental Policy', *Political Studies*, 44(4): 686–703.

Goodhart, C. A. (2006). 'Replacing the Stability and Growth Pact?', *Atlantic Economic Journal*, 34(3): 243–59.

Goodhart, C. A. and Smith, S. (1993). 'Stabilization', in *The Economics of Community Public Finance*. European Economy Reports and Studies 5. Brussels: European Commission, pp. 356–73.

Grant, C. (1994). *Delors: Inside the House that Jacques Built*. London: Nicholas Brealey.

Groeben, H. von der (1982). *Aufbaujahre der Europäischen Gemeinschaft: Das Ringen um den Gemeinsamen Markt und die Politische Union (1958–1966)*. Baden-Baden: Nomos Verlag.

Gros, D. and Thygesen, N. (1998). *European Monetary Integration: From the European Monetary System to Economic and Monetary Union*. London: Longman.

Guindey, G. (1973). *Mythes et réalités de la crise monétaire international*. Paris: J. Delmas.

Habermas, J. (2013). *The Crisis of the European Union: A Response*. Chichester: John Wiley.

Hall, P. A. (1993). 'Policy Paradigms, Social Learning, and the State: The Case of Economic Policymaking in Britain', *Comparative Politics*, 25(3): 275–96.

Hayek, F. von (1953). *Scientisme et les sciences sociales: Essai sur le mauvais usage de la raison*, trans. Raymond Barre. Paris: Plon.

Hayek, F. von (1976a). *Choice in Currency: A Way to Stop Inflation*. London: Institute of Economic Affairs.

Hayek, F. von (1976b). *Denationalization of Money—The Argument Refined: An Analysis of the Theory and Practice of Concurrent Currencies*. London: Institute of Economic Affairs.

Heads of State or Government (1972). 'Meetings of the Heads of State or Government', Paris, 19–20 October. Compendium of Community Monetary Texts, 1974.

Heipertz, M. and Verdun, A. (2010). *Ruling Europe: The Politics of the Stability and Growth Pact*. Cambridge: Cambridge University Press.

Heisbourg, F. (2013). *La fin du rêve européen*. Paris: Stock.

Helleiner, E. (2009). 'Central Bankers as Good Neighbours: US Money Doctors in Latin America during the 1940s', *Financial History Review*, 16(1): 5–25.

Henning, C. (1994). *Currencies and Policies in the United States, Germany, and Japan*. Washington, DC: Institute for International Economics.

Hentschel, V. (1996). *Ludwig Erhard: Ein Politikerleben*. Munich: Olzog.

Hiepel, C. (2003). 'In Search of the Greatest Common Denominator: Germany and The Hague Summit Conference 1969', *Journal of European Integration History*, 9: 63–81.

HM Treasury (1989). *An Evolutionary Approach to Economic and Monetary Union*. London: HMSO.

Hodjera, Z. (1973). 'International Short-Term Capital Movements: A Survey of Theory and Empirical Analysis', *IMF Staff Papers*, 20: 683–740.

Hodson, D. (2009). 'EMU and Political Union: What, if Anything, Have We Learned from the Euro's First Decade?', *Journal of European Public Policy*, 16(4): 508–26.

Hoeksma, J. and Schoenmaker, D. (2011). 'The Sovereign Behind the Euro', Duisenberg School of Finance Policy Paper No. 15.

House of Lords (2014). *Euro Area Crisis: An Update*. European Union Committee, 4 April.

Howarth, D. (2001). *The French Road to European Monetary Union*. Basingstoke: Palgrave Macmillan.

Hutton, W. (2008). *The World We're In*. London: Hachette.

Iozzo, A. (2012). 'From the ECU to the EURO', in J.-C. Koeune and A. Lamfalussy (eds.), *In Search of a New World Monetary Order*. Brussels: Peter Lang, pp. 137–8.

Issing, O. (2008). *The Birth of the Euro*. Cambridge: Cambridge University Press.

Issing, O. (2013). 'Wir brauchen die Kontrolle durch die Märkte', *Handelsblatt Wirtschafts- und Finanzzeitung*, 22 July.

Jaffé, W. (1935). 'Unpublished Papers and Letters of Léon Walras', *Journal of Political Economy*, 43: 187–207.

James, H. (2012). *Making the European Monetary Union: The Role of the Committee of Central Bank Governors and the Origins of the European Central Bank*. Cambridge, MA: Harvard University Press.

Jenkins, R. (1978). 'Europe: Why Social Democrats Should Support a New Advance'. The Rita Hinden Memorial Lecture, London, 4 February. Brussels: European Commission.

Jenkins, R. (1989). *European Diary, 1977–1981*. London: Collins.

Jenkins, R. (1991). *A Life at the Centre*. London: Macmillan.

Joerges, C. (2010). 'Unity in Diversity as Europe's Vocation and Conflicts Law as Europe's Constitutional Form', LEQS Paper, No. 28, London School of Economics, revised version April 2013.

Johansson, K. M. (2002). 'Another Road to Maastricht: The Christian Democrat Coalition and the Quest for European Union', *Journal of Common Market Studies*, 40(5): 871–93.

Jönsson, C. and Hall, M. (2003). 'Communication: An Essential Aspect of Diplomacy', *International Studies Perspectives*, 4(2): 195–210.

Kahn, J.-F. (1996). *La pensée unique*. Paris: Hachette.

Kaiser, W. (2007). *Christian Democracy and the Origins of European Union*. Cambridge: Cambridge University Press.

Kaplan, J. and Schleiminger, G. (1989). *The European Payments Union: Financial Diplomacy in the 1950s*. Oxford: Clarendon Press.

Karamouzi, E. (2014). *Greece, the EEC and the Cold War, 1974–79*. Basingstoke: Palgrave Macmillan.

Kitzinger, U. (1973). *Diplomacy and Persuasion: How Britain Joined the Common Market*. London: Thames and Hudson.

Koeune, J.-C. (2015). 'Challenges and Prospects of EMU', in E. Danescu and S. Muñoz (eds.), *Pierre Werner, une vision pour l'Europe: pensée, action, enseignements/Pierre Werner and Europe: His Approach, Action and Legacy*. Brussels: Peter Lang, pp. 301–5.

Kohl, H. and Mitterrand, F. (1990). 'Letter by the German Federal Chancellor Helmut Kohl and French President François Mitterrand to the Irish Presidency of the EC, 19 April 1990', *Agence Europe*.

Kowitz, R. (1998). *Alfred Müller-Armack. Wirtschaftspolitik als Berufung. Zur Entstehungsgeschichte der Sozialen Marktwirtschaft und dem politischen Wirken des Hochschullehrers*. Cologne: Deutscher-Institutsverlag.

Krugman, P. (1993). 'What Do We Need to Know about the International Monetary System?', in *Essays in International Economics*, No. 190. Princeton, NJ: Princeton University Press.

Laitenberger, V. (1986). *Ludwig Erhard: Der Nationalökonom als Politiker*. Göttingen: Muster-Schmidt.

Lamfalussy, A. (1961). *Investment and Growth in Mature Economies: The Case of Belgium*. London: Macmillan.

Lamfalussy, A. (1963). *The United Kingdom and the Six: An Essay on Economic Growth in Western Europe*. London: Macmillan.

Lamfalussy, A. (1971). 'Le système monétaire international, l'intégration européenne et le régime des taux de change'. In Centre d'études bancaires et financières, *Cahiers des conférences* 183: pp. 3–28.

Lamfalussy, A. (1976). 'Monetary and Fiscal Integration', in F. Machlup (ed.), *Economic Integration Worldwide: Regional, Sectoral*. London: Macmillan, pp. 218–45.

Lamfalussy, A. (1979). 'The Possible Consequences of the Establishment of the European Monetary System (EMS) for the Working of the International Monetary System'. Meeting of the Consultative Group on International Economic and Monetary Affairs in Bermuda, 17–19 February. BISA, file 7.17—Speeches.

Lamfalussy, A. (1984). 'What Role for Monetary Policy Today?' Conference on Monetary Conditions for Economic Recovery, 14–16 November, Amsterdam. BISA, file 7.17—Speeches.

Lamfalussy, A. (1985). 'The Changing Environment of Central Bank Policy', *American Economic Review*, 75(2): 409–14.

Lamfalussy, A. (1988). 'The ECU Banking Market', *Collection of Papers: Committee for the Study of Economic and Monetary Union*. Luxembourg, 1989, pp. 201–8.

Lamfalussy, A. (1989a). 'Macro-Coordination of Fiscal Policies in an Economic and Monetary Union in Europe', *Collection of Papers: Committee for the Study of Economic and Monetary Union*. Luxembourg, January, pp. 91–126.

Lamfalussy, A. (1989b). 'A Proposal for Stage Two under which Monetary Policy Operations would be Centralized in a Jointly-Owned Subsidiary', *Collection of Papers: Committee for the Study of Economic and Monetary Union*. Luxembourg, January, pp. 213–20.

Lamfalussy, A. (1993). 'International Central Bank Co-operation: What It Can—and Cannot—Achieve', in A. Steinherr and D. Weiserbs (eds.), *Evolution of the International and Regional Monetary Systems: Essays in Honour of Robert Triffin*. New York: St. Martin's Press, pp. 35–45.

Lamfalussy, A. (1997). 'Securing the Benefits of EMU'. London School of Economics, 10 March.

Lamfalussy, A. (1998). 'Back to Fundamentals: Why a Monetary Union for Europe?', in G. Báger and M. Szabó-Pelsöczi (eds.), *Global Monetary and Economic Convergence: On the Occasion of the Fiftieth Anniversary of the Marshall Plan*. Aldershot: Ashgate, pp. 35–41.

Lamfalussy, A. (2000). *Financial Crisis in Emerging Markets: An Essay on Financial Globalisation and Fragility*. New Haven, CT: Yale University Press.

Lamfalussy, A. (2001). 'Preface', in A. Lamfalussy, B. Snoy, and J. Wilson (eds.), *Fragility of the International Financial System*. Brussels: Peter Lang, p. 9.

Lamfalussy, A. (2004). *Central Banks and Financial Stability*, 2nd Pierre Werner Lecture. Luxembourg: Banque Centrale de Luxembourg.

Lamfalussy, A. (2006). 'Monetary Policy and Systematic Risk Prevention: Challenges ahead for Central Banks'. The Bank of Greece Zolotas Lecture, Athens, 29 September.

Lamfalussy, A. (2011). 'Dinner Address', in M. Jarocinsky et al. (eds.), *Approaches to Monetary Policy Revisited: Lessons Learned from the Crisis*. Sixth ECB Central Banking Conference. Frankfurt am Main: ECB, pp. 168–73.

Lamfalussy, C., Maes, I., and Péters, S. (2014). *Alexandre Lamfalussy: The Wise Man of the Euro. A Conversation with Christophe Lamfalussy, Ivo Maes and Sabine Péters*. Preface by Jacques de Larosière. Leuven: LannooCampus, February.

Lawson, N. (1992). *The View from No. 11: Memoirs of a Tory Radical*. London: Bantam.

Lequesne, C. (2010). 'Le commissaire européen', in Académie des Sciences Morales et Politiques, FNSP, Aspen France, *Raymond Barre, Un homme singulier dans la politique française*. Paris: Éditions de Fallois, pp. 57–68.

Löffler, B. (2003). *Soziale Marktwirtschaft und Administrative Praxis*. Stuttgart: Franz Steiner Verlag.

Loriaux, M. (1991). *France after Hegemony: International Change and Financial Reform*. Ithaca, NY: Cornell University Press.

Loughlin, J. (1993). 'Federalism, Regionalism and European Union', *Politics*, 13(1): 9–16.

Ludlow, P. (1982). *The Making of the European Monetary System: A Case-Study of the Politics of the European Community*. London: Butterworth.

Ludlow, P. (2010). 'In the Last Resort: The European Council and the Euro Crisis', *Eurocomment Briefing Notes*, 7(7/8): 16.

Ludlow, P. (forthcoming). 'Navigating the European Stream at Full Flood: Jacques Delors as Commission President (1985–95)', in J. van der Harst and G. Voerman (eds.), *The Presidents of the European Commission*. Biggleswade: John Harper.

Lynch, F. (1997). *France and the International Economy: From Vichy to the Treaty of Rome*. London: Routledge.

McKinnon, R. (1997). 'Market-Preserving Fiscal Federalism in the American Monetary Union', in M. Blejera and T. Ter-Minassion (eds.), *Macroeconomic Dimensions of Public Finance*. London: Routledge, pp. 73–93.

McLendon, M. L. (2006). 'Tocqueville, Jansenism, and the Psychology of Freedom', *American Journal of Political Science*, 50(3): 664–75.

McNamara, K. (1998). *The Currency of Ideas: Monetary Politics in the European Union*. Ithaca, NY: Cornell University Press.

Maes, I. (1992). 'Optimum Currency Area Theory and European Monetary Integration', *Tijdschrift voor Economie and Management*, 37(2): 137–52.

Maes, I. (1998a). 'Macroeconomic Thought at the European Commission in the 1970s: The First Decade of the Annual Economic Reports', *Banca Nazionale del Lavoro Quarterly Review*, 207: 387–412.

Maes, I. (1998b). 'Projets d'intégration monétaire à la Commission européenne', in E. Bussière and M. Dumoulin (eds.), *Milieux économiques et intégration européenne en Europe occidentale au XXe siècle*. Arras: Artois, Presses Université, pp. 35–50.

Maes, I. (2002). *Economic Thought and the Making of European Monetary Union*. Cheltenham: Edward Elgar.

Maes, I. (2004). 'On the Origins of the Franco-German EMU Controversies', *European Journal of Law and Economics*, 17: 21–39.

Maes, I. (2006). 'The Ascent of the European Commission as an Actor in the Monetary Integration Process in the 1960s', *Scottish Journal of Political Economy*, 53(2): 222–41.

Maes, I. (2007). *Half a Century of European Financial Integration: From the Rome Treaty to the 21st Century*, foreword by Ph. Maystadt. Brussels: Mercatorfonds.

Maes, I. (2008). 'The Spread of Keynesian Economics: A Comparison of the Belgian and Italian Experiences (1945–1970)', *Journal of the History of Economic Thought*, 20(6): 1122–50.

Maes, I. (2009a). 'The Young Lamfalussy: An Empirical and Policy-Oriented Growth Theorist', *Revue bancaire et financière/Bank- en Financiewezen*, 73(5): 286–300.

Maes, I. (2009b). 'On the Origins of the BIS Macro-Prudential Approach to Financial Stability: Alexandre Lamfalussy and Financial Fragility', *PSL Quarterly Review*, 63 (254): 265–92.

Maes, I. (2011a). 'Alexandre Lamfalussy et les tentatives de la BRI de prévenir un endettement excessif de l'Amérique latine dans les années 1970', *Histoire, économie et société*, 30: 52–77.

Maes, I. (2011b). 'The Evolution of Alexandre Lamfalussy's Thought on European Monetary Integration (1961–1993)', *Oeconomia*, 1(1): 489–523.

Maes, I. (2012). 'Triffin et l'analyse du système monétaire international', in J.-C. Koeune and A. Lamfalussy (eds.), *À la recherché d'un nouvel ordre monétaire mondial*. Brussels: Peter-Lang, pp. 55–71.

Maes, I. (2013a). 'On the Origins of the Triffin Dilemma', *European Journal of the History of Economic Thought*, 20(6): 1222–50.

Maes, I. (2013b). 'Tommaso Padoa-Schioppa: Macroeconomic and Monetary Thought, and Policy-Making at the European Commission', *History of Economic Thought and Policy*, 2(2): 21–43.

Maes, I. and Buyst, E. (2004). 'Triffin, the European Commission and the Project of a European Reserve Fund', in M. Dumoulin (ed.), *Réseaux économiques et construction européenne/Economic Networks and European Integration*. Brussels: Peter Lang, pp. 431–44.

Maes, I. and Buyst, E. (2005). 'Migration and Americanization: The Special Case of Belgian Economics', *European Journal of the History of Economic Thought*, 12(1): 73–88.

Maes, I. and Moss, F. (eds.) (2014). *'Progress through Crisis?' Proceedings of the Conference for the 20th Anniversary of the Establishment of the European Monetary Institute.* Frankfurt am Main: European Central Bank.

Maes, I. and Quaglia, L. (2004). 'France and Italy's Policies on European Monetary Integration: A Comparison of "Strong" and "Weak" States', *Comparative European Politics*, 2(1): 51–72.

Mamou, Y. (1988). *Une machine de pouvoir: La Direction du Trésor.* Paris: La Découverte.

Manow, P. (2001). 'Ordoliberalismus als ökonomische Ordnungstheologie', *Leviathan*, 29(2): 179–98.

Marcussen, M. (2000). *Ideas and Elites: The Social Construction of Economic and Monetary Union.* Aalborg: Aalborg University Press.

Marjolin, R. (1965). Extract from the statement on certain monetary matters [international monetary system] made by M. Robert Marjolin, Vice-President of the Commission of the European Economic Community, to the European Parliament. Strasbourg, 23 March. <http://aei.pitt.edu/id/eprint/13528>.

Marjolin, R. (1986). *Architect of European Unity: Memoirs 1911–1986.* London: Weidenfeld & Nicolson.

Marsh, D. (1992). *The Most Powerful Bank: Inside Germany's Bundesbank.* New York: Times Books.

Marsh, D. (2009). *The Euro: The Politics of the New Global Currency.* New Haven, CT: Yale University Press.

Masini, F. (2004). *SMEmorie della lira: Gli economisti italiani e l'adesione al Sistema Monetario Europeo.* Milan: Franco Angeli.

Masini, F. (ed.) (2009a). 'Dalla moneta alla costituzione: Storia e prospettive dell'integrazione europea (1979–2009)', *Il Ponte*, 65(5).

Masini, F. (2009b). 'Per un'economia politica dell'interdipendenza globale. Beni collettivi, mercati e istituzioni pubbliche', in Masini (ed.), 'Dalla moneta alla costituzione: Storia e prospettive dell'integrazione europea (1979–2009)', *Il Ponte*, 65(5): 136–55.

Masini, F. (2010). 'Alternative Routes to Monetary Integration in the British Economic and Political Debate (1989–91)', *Storia del Pensiero Economico*, 1: 71–97.

Masini, F. (2012a). 'Luigi Einaudi and the Making of the Neoliberal Project', *History of Economic Thought and Policy*, 1(1): 39–59.

Masini, F. (2012b). 'Designing the Institutions of International Liberalism: Some Contributions from the Interwar Period', *Constitutional Political Economy*, 23(1): 45–65.

Masini, F. (2014). 'European Integration: Contrasting Models and Perspectives', in R. Fiorentini and G. Montani (eds.), *The European Union and Supranational Political Economy.* Abingdon: Routledge, pp. 44–64.

Masini, F. (2015). 'Padoa-Schioppa, Tommaso', in L. P. Rochon and S. Rossi (eds.), *The Encyclopedia of Central Banking.* Cheltenham: Edward Elgar, pp. 399–400.

Mauduit, L. (1995). 'Convergences électorales pour repousser le lancement de la monnaie unique', *Le Monde*, 28 February.

Mayer, T. (2012). *Europe's Unfinished Currency: The Political Economics of the Euro.* London: Anthem Press.

Maystadt, P. (2014). *Europe: le continent perdu?* Waterloo: Avant propos.
Meade, J. (1957). 'The Balance of Payments Problem of a European Free Trade Area', *Economics Journal*, 67: 379–96.
Milési, G. (1995). *Jacques Delors: l'homme qui dit non*. Paris: Édition 1.
Milward, A. S. (1984). *The Reconstruction of Western Europe, 1945–51*. Berkeley, CA: University of California Press.
Ministère des Finances (1970). 'Un Plan de Solidarité Monétaire Européenne en Trois Étapes 1971–1977', reprinted in *Europe Documents*, 11 March.
Modigliani, F. (1978). 'I pro e contro per l'Italia', *Corriere della Sera*, 1 December.
Modigliani, F. and Padoa-Schioppa, T. (1977). 'La politica economica in un'economia con salari indicizzati al 100% e più', *Moneta e credito*, March: 3–53.
Moitroux, J.-M. (1995). *Een bank in de Geschiedenis*. Brussels: BBL.
Monnet, J. (1976). *Mémoires*, Tome 2. Paris: Fayard.
Moore, C. (2011). 'Jacques Delors interview: Euro Would Still Be Strong if It Had Been Built to My Plan', *Daily Telegraph*, 2 December.
Moravcsik, A. (1998). *The Choice for Europe: Social Purpose and State Power from Messina to Maastricht*. Ithaca, NY: Cornell University Press.
Morelli, U. (1990). *Contro il Mito dello Stato Sovrano: Luigi Einaudi e l'Unità Europea*. Milan: Franco Angeli.
Mourlon-Druol, E. (2012). *A Europe Made of Money: The Emergence of the European Monetary System*. Ithaca, NY: Cornell University Press.
Müller-Armack, A. (1956). 'Soziale Marktwirtschaft', in *Handwörterbuch der Sozialwissenschaften*. Stuttgart: Fischer, pp. 243–50.
Mundell, R. (1961). 'A Theory of Optimum Currency Areas', *American Economic Review*, 51(4): 657–65.
Mundell, R. (1963). 'Capital Mobility and Stabilization Policy under Fixed and Flexible Exchange Rates', *Canadian Journal of Economics and Political Science*, 29(4): 475–85.
Nora, P. (1987). *Essais d'ego-histoire*. Paris: Gallimard.
Nussbaum, M. (2013). *Political Emotions: Why Love Matters for Justice*. Cambridge, MA: Harvard University Press.
Nussbaum, M. and Sen, A. (eds.) (1993). *The Quality of Life*. Oxford: Clarendon Press.
Padoa-Schioppa, T. (1981). 'L'ECU e il Sistema monetario europeo'. Speech at the conference on 'Un mercato finanziario italiano in euroscudi', University of Trieste, March. Reprinted in Padoa-Schioppa, *L'Europa verso l'unione monetaria: Dallo Sme al trattato di Maastricht*. Turin: Giulio Einaudi, 1992, pp. 23–33.
Padoa-Schioppa, T. (1982). 'Mobilità dei capitali: perchè la Comunità è inadempiente?' Conference in Milan, June. Reprinted in Padoa-Schioppa, *L'Europa verso l'unione monetaria: Dallo Sme al trattato di Maastricht*. Turin: Giulio Einaudi, 1992, pp. 34–54.
Padoa-Schioppa, T. (1983). 'Regole e istituzioni nelle economie pluristatali', in L. Tsoukalis (ed.), *The Political Economy of International Money*. London: Sage. Reprinted in Padoa-Schioppa, *L'Europa verso l'unione monetaria: Dallo Sme al trattato di Maastricht*. Turin: Giulio Einaudi, 1992, pp. 5–22.
Padoa-Schioppa, T. (1985). 'Che cosa ci ha insegnato lo SME'. Reprinted in Padoa-Schioppa, *L'Europa verso l'unione monetaria: Dallo Sme al trattato di Maastricht*. Turin: Giulio Einaudi, 1992, pp. 55–76.

Padoa-Schioppa, T. (1987a). 'Dopo l'Atto unico: efficienza, stabilità ed equità'. Reprinted in Padoa-Schioppa, *L'Europa verso l'unione monetaria: Dallo Sme al trattato di Maastricht*. Turin: Giulio Einaudi, 1992, pp. 79–90.

Padoa-Schioppa, T. (1987b). 'L'ECU verso la maggiore età'. Reprinted in Padoa-Schioppa, *L'Europa verso l'unione monetaria: Dallo Sme al trattato di Maastricht*. Turin: Giulio Einaudi, 1992, pp. 91–110.

Padoa-Schioppa, T. (1987c). 'Lo SME non basta più: ci vuole l'unione monetaria'. Reprinted in Padoa-Schioppa, *L'Europa verso l'unione monetaria: Dallo Sme al trattato di Maastricht*. Turin: Giulio Einaudi, 1992, pp. 111–33.

Padoa-Schioppa, T. (ed.) (1987d). 'Efficiency, Stability, and Equity: A Strategy for the Evolution of the Economic System of the European Community; Report of a Study Group Appointed by the Commission of the European Communities'. Brussels: European Commission.

Padoa-Schioppa, T. (1988). 'Vigilia di Hannover'. Reprinted in Padoa-Schioppa, *L'Europa verso l'unione monetaria: Dallo Sme al trattato di Maastricht*. Turin: Giulio Einaudi, 1992, pp. 156–65.

Padoa-Schioppa, T. (1989). 'Il Rapporto Delors: dale intenzioni all'azione'. Reprinted in Padoa-Schioppa, *L'Europa verso l'unione monetaria: Dallo Sme al trattato di Maastricht*. Turin: Giulio Einaudi, 1992, pp. 169–84.

Padoa-Schioppa, T. (1990). 'Unione e concorrenza monetaria'. Reprinted in Padoa-Schioppa, *L'Europa verso l'unione monetaria: Dallo Sme al trattato di Maastricht*. Turin: Giulio Einaudi, 1992, pp. 185–202.

Padoa-Schioppa, T. (1991a). 'Unione monetaria e unione politica'. i Reprinted in Padoa-Schioppa, *L'Europa verso l'unione monetaria: Dallo Sme al trattato di Maastricht*. Turin: Giulio Einaudi, 1992, pp. 203–10.

Padoa-Schioppa, T. (1991b). 'Vigilia di Maastricht'. Reprinted in Padoa-Schioppa, *L'Europa verso l'unione monetaria: Dallo Sme al trattato di Maastricht*. Turin: Giulio Einaudi, 1992, pp. 211–25.

Padoa-Schioppa, T. (1991c). 'Agenda per la fase due'. Reprinted in Padoa-Schioppa, *L'Europa verso l'unione monetaria: Dallo Sme al trattato di Maastricht*. Turin: Giulio Einaudi, 1992, pp. 226–64.

Padoa-Schioppa, T. (1991d). 'European Monies and European Monetary Union', in A. Steinherr and D. Weiserbs (eds.), *Evolution of the International and Regional Monetary System*. London: Macmillan, pp. 201–6.

Padoa-Schioppa, T. (1992a). 'Introduzione', in Padoa-Schioppa, *L'Europa verso l'unione monetaria: Dallo Sme al trattato di Maastricht*. Turin: Giulio Einaudi, pp. ix–xxxv.

Padoa-Schioppa, T. (1992b). *L'Europa verso l'unione monetaria: Dallo Sme al trattato di Maastricht*. Turin: Giulio Einaudi.

Padoa-Schioppa, T. (1994; repr. 2000). 'The ECU's Coming of Age', in Padoa-Schioppa, *The Road to Monetary Union in Europe*. Oxford: Clarendon Press, pp. 62–80.

Padoa-Schioppa, T. (1995). 'Economic Federalism and the European Union', in K. Knop, S. Ostry, R. Simeon, and K. Swinton (eds.), *Rethinking Federalism: Citizens, Markets, and Governments in a Changing World*. Vancouver: UBC Press, pp. 154–62.

Padoa-Schioppa, T. (1997). *Il governo dell'economia*. Bologna: Il Mulino.

Padoa-Schioppa, T. (1998). Hearing of Mr Tommaso Padoa-Schioppa, candidate for the Board of the ECB. European Parliament. <http://www.europarl.europa.eu/hearings/19980507/ecb/05_en.htm>.

Padoa-Schioppa, T. (2000a). *Licensing Banks: Still Necessary?* Washington, DC: The Group of Thirty.

Padoa-Schioppa, T. (2000b). *The Road to Monetary Union in Europe: The Emperor, the Kings, and the Genies*. Oxford: Oxford University Press.

Padoa-Schioppa, T. (2001). *Europa, forza gentile: Cosa ci ha insegnato l'avventura europea*. Bologna: Il Mulino.

Padoa-Schioppa, T. (2002). 'A European Economic Constitution', *The Federalist*, 44(3): 190–7.

Padoa-Schioppa, T. (2004a). *La lunga via per l'euro*. Bologna: Il Mulino.

Padoa-Schioppa, T. (2004b). *L'euro e la sua banca centrale: L'unione dopo l'unione*. Bologna: Il Mulino.

Padoa-Schioppa, T. (2007). 'Pensare l'internazionalizzazione'. Inaugural Lecture of the 145th Academic Year, Milan: Politecnico of Milan, 12 November, typescript.

Padoa-Schioppa, T. (2008). 'Interdependence and Cooperation: An Endangered Pair?', in C. Borio, G. Toniolo, and P. Clement (eds.), *Past and Future of Central Bank Cooperation*. Cambridge: Cambridge University Press, pp. 211–20.

Padoa-Schioppa, T. (2010a). 'Athens Must not be Left to Stand Alone', *Financial Times*, 19 February. <http://www.tommasopadoaschioppa.eu/europa/athens-must-not-be-left-to-stand-alone-2>.

Padoa-Schioppa, T. (2010b). 'L'ombre de Bancor: la crise et le désordre monétaire mondial'. Exposé à la Fondation internationale Triffin, Louvain-la-Neuve, 25 February.

Papadia, F. (2014). 'Biografia di Tomaso Padoa-Schioppa', in *Dizionario Biografico degli Italiani*, Volume 80. Rome: Enciclopedia Treccani.

Papadia, F. (2015). Notes on the typescript 'Tommaso Padoa-Schioppa: EMU as a Crucial Building Stone for a Federal Europe' by Fabio Masini.

Parr, H. (2006). 'Saving the Community: The French Response to Britain's Second EEC Application in 1967', *Cold War History*, 6: 425–54.

Peacock, A. and Willgerodt, H. (eds.) (1989). *Germany's Social Market Economy: Origins and Evolution*. London: Macmillan.

Peterson, J. (1994). 'Subsidiarity: A Definition to Suit any Vision?', *Parliamentary Affairs*, 47(1): 116–32.

Polanyi, K. (1944). *The Great Transformation*. Boston, MA: Beacon.

Popkin, J. (2005). *History, Historians, and Autobiography*. Chicago, IL: University of Chicago.

Quaglia, L. (2007). 'The Politics of Financial Service Regulation and Supervision Reform in the European Union', *European Journal of Political Research*, 46(2): 269–90.

Raymond, R. (2014). 'From the Maastricht Treaty to the Euro: The Role of the EMI', in I. Maes and F. Moss (eds.), *Progress through Crisis? Proceedings of the Conference for the 20th Anniversary of the Establishment of the European Monetary Institute*. Frankfurt am Main: ECB, pp. 71–7.

Rollat, A. (1993). *Delors*. Paris: Flammarion.

Rose, A. (2000). 'One Money, One Market: Estimating the Effect of Common Currencies on Trade', *Economic Policy*, 30: 9–45.

Ross, G. (1995). *Jacques Delors and European Integration*. Cambridge: Polity Press.

Rotondo, R. (2007). 'Una pazienza attiva. Intervista a Tommaso Padoa-Schioppa', *30 Giorni*, 64. <http://www.tommasopadoaschioppa.eu/wp-content/uploads/2009/10/20070403_9723_1.pdf>.

Rueff, J. (1947). 'The Fallacies of Lord Keynes' General Theory', *Quarterly Journal of Economics*, 61(3): 343–67.

Rueff, J. (1948). 'The Fallacies of Lord Keynes' General Theory: Reply', *Quarterly Journal of Economics*, 62(5): 771–82.

Saccomanni, F. (2005). 'Farewell Speech for Tommaso Padoa-Schioppa'. Frankfurt: ECB, 26 April, manuscript.

Saint-Ouen, F. (1990). *Les partis politiques et l'Europe, une approche comparative*. Geneva: Publication de l'Institut universitaire d'études européennes, Presses Universitaires de France.

Samuelson, P. (1951). 'Schumpeter as a Teacher and Economic Theorist', *Review of Economics and Statistics*, 33(2): 98–103.

Sandbu, M. (2015). *Europe's Orphan: The Future of the Euro and the Politics of Debt*. Princeton, NJ: Princeton University Press.

Sapir, A. (2014a). 'Still the Right Agenda for Europe? The Sapir Report Ten Years On', *Journal of Common Market Studies*, 52: 57–73.

Sapir, A. (2014b). 'Financial Crises under two Monetary Regimes: EMU vs. EMS', in I. Maes and F. Moss (eds.), *Progress through Crisis? Proceedings of the Conference for the 20th Anniversary of the Establishment of the European Monetary Institute*. Frankfurt am Main: ECB, pp. 33–67.

Sapir, A. and Wolf, G. (2015). 'Euro-Area Governance: What to Reform and How to Do It'. Policy Brief, 27 February. Brussels: Bruegel.

Sarcinelli, M. (2004). 'Europe's Federation and Currency: The Contribution of Luigi Einaudi', *Banca Nazionale del Lavoro Quarterly Review*, 57(229): 109–30.

Scharpf, F. (1999). *Governing in Europe: Effective and Democratic?* Oxford: Oxford University Press.

Schäuble, W. and Lamers, C. (1994). CDU/CSU-Fraktion des Deutschen Bundestags, 'Überlegungen zur europäischen Politik', Bonn, 1 September.

Scheller, H.-P. (2011). 'Le Comité des gouverneurs des banques centrales de la CEE et l'unification monétaire européenne', *Histoire, économie et société*, 30(4): 79–100.

Scheller, H.-P. (2014). 'The Design of the ECB's Toolbox: Fitting the EMI Blueprint into a Deeper EMU', in I. Maes and F. Moss (eds.), *Progress through Crisis? Proceedings of the Conference for the 20th Anniversary of the Establishment of the European Monetary Institute*. Frankfurt am Main: ECB, pp. 113–28.

Scheller, H. (2015). 'The Werner Plan and the Delors Report: One or Two Approaches to EMU?', in E. Danescu and S. Muñoz (eds.), *Pierre Werner, une vision pour l'Europe: pensée, action, enseignements/Pierre Werner and Europe: His Approach, Action and Legacy*. Brussels: Peter Lang, pp. 277–98.

Schmidt, H. (1996). 'Die Bundesbank—kein Staat im Staate', *Die Zeit*, 46, 8 November.

Schwarz, H.-P. (1997). *Konrad Adenauer, Volume II: 1952–1967*. Oxford: Berghahn Books.

Seux, D. (2014). 'Déficit public: L'histoire secrète du 3%', *Les Echos* Blog, 3 October. <http://blogs.lesechos.fr/dominique-seux/l-histoire-du-critere-de-3-a15011.html#owZft Oxcc55227vM.99>.

Smets, J., Michielsen, J., and Maes, I. (2003). 'Belgium and the Creation of the Euro', in M. Dumoulin, G. Duchêne, and A. Van Laer (eds.), *La Belgique et l'Europe du XXe au XXIe Siècle*. Brussels: Peter Lang, pp. 295–318.

Smith, W. L. (1965). 'Are There Enough Policy Tools?', *American Economic Review*, 55: 208–20.

Soutou, G.-H. (2010). 'Raymond Barre et l'Europe', in Académie des Sciences Morales et Politiques, FNSP, Aspen France, *Raymond Barre, Un homme singulier dans la politique française*. Paris: Éditions de Fallois, pp. 69–82.

Spicker, P. (1991). 'The Principle of Subsidiarity and the Social Policy of the European Community', *Journal of European Social Policy*, 1(1): 3–14.

Spinelli, A. (1978). 'Reflections on the Institutional Crisis in the European Community', *West European Politics*, 1(1): 77–88.

Streeck, W. (2013). *Gekaufte Zeit: Die vertagte Krise des demokratischen Kapitalismus*. Berlin: Suhrkamp.

Szász, A. (1999). *The Road to European Monetary Union*. Basingstoke: Macmillan.

Szenberg, M. (ed.) (1992). *Eminent Economists: Their Life Philosophies*. Cambridge: Cambridge University Press.

Szenberg, M. (ed.) (1998). *Passion and Craft: Economists at Work*. Ann Arbor, MI: University of Michigan Press.

Tallberg, J. (2008). 'Bargaining Power in the European Council', *Journal of Common Market Studies*, 46(3): 685–708.

Taverne, D. (1971). *Monetary and Economic Union in Europe, Europe and You*. London: Labour Committee for Europe.

Taverne, D. (2004). 'Chancellor of the Exchequer', in A. Adonis and K. Thomas (eds.), *Roy Jenkins: A Retrospective*. Oxford: Oxford University Press, pp. 85–106.

Thatcher, M. (2011). *The Downing Street Years*. London: HarperCollins.

Thygesen, N. (1989). 'The Delors Report and European Economic and Monetary Union', *International Affairs*, 65(4): 637–52.

Tietmeyer, H. (1971). 'L'union économique et monétaire au centre du débat politique'. Hefte. No. 1/197. Köln: Institut für Wirtschaftspolitik Press.

Tietmeyer, H. (1988). 'The Political Consequences of Monetary Union'. Speech delivered to the Social Congress of the Commission of Bishops' Conferences of the European Community, Brussels, 20 February.

Tietmeyer, H. (1994). 'On the Architecture of EMU', in A. Steinherr (ed.), *30 Years of European Monetary Integration: From the Werner Plan to EMU*. Harlow: Longman, pp. 31–7.

Tietmeyer, H. (1999). *The Social Market Economy and Monetary Stability*. London: Economica.

Tietmeyer, H. (2002). 'Kirche und Wirtschaft: Felder der Kooperation und des Konflikts im Zeitalter der Globalisierung', in K. Gabriel (ed.), *Kirche—Staat—Wirtschaft auf dem Weg ins 21. Jahrhundert*. Münster: Lit Verlag.

Tietmeyer, H. (2003). 'Der Bericht der Werner-Gruppe von 1970 und der Bericht der Delors-Gruppe von 1989—Ein Vergleich', in W. Hankel, K. Schachtschneider, and

J. Starbatty (eds.), *Der Ökonom als Politiker: Festschrift für Wilhelm Nölling*. Stuttgart: Lucius, pp. 345–59.

Tietmeyer, H. (2005). *Herausforderung EURO: Wie es zum Euro kam und was er für Deutschlands Zukunft bedeutet*. Munich: Hanser.

Tietmeyer, H. (2015). 'Der Werner-Bericht als Wegweiser für die Wirtschafts- und Währingsunion', in E. Danescu and S. Muñoz (eds.), *Pierre Werner, une vision pour l'Europe: pensée, action, enseignements/Pierre Werner and Europe: His Approach, Action and Legacy*. Brussels: Peter Lang, pp. 57–91.

Tobin, J. (1984). 'On the Efficiency of the Financial System', *Lloyds Bank Review*, 153: 1–15.

Tomlinson, J. (2004). *The Labour Governments 1964–70*, vol. 3. Manchester: Manchester University Press.

Toniolo, G. (with the cooperation of P. Clement) (2005). *Central Bank Cooperation at the Bank for International Settlements, 1930–1973*. Cambridge: Cambridge University Press.

Triffin, R. (1935). 'Les mouvements différentiels des prix de gros en Belgique de 1927 à 1934: Calcul et interprétation d'indices de groupes comparables', *Bulletin de l'Institut des Sciences Economiques*, 6(3): 267–95.

Triffin, R. (1937). 'La théorie de la surévaluation monétaire et la dévaluation belge', *Bulletin de l'Institut de Recherces Economiques*, 9(1): 19–52.

Triffin, R. (1941). *Monopolistic Competition and General Equilibrium Theory*. Cambridge, MA: Harvard University Press.

Triffin, R. (1944). 'Central Banking and Monetary Management in Latin America', in S. Harris (ed.), *Economic Problems of Latin America*. New York: McGraw-Hill, pp. 93–116.

Triffin, R. (1947). 'National Central Banking and the International Economy', in R. Triffin, L. Metzler, and G. Haberler (eds.), *International Monetary Policies*. Postwar Economic Studies 7. Washington, DC: Board of Governors of the Federal Reserve System, pp. 46–81.

Triffin, R. (1950). *La multilatéralisation progressive des devises en Europe*, 1 March, NBBA, Brussels.

Triffin, R. (1953). *Convertibility and EPU*. NBBA, Brussels.

Triffin, R. (1954). 'Convertibilité ou integration', *Economie appliquée*, 7(4): 359–75.

Triffin, R. (1957). *Europe and the Money Muddle*. New Haven, CT: Yale University Press.

Triffin, R. (1958). 'La monnaie et le Marché Commun: Politiques nationales et intégration régionale', *Cahiers de l'Institut de Sciences Economiques Appliquées*, 74: 1–17.

Triffin, R. (1960a). *Gold and the Dollar Crisis*. New Haven, CT: Yale University Press.

Triffin, R. (1960b). 'Pour un Fonds européen de réserves'. Lausanne: Centre de recherches européennes.

Triffin, R. (1973). 'Le système monétaire international. Intervention devant la Commission des Finances de l'Assemblée Nationale', *Revue du marché commun*, November : 424–6.

Triffin, R. (1977). 'A European Parallel Currency as a Shelter against Exchange-Rate Instability', *Bulletin de l'IRES*, 45.

Triffin, R. (1979). 'Introduction: The Emerging European Monetary System', *Bulletin de la Banque Nationale de Belgique*, 65(4): 9–10.

Triffin, R. (1981). 'An Economist's Career: What? Why? How?', *BNL Quarterly Review*, 138(3): 239–59.

Triffin, R. (1989). 'Preface', in J. van Ypersele and J. C. Koeune, *Le Système Monétaire Européen*, 3rd edition. Luxembourg: CECA.

Triffin, R. and Swings, A. (eds.) (1980). *The Private Use of the ECU*. Brussels: Kredietbank.

Tudor, B. (1994). 'M. Pons demande des "explications" à la SOFRES sur un sondage défavorable à M. Chirac', *Le Monde*, 12 December.

van den Berg, C. C. A. (2004). *The Making of the Statute of the European System of Central Banks: An Application of Checks and Balances*. Amsterdam: Dutch University Press.

Van Rompuy, H. (2012). *Towards a Genuine Economic and Monetary Union: Report by the President of the European Council*. Brussels: European Council.

Van Yperseele, J. and Koeune, J.-C. (1988). *Le système monétaire européen*. Luxembourg-Brussels: Perspectives européennes.

Verdun, A. (1999). 'The Role of the Delors Committee in the Creation of EMU: An Epistemic Community?', *Journal of European Public Policy*, 6(2): 308–28.

Vigo, G. (1986). 'Introduzione', in L. Einaudi (ed.), *La guerra e l'unità europea*. Bologna: Il Mulino, pp. 7–13.

Visco, I. (2011). 'Tommaso Padoa-Schioppa', personal remark at the Ceremony in Memory of Tommaso Padoa-Schioppa, European University Institute, Badia Fiesolana, 28 January. <http://www.bis.org/review/r110131g.pdf>.

Wall, S. (2012). *The Official History of Britain and the European Community. Volume II: From Rejection to Referendum, 1963–1975*. Abingdon: Routledge.

Wall Street Journal Europe (1988). 'Poehl Doubts European Unity is Likely Soon', 6 May.

Warlouzet, L. (2008). 'Relancer la CEE avant la chaise vide: Néo-fonctionnalistes vs. fédéralistes au sein de la Commission européenne (1964–1965)', *Journal of European Integration History*, 14(1): 69–86.

Warlouzet, L. (2011). *Le choix de la CEE par la France: L'Europe économique en débat de Mendes France a de Gaulle (1955–1969)*. Paris: Comité pour l'histoire économique et financière de la France.

Weintraub, R. (1991). *Stabilizing Dynamics: Constructing Economic Knowledge*. Cambridge: Cambridge University Press.

Weintraub, R. and Forget, E. (eds.) (2007). *Economists' Lives: Biography and Autobiography in the History of Economics*. Durham, NC: Duke University Press.

Werner, P. (1960). 'Significations d'une intégration monétaire', *Documentation bulletin*, No. 15, December. Luxembourg: SIP, pp. 3–11.

Werner, P. (1962). 'Problèmes de l'intégration financière de l'Europe'. Talk given in Brussels by Pierre Werner, Minister of State, President of the Luxembourg Government and Finance Minister, to the members of the Association des Amitiés Belgo-Luxembourgeoises and the Cercle Royal Gaulois. Brussels: Cercle Royal Gaulois. Source: Pierre Werner family archives.

Werner, P. (1966a). 'Exposé sur la politique monétaire européenne'. Lecture given in Brussels by Pierre Werner, Minister of State, President of the Government and Minister for the Treasury and the Civil Service, at the invitation of the American and Common Market Club, Brussels, 5 June. *La Libre Belgique*, 6 June.

Werner, P. (1966b). 'Address by Pierre Werner, President of the Councils of the European Communities, to the European Parliament in Strasbourg, 28 June', *Documentation bulletin*, No. 9, 1 July. Luxembourg: SIP, pp. 8–12.

Werner, P. (1968a). 'Perspectives de la Politique Financière et Monétaire Européenne'. Address given at the CDU Economic Congress in Saarbrücken on 26 January. Source: Pierre Werner family archives. Also in *Documentation bulletin*, No. 2. Luxembourg: SIP, pp. 3–9.

Werner, P. (1968b). 'Benelux et les perspectives de la politique financière européenne'. Address given in The Hague by Pierre Werner, Minister of State, President of the Government and Minister for the Treasury, to the Benelux Committee, 1 April. *Documentation bulletin*, No. 6, 30 June. Luxembourg: SIP, pp. 8–11.

Werner, P. (1968c). 'Address given in Rotterdam by Pierre Werner, President of the Government, Minister for the Treasury, at the meeting of the Council of Finance Ministers of the EEC, 10 September 1968. *Documentation bulletin*, No. 8, September. Luxembourg: SIP, pp. 4–6.

Werner, P. (1969). 'Statement by Mr Pierre Werner, Minister of State, Prime Minister of Luxembourg, at the conference of the Heads of State or Government, The Hague, 1 December 1969'. *Documentation bulletin*, No. 14, 10 December. Luxembourg: SIP, pp. 3–7.

Werner, P. (1970a). 'L'Europe en route vers l'Union Monétaire', *Documentation bulletin*, No. 1, 28 February. Luxembourg: SIP, pp. 5–12.

Werner, P. (1970b). 'Statement by Pierre Werner to the Council of Ministers, Luxembourg, 26 October 1970', *Documentation bulletin*, No. 6. Luxembourg: SIP, pp. 4–5.

Werner, P. (1972). 'L'union économique et monétaire en tant qu'étape vers l'Europe politique', in *Liber amicorum Fernand Collin*. Brussels: Kredietbank, pp. 263–8.

Werner, P. (1989). 'L'Union économique et monétaire d'un rapport à l'autre'. September. Source: Archives familiales Pierre Werner.

Werner, P. (1990). 'Der Werner-Bericht und der Delors-Bericht zur Europäischen Wirtschafts- und Währungsunion im Vergleich', in O. Franz (ed.), *Die Europäische Zentralbank*. Bonn: Europa Union Verlag, pp. 175–84.

Werner, P. (1992). *Itinéraires luxembourgeois et européens: Évolutions et souvenirs 1945–1985*, 2 vols. Luxembourg: Saint-Paul.

Wester, R. (1992). 'The European Commission and European Political Union', in F. Laursen and S. Vanhoonacker (eds.), *The Intergovernmental Conference on Political Union: Institutional Reforms, New Policies and International Identity of the European Community*. Maastricht: Martinus Nijhoff Publishers, pp. 163–78.

Wolf, M. (2014). *The Shifts and the Shocks: What We've Learned—and Have Still to Learn—from the Financial Crisis*. London: Allen Lane.

Young, H. (1999). *This Blessed Plot: Britain and Europe from Churchill to Blair*. Basingstoke: Macmillan.

Name Index

Subject Index

The manufacturer's authorised representative in the EU for product safety is Oxford University Press España S.A. of El Parque Empresarial San Fernando de Henares, Avenida de Castilla, 2 - 28830 Madrid (www.oup.es/en or product.safety@oup.com). OUP España S.A. also acts as importer into Spain of products made by the manufacturer.
Printed and bound by CPI Group (UK) Ltd, Croydon, CR0 4YY
14/09/2026
02216304-0008